To S.S.F.
but for whom this book would never have been started
and to S.M.W.
but for whom it would never have been finished

The Towns of Roman Britain

JOHN WACHER

B.T. BATSFORD LTD London

© John Wacher 1974

First published 1975
ISBN 0 7134 2794 9

Filmset by Tradespools Ltd, Frome, Somerset
Printed by The Anchor Press Ltd, Tiptree, Essex

for the Publishers
B. T. Batsford Ltd, 4 Fitzhardinge Street, London W1H 0AH

Contents

Acknowledgement

This book was written between 1970 and 1973, and incorporates as much up to date information as possible, which was available to the end of 1972. I should have been quite unable to do so without the ready cooperation of a large number of archaeologists and field-workers, who willingly made available the results of their most recent work, and discussed it where necessary. It is gratifying to record that only two requests for information met with a blank refusal, and it is therefore one of my most pleasurable duties to be able to thank all those who have helped, and who have made my task easier and more worthwhile: Michael Apted, Martin Biddle, George Boon, John Casey, Dorothy Charlesworth, David T.-D. Clarke, John Collis, Christina Colyer, Barry Cunliffe, Alec Down, Paul Drury, Rosalind Dunnett (Mrs Niblett), Aileen Fox, Barbara Green, Michael Griffiths, Henry Hurst, Barri Jones, Jeremy Knight, Don Mackreth, Alan McWhirr, Peter Marsden, Jean Mellor, Ralph Merrifield, David Neal, Bill Putnam, Herman Ramm, Hugh Thompson, Graham Webster, Ben Whitwell and John Peter Wild. More especially, I owe a very real debt of gratitude to both Sheppard Frere and Joyce Reynolds, who read the full text in draft, and who were able to suggest many improvements.

No book of this type can be written without the inclusion of thoughts and ideas unconsciously gleaned in the course of conversation with friends and colleagues. If someone among this unacknowledged band should recognise one for his own, I hope he will accept my sincere apologies.

In addition, I am most grateful for all those museums, government departments and other people who have so kindly allowed me to reproduce drawings or photographs, often in advance of their own publications, and who are acknowledged individually elsewhere. I must thank Mrs Chris Boddington for producing the finished drawings for each town plan, and Mrs P. A. Walker for devoting so much care to the typescript.

Despite all the help which I have received, I must reserve to myself all errors or omissions which may appear, as the result of holding my own opinions in the face of opposition. In archaeology, as in most subjects, it is impossible to agree with everyone all the time.

Finally, I would like to thank the University of Leicester for giving me a term's leave of absence so that I was able to complete this book within a reasonable time.

J. S. WACHER

Leicester
6 December 1972

Plates

Figures

NOTE

Numerals in square brackets, at the head of each page, refer to the page numbers on which the relevant notes can be located.

Preface

The aims of this book are threefold: to examine and define the functions of towns in Roman Britain and to apply the definition so formed to Romano-British sites; to consider the towns' foundation, political affiliations, development and decline; and to illustrate where possible both their individual characters and their surroundings. It is not, and has never been, my intention to provide a complete inventory of all discoveries, which can in most cases readily be obtained from published sources, but full references are given wherever possible.

I have thought it necessary to define the term *town* as applied to Roman Britain because of the confusion which seems to reign in many quarters about what can or cannot be called a town. To a great extent, the definition so developed can be applied to most provinces of the western Empire, because it is based on criteria associated with their functions. Providing *all* these criteria are satisfied for a particular site it is probably safe to call it a town, although there are bound to be borderline cases. It should not be thought, however, that the Roman Empire was necessarily conscious of the functions now attributed to its towns by the process of modern geographical reasoning, or that the towns were necessarily planned with these functions in mind. In many cases they were assumed long after foundation had taken place.

A note of caution might perhaps be sounded here. No quantitative methods have been used to define the relative importance or spheres of influence of any towns. Some attempts have recently been made to do so without conspicuous success.[1] Such methods can only be successful if the calculations are, to a great extent, based on factual observations. Analysis all too readily shows that many of the so-called 'facts' about Romano-British towns are compounded of a mixture of inference, analogy, extrapolation, surmise and presumption. In no aspect is this more so than when dealing with questions of economics and population. To apply quantitative methods in our present state of knowledge is, therefore, not only misguided but probably also misleading, since it cloaks the information that we have with a spurious authenticity.

Much of the confusion over what can or cannot be called a town arises from the actual terminology. In the descriptions of Latin authors and in other sources, no less than six different words with urban connotations are applied to sites in Britain, to which we can add one Greek word used by Ptolemy. These can be briefly considered:

1. *Civitas* means primarily citizenship, either of a Roman or of any peregrine (e.g. non-Roman) community. It was also used to describe the communities themselves, and, under the principate, it was very commonly used to describe peregrine communities.

2. *Colonia*, in the early Empire, was used to describe towns inhabited either by Roman or Latin citizens,[2] who might be retired army veterans. The constitution, based on that of Rome itself, was governed by a charter. Increasingly, as time passed, towns of lower grade were sometimes promoted to this rank.

3. *Municipium*, again in the early Empire, described towns whose constitution was likewise governed by charter. The inhabitants would have been of Roman or Latin status according to the grade of the municipium. Later, however, a town with only Latin rights might have received full Roman rights and subsequent promotion to *colonia* was not unknown.

4. *Oppidum*, although meaning literally a town, was used loosely by Caesar and other authors to describe fortified native sites in Britain and Gaul. As normally used in the principate, it had no precise legal meaning.

5. *Urbs* is normally translated as city, and it was used to describe a settlement of higher status than one which might be called an *oppidum*.

6. *Vicus* has probably the widest range of meanings yet considered. It can refer to districts or quarters of a town; to villages, particularly where evidence connects them with forts, or to private or imperial estates. It was also used to describe the central towns of some peregrine *civitates*. It had, therefore, the lowest legal status accorded to a built-up area, as distinct from a *pagus*, which formed a country district. Arguments have taken place as to whether a *vicus* (district) can exist in a *vicus* (civitas capital).

7. Πόλις, was originally used to describe the city states of Greece. Consequently, ancient historians have tended to equate it with *civitas* when it is used by authors writing under the Roman principate. As applied to Britain, its use was more in the manner of *oppidum*. It is here, when Greek overtones are added to the Roman notions of a British town, that confusion is at its worst.

The above section summarises urban terms, both legal and other, which were applied, sometimes not too accurately, to British sites. It is in trying to equate them with modern terminology that there is the greatest difficulty, for in English there are just as many terms to describe the status, function and inhabitants of urban settlements: town, city, urban district, municipality, county borough, borough; citizen, citizenship. Of these, the first has no specific legal meaning and is applied generally to urban sites, but not to villages. Citizen and citizenship have many shades of meaning in both modern and Roman worlds. The remaining urban terms are only applied to towns with the appropriate status in the modern local government hierarchy. Since, however, they have quite specific meanings, it seems wrong that any should be applied to ancient sites, which had their own quite different organisations. Instead, therefore, of applying the English word city to distinguish certain types of ancient site from other towns, as is done by some classical archaeologists and ancient historians, it seems better to use only the word town to describe *all* urban settlements of the period, leaving the Latin or Greek terms to define themselves from their characteristic functions and institutions. This approach has been adopted in the following pages; all classes of urban settlements have been called towns, and the term city has been rejected.

We are then left with finding an appropriate terminology for the large number of minor settlements, such as those which are euphemistically called 'small towns' and those which are nucleated but unfortified. Many, but not necessarily all, probably held the status of *vicus*; others for the present defy definition. But, if we require an English equivalent, it is probably better that they should be referred to as villages, and they can be further distinguished by calling them fortified or unfortified, as may be.

I am quite aware that many scholars and students will not necessarily agree with these proposals, but they are at least a start in clearing up confusion and misunderstanding. If further refinements or more credible alternatives can be suggested, so much the better.

I

What were towns and how did they develop?

There are three types of town to be considered in this book. They are those which had a certain status as administrative centres and were therefore genuine towns in ancient eyes: they can be classified as *coloniae*, *municipia* and the planned *vici* which became civitas capitals.

During the later years of the Republic it had become the custom often to give allotments of land to retiring legionaries. Augustus introduced the practice of cash gratuities, although land allotments were still made. In order to regulate these grants when a large number of men were discharged in the same area simultaneously, special towns called *coloniae* were founded from time to time as acts of government policy; each legionary would receive a plot of land in the town together with another in the *territorium*, the country surrounding the town and attributed to it, the size of the plots depending on rank. The population of a *colonia* was essentially of Roman citizens, although a non-Roman element, called *incolae*, was sometimes present as well. On foundation these towns probably received a 'charter' (*lex coloniae*) from the central government (but see Chapt. II, footnote 5, p. 427), and their institutions and administration were based on those practised in early imperial Rome itself. In AD 49, the first *colonia* in Britain was established at Colchester for veterans of one or perhaps more of the legions then serving in the province. It is unlikely that this, the *colonia (Claudia?) Victricensis* (p. 79), was deliberately intended to be the provincial administrative capital of Britain; a variety of factors prevented it from adequately fulfilling this function and it was soon replaced by London (p. 80). Later in the first century two more *coloniae* were founded: supposedly between AD 96–8 at Gloucester (*colonia Nervia Glevensium*) for veterans of Legio II Augusta (p. 137), and, probably slightly earlier, at Lincoln (*Lindum colonia*) for veterans of Legio IX Hispana (p. 120). It should be noted that at least two, and probably all three, occupied the actual sites of earlier legionary fortresses, so that their foundation would primarily have involved land which had been expropriated by the government, and was already imperial property.

Apart from establishing *coloniae* as new towns, it was also the practice to promote existing settlements which would then be constituted into communities organised on the Roman model. This had been done extensively by Julius Caesar in Gallia Narbonensis, and ultimately it became a fairly common practice to upgrade tribal towns and some other *vici* to the rank of *municipium*, followed perhaps by promotion later to *colonia*. At York, an extra-mural settlement, probably distinct from the *canabae*, had grown on the opposite bank of the river Ouse to the legionary fortress. It is known to have been a *colonia* by AD 237, but it is likely that the act of promotion was made earlier by Septimius Severus in the first decade of the third century (p. 156). What is not known for certain, however, is whether the grant of colonial status had been preceded, at some time in the second century, by intermediate promotion to a *municipium*, as often happened elsewhere in the Empire.[1] A reference by Aurelius Victor, in his account of the death of Severus, describes it as such, but is not entirely reliable.[2]

Another town which may have been treated in the same way as York was the provincial capital of London (p. 87). While there is no epigraphic evidence relating to its civic status, it would seem inconceivable that a site which became one of the largest towns in the western Empire, which, from about AD 60, became the headquarters of the imperial procurator, which, by the early second century at latest, had become the seat of the provincial governor, and which had a fort specially provided for soldiers attached to the governor's staff, should not have received a 'charter'. The most likely suggestion to make, in the absence of detailed evidence, would be that it became a *municipium* late in the first or early in the second century, followed by promotion to a *colonia* perhaps in the late second or early third century to account for the additional title of Augusta, which it is known to have held by the fourth.

It will have been gathered from the paragraph above that a *municipium*, although still a 'chartered' town, was lower in rank than a *colonia*. There were, however, additional differences, as *municipia* could either have full Roman rights or only Latin rights, and, in addition could retain some native laws alongside the *ius civile* of Rome. The former were towns inhabited mainly by Roman citizens, and therefore differed only in degree from *coloniae*, although it should be remembered that some *coloniae* had no more than Latin rights. But promotion to municipal status with only Latin rights could be achieved by an existing town whose inhabitants were predominantly non-citizens. Citizenship would, however, be given to the town's magistrates, together with their families, so in time the number of citizens might be expected slowly to grow. From the second century, grants were also made in which citizenship might be conferred on the whole council in addition to the magistrates.

Verulamium is the only town in Britain for which there is some evidence suggesting the grant of a municipal 'charter', probably with Latin rights (p. 202). Although it probably received its 'charter' in the first century, the precise date is not known. According to Tacitus it was a *municipium* at the time of the Boudiccan rebellion in AD 60,[3] and Frere has suggested[4] that promotion was given under Claudius. However, he argues elsewhere[5] that the physical indication of the

higher classes of a self-governing community, at least in Britain, was the possession of a forum with basilica, and it is known that these buildings at Verulamium
date to the early Flavian period.[6] Was there an earlier forum, not yet touched by
excavation (perhaps smaller in size than the later?) which had been burnt by
Boudicca and which was being rebuilt, like some other parts of the town, after
a considerable delay, or was the promotion perhaps not given until early in
Vespasian's principate? Rivet suggests that Tacitus may have been using the
word anachronistically[7] of a town which was a *municipium* by the time he was
writing, but not at the time of the event he was writing about. It must be admitted
that, even given very rapid development of the town in the first few years after
the conquest, there cannot, under Claudius, have been a great deal in existence
to promote. It might be better to consider that municipal status was conferred
by Vespasian on a definite, established town, as was usually the case, than by
Claudius on a town in embryo.[8] It is also known that Vespasian was responsible
for urban promotions in other provinces, *Aventicum* being but one example.

'It would be surprising if some other towns in Britain had not been promoted
in later years. Some indeed may have been, but the evidence is slight and un-
satisfactory. In the Antonine Itinerary, a route-list compiled for official purposes
in the early third century, the majority of civitas capitals are listed, together with
their distinctive tribal suffixes, such as *Venta Silurum* (Caerwent). There are,
however, a small number which lack these suffixes; Verulamium, Canterbury,
Dorchester, Leicester and Wroxeter, and this is sometimes considered as a pointer
to promotion. Since Verulamium is included, there may be some substance in
the suggestion, as we have seen that it was probably a *municipium*. It should be
noted that Cirencester is unfortunately omitted from the list altogether, but
there are other reasons which might suggest that it too had received promotion
(see p. 84).

Normally a *municipium*, like a *colonia* would have a *territorium* attributed to it.
Unfortunately in Britain there is no evidence for the size of these land allotments.
Rivet has drawn attention to the fact that the chief concentrations of villas tend
to lie in areas adjacent to fortified *vici* and not in the areas around civitas capitals.[9]
He goes on to suggest that the land around the capitals was worked actually from
the towns, which is a distinct possibility. But it could mean only that this land
was organised in larger estates, and larger estates could mean fewer and more
widely scattered villas.

Round certain towns, notably Cirencester, Leicester, Verulamium, Dorchester
and Canterbury, lies a well-defined area free of villas, except that for the first four
towns, the areas contain *one* villa only, placed quite close to the town boundaries.
Frere has noted[10] that there are at least fifteen villas within a ten-mile radius of
Cirencester; but cut the radius to four miles and there is only one, at the Barton
Farm[11] near the north-west boundary, although four more lie close to the four-
mile circumference. At Verulamium there is a villa situated at Gorhambury[12]
just outside the Chester Gate, and at Leicester at the Cherry Orchard,[13] less than
a mile from the south-west boundary. At Dorchester there is one at Olga Road.[14]

That three of these towns are listed in the Antonine Itinerary without the tribal suffix is perhaps more than just coincidence, while Cirencester must be considered a strong claimant for promotion on the grounds of its size and its later history. Although there would seem to be some common factor present at all these towns, it is not at present possible to envisage the character or organisation of *territoria*. Towns which may have achieved such promotion,[15] probably still continued to act as the administrative centres for their *civitates*.

We have so far used 'town' to describe the first two classes of sites of which we are writing: *coloniae* and *municipia*. It remains to justify its use for the third class, the civitas capitals, or planned *vici*, and it is here that confusion can arise because of misconception.

The word 'town' as applied to settlements in Roman Britain has become synonymous with a fortified settlement of civilian character.[16] This definition, though popular, is inaccurate. In a strict Roman legal sense there is no precise equivalent. If, however, it is to be used at all it might most appropriately be restricted to 'chartered' towns, both *coloniae* and *municipia*. But it is difficult in Britain to define the term so closely; many others exceeded the 'chartered' towns in size and wealth, and apparently differed from them only in legal status. Equally, it is clear that not all contemporary writers were precise in their use of terms for town, and Ptolemy described many sites in Britain, including hill-forts, as πόλεις, while Pliny refers to them as *oppida*, when few if any can have had higher status than that of *vicus* or village. This difficulty of definition becomes most acute when comparing the so-called 'small towns' with unfortified civil settlements of similar or larger size. There seems no good reason why a settlement, covering no more than a few acres but bounded by a bank or wall, should be called a town, when one, undefended, of similar or perhaps greater size is not. Both would almost certainly have had the same status of *vicus*, and should be so called, the provision of fortifications being a function of the use to which it was put rather than of its status. Resistance has grown in the last two or three decades to the use of the word village in a Romano-British context, in parallel with its virtual abandonment by prehistorians in Iron Age contexts. Happily this retreat has now been halted to some extent, and the late Sir Ian Richmond drew attention to many sites in Roman Britain which should properly be called villages,[17] covering a great number and variety of settlements. That being so, it would be inappropriate to consider in this book the majority of what have, until now, been called 'small towns', as in almost every case, defended or not, they were no more than villages. But again, if too strictly adhered to, such an exclusion would prohibit other sites from being included, as many of the civitas capitals started as *vici*, often outside forts established in the early years of the conquest, and many, at least, can never have progressed beyond that legal status. The evidence for possible later promotion of these *vici* is very slight or even non-existent for the majority and it is probably right to assume that most were never promoted. Nevertheless distinctions can still be drawn between them and the true village settlements, even though both may have possessed the same status.

The establishment of civitas capitals in Britain to act as the administrative centres for local government closely followed the pattern already established by the Romans in Gaul. Most of the newly-constituted *civitates* were formed from Iron Age tribal groups. The selection of a site as the centre for a *civitas* may therefore be seen as a deliberate act, involving the choice of what was probably already either a pre-existing native centre or a newly-formed village outside a fort. Subsequently, development was chiefly left to the inclinations of the natives, although some governors, notably in the Flavian period, pursued a more active policy of romanisation and showed greater concern over the rate of progress.[18] The chief difference therefore between a *vicus* which grew for purely economic reasons and one selected for development as a civitas capital is likely to be in planning. It is obvious from the plans of those British capitals which are known that conscious efforts were made from the first to produce towns cast in the Mediterranean mould, even if the final result fell short of expectations. These plans contrast sharply with the haphazard and piecemeal development of the true village.[19] The evidence for coordinated planning provided by civitas capitals entitles them to be called towns, even if their earliest legal status was still that of a *vicus*. Apart from planning, these 'developed' *vici* were also conceived as towns in a social, economic, political and administrative sense, but in a way that adapted Mediterranean usage to a newly-conquered and unromanised province.

If the selection of civitas capitals owed much to official policy, then the variations in plan which occur between one capital and another must be a measure of local wealth and opinion, otherwise there would have been a greater degree of standardisation between sites. This is an argument against the imposition of a standard plan, and illustrates the degree to which the natives were allowed to pursue their own course, with the minimum interference from above. To effect a true comparison, however, between the sizes of towns and, for instance, their public buildings, it is necessary to know the position of the town boundary when the buildings were erected. It is not strictly accurate for instance to associate the Flavium forum at Cirencester, measuring 550ft (167m) by 345ft (105m), with a town of 250 acres (101ha), for that was the area enclosed only by the late second-century defences. It is not yet known if Flavian Cirencester was the same size. But it is known that the area of some towns, as enclosed by successive systems of fortifications, altered radically over the years. That being so, it would be unwise to infer that an early town boundary was always the same as that on which defences were erected, often more than 100 years after the town's foundation. Verulamium is one of the very few towns where successive sizes at various times can be estimated: the first-century town is known to have covered 119 acres (48ha), the late-Antonine town expanded to 225 acres (91ha), and the third and fourth-century town contracted to an area of 200 acres (81ha), each defined by a different line of fortification. These changes show growth or contraction caused by varying economic pressures which must have superceded official policy as the controlling factor after foundation, and to which in the end would be owed the familiar shapes and sizes of the towns of Roman Britain. While a town possessed no fortifications, or at best only an earthwork, there was little to prevent its expansion. But once it was ringed with a stone wall, it became crystallised; so the provision of walls would have made further expansion possible only at great cost. An example is, of course, Lincoln, where the new town was walled separately and at a later date. After walls were built, economic forces would tend no longer to affect the size of a town, but only the standard, size and density of its internal structures.

These remarks about the civitas capitals have indicated the course development took, but it should be noted that the choice of a suitable site for one was influenced by more varied causes than lay behind the foundation of a *colonia*.

Of the twenty-three tribal areas for which there is evidence in Britain during the Roman period, at least sixteen seem to have been released wholly or in part from military control and became self-governing *civitates peregrinae*. At least three of these (Belgae, Regnenses and Cantiaci) seem to have been artificially formed either by joining together a number of smaller tribes, or by carving out an area from a larger tribal territory. But only eleven civitas capitals are directly attested: *Calleva Atrebatum* (Silchester), *Corinium Dobunnorum* (Cirencester), *Durovernum Cantiacorum* (Canterbury), *Isca Dumnoniorum* (Exeter), *Isurium Brigantum* (Aldborough), *Noviomagus Regnensium* (Chichester), *Ratae Coritanorum* (Leicester), *Venta Belgarum* (Winchester), *Venta Icenorum* (Caistor-by-Norwich), *Venta Silurum* (Caerwent) and *Viroconium Cornoviorum* (Wroxeter). Three more can be suggested with reasonable certainty: *Petuaria* (Brough-on-Humber) at first for the Parisi, *Durnovaria* (Dorchester) for the Durotriges and *Moridunum* (Carmarthen) for the Demetae. That leaves two other *civitates*: the Catuvellauni, who were probably administered from the *municipium* at Verulamium, and the Trinovantes. It is not yet known with certainty if the latter had their own centre, and opinion is divided. *Caesaromagus* (Chelmsford) may have started as the capital,[20] but it is not impossible that later the *civitas* was administered from the *colonia* at Camulodunum, while remaining separate from the *territorium*, as probably with the Helvetii and Ubii. A third but less likely alternative might envisage the whole tribal area, perhaps as a punishment for their part in the Boudiccan rebellion, being attributed to the *colonia*, as happened to the Salassi in northern Italy.

Some *civitates* were subdivided into smaller units at a later date, perhaps by the promotion of *pagi* to the full rank of *civitas*, as seems to have happened in Gaul. The *civitas Carvetiorum* is an example which was probably formed from the north-west section of the Brigantes,[21] with a centre at Carlisle. Another possible subdivision may have affected the northern part of the Catuvellauni, which with part of the Coritani may have been fused to form the *civitas Corielsoliliorum*,[22] and which is attested in an informal inscription on a fragment of tile from *Tripontium*, with perhaps a centre at Water Newton. The Durotriges also seem to have been split into two sections, with the *Durotrages Lindinienses* presumably formed into a separate *civitas* centred on Ilchester.[23] Other examples may well be forthcoming in the future as more evidence is gathered.

1   The towns of Roman Britain

Civitates peregrinae, self-governing districts of non-citizens,[24] and their capital towns would normally have been set up by the provincial administration in Britain as each area was freed from military control. Each would have been formed by agreement reached between the leaders of the community and the government. In this way the constitution and administration of the *civitas* would have been regulated. The agreement reached, however, was probably weighted heavily in favour of the government, so that at any time, if need arose, it could have been revoked unilaterally by the governor. This would imply an informal arrangement, giving rise to conditions which probably differed only in degree from those which had been enforced under direct military occupation. The same people, who in the main were the tribal rulers and who had received orders from local military commanders, probably continued to hold sway over the *civitas*, subject, of course, to the governor's veto on undesirable persons; at lower levels in society the changes were probably negligible in practice, and would have made little difference to the general way of life. Moreover, there were ever present the demands of the imperial procurator and the threat of government interference in local affairs, or even, in extreme cases, of the reimposition of military occupation, as happened in parts of Brigantia during the second century. A provincial governor had very arbitrary powers in this respect, even if, in a small province like Sardinia, he sometimes had difficulty in enforcing his will over obstreperous municipalities.

Recently, two opposing views on the nature of *civitates* have been argued, which are to some extent a revival of the contrasting but not contemporary opinions of Th. Mommsen and A. H. M. Jones. Rivet contends that *civitates* existed physically both before and after the conquest; Frere argues that they were only created after military control had been removed from an area.[25] The truth probably lies, as always, somewhere between these two extremes, although it is not easy to grasp, and it will have depended on the Roman ability to adopt and compromise. Despite the strong element of continuity which can be envisaged as having existed, there was an unquestionable distinction between an area under direct military occupation and a *civitas* constituted after that occupation had ceased. Some major modifications can be observed in the administrative and social structure, leading to the formation, from the tribal aristocracy, of a specific romanised social class—the *curiales*—and the introduction of the higher grades of magistracies. Also, under military control, much discretion would have been allowed to local commanders and instructions from the imperial government were probably relayed through them, whereas later they could be sent by the governor direct to the magistrates and council, who would be expected to assume a greater degree of responsibility. At this stage the *civitas peregrina* would become, as A. H. M. Jones has pointed out, formally recognised as a responsible organisation within the provincial framework of administration, with closely prescribed legal rights and duties, although any of them might be subject to revoke by the governor. The newly-constituted *civitas* was matched by the concentration of local government in its capital, with buildings designed appropriately for administrative purposes. Here we might argue, as Frere has done,[26] but in a modified form, that the *forum* and its attached *basilica* was the physical manifestation of this particular level of local government under the Roman provincial administration in Britain, at least during the later first and second centuries. It might be correct to say that the *curia* was the necessary visible evidence, especially in the earlier decades. But it should be remembered that the reverse was not always true. At least one *colonia* and one, and possibly other, *civitates* managed seemingly for a time without a forum, so that absence of a forum cannot be taken to imply the non-existence of a self-governing community.

The early situation in Britain was, however, complicated by the acceptance of two tribal states as client kingdoms (fig. 2): the Iceni, ruled by Prasutagus or,

2   Claudio-Neronian civitates and client kingdoms

perhaps at first, by a predecessor, and the kingdom of Cogidubnus. Since these kingdoms were probably only subject to the governor, they are unlikely to have been constituted as *civitates peregrinae*, and would have only become so on their dissolution, which, with the Iceni, took place in AD 60. The kingdom of Cogidubnus, enlarged during the sixties, was split into three parts on his death in the Flavian period to form the *civitas Regnensium*, the *civitas Atrebatum* and the *civitas Belgarum*.

If allowance is made for these two client kingdoms, then the remaining areas to have been freed from military control soon after the invasion were those occupied by the Trinovantes, the south-eastern part of the Catuvellauni, and the smaller tribes of Kent. We have already seen that the land of the Trinovantes was the first in Britain to be selected for an exercise in urbanisation with the foundation of the *colonia* at Colchester in AD 49. Direct military control may have been removed, but control by army veterans was apparently no less severe, as Tacitus makes clear.[27] The establishment of a separate *civitas* is perhaps doubtful, but nevertheless should be considered as a possibility. The treatment of the Trinovantes was, however, exceptional in Britain. The period which saw the foundation of the new *colonia* probably saw also the constitution of the *civitas Catuvellaunorum* in the south-east midlands, and the *civitas Cantiacorum*, a new unit formed out of the tribes living in Kent (fig. 2). Both *civitates* were provided with capitals: at Verulamium and Canterbury respectively. On these grounds alone Verulamium might have had a pre-Boudiccan *curia*, even if it was not then a *municipium* (see p. 18, above). Canterbury too might be expected to have had one as early, although no satisfactory evidence has yet been found. Nevertheless the foundation of these two towns enables us to see some of the reasons behind the choice of site for a civitas capital. In Kent at the time of the conquest there were several Iron Age centres, of which Rochester and Canterbury were but two of the most important. Both lay close to river crossings, and both were associated with gaps through the North Downs. Geographically therefore there was little to choose between the two sites, except perhaps that Canterbury, with its easier connexion by water direct to the supply base and port of Richborough, may have had a slight advantage. This advantage would undoubtedly have been strengthened when the roads to Richborough, Dover and Lympne were constructed,[28] as all three met at Canterbury, so creating an important road junction. So the reasons behind the selection of Canterbury as the new civitas capital begin to emerge: it was already a native settlement of some consequence, set in a good geographical position, and, more important, its geographical position coincided with the new requirements imposed by communications along road and river. Rochester simply did not have this combination of factors.

The choice of Verulamium must have depended on very similar reasons. However, slight differences can be detected here. The native centre had overflowed from a low hill, about $\frac{3}{4}$ mile (1·2km) from the river Ver, down into the valley below. For a time a fort was held only a short distance from the river and presumably inside the native settlement; the new main road, Watling Street, was aligned on this fort. The duration of the military occupation though was probably too short to have any profound local effect, so that, with the fort's evacuation, the new town was planned to overly much the same area as the native settlement on the lower slopes of the hill. Again we see the combination of an important native centre with a good geographical position, although in this case the latter was slightly adapted to meet the new requirements. Compared however with some other examples, the migration was very slight.

The period between about AD 50–70 probably saw the constitution of only one new *civitas*, as the frontier region based on the Severn–Trent line was comparatively stable. When the client king Prasutagus died in *c.* AD 60, the absorption of the Iceni into the province, presumably as a new *civitas peregrina*, led directly to the Boudiccan rebellion. After the rebellion had been suppressed, the tribe would have been in no fit state for self-government. A period of direct military occupation would have been the result, although the forts known in or near Icenian territory would seem to have been intended to control the tribe by isolating them from their neighbours rather than by occupation. Perhaps one can detect here the more humane policy of Petronius Turpilianus and Trebellius Maximus, for forts placed well inside the tribal territory would undoubtedly have acted as a continued irritant. However, the civitas capital for the Iceni does not seem to have been developed much before the end of the first century. Therefore an intermediate period, perhaps under a *praefectus civitatis*, an army officer, under whose direction the tribal leaders would acquire the arts of local government as understood by Rome, might be envisaged after full military occupation had ceased.[29] Not enough is known about the early history of the site at Caistor-by-Norwich (*Venta Icenorum*) for the reasons which lay behind its choice to be examined. It would seem to have been a site which was selected solely for its geographical position and which bore little relationship to any native centre.

Two events in the Flavian period probably led to the constitution of at least eight more *civitates peregrinae* (fig. 3). The death of Cogidubnus *c.* AD 80 would have caused the splitting up of his kingdom, its absorption into the province and the emergence of the *civitas Regnensium*, the *civitas Atrebatum* and the *civitas Belgarum*. The resumption of the military advance into the north and west under the first three Flavian governors, and the repercussions which followed, would have required the release of an increasing number of army units from rearward areas, both to make up the necessary campaign forces and also to provide garrisons for the new conquests. By this time, the tribes in the south-west and in the midlands had probably accepted a degree of romanisation. The provincial administration would, therefore, have had to set up self-governing *civitates*, to take over from the military authorities, before these regiments could be released for service elsewhere. The *civitates* then to emerge were the *civitas Dumnoniorum*, the *civitas Durotrigum*, the *civitas Dobunnorum*, the *civitas Coritanorum* and slightly later the *civitas Cornoviorum*. The extra work following these actions, could well have swamped successive governor's staffs, especially as major military campaigns

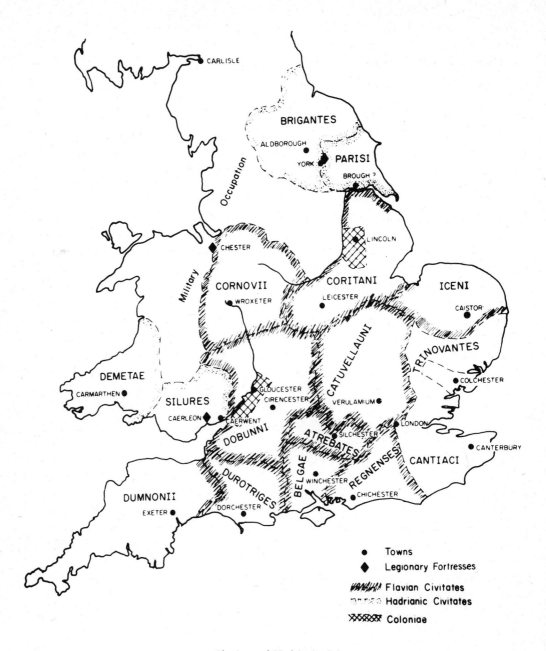

CARLISLE

BRIGANTES

ALDBOROUGH

YORK   PARISI

BROUGH ?

Occupation

LINCOLN

Military

CHESTER

CORNOVII   CORITANI   ICENI

WROXETER   LEICESTER   CAISTOR

TRINOVANTES

DEMETAE   CATUVELLAUNI   COLCHESTER

CARMARTHEN   GLOUCESTER   VERULAMIUM

SILURES   CIRENCESTER   LONDON

CAERLEON   CAERWENT   SILCHESTER

DOBUNNI   ATREBATES   CANTERBURY

CANTIACI

BELGAE   REGNENSES

DUROTRIGES   WINCHESTER   CHICHESTER

DUMNONII

EXETER   DORCHESTER

●   Towns
◆   Legionary Fortresses
〰〰〰 Flavian Civitates
⌐⌐⌐⌐ Hadrianic Civitates
✕✕✕✕ Coloniae

3   Flavian and Hadrianic civitates

were being carried out for much of the time. It is not surprising therefore that
we find two lawyers, each of some eminence and seniority, being appointed
successively to the newly-created post of *legatus iuridicus*, or law-officer, to the
governor's staff between AD 80–6, just when this work would be starting.

Suggestions have already been made that these appointments were to do with the fragmentation of the kingdom of Cogidubnus into three *civitates*[30] after his death. Holders of the office were not only to be found in Britain; but, when it is realised that in the last twenty years of the first century no less than eight *civitates* were probably being set up, together with the *coloniae* at Lincoln and Gloucester, then the presence of these law-officers in Britain would have been doubly necessary, not only to resolve the initial legal problems, particularly connected with the *coloniae*, but also to cope with the large amount of extra judicial work involved.

These eight new *civitates* would also require capitals, and the sites chosen illustrate even better the varied reasons, already partly discussed for Verulamium and Canterbury, which led to their selection.

In the kingdom of Cogidubnus the three sites selected were Chichester (*Noviomagus Regnensium*), Silchester (*Calleva Atrebatum*) and Winchester (*Venta Belgarum*), and it is not difficult to see the reasons behind the choice. Both Silchester[31] and Winchester[32] had been major Iron Age settlements before the conquest, and both had become principal centres of the new kingdom, receiving defences when few other sites in Britain were fortified. By AD 80 Silchester already had the makings of a town, and probably possessed a public bath-house. That both sites also occupied excellent geographical situations, capable of being integrated into the new road system without change, must have been an added attraction, and in neither case can there have been much difficulty of choice. Chichester was slightly different. There is no evidence for pre-Roman occupation of the site, and indeed the settlement at Selsey should rightly be seen as its Iron Age predecessor. But by the new standards, Selsey was inconveniently placed near the end of a promontory jutting out into the English channel. In the first few years after the invasion, a harbour and supply base grew at Fishbourne at the head of an inlet west of Selsey Bill. It is not surprising therefore that Cogidubnus selected for his capital a new site about a mile (1·6km) east of the harbour with all its facilities, rather than isolated Selsey. Such evidence as there is of early Chichester has been taken to suggest rapid progress towards romanisation, following a military occupation, and many of the inhabitants of Selsey would probably have drifted gradually to the new town (see Cirencester below, p. 30). When the time came for the Regnenses to adopt a civitas capital, Chichester was the obvious and only choice.

In the other five new *civitates* outside Cogidubnus' kingdom, military occupation would have been continuous from the conquest, with forts placed at intervals throughout their territories. As the siting of some of these forts affected later developments, they must be considered first. There is definite evidence for forts or fortresses having been built at Exeter,[33] Cirencester,[34] Leicester[35] and Wroxeter,[36] while another is implied by finds of military equipment at Dorchester.[37] These forts and fortresses would have been envisaged in or near their respective positions in accordance with the general strategy pursued by the two governors of Britain, Aulus Plautius and Ostorius Scapula, in laying out the first frontier. Their actual placing would nevertheless have owed much to the tactical requirements of the locality in which they were put. At Leicester, for instance, it coincided almost exactly with a major native settlement, but such a coincidence must have been largely accidental, as can be seen from the other four examples, and probably played only a secondary part in siting the fort. At Cirencester, Dorchester and Wroxeter the tactical requirements dictated their being placed some miles away from principal native settlements, while at Exeter no obvious site anywhere near can be interpreted as a native capital. How then did these five sites emerge as civitas capitals? The way is probably best shown by considering the specific example of Cirencester (*Corinium Dobunnorum*).

A fort, or possibly a 30-acre (12ha) fortress, was established at Cirencester a year or so after the invasion, and a study of the earliest roads in the vicinity shows that they were aligned on the fort (fig. 4). About AD 49 the site was moved fractionally to the north-west and a new fort built for a cavalry regiment. These forts fitted strategically into a series placed along, behind and in advance of the Fosse Way to form a frontier zone of some depth. The nearest neighbour seems to have been the fort, and later the fortress, at Gloucester. The tactical siting of the fort would have been influenced by a number of local factors, the most important being geography, and another the political situation. Geographically the fort was built in a position often favoured by Roman military engineers: on a low plateau connected with higher ground to the south and west, but over-looking lower, possibly marshy ground elsewhere. The meeting of the Fosse Way with Akeman Street and an intersection with Ermin Street also created an important road junction. Additionally there would have been a bridge carrying the Fosse Way over the river Churn to be guarded. The political factors would have been centred on the large native *oppidum* at Bagendon (*Corinion?*), about 3 miles (4·8km) north of Cirencester. Mrs Clifford's excavations[38] have shown it to be almost certainly the capital of the eastern half of the Dobunni, whose king Boduocus was one of the first to surrender to Plautius in AD 43. This piece of diplomacy may have earned for him a short continued reign and the status of an ally. The western and possibly less philo-Roman part of the Dobunni, with their king Corio. . .[39] may have met the Romans with force, and, as a result, may later have lost their identity in the *civitas Belgarum*. The placing of a fort at Cirencester would therefore fulfil all the tactical requirements and, at the same time, would be able to supervise the local capital while protecting it from any possible attack by hostile people to the west.

Although no attempt seems to have been made to move the inhabitants from Bagendon, we can be sure that a cavalry fort only 3 miles (4·8km) away would have had a profound economic effect on them. Cavalrymen were better paid than auxiliary infantrymen and, by native standards, they would have had a considerable sum of money to spend on local goods and services. At first the natives might have travelled periodically to the fort to sell their goods, but it would not have been long before the advantages of living closer were recognised. Excavation has shown that from about AD 60, or perhaps slightly earlier, timber-

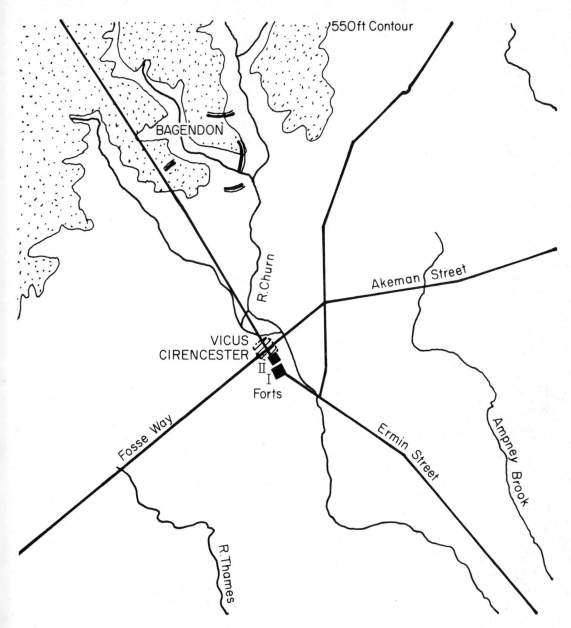

4   Roman forts at Cirencester

framed buildings and huts were being erected and streets laid out in the area immediately north-west of the fort.[40] As at least one of the streets was constructed parallel to the fort defences, either a degree of official encouragement and help or native imitation of Roman ways might be implied, so that, when the settlement became large enough, it would probably have been given the legal status of a *vicus*, and allowed to manage its own purely internal affairs under the supervision of the prefect of the fort. It can hardly be coincidence that, at precisely the time when it can be shown that the *vicus* was expanding, Mrs Clifford's excavations have shown that occupation at Bagendon was declining, until it finally ended between *c.* AD 60 and 70.[41] Bagendon had now been deserted in favour of the new *vicus*. No compulsion would have been needed save the money in the soldiers' pockets, which, then as now, provided the incentive wherever a garrison of troops has been established for any length of time. So, when the fort was evacuated, probably in the late seventies, a flourishing trading settlement would have been in existence and it is likely that it already acted as a market for any nearby farms. Its direct links with the old capital, the connexions which the majority of the tribal notables from Bagendon would have had there, and its excellent position with respect to the new road system, would have made it the obvious choice for a capital when the *civitas Dobunnorum* was set up. Within a decade the new town had been laid out, which, with its regular street-pattern and numerous new shops and houses, had extended over both the *vicus* and the abandoned fort, so showing complete transfer of government land to the *civitas*. At the centre, the forum and basilica were built, perhaps with more haste than good judgment (see p. 298), on a scale which outstripped in size all others in Britain except London. Even at this early stage the Dobunni were investing lavishly in 'romanitas'.

At Dorchester, Exeter and Leicester similar processes, but with minor variations, can be discerned. The great hill-fort of Maiden Castle is only just over 2 miles (3·2km) from where the first fort may have been built at Dorchester (*Durnovaria*). It is often claimed that there is no evidence on which to assume that Maiden Castle was the chief Durotrigan centre, as so many other large hill-forts are known in their territory. Such claims may or may not be correct, but they cannot deny the hill-fort's size and relative importance. It is also possible to surmount these claims by arguing backwards from the foundation of the civitas capital. Given a number of sites of equal potential, that most likely to be selected would probably have been one where there was already a preponderance of influential tribal notables, as suggested above for Cirencester. If the *vicus* at Dorchester was chosen as the capital then it would probably follow that the most important tribesmen came originally from Maiden Castle and not for instance from Hod Hill, Badbury Rings or Ham Hill.[42]

At Exeter (*Isca Dumnoniorum*) the same forces would have been at work with an added simplification: with few forts in Dumnonian territory there would have been less choice of *vici* and, moreover, there was no obvious native centre to perpetuate. Moreover, a legionary fortress would have exerted more influence than an auxiliary fort and consequently may have attracted a larger *vicus*.

The coincidence of fort and native centre at Leicester (*Ratae Coritanorum*) will also have reduced the possibilities, although the constitution of the *civitas Coritanorum* may have been complicated by the foundation of *Lindum colonia* in the northern sector of the tribal region. Emphasis would in consequence have been placed on the southern half, with the selection of a capital at Leicester rather than at some other major centre such as Old Sleaford. It is probable that the military occupation of the Coritani ended at about the same time as that of their south-western neighbours and the fort at Leicester does not seem to have been occupied much after AD 75.[43] The constitution of the *civitas* would presumably have been again carried out on the removal of military control. But, although the streets of *Ratae* were laid out, a vacant insula at the centre was left for the forum, which was not built until the Hadrianic-Antonine period.[44] However no doubt can attach to the earlier existence of the *vicus* even without a forum, as a military diploma of AD 106 refers to a Roman citizen's *origo* as *Ratis*.[45]

If Frere is right in his suggestion that Legio XX did not leave Wroxeter until *c*. AD 90,[46] as seems likely, then the *civitas Cornoviorum* cannot have been formed before the last decade of the first century, or possibly even later. The reasons for the choice of Wroxeter (*Viroconium Cornoviorum*) as the civitas capital were much the same as those which applied to Dorchester. Although the legionary fortress was not far from the Wrekin, there is less evidence to suggest the pre-eminence of this hill-fort among Cornovian native sites than there was for Maiden Castle. The date of completion of the forum at Wroxeter, as provided by the inscription dedicated to Hadrian, is AD 129/30.[47] If we accept that the provision of a basilica is the physical evidence of local self-government at *civitas* level, then the gap of thirty or more years which elapsed between the earliest possible date for the foundation of the two *civitates* of the Coritani and Cornovii and the completion of their fora is difficult to explain. Certainly some allowance must be made for the planning and construction of a major building, for which ten years would seem to be more than enough; but for a generation and a half, or more, to elapse, would seem to point to other reasons for delay. It is difficult to plead for these two *civitates*, as perhaps we might for the Iceni, that poverty was the reason for the time-lag, as both had developed rich and flourishing capitals by the mid-second century. Possibly sheer inertia, coupled with the slackening of interest in Britain under Trajan, was the cause. During this principate, interest was centred on Dacia and the eastern Empire, and Trajan himself was no great promoter of new towns in the west; perhaps only in the more bracing atmosphere following Hadrian's visit to Britain was interest revived and work resumed. Other alternatives might envisage the continuation of military government for the Cornovii and delay until the Hadrianic period of the award of self-government, while the Coritani may have been, for a short time, administered from the *colonia* at Lincoln.

Doubt must also surround the date at which the *civitas Silurum* was formed. It has been suggested[48] that Caerwent (*Venta Silurum*) was established *c*. AD 75, but this must be viewed with caution, since the evidence would apply just as well to a fort with an attached *vicus* as to a town.[49] The Silures were openly hostile to Rome until they were finally defeated by Julius Frontinus between AD 75 and 79. Full military occupation would certainly have been maintained for a time, which, in view of their hostility, might be expected to have been longer than for a friendly tribe. Indeed, at least one new fort, at Gelligaer, was being built in their territory soon after the turn of the first century[50] and, while it is conceivable that this construction was intended to help protect the *civitas* from the unruly elements of central Wales, there is certainly no good reason to suggest its constitution before the second century at the earliest. Too little is known about the early history of Caerwent for sound reasons to be advanced for the choice of site, although it has been suggested that Llanmelin was its native predecessor.

The last group of principal *civitates* to be considered is that containing the Parisi, Brigantes and Demetae (fig. 3). At present, decisive information is only available on the first. That the civitas capital of the Parisi was for a time situated near Brough-on-Humber (*Petuaria*) is now almost certain,[51] in spite of attempts to show that the tribe was divided into four parts, each with its own centre. The selection of *Petuaria* as the capital followed closely the reasons already set out for Cirencester. A fort was established by Petillius Cerialis *c.* AD 71–2 not far from a major native settlement at North Ferriby. After an initial evacuation and re-occupation, the fort was finally abandoned *c.* AD 125, by which time a *vicus* appears to have grown nearby. The *civitas Parisorum* was probably constituted shortly afterwards; it was almost certainly in existence by AD 144.[52]

Not sufficient is yet known about the early history of Aldborough (*Isurium Brigantum*) for there to be any certainty as to the date of its foundation and the organising of the *civitas Brigantum*. But there are sufficient similarities to Brough-on-Humber and the Parisi for an early or mid-Hadrianic date to be suggested. A date then would also be consistent with the evacuation of at least eight forts in Brigantian territory, especially in the area round the Vale of York, and the loosening of military control which this would imply.[53]

Even less can be said about the Demetae. The suggestion that they were organised into the *civitas Demetarum* with a capital at Carmarthen (*Moridunum*) is of recent origin.[54] Excavation has shown that there was a Flavian fort, that a *vicus* was connected with it, and that the *vicus* probably developed into the civitas capital early in the second century. The most marked similarities exist between the Demetae and the scattered tribe of the Dumnonii, so that the choice of Carmarthen would have been made on much the same grounds as the choice of Exeter.

Two other probable civitas capitals, Carlisle (*Luguvalium*) and Ilchester (*Lindinis*) were the product of the subdivision of the Brigantes and Durotriges respectively. As they were not from the first apparently 'planned *vici*', they lie for the present outside our definition of what is a town, and will therefore be considered in a later chapter, with some other exceptions.

That there were certain common factors behind the foundation of each and every town in Roman Britain will, by now, be apparent. But, once founded, each town tended to assume its own individual pattern of development, which was brought about by different circumstances in each case. The subsequent history of these towns is therefore discussed in later chapters under individual headings, although attention is drawn to such similarities as may exist between them. The only event of later years which should have affected all towns alike, was the Edict of Caracalla in AD 212, which awarded Roman citizenship to all free-born inhabitants of the Empire. The Edict—the *constitutio Antoniniana*—would have made it necessary for all these to give a specific town as *origo*, whereas before, it had been sufficient for a non-citizen to give only his *civitas peregrina*. So would come about a subtle change in emphasis from a whole district to the town at its centre, which might in time assume an ascendancy in peoples' minds, even if it was not accompanied by a change in status.

2

What part did
towns play in the province?

To many Romans civilised life was focused on the town. It was at once the centre for administration, education, trade, amusement, amenity and protection. Although country life may have appealed to some, such as Vergil, it had equally little attraction for many others. Indeed Pliny speaks out against such retirement; both Varro and Columella considered that it was necessary for a land-owner to know what was happening on his farms, although neither suggested that he should live there permanently. But this was the upper class view, and not all would subscribe to it. The Roman world was full or people living permanently on farms, although even they would have recognised the importance of towns in their society. Iron Age society in Britain, like that in many parts of Gaul, presented something of a contrast, revolving almost entirely round individual farms, fortresses and villages with only comparatively few larger collective settlements. But even these settlements could not be called towns in the Mediterranean sense, and the use of the word 'oppida' by Caesar, Suetonius and other authors to describe them was, we cannot but feel, little more than a courtesy title for something for which the Romans were at a loss for a name. An oppidum might have been a large area enclosed by a series of dykes, such as those at Camulodunum, Bagendon or Stanwick (N. Yorks.), or it might have been a hill-fort like one of the twenty oppida which Vespasian, when legate of Legio II Augusta, captured during his campaign in southern England immediately after the invasion.[1] All attracted the same name at the hands of Latin authors, yet none, whether hill-fort or dyked enclosure, would have contained more than a haphazardly-placed collection of huts, and none would have fulfilled the functions which were expected of a town by the Roman provincial administration.

This radical difference in outlook could have been the cause of much friction between conquerors and conquered. It was natural that the imperial government would hope for the cooperation of the natives in establishing towns, for not only were they an essential part of the Roman way of life, which the natives were encouraged to emulate, but they also made the tasks of administration, tax collection, education and policing much easier. It might be claimed that one of the main achievements, by which the success of the Roman administration in Britain can be judged, was its ability to persuade a population, totally committed to a rural way of life, to accept the alien, urban settlements in its midst. Admittedly, the process of assimilation was not a new problem, having already been tried in other provinces, especially in Gaul, with general success; but Britain, although very similar to Gaul, was still different in many respects. Admittedly, all attempts at urbanisation in Britain were not the unqualified success that no doubt the provincial administration hoped they would be. Admittedly also, there were mistakes and failures, especially at first, but there were more successes: and in this context a successful town represented a success for the provincial administration in pacifying the country. Conquest was only the start of Roman intervention in Britain; acceptance of the conquest by the native population was altogether another matter, and the growth of towns was proof of that acceptance. Equally, it might be said that continuance or re-imposition of military occupation represented a failure. A fort or fortress might have been occupied entirely by Roman citizens, but it was an island in, or on the edge of, potentially hostile foreign territory, which had refused to accept romanisation except possibly at a very low level. A town might have been inhabited almost entirely by non-citizens, it might have been but a poor imitation of Rome in a very makeshift and diluted form, yet that town represented acceptance of Rome in a way that no fort or fortress ever could do.

Towns then were used to further the acceptance of the Roman conquest. In a province such as Britain, which was not familiar with urbanisation, this could only be done by the creation of models to serve as examples for the native population, and the first to be planned was the *colonia* at Camulodunum. Included in it were all the main types of buildings normally associated with civilised Roman town life.[2] If they dazzled and inspired awe among the natives and provided a local image of Rome's power and magnificence, it would cause a much greater impression. A secondary reason for the foundation of this particular *colonia* is also apparent. Only a year or so before work was started, a minor revolt had broken out among the Iceni, and with the removal of the last major army unit, Legio XX, from the south-east in AD 49 it was necessary to replace it with a reliable reserve. These two principal functions of the *colonia* were not entirely compatible. The retired legionary veterans, who formed the main part of the population, did not make the best salesmen for model urban life; yet there was an undoubted need for their presence. That this same reserve of legionary veterans then failed to heed the warning signs of AD 60, and indeed added to the danger by their arrogant behaviour, cannot be taken as evidence for the failure of the policy which prescribed the model. The policy was not so much at fault as its executors; nevertheless the Boudiccan rebellion was a very serious set-back. These two functions were supplemented by a third, which was specific to Colchester. The provincial administration established there the headquarters of the imperial cult. By choosing a site close to the old capital of Cunobelin, it was probably felt that the loyalties of most British people would be perpetuated and transferred to the new town. The decision was not entirely good; the administrative capital later grew in London (p. 80), even though the chief centre of the imperial cult probably remained at Colchester. The cult itself was yet another facet of imperial policy and tended to be something of a unifying force in a heterogeneous Empire. In consequence, an oath of loyalty to the Emperor's *numen* or to the *Domus Divina* probably had both secular and religious meanings. The setting up of a cult centre was therefore an important act in a new and uncivilised province. Once more the provincial administration followed precedents already established in Germany and also in Gaul, where the religious centre for the three northern Gaulish provinces had been founded on a site close to the *colonia* of Lyons (*Lugdunum*) in the confluence between the rivers Rhône and Soâne. There was built first an altar and then a temple dedicated to Rome and Augustus, and the apparent success of this centre was probably the reason for the adoption of a similar scheme in Britain, even though the German attempt had been a failure. But perhaps the British counterpart was carried through with too great an excess of zeal and officiousness, or perhaps the British were demonstrating once more the differences between themselves and the Gauls. The great temple and the associated altar which was constructed at Colchester attracted unwelcome attention even in Rome, while in Britain it seems to have become the focus of disenchantment for precisely those disruptive elements in the population which it was intended to unite.[3] Again it might be said that the executors were at fault and not imperial policy. The policy itself was vindicated when the temple had been rebuilt after the Boudiccan rebellion had destroyed it: in later years the cult is attested in a wide variety of contexts, showing that it had become generally accepted.

Except for its central religious role, the part played by the *colonia* at Colchester in forming a model for urban development was followed by the two later foundations at Lincoln and Gloucester. The distribution of these three *coloniae* could not have been bettered, had it been intended deliberately to show the largest number of people in Britain the desirability of urban life. It might be said therefore that these three towns played an educational part in furthering urbanisation in the province. Naturally, however, this role would have lessened as time went on, and as other towns were established and developed. Ultimately all towns, no matter what their status, would assume the same basic functions which would only vary in very special circumstances: as indicated at the start of this chapter, they provided facilities for administration, education, trade, amusement, amenity and protection.

The administrative unit of a *colonia*, and probably also of a *municipium*, consisted of the town and its *territorium*, which was treated as being an extension of the town. The towns themselves were almost certainly divided into wards, also called *vici*, and possible evidence for two such *vici* is provided by inscriptions from Lincoln;[4] others probably existed there and in the other two *coloniae*. The administration was regulated by a foundation 'charter' (*lex coloniae*) supposedly

granted by the central government.[5] We have no knowledge of the individual
'charters' of the British *coloniae*; but, by referring to examples from other
provinces, in particular from Spain, and to the *Digest*, it is possible to draw
tentative conclusions about the way in which they were administered. However,
it should be remembered that each 'charter' was drafted separately and may have
differed in detail from others, although all would probably have drawn heavily
on established precedent.

The supreme authority in a town was nominally the *ordo*, a council of about
100 *decuriones*,[6] elected from among citizens, who were normally at least 30
years old and who had a specified level of personal wealth and property.[7] Initially,
election was by the general assembly of the town, but by the second century the
ordo and the magistrates had become virtually self-perpetuating. It is also probable
that a *decurion* had to reside within a certain distance of the town.[8] The *ordo* was
responsible for the annual appointments of magistrates, of which there were two
pairs. These pairs of officers, the *duoviri iuridicundo* and the *aediles* were the chief
executives of the town. Ostensibly, they were subject to the *ordo* and apparently
they could be called to account by the *decuriones* on any matter concerning public
affairs. In practice they probably possessed greater powers than this arrangement
suggests and at least one case is known from the *colonia Julia Vienna* (Vienne)
where a *duovir* exceeded his authority and ordered the complete abolition of the
games. It was alleged on appeal to Rome that he had no power to make such an

1   Centuriated area 17 miles (27km) north of Orange (*colonia Arausio*) as represented on the cadastre. The
area lies east of the river Rhône, with the river Berre running east-west (from top to bottom) through it.
The plots represented are DD XVI to DD XX and CK I to CK II (*Orange Museum*)

order, but his action was upheld.[9] Also, if a *decurion* was accused of being unfit for his position, a *duovir* could be called upon to pass judgment on him; if he gave an adverse decision that person ceased to be a *decurion* forthwith.[10] The *duoviri* were the senior pair and it is probable that they would have been elected members of the *ordo* before appointment. They sat as magistrates in the local court trying cases of petty crime and civil cases on which an upper monetary limit was placed; serious criminal cases and civil cases involving sums of money above the limit were remitted for trial in the governor's assize courts (*conventus*). But by the later period hardly any power of correction in the criminal courts had been left to local magistrates. One or other also acted as chairman at meetings of the *ordo*, and they had various other legal and non-legal duties, such as those connected with the supervision of the imperial cult, public ceremonies, the local militia, and supervision of the junior officers. For a decree of the *ordo* to be valid, the magistrates' presence was essential, although a right of appeal to the council lay with anyone fined in the courts. Every fifth year was deemed to be of special importance, when outstandingly eminent people were appointed as *duoviri* and received the title of *quinquennales*. They had extra duties to undertake, which included the filling of vacancies in the *ordo*, the renewal of public contracts and the assessment of new levels of tax liability, occasioned either by change of ownership or circumstances. Normally at this stage any ex-magistrates with the necessary qualifications, who were not already members, would have been elected to the *ordo*.

The junior officers or *aediles* could be appointed at the age of 25, so that simultaneous election to the *ordo* would not be automatic. They were mainly responsible for the upkeep of public buildings, roads and streets, the aqueduct and its distributive system, sewers and other works. Apparently an aedile could also sit as a magistrate in place of a *duovir*,[11] although the more normal practice was for a prefect to be appointed if the *duovir* had to be absent for more than a day.

For some of the larger *coloniae* at least, there were probably a pair of financial officers (*quaestors*) whose duties were akin to the modern city treasurer and who were responsible to the *duoviri*.

The *seviri augustales*[12] were in charge, under the magistrates' supervision, of ceremonies connected with the imperial cult. They were normally elected by the decurions from among the most wealthy of the freedmen in a town, who were prohibited from election either to magistracies or to the *ordo*. It was a post which required a considerable amount of personal expenditure on games and festivals and most holders of the office would have been rich merchants. Indeed, few of the officers mentioned above would have escaped such expenditure, for, on election, they not only had to pay a fee to the municipal treasury, but they were also expected to donate a handsome gift to the town, which often took the form of some useful structure, or a public show.[13] In order ostensibly to protect its wider interests a town, acting through its decurions, could elect patrons, who were usually influential in military or government affairs in Rome. Although patrons would only be honorary members of the *ordo*, they were often considerable benefactors to the town (cf. below p. 381). Hence a system by which most public works were erected and maintained by private subscription enabled local taxation to be kept at a low level. Revenues for the most part were obtained by renting land or buildings and, to a lesser extent, by selling water from the aqueduct to private consumers, by fines, and by dues on goods brought into the town.

The *territorium* of a *colonia* or *municipium* would be organised and administered as part of the town. In a great many places in other parts of the Empire the land was divided up into plots by a rigid grid system of accommodation roads. The basic measurement was the *iugerum* ($\frac{5}{8}$ acre = 0·25ha), and 200 *iugera* made up one square *centuria quadrata*, with sides of 20 *actus* (776yds = 709m). Unfortunately, no satisfactory evidence seems to have survived for the existence of centuriation outside any of the British *coloniae*. Indeed, Richmond has gone so far as to suggest that it need not be expected at Colchester, as the land, as captive land, was distributed haphazardly among the veterans; any authorised person could take as much as he pleased.[14] It is possible that the land apportionment was better regulated after the Boudiccan rebellion and the refounding of the *colonia*, but no reliable evidence is available, in spite of Haverfield's, and, later, Stevens' attempts to show its existence.[15] The same paucity of information applies to the other *coloniae*, although there the use of centuriation might be more readily expected. Whether centuriation existed or not, the plan of the *territorium* would probably have been recorded in the town archive, with possibly an engraved marble or bronze plan set up in the forum of the town. One example (pl. 1) of such a record comes from *colonia Arausio* (Orange) in Gallia Narbonensis.[16] Dated to AD 77 in Vespasian's principate it is marked off in rectangular areas representing 200 *iugera*. Additional subdivisions are inscribed with the plot number, the legal description of the land, the individual landowner, where one existed, and sometimes its valuation and state—whether cultivated or not.

The administration of a *municipium* was almost identical with that of a *colonia*, except that a *municipium* could retain some of its native laws whereas a *colonia* had to use Roman law. It is probable that a basically similar system to that used in *municipia*, but normally lacking *quaestors*, would have been used for the *civitates*, although considerable variations are known.

The size of many *civitates* in both Britain and Gaul would have made necessary smaller units within them. A *civitas* was therefore usually split into a number of country districts or *pagi*, and, although there is no direct evidence for their existence in Britain,[27] it is most likely that the Gallic practice was followed. In addition, the civitas capital and all the principal villages would have received the rank of *vicus*, but the former might, if large enough, be made up of a number of wards, which were also called *vici*, hence giving rise to some confusion in modern arguments.[18] These *vici* were also allowed a measure of self-government and were allowed to elect two *magistri* and a council of *vicani*, while some civitas capitals certainly had *aediles* as well.[19] A single civitas capital, therefore, would be representative of several levels of local government: the *vicus*, and possibly constituent *vici*, and the *civitas*, to which all *vici* and *pagi* would be subordinate. *Civitates*, like *coloniae* and *municipia*, were probably able to elect patrons, although

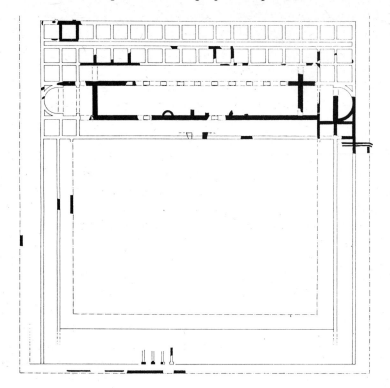

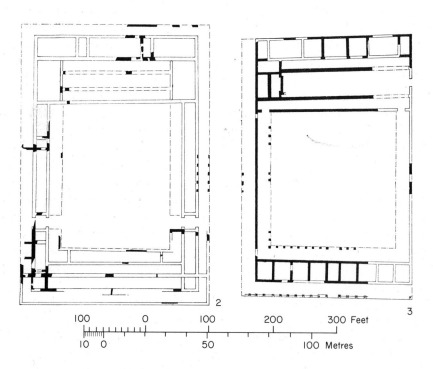

5   Plans of fora: (1) London; (2) Leicester; (3) Wroxeter (*after D. Macketh*)

none are known from Britain. Other benefactors must have existed; an inscription on a statue-base from Caerwent[20] records that it was set up 'by decree of the council of the *civitas Silurum*' to Tiberius Claudius Paulinus, who for a time was legate of Legio II Augusta at Caerleon, before going on to be governor successively of Narbonensis, Lugdunensis and Britannia Inferior. It is probable that he formed connections with the town during his service at Caerleon, and in some way became a benefactor, which was marked by a statue erected in his honour before he succeeded to the last post *c*. AD 220.

As time passed various changes took place in the functions and titles of the administration of towns and *civitates*. For instance members of the *ordo* were more commonly referred to by the name *curiales* in the later Empire, although *decurio* never fully went out of use; occasionally in the fourth century a decurion is referred to as a *senator*, as on the tombstone of Flavius Martius, a council member of the *civitas Carvetiorum*.[21] From the second century onwards a new post of *curator* was being created. At first these officers were occasional appointments to meet some special need in matters of finance; by the third century they were being appointed as regular magistrates and full-time officials, *curatores rei publicae* or *civitatis*, and by the fourth century they had become universal. Apart from being pre-eminent in financial matters they also took the place of the *duoviri* as chairmen of the *curiales*,[22] and it is clear from other evidence that the decurions now had to refer all matters relating to public works and buildings to the *curator* before decisions could be reached. No *curatores* have been attested for Britain, but several inscriptions from Gallia Belgica show their existence in similar circumstances, and include also examples of *curatores vici*.[23] The growing tendency towards the appointment of imperial placemen in place of lay-magistrates and officials was, of course, being matched in other quarters, and by the fourth century the ranks of imperial, provincial and local government civil servants had all swollen considerably. The reorganisation and fragmentation of certain provinces in the Empire, first under Septimius Severus and later again under Diocletian helped the process and resulted in the creation of a carefully-graded hierarchy of officials and the multiplication of offices. Nevertheless, the decurions seem to have retained their importance, although the post became increasingly unpopular. It has been argued that, at the moment when election to magistracies was carried out by the *ordo* and not by the popular assembly, the supply of purely voluntary candidates had dwindled almost to vanishing point. If too few or no candidates presented themselves, the magistrate was required to make out for election a list of sufficient and fit persons, who could in turn nominate others.[24] The decurions had always been responsible for the collection of taxes and for their forwarding to the proper authority. This responsibility was extended by Diocletian, who made them personally liable for the taxes of defaulters. By now, also, the level of taxation had risen considerably and the number of people who could not meet their liabilities and so defaulted must have increased with it. Few persons would have voluntarily undertaken the duty of decurion with such personal and public liabilities, so that an office which for long had been compul-

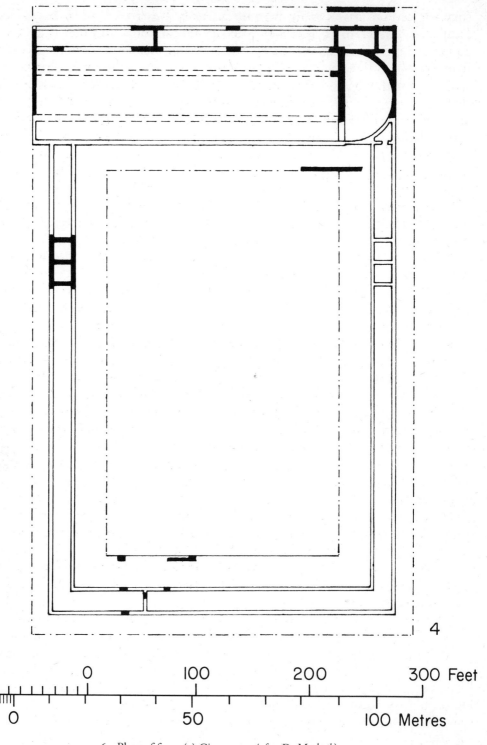

100   0   100   200   300 Feet

10   0   50   100 Metres

6   Plans of fora: (4) Cirencester (*after D. Macketh*)

sory for certain classes, now became virtually hereditary. In their anxiety to escape the burden, those who were still rich bought or bribed their way into the equestrian order, whose members, being of a higher social class, were exempt from service as *curiales*. Eventual bankruptcy must have been the fear of many who remained. It has been argued that the wealth of villas in Britain in the fourth century does not reflect a decline in wealth of the curial class. But the evidence is unbalanced; the villas belonged to those who either survived or escaped from their obligations. We cannot expect to find evidence of those who went bankrupt. There must have been at least 2000 decurions in Britain at any one time, and as we have already seen (p. 427, n. 7) bankruptcy did not relieve them of their positions, while only about 600 villas of all types are known.

It has already been noted in Chapter I that the presence in a British town of a forum, with its associated basilica, probably indicates the existence of a self-governing community. The basilica was a large aisled hall stretching the full length of one end of the forum; it would have been the chief administrative centre (figs. 5–7). The hall itself would certainly have been used for public meetings and assemblies and also as a gathering place for litigants and witnesses waiting for cases to be heard. It also served as the law court itself, either for the local magistrates or, in the case of certain towns, which are not known in Britain, for the assizes (*conventus*) of the governor, the 'bench' being seated on a tribunal. The latter was placed at one end of the nave, and commonly it was matched by another at the opposing end. It is possible that the magistrates also had private offices, where business of a less judicial nature could be conducted, but which, no doubt, could also be used for hearing applications 'in chambers'. A series of rooms which ran down the basilica on the side away from the forum probably provided these offices; others served a variety of purposes. One room, by no means always the largest in the range, is usually placed symmetrically at the centre; it is sometimes called the *curia*, or council chamber, but Frere has pointed out[25] that in the majority of cases it would be too small to seat the members of the *ordo* even if their number was, as sometimes, less than a hundred. It is more likely to have been a shrine dedicated to the local deity and may also have contained imperial statues. Indeed the *curia* would probably have been the largest room of all, while the remainder would have served as offices and record rooms. At Wroxeter one such room was found to contain writing materials, traces of wooden chests and part of a military diploma.[26]

If towns acted principally as administrative centres their role in fostering civilised life was almost equally important. In the *coloniae*, civilised life was predominantly romanised from the start, but in the early civitas capitals it was something new, which the natives had to learn, and the life there might at first be better described as progress towards romanisation. The foundation of towns in Britain probably had the effect of syphoning off from the countryside the go-ahead, ambitious people, leaving the more conservative behind. We can see much the same process working today, with the foundation of new towns in various parts of the country. The increased opportunities offered are undoubtedly

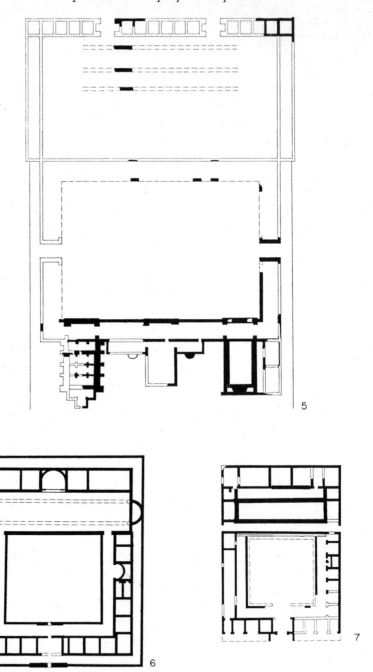

5

6

7

100   0   100   200   300 Feet

10 0   50   100 Metres

7   Plans of fora: (5) Verulamium; (6) Silchester; (7) Caerwent (*after D. Macketh*)

their main attraction. Such people would be more ready to accept the new standards, if by so doing they advanced their own prospects. This could be one of the reasons why romanisation proceeded more rapidly in towns than in the country.

The new social classes which emerged in towns did not differ fundamentally from the oligarchic Celtic society of the Iron Age. What changes there were probably came about through a greater degree of social mobility, the creation of some new classes, such as merchants and shopkeepers and finer distinctions between classes. We have already seen that the curial class was confined to free-born men possessing a certain level of wealth, but there was nothing in law to prevent the sons of a rich freedman from becoming members of that class and so reaching a higher social standing than their father. In the earlier years, too, both these classes would be cut across by the distinction between non-citizens and Roman citizens, who would, among other things, be bound by a different legal code. Among the lower classes there would be yet another distinction between free-born and slave. A slave who was manumitted and perhaps set up in business, either on his own account, or as a tenant of his master, often had a greater chance of success than a free-born artisan or shopkeeper, and might in time accumulate great wealth. Often, also, a master who freed a slave and allowed him perhaps to become a tenant of a shop received a better return than if he had retained him as a slave. We can probably assume therefore that, at least during the first two centuries, a greater degree of social mobility occurred in Britain than had before. We do not know to what extent this was aided by the patronage system, so common in other parts of the Empire; a rich patron, in return for various gifts, would help to prosper a less wealthy client, who certainly stood lower in the social order. Changing economic patterns and far-reaching controls imposed from above may later have reduced mobility just as the general award of Roman citizenship in the early third century reduced the number of classes.

The rate at which romanisation proceeded is difficult to estimate. As Frere has most recently pointed out, the evidence is mainly material.[27] That it ultimately spread deeply in towns cannot be doubted; it was the intention of Rome that it should. Nevertheless a degree of native British culture, which varied in strength from place to place, still remained and often fused completely with the Roman. Much has already been written about the use of Latin in Roman Britain, and several different conclusions have been reached.[28] The general opinion seems to be that it was the language of officialdom and cultured society, with many of the upper classes being bilingual, but that it was a language acquired by teaching at school; in the towns, artisans had some knowledge of Latin, but in the country little or none.

The test of how natural is a language to its user surely depends on the ability to think in that language, without first having to think in a different tongue and then translate the thoughts. Naturally this is difficult to assess, when little or nothing of these thoughts survive, but it might be argued that, if an adult could scratch obscene epithets in Latin on the wall of a derelict house in Leicester,[29] then it is probable that he could swear in Latin speech. The use of expletives might be taken to suggest that the user was thinking in the same language, so in turn implying a familiarity stretching back to before the schoolroom. The widespread use of Latin names, even if some do have Celtic stems, would seemingly point in the same direction. The cosmopolitan nature of many British towns and villages, where inscriptions attest the presence of Gauls, Germans, Greeks and Syrians would of necessity require some common language, which Latin would best fulfil. Apart from language, it is probable that the people who came to Britain from other provinces of the Empire, made a considerable contribution to the process of romanisation and transmitted ideas for the new way of life. Nevertheless the British language did survive, chiefly, we must assume, among countrymen, and there is much evidence of cross-fertilisation between the two languages, so that we might wonder whether the variety spoken at the end of the fourth century would have been intelligible to an inhabitant of pre-Roman Britain.

The spread of civilised manners and customs in the towns could only take place with, and indeed would be encouraged by, the provision of amenities. High on the list ranked the public bath-house (figs. 8–9), with its facilities for relaxation and exercise as well as hygiene; for, in the Roman world, the town baths were akin to a good club. These buildings have still to be identified in many of the earlier towns such as Chichester and Winchester, but at Silchester one was built during the first century. Leicester, perhaps in keeping with its later development as a civitas capital, was not provided with one until the middle of the second century. The size of some civic bath-houses in Britain has sometimes led to questions being asked about their operation. Suggestions have been made that they could not be maintained permanently in full operation, as the expense would be too great, and that there would not be the demand. But with an estimated population of about three or four thousand for Leicester, even a weekly visit on the part of each inhabitant to the Jewry Wall baths would mean nearly 500 people a day passing through its doors, or perhaps between sixty or seventy an hour. Moreover such a massive building would require very large quantities of fuel initially to raise the temperature of the various rooms to their correct level. The thickness of the walls and roof would ensure minimum heat loss, so that once hot, much smaller quantities of fuel would be needed to maintain a level temperature. To light the fires intermittently would, in the long run, have wasted far more fuel than it would have saved.

A large bath-house could only work satisfactorily if a copious supply of running water was available, so that, at the same time if not before, an aqueduct would be constructed, and urban aqueducts are known at Dorchester, Wroxeter, Leicester and Lincoln; others probably existed at least at London, Silchester, Cirencester, Caerwent and Verulamium, where the presence of the distribution pipes inside the towns is known. Once constructed they could be used to supple-ment other sources of domestic water, frequently drawn from wells; so public water tanks would be set up at intervals in the streets. Householders and shop-

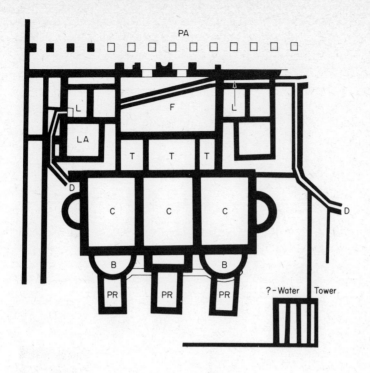

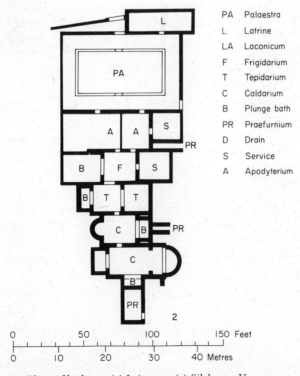

PA Palaestra

L Latrine

LA Laconicum

F Frigidarium

T Tepidarium

C Caldarium

B Plunge bath

PR Praefurnium

D Drain

S Service

A Apodyterium

8 Plans of baths at: (1) Leicester; (2) Silchester V

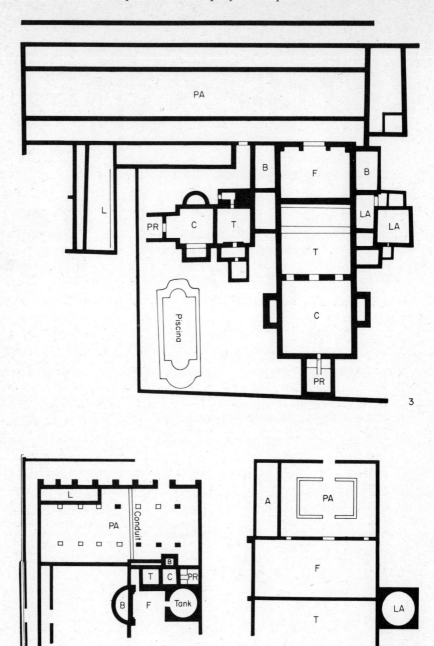

9   Plans of baths at: (3) Wroxeter; (4) Caerwent; (5) Caistor-by-Norwich

keepers might, if the flow was sufficient, and by payment of a fee, be supplied too, as at Wroxeter and Verulamium, while any excess was allowed to run into the sewers to ensure adequate flushing. Richmond has argued that few of the civitas capitals in Britain possessed proper sewers.[30] One of the finest examples in any town is the system which ran beneath the streets of Lincoln, which also possessed an aqueduct. It should be remembered that if a free flow of water enters a town in an aqueduct, then sewers of almost equal capacity must be provided to carry away the surplus and the waste after use; the reverse is frequently true, and a high-capacity sewage system should imply the presence of an aqueduct, or at least a copious source within the town. That being so, any town with a proved aqueduct and distribution system, which has not yet produced evidence for sewers, would be worth re-examination. Not all sewers were constructed on the monumental pattern of Lincoln, and one recently found[31] running down the centre of part of Ermin Street in Cirencester had a cross-sectional area about two feet square (0·2 sq. m) but had been lined entirely with timber. In the aerial photographs of some other towns, notably Caistor-by-Norwich, suspicious dark lines can be seen running centrally down some streets, and these might well represent sewers of the Cirencester type.

The comfortable town-house, with its dining-room and separate servants' wing, must also have ranked high among the amenities. Not a great deal is known about these houses in the first century, but, by the second century, houses of the curial class become sufficiently distinctive in plan to be readily identifiable. Still in some cases constructed with timber frames and wattle and daub walls they had to eschew the refinement of central heating. Nevertheless, mosaics and frescoes decorated the floors and walls at least of the dining room; adequately warmed by braziers, the householder could entertain his guests to dinner in some degree of fashion and, while sampling the products of a more varied diet, they could discuss, in Latin, the subject of his new wall-painting. With the improvement of building materials and the use of more brick and stone in place of wood, the braziers could be replaced by ducted, underfloor heating with additional channels carrying the heat up through the walls, so helping to reduce condensation in winter. These houses, for all their comforts, rarely had private bath-wings, of the type which are associated with so many country villas. Only the richest could afford them, and even they, like all other inhabitants of the town, might have made use of the public baths, and a visit often assumed the guise of a social event. Even slaves might be sent to the baths by their master, while under a decree of Hadrian, and as the result of scandalous behaviour during mixed bathing, separate times of the day were set aside for the use of men and women.

Civilised living required entertainment as well as amenity. In British towns the amphitheatre was the principal place of entertainment, with surviving examples at Cirencester, Dorchester, Silchester, Chichester, Carmarthen and probably Caerwent, and with others possibly implied at York and Leicester by inscriptions (figs. 14–16). The size of these buildings often dictated that they should be constructed near the edges of a town's built-up area; consequently

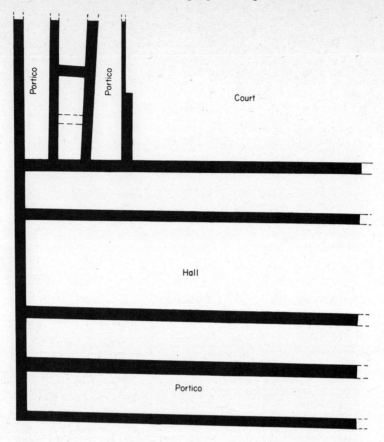

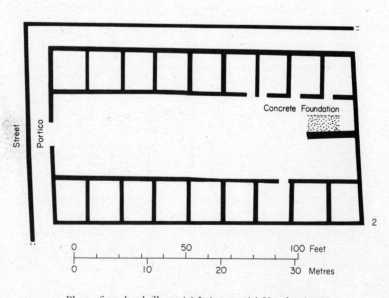

10   Plans of market halls at: (1) Leicester; (2) Verulamium I

when the towns were walled they were often left outside the fortifications for reasons of economy, and it is not strictly true to say, as is sometimes done, that amphitheatres were built outside the walls. The only example of an amphitheatre likely to post-date the construction of defences is that of Caerwent, and it is interesting that it should have been placed within the walls. Apart from the examples quoted above, other towns such as the *coloniae* would probably have been provided with them. They were sometimes of simple earth-bank construction with the banks and entrances revetted with wooden walls, which often survived for the life of the building, timbers being replaced as they rotted (e.g. Dorchester). In

2   Heavy bronze helmet, perhaps of a gladiator, from Hawkedon, Suffolk (*British Museum*)

other examples such as that at Cirencester, the initial timber construction was replaced by masonry; but in both types the seating would have been of planks supported on the banks surrounding the arena. It is not known precisely what type of show was staged in these amphitheatres. A graffito on a sherd of pottery from Leicester attests a gladiator, while a gladiator's helmet has recently been found in Suffolk (pl. 2). There is also the mosaic from the villa at Bignor showing various scenes of cupids dressed as gladiators undergoing training, which is at least evidence for an interest in these shows, even if it cannot be taken as evidence for the performances themselves. But such entertainments, being expensive, were probably rare in Britain, and the audiences would most likely have had to be content with bear-baiting and cheaper shows. However, it should not be forgotten that certain criminals were commonly condemned to death 'ad bestias' (pl. 3) and the sentence carried out publicly in the amphitheatre; in a more robust age this was considered excellent entertainment.

The Roman theatre proper seems to have been much rarer in Britain than the amphitheatre. The sites of only three, at Canterbury, Verulamium and Gosbecks Farm, Colchester, are known (figs. 12, 13). That at Verulamium is an adapted form, while the third lies outside the *colonia* at Colchester and is not strictly a town theatre. Two others are attested: the first by Tacitus inside the pre-Boudiccan *colonia* at Colchester, the second by an inscription at Brough-on-Humber, but neither building is known. It would be natural to expect others at

3   Mosaic from Zliten, Lepcis Magna, North Africa, showing criminals condemned 'ad bestias' (*Roger Wood Studios*)

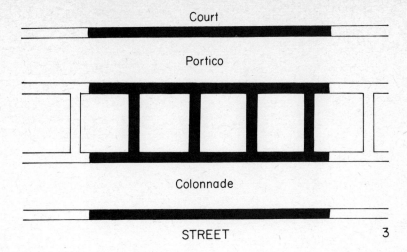

Court

Portico

Colonnade

STREET

3

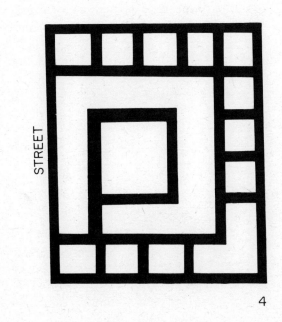

STREET

4

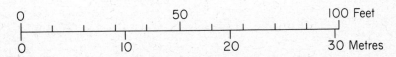

0　　　　　　　50　　　　　　100 Feet

0　　　　10　　　20　　　30 Metres

11　Plans of market halls at: (3) Cirencester; (4) Wroxeter

Lincoln and Gloucester, and probably also at London and York. Of the known examples, only the later theatre at Canterbury matches the style of the larger Gallic theatres in both scale and construction. The theatre at Gosbecks Farm, although superficially of Roman plan, has a very small stage and no proper stage building; it also effects a compromise in the construction, the seating being carried on earth banks instead of masonry vaults, and the whole is reminiscent of Romano-Celtic types. The adapted form at Verulamium is a better British example of this type, which have a distribution mainly in north-west Gaul. The orchestra at Verulamium, instead of being semi-circular as in the Roman theatre, was enlarged almost to a full circle with the stage forming a chord across one side; the position and arrangement of the entrances was also different. It is commonly assumed that this type of theatre was intended to double as an amphitheatre when necessary, and, if so, it would represent a wise economy for a town with perhaps limited means and uncertain of the reception which would be accorded other forms of entertainment. But at the same time it indicates a slightly higher degree of romanisation than the town with only an amphitheatre and little or no obvious interest in drama, mimes, singing or recitation. Many theatres in the Empire were closely connected with shrines or temples, and at least two, at Verulamium and Gosbecks Farm, show the same affinity. Not enough is known about the area surrounding the theatre for there to be any certainty at Canterbury about a similar association, or for that matter at Brough-on-Humber; but Brough undoubtedly had a religious centre of a sort, for the grave of a priest was found not far from the naval base.[32] The interrelation of temple and theatre in so many cases was deliberate.[33] The theatre would indicate the presence of large gatherings and the obvious popularity of the deity concerned. In both cases where the associated temples are known, at Verulamium and Gosbecks Farm, they are Romano-Celtic in type, implying a dedication to some native god, perhaps identified with a classical deity. This conjunction of temple and theatre would seem to hint at the performance of both religious and secular entertainments. Other evidence in the form of an ivory tragic mask found at Caerleon, and certainly an import, implies perhaps the presence there of a travelling theatre company.[34] Other masks are known from Catterick and Baldock (pls. 5, 6). A second-century house in Leicester was decorated with frescoes incorporating architectural features; at least two of the panels contained paintings of tragic masks (p. 348), and there is a strong resemblance to a theatrical fresco at Herculaneum,[35] perhaps suggesting an interest in dramatic spectacles on the part of the owner (pl. 4). Another point of interest, seldom considered for Britain, is the capacity of theatres and amphitheatres. It is probably right to assume that an amphitheatre could seat most of the adult population of a town, probably together with visitors and people from the surrounding countryside; it is not difficult to imagine in them types of show which would attract a full house. But the later theatre at Canterbury would, on the same basis, seat at least seven thousand spectators. Even allowing for a greater population than Silchester,[36] it is hard to believe that so many would show an interest in dramatic spectacles. Either

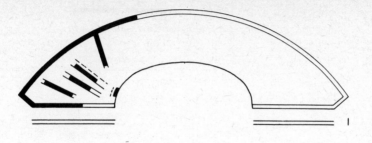

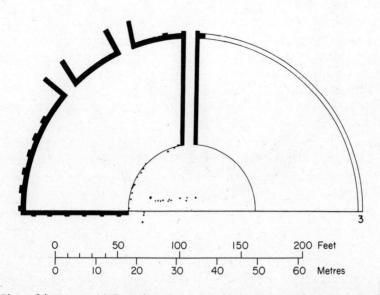

12   Plans of theatres at: (1) Canterbury I; (2) Canterbury II; (3) Gosbecks Farm, Colchester

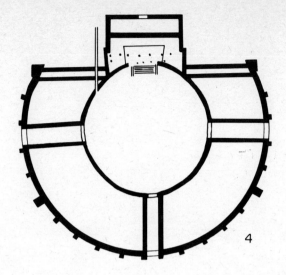

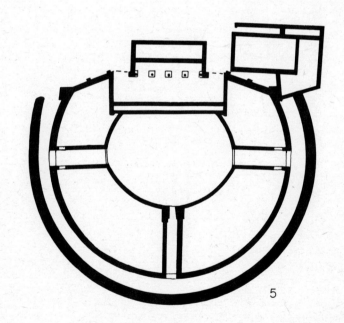

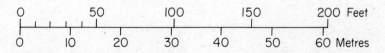

13   Plans of theatres at: (4) Verulamium I; (5) Verulamium IV

the theatre would have become a municipal white elephant, or, more likely, it was connected with important religious festivals, as took place in the theatres at Gosbecks Farm and Verulamium, catering as well for the country population around the town. Further, it can be argued that the rebuilding on a massive scale in the early third century, of the early theatre at Canterbury, points not just to a continuing demand for accommodation but to a demand that was actually increasing.

The third form of popular entertainment in the Roman world was centred on the *circus*, used for chariot racing. No buildings for this sport have yet been identified in Britain; the only indications of interest in it are a mosaic graphically depicting a scene during a race from a villa at Horkstow (Lincs.),[37] which is now in the British Museum, and part of a relief showing a boy charioteer from the *colonia* at Lincoln,[38] with other oblique references from the villa at Chedworth, and the *colonia* at York.[39]

The commercial life of a town, as we have already seen in Chapter I, was paramount in shaping its progress and development. No matter how much official help a town might have received at its inception, all would come to nothing unless there was a sound economic reason for its continued existence. The factors which governed a town's growth and decided whether it would increase or decrease in size, or perhaps even wither altogether, might therefore be different from those which governed the initial choice of a site. Much would depend on the potential wealth or otherwise of the area it served; important too would be the drive and enthusiasm of its individual inhabitants and the type and diversity of the goods and services which they provided. Ultimately then, it was not necessarily a good geographical position which made a town prosperous but its inhabitants. Nor should it be forgotten that prosperity is fickle and can desert a town as quickly as it can build one. The two *coloniae* of Lincoln and Gloucester could be said to have begun with equal opportunities; they were almost twins and nearly identical in size, in date of foundation and in the type of people who started them; both had equal opportunities in the country surrounding them. Yet Lincoln appears to have doubled its official size while Gloucester did not; Lincoln probably became a market centre for a large area of country, while Gloucester seemingly allowed Cirencester to capture the rich markets of the Cotswolds. There must therefore have been some essential difference between them which it is almost impossible to trace at this distance in time. Apart from the fact that Lincoln possibly had greater opportunities as a port, the only apparent difference would seem to be that it was situated on a bracing hill-top near the east coast, while Gloucester lay at sea level in a river valley in the west country. Was this difference in climate sufficient in itself to create the divergent development patterns; or were there other reasons, still to seek? It is more than likely, but we shall probably never know (but see p. 86 for discussion of one possible reason).

The importance of trade to a town is indicated by the speed with which shops appeared in the very earliest years after its foundation; Claudian shops have been excavated at Verulamium, London and Colchester, and Flavian shops at Cirencester and Leicester. Official encouragement came with the provision of forums and market-halls (*macella*), in which were shops that could be rented by tenants and where the temporary stalls of itinerant traders could be set up on market day.[40] The magistrates had power to intervene if a trader was suspected of fraudulent practices, and standard measures of length and volume can still be seen in the forum at Pompeii and in the *macellum* at Lepcis Magna in Tripolitania.[41] Later, magistrates also had to fix prices and had to attempt for a short time the enforcement of Diocletian's edict of standard prices. The forum which, with the basilica, usually occupied the central insula of a town in Britain, was a large open court surrounded on three sides by a portico, on to which opened a series of rooms that could either be used as offices by the authorities, or sometimes as shrines, or else be let out as shops. The basilica lay on the fourth side, while entrances into the court might be placed in one or more of the others. In some cases a portico also enclosed the whole or part of the building on the outside. Both porticoes and also the court could be used for temporary stalls (figs. 5–7).

This type of forum, which is common in Britain but not in Gaul, owes much to the plans of military *principia* and emphasises the assistance that military architects and engineers would have given during the early years of a town's development. Only at Verulamium and possibly Colchester are there indications implying forums of another type, in which the *capitolium*, or main religious centre, formed part of it.

Sometimes, in addition to the forum, a town might possess a separate market-hall or *macellum* (figs. 10, 11). At Verulamium one was erected in the Flavian period facing an open space, later to be used for the theatre, and in front of a major temple;[42] it contained two rows of shops facing each other across a court-yard. Cirencester was provided with a market-hall in Hadrian's principate;[43] not all has yet been excavated, but part of its plan strongly resembles the wing of a forum and, but for the prior identification of the latter in the next insula to the north-east, confusion of identity could have arisen. A number of pits, which were packed with bones, had been dug in and around the building; the bones had been sawn and cut and would appear to have come from butchers' shops, implying perhaps that this part of the building was a meat market.[44] Leicester was another town where a separate market was built, probably early in the third century, when a great basilican hall was constructed on the site of a derelict house adjacent to the forum; from the west end of the hall a wing containing rows of shops between porticoes projected northwards, to be matched probably by another wing at the east end.[45] Again the similarity of this building and the basilica proper could give rise to confusion; it was, however, little more than half the length of the latter and no provision had been made for a tribunal, leaving its purely commercial function in no doubt. These three *macella* are unlikely to be the only British examples of a type of structure that is comparatively common in the larger towns of other provinces, and it is likely that the building at Wroxeter, near the baths, had a similar function.

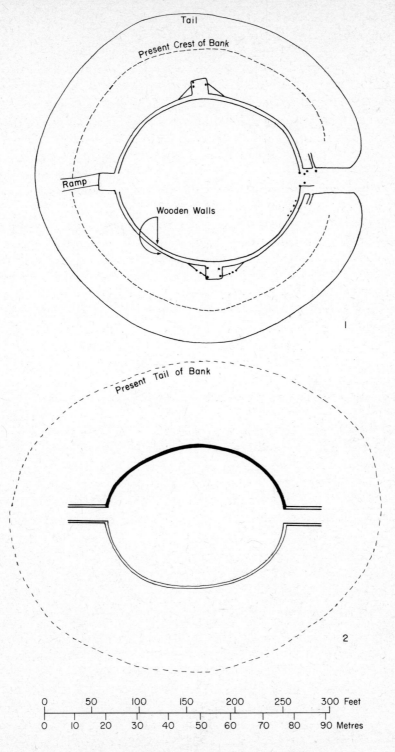

14   Plans of amphitheatres at: (1) Dorchester; (2) Chichester

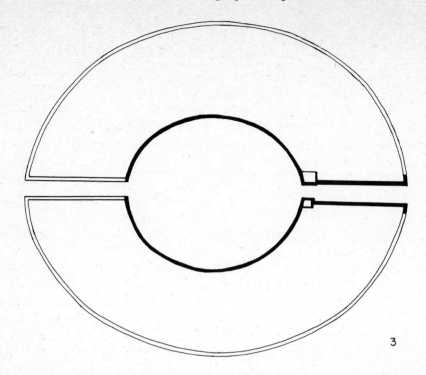

3

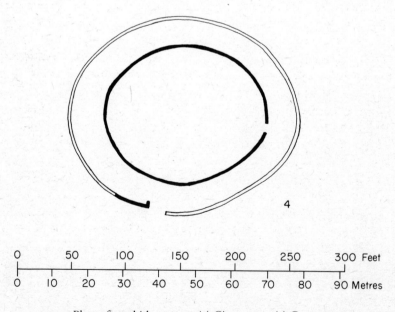

4

0   50   100   150   200   250   300 Feet

0   10   20   30   40   50   60   70   80   90 Metres

15   Plans of amphitheatres at: (3) Cirencester; (4) Caerwent

The great majority of tradesmen in the towns carried on their business either from residential shops or from rented premises in the forum or market, probably leaving the porticoes and open spaces in the public markets for itinerant merchants or country folk. But there would be nothing to prevent local tradesmen taking a temporary stall for market day and so reaping extra benefit. The shops often cluster together in the centres of towns to form whole streets, whose commercial character is left in no doubt by their presence. Three main types of shopkeeper can be envisaged: the owner, the freedman-tenant and the slave-manager. A fourth type might possibly be envisaged for Britain: free-born retainers of humble origin, derived from the old Celtic society, being used as managers or even tenants. The first two categories can be suggested for the shops already mentioned (p. 59) as having been built at Cirencester and Verulamium respectively in their early years. At Cirencester, excavation has shown that a row of shops opposite the market-hall had been rebuilt on a piecemeal basis; as each owner amassed enough capital, he rebuilt his shop in stone instead of wood, so that for a time timber shops were mixed side-by-side with those built in stone and only by the fourth century were all of stone.[46] Development of this sort implies that each plot was separately owned, probably by the shopkeeper in person. At best, two adjacent shops were sometimes joined together with communicating doors, suggesting a man in a rather more prosperous business. The emphasis seems to be on personal ownership with a variety of gradations showing different degrees of success. At Verulamium, Frere has shown that the block of shops in Insula XIV,[47] first built in the early Claudian period, were almost certainly erected as a business venture by one or more prominent local landowners, who probably let out individual premises to freed slaves or retainers. After being burnt by Boudicca they were rebuilt on a very similar pattern, but later rebuilding (viz. Period IIC, *c.* AD 130–50) began to show fragmentation of the original land-holding; later (viz. Period IID, *c.* AD 150–5) there are at least three or four alleys dividing them into four or five blocks. Lastly these blocks were reduced to two. Management by a slave is best illustrated by the inscription from Norton (Yorks.) referring to a goldsmith's shop.[48]

Most shops were narrow buildings with their long axes at right angles to the street onto which they opened. When placed close together this naturally fitted as many as possible into a given length of street, so making the best use of the more favoured frontages near the town centre. Not all, however, were of this type and more spacious examples are known at Verulamium, Wroxeter and possibly also at Silchester. The end fronting the street usually contained a single wide door which could be closed with wooden shutters. To protect the fronts from rain when open, and also to give cover for customers, porticoes were often provided in the larger towns. Internal divisions tended to follow a pre-set pattern, depending on whether there was an upper storey. Richmond believed that upper floors existed and quoted the example visible on Trajan's Column.[49] If so, then the residential quarters of the shopkeeper would most probably have been on the first floor, while the ground floor was kept for business. But an upper storey

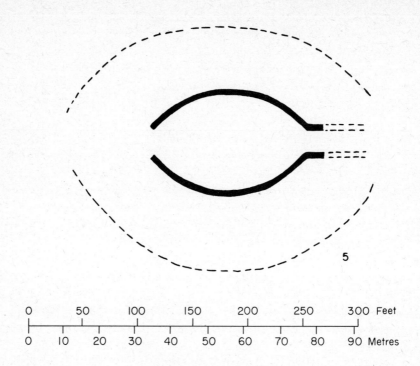

5

```
0        50       100      150      200      250      300 Feet
├────┼────┼────┼────┼────┼────┼────┼────┼────┼────┤
0    10   20   30   40   50   60   70   80   90 Metres
```

16   Plan of amphitheatre at Carmarthen

could also have been used as a storage loft, either in whole or in part. The ground floor is often divided between a reasonably large, open area at the front and a number of smaller rooms behind; if an upper floor was used for storage, or did not exist, these rooms at the rear would have provided accommodation on the ground floor. When shops were packed closely together, the only possible way to expand was by extending the premises to the rear, which is precisely what can be seen on the plan of the Insula xiv shops at Verulamium in the mid-second century.

The way in which business was carried out in these shops has been summarised most succinctly by Richmond: 'It is the direct antithesis of the multiple store: not large-scale industry engaged in mass production of large stocks of standard goods, but a small concern producing to individual requirements goods specifically ordered, such as might be commissioned on one market-day and ready on the next.'[50]

The trade itself might be considered, as today, in two sections: goods and services. The former would include the sale, and possible manufacture on the spot, of a very wide range of materials. Unfortunately, we can rarely, if at all, determine in what goods or services a particular shop dealt. Normally, before a shop was pulled down, all the goods would have been sold already, or at least packed, with a view to reopening the business in a new building. Little would be left to indicate what had been there. Even if something had been accidentally left, only hardware like pottery, glass and metals could be expected to survive in British soil conditions; unless the ground rapidly became waterlogged and remained so, organic materials would not be found in an excavation. Fittings and fixtures like hearths, ovens, or waste-bins might help to solve the problem, but who is to say, in the absence of other evidence, to what special purpose a simple oven was put, when a whole series of semi-industrial processes might be suggested for it. Only if the shop suffered a disaster like a fire, would one expect to find the contents still in it. Despite this rather gloomy picture, there is still some evidence for a variety of activities, even if it is widely scattered and cannot be attributed to one town alone. A secondary source of information is fortunately provided by pictorial representations on funeral monuments, mainly, however, from other provinces. In the Vatican museum there is an excellent representation on a tombstone of a cutler's shop, while another in Dresden Museum shows a butcher's shop which would not be out-of-place in a town today, and is a reminder of the Cirencester market hall.

Direct evidence for pottery and glassware shops has been found at Colchester, where also a coppersmith, Cintismus, had his workshop. Another coppersmith, Glaucus, signed his name on a statuette found at Martlesham (Suffolk); yet a third, Celatus, probably worked in Lincoln.[51] Coppersmiths' workshops themselves have been identified at Verulamium and Catterick. A goldsmith has already been mentioned at Norton (Yorks.), and another's shop has been found at Verulamium; there were also goldsmiths at London and Cirencester. A glass-maker set up in business in the Leicester market-hall during the fourth century, where, as a sideline, he seems also to have been engaged in the highly illegal activity[52] of melting down the base silver coinage to recover the silver. A silver-smith ran a large establishment at Silchester, which was equipped with its own cupellation furnace for silver recovery. Other, often profitable information, comes from altars or building dedications. An altar from Cirencester mentions Sulinus, a *sculptor* or superior stone-mason, who also worked at Bath.[53] Ordinary stone-masons or *lapidarii* have left samples of their work at Bisley (Glos.) as well as Bath.[54] Wine-merchants are known from both the *coloniae* at York and Lincoln. Finds of ironwork at Silchester, Verulamium and Great Chesterford imply the presence of blacksmiths, while a tombstone showing one at work is known at York. The agricultural implements, which are included in these hoards, serve as a reminder that probably most farmers, unless they were fortunate enough to be the tenant of a large landowner with a resident smith on the estate, would have had to go to the nearest town or village to buy new implements or have old ones repaired—a theme which will be developed more fully below. There were glassworks at Mancetter, Wilderspool and at Caistor-by-Norwich, which seem to have produced window glass and possibly common domestic vessels. Pottery was manufactured outside many towns, such as Lincoln and Colchester, and was probably on sale in shops or stalls in the towns; merchants selling *mortaria* and samian ware had stalls in one of the porticoes of the Wroxeter forum. Some towns, such as Gloucester, also possessed their own brickworks.

Buildings at Silchester have been interpreted as a dye-works from the circular furnaces they contained, but such furnaces would fit some other trades just as adequately. It is not known to what extent bakers' shops existed, since much grain was home-ground and also probably home-baked, but large donkey-driven millstones from London and Canterbury, part of two shafts from mill-wheels from Lincoln and fragments of mechanically-driven millstones from a number of places imply their existence, since bakers ground their own corn. A large iron slice for turning loaves while in the oven has been found at Verulamium, while an ornamental mould for impressing cakes or loaves comes from Silchester. The list can be extended further but begins to become tenuous when such occupations as brewers, cobblers, tanners, tailors and suchlike trades are considered.

What might be called the 'service' trades often tended to overlap with the production of goods; blacksmiths repaired as well as manufactured ironwork, fullers not only treated and prepared new cloth but also acted as launderers. But there must have been snack-bars and hostelries in many towns, although, apart from the official *mansiones*, they are difficult to identify. There is, however, an indication of a snack-bar in the forum at Caerwent whose main item on the menu seems to have been oysters. A bank was the suggestion made for one of the rooms in the forum at Silchester, while an enterprising shopkeeper at Verulamium increased his profits by providing a row of public lavatories.

There is one common aspect in all these trading activities which, because there is little direct evidence, is more often than not taken for granted and therefore possibly underestimated. It might be called in modern terminology, an 'invisible export' from the towns to the countryside: the flow or sale of ideas. We have already suggested earlier in this chapter that the new towns would tend to attract the more go-ahead and ambitious people, who would be prepared to accept and develop new techniques to do with farming, building and other processes. The provincial administration often encouraged towns to be centres of education, but presumably not only in Latin and civilised manners; romanisation implied more than that.

It was also the responsibility of the administration to collect taxes. But they knew very well that you could not tax what did not exist; hence the anxiety of Classicianus after the Boudiccan rebellion,[55] and Agricola's lessening of the tax burden.[56] Complete expropriation of all produce might have answered for Caesar during his expeditions, but it was not a suitable policy for a lengthy occupation. It was presumably known also that there was a point beyond which, if tax was increased, total revenue declined, a factor familiar to every modern Chancellor of the Exchequer, even if in the fourth century the margin was some-

4   Theatrical fresco from a house at Herculaneum (*Scala Instituto Fotografico Editoriale*)

times run close or exceeded. It was therefore very much in the interests of the administration to encourage increased production especially of agricultural goods. New ideas or techniques to achieve this aim would presumably, and in the main, have first reached the towns by the activities of travelling salesmen, whence they would gradually have become copied and then disseminated in the country.

In any society, but especially in those which depend more on the spoken than on the written word, gossip is one of the most potent ways of circulating news, whether true or untrue, garbled or concise. Gossip would have been a normal part of every market-day in every town or village in Roman Britain. So, in time,

5   Part of a theatrical tragic mask, made of pottery, from Baldock (*Crown Copyright—reproduced with permission of the Controller of Her Majesty's Stationery Office*)

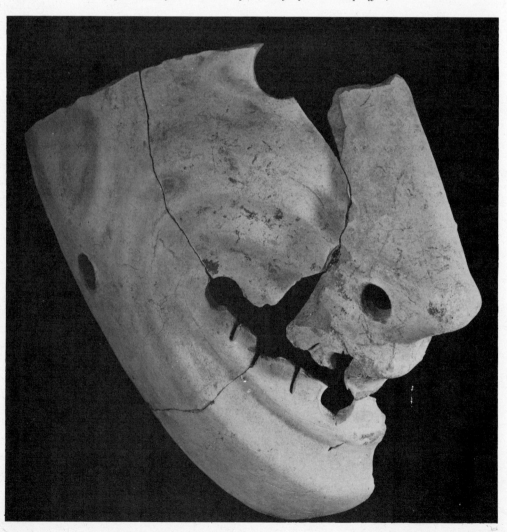

6   Similar mask, probably made near Water Newton, from Catterick (*Crown Copyright—reproduced with permission of the Controller of Her Majesty's Stationery Office*)

news of more and better agricultural implements or practices would filter through to the country farmers, followed probably by the implements themselves, for the earliest examples would probably have been made and sold by a town blacksmith.

It is frequently stated that the Romans brought little fresh knowledge of agriculture to Britain, that what was new produced only marginal advances, and that it was chiefly improved by indirect means such as better roads, markets and administration. In many ways this is true, but to say so is to overlook in part the *total* sum of the improvements. Rivet has calculated that a minimum of 106,000 acres (42,900ha) of cereal crops alone would have been required to feed the army in Britain during the first century,[57] and this figure does not allow a profit to the producer. Such a figure must imply a tremendous increase in production, especially with the growing markets in the towns and villages to be supplied as well. By any standards this was a great improvement, even a great achievement, simply because more land was being used with greater efficiency than before: what had been untilled waste was now under cultivation. But it was achieved strictly within the bounds of the agricultural knowledge of the day. To look for more will not carry us much further; to expect more, is like blaming the Romans for not making use of the aeroplane to improve their communications! In the last 2000 years of agriculture the only real revolution has been brought about by the internal combustion engine; almost all other changes have been concerned with marginal alterations to well-established, traditional methods.

Reduced to its essentials it might be said that the ploughs of Roman Britain were not necessarily very much *better* than the Celtic ploughs, but that there must have been far *more* of them in use, and that they must have been distributed more widely among all classes of farmers. If a man, who had used a spade or hoe to cultivate a plot of ground, bought a plough, and by so doing was able to cultivate not only the original plot but another twice the size, then who can deny that this was an improvement? It could be argued that such changes might have come in time even without Roman intervention in Britain, or that they might have been produced by an occupation of a totally military nature. However, places uneffected by the Romans, where Celtic agriculture continued unchanged, do not encourage acceptance of the first argument, while it is difficult to see how compulsion under military government could ever have produced the increase in cultivation which took place. There must therefore have been a voluntary acceptance pattern in the countryside as well as in the towns. The rate of acceptance, however, would not have been evenly spread and some parts of the country were slower than others to adopt new ways. Moreover, it is apparent that the most rapid acceptance took place round towns and villages, and that areas where these were sparsely distributed or non-existent often remained far longer in a more primitive agricultural state.

We started this discussion by considering the 'export' of ideas from towns and proceeded by way of education, taxation and increased agricultural production until we have now arrived back at the towns. Two hundred years ago Adam Smith reported that the most highly-developed agricultural nations were precisely those in which industry and commerce were also developed to an equal or greater degree. He also noted that the most prosperous country areas were to be found near cities, with the poorest agriculture further away.[58] To some extent these observations are still true today, while they describe almost exactly the situation in Roman Britain.

But while it is easy to observe facts, drawing correct deductions from them is often fraught with difficulty. However, it would appear that towns, and to a lesser extent villages, were an essential prerequisite to the development of pros-

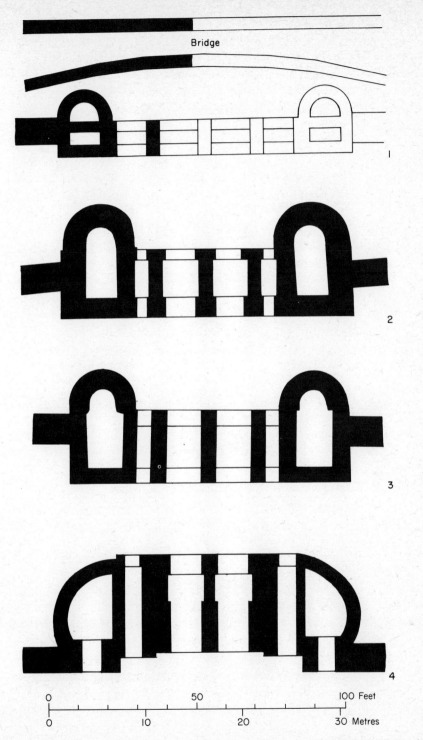

Bridge

17 Plans of gates at: (1) Cirencester, Verulamium gate; (2) Verulamium, London gate; (3) Verulamium, Chester gate; (4) Colchester, Balkerne gate. Exterior to top of the page

perous farming, not so much because they provided a market for agricultural produce—the necessary surplus to feed the towns can only have come *after* they started to develop—but because they would have been the first to adopt new ideas and techniques and put them into practice. A measure of proof is provided by the events of the fifth century, when the towns were quite capable of looking after themselves, long after communications with the farms had been cut or rendered unsafe. It might be said that at the centre of each developing country area there was a town providing the impetus; with the situation reversed and in decay, it was the town at the centre which was capable of surviving longest. The interdependence between the towns and the countryside is often stressed, and we can see now the nature of the relationship, which was heavily weighted in favour of the towns; the pattern of agricultural settlement that emerged in Roman Britain could not have been produced without the towns and villages and could not have survived, indeed did not survive, in isolation.

This is a far cry from Collingwood's view: 'Economically, the towns were parasitic on the countryside. They had to be fed by it, and the goods they produced, together with the services they rendered as markets and trading-centres, were no adequate return for the food they consumed and the expenditure which they demanded for the upkeep of their public services. They had their industries; but these consisted only to a small extent in the production of goods needed in the country; most of them were luxury-trades whose produce was mostly used in the towns themselves. They did a large business in retail trade, selling pottery made in Gaul and other imports, but, here again, the total quantity of these goods which found its way into the country districts was the barest fraction of what the towns consumed. From the strictly economic point of view the towns were a luxury.'[59] Now that we have so much more information than was available to Collingwood, we can see the shortcomings of his view of the part played by towns in the province.

In the opening sentence of this chapter it was stressed that towns also acted as centres for protection, a function which they often shared with fortified villages. Much has been written about these fortifications, both in sum and individually, and it is only necessary here to summarise the current views at present obtaining on town defences in general.[60]

Few towns in Britain were fortified during the first century. Not only were defences unnecessary by virtue of the military situation, but also they could be obtained only by a petition to the Emperor,[61] who, in normal circumstances, would have been unlikely to grant the request. Only at Verulamium, Winchester and Silchester have defensive circuits, dating to the first century, been positively identified. There is some evidence for early fortifications at Colchester, and both Lincoln and Gloucester may have been given narrow gauge walls early in the second, if not in the late first century. In both the latter cases the walls were inserted into the front of the pre-existing legionary fortress ramparts. Here we may read pride as providing the probable motive for their erection; as chartered towns they could more readily qualify for imperial permission as others, such

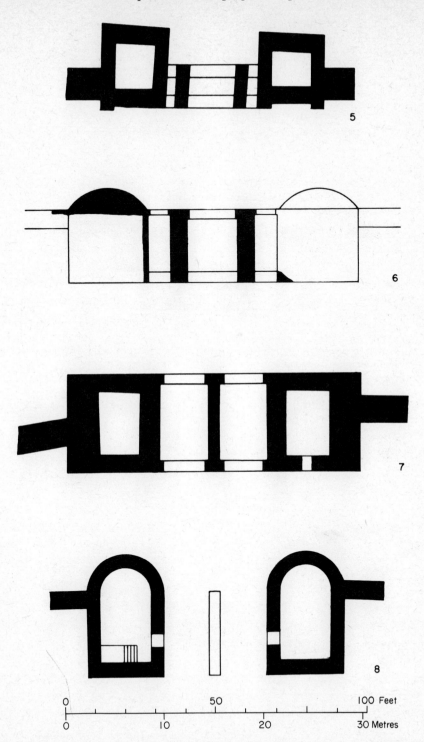

18 Plans of gates at: (5) Verulamium, Silchester gate; (6) Lincoln, north gate, old town; (7) London, Newgate; (8) Lincoln, east gate II, old town. Exterior to top of the page

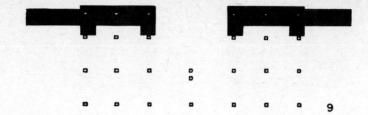

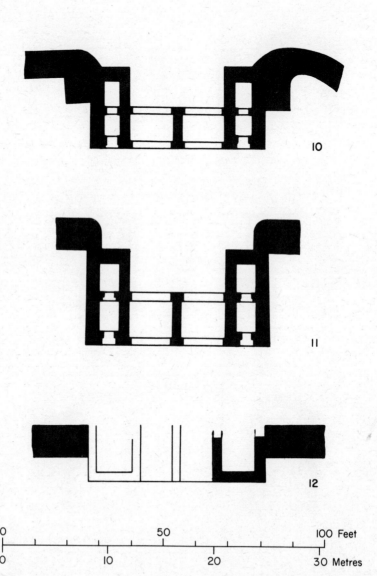

19   Plans of gates at: (9) Lincoln, east gate I, old town; (10) Silchester, west gate; (11) Silchester, east gate; (12) Exeter, south gate. Exterior to top of the page

as Arles, Nîmes and Aosta, had qualified under Augustus, although Aosta probably needed them as protection from Alpine tribes.

The end of the second century saw many towns and some villages being fortified. The great majority were only provided with earthworks, although there are indications that work on masonry gates and towers may have already been started at Silchester, Cirencester, Verulamium, Caerwent and Exeter, and it is also possible that London was from the first provided with a stone wall. It was probably Clodius Albinus, anticipating the day when he knew he would have to contest his claim to the purple outside Britain, who foresaw the likely defensive need of the towns in the absence of most of the British garrison, and who gave the orders for their construction. Lack of time, perhaps coupled with an insufficiency of skilled masons, might, therefore, explain why earthworks were built when stone walls were altogether more desirable fortifications.

The provision of stone walls for hitherto unfortified towns, and for those previously fortified only by earthworks, appears to have begun in the earlier third century, and continued for several decades, possibly for as long as fifty years. The reasons for commencing this huge construction programme are obscure, but they may have been connected with the desire to make more permanent the earlier earthworks. It is clear from evidence now available that the work was carried out at an uneven rate, with possible interruptions and changes of plan, but by the fourth century all towns and most villages in Britain had been given permanent linear fortifications, made up of three main elements. The stone wall itself was anything from four to ten feet thick and was backed by a solid bank of earth, which usually, but not always, incorporated any preexisting earthwork: the total width of rampart could vary from about 15ft (4·6m) up to 40ft (12m) or more. In front of the wall was a system of ditches, usually limited to one or two, but occasionally incorporating more. Some towns are known, such as Canterbury, Cirencester, Gloucester, Lincoln and Verulamium, where square interval towers were attached to the inner face of the wall. Gates, with few exceptions, normally had one or two portals; whether towers were placed over them, or omitted altogether, was usually governed by the number and placing of the portals (figs. 17–21).

Changing patterns of military strategy and tactics during the fourth century ultimately brought about the modification of town defences. Count Theodosius, the restorer of Britain's fortifications in the years immediately following the barbarian conspiracy and invasion of AD 367,[62] was probably responsible for originating the work. It took the form of adding external towers to the curtain wall at frequent intervals round the perimeter. To do this, however, the inner ditch had to be filled completely, or at least in part, which in turn necessitated another, usually wider ditch being dug further away from the wall. The purpose of these towers was to provide for the easier and more effective deployment of artillery. It should be noted however that no towns, apart from Lincoln, appear to have had towers added immediately beside gates; if projecting towers are found attached to gates, as at Cirencester and Verulamium, they are almost

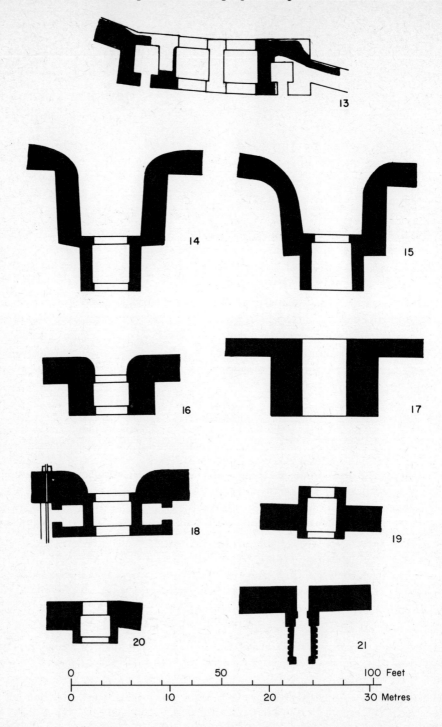

20   Plans of gates at: (13) Canterbury, Riding gate; (14) Silchester, south gate; (15) Silchester, north gate;
(16) Colchester, north-east gate; (17) Lincoln, west gate; old town; (18) Caistor-by-Norwich, south gate;
(19) Caerwent, south gate; (20) Caerwent, north gate; (21) Silchester, sluice gate. Exterior to top of the page

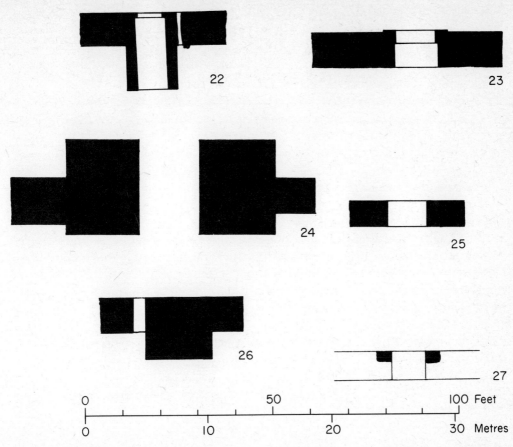

21   Plans of gates at: (22) Canterbury, London gate; (23) Silchester, south-west gate; (24) Lincoln, west gate, new town; (25) Silchester, amphitheatre gate; (26) Colchester, south-west postern; (27) Canterbury, Quenin gate. Exterior to top of the page

invariably part of the original structure, and such gates usually belong to an earlier phase of fortification. It might be thought that gates, being the most vulnerable part of a walled circuit would have most readily qualified for them, until it is realised that the placing of towers is by no means consistent. Some towns are well-provided, others have few, often irregularly spaced, while a small minority appear to have none. Sometimes they are placed at corners, sometimes not. A number of different shapes and sizes can also be observed. Indeed, this very lack of consistency might point towards careless supervision over the task of strengthening defences, and to an indifferent understanding of the tactics involved.[63]

The provision of bastions for the use of artillery must imply the deployment of personnel trained in its use. We know nothing of either the strength or composition of garrisons provided for this purpose; nor do we know anything of the way in which such defences were manned before bastions were constructed. No town in Britain has yet produced evidence for buildings which might be interpreted as the quarters of a garrison. Before trained garrisons were required for artillery it may be that the townspeople themselves provided the guardians for their fortifications. Moreover it would appear likely that all would have been billeted among householders in the town, and not in special barracks.[64]

The suggested existence of specialist garrisons for artillery might explain why some towns do not appear to have been given bastions, while others are deficient in numbers. Given the known shortage of trained manpower in the army towards the end of the fourth century, it is likely that there were just not enough men to go round, and that they would have been distributed wherever the need was greatest.

It is difficult to assess the overall effect of the construction of town defences. At first it was probably very slight, but with the growing insecurity of the third and fourth centuries they would have undoubtedly given a comfortable feeling to the inhabitants. Apart from giving protection to essential administrative centres with their records, they would also have protected much individual wealth, as well as official supplies of food, from brigands and robbers. Their existence probably provided much-needed confidence for farmers and country dwellers who continued to occupy unprotected settlements. Town fortifications, however, as a major investment, did not fully pay dividends until the fifth century. Then, the collapse of central government meant that many towns were henceforth on their own. There is more than enough evidence to show that most managed tolerably well behind the protection of their walls guarded by garrisons of German *foederati*. Short of treachery, famine or plague they were more than a match for the Anglo-Saxon raiders, who were unable to engage in lengthy siege warfare. Now also they must have become refuges for the inhabitants of outlying farms and unfortified villages. In many cases these farmers not only had to contend with dangerous situations, but also had to face an almost complete loss of earnings owing to the breakdown in communications.

The protective function of towns, therefore, although always present to some extent from the first, became only of prime importance during the evening of their existence. Towns have been described as the last bastions of Romano-British civilisation;[65] as bastions they protected that civilisation until, for a variety of reasons, it no longer survived.

3

Towns as
Provincial Capitals

It is unlikely that the Romans had at first any clear ideas for the foundation in Britain of a provincial capital of a type which later emerged at London. The establishment of the headquarters of the imperial cult at Colchester under Claudius should in no way be taken to indicate that the town was intended also to act as the administrative centre for the province. As the only site, before the conquest, which might with justification be called the 'capital' of Britain, it was the obvious choice for the cult centre, for there the cult would have made the greatest impact on the native Britons. Camulodunum had become the capital of Cunobelin about AD 10 and ultimately, due to his conquests, the 'capital' of most of southern Britain. But it would not follow that what suited Cunobelin, and the general economic way of life of Belgic Britain, would necessarily provide the same facilities in the changed conditions after the conquest. Naturally though, Camulodunum, as the British 'capital', was also the most attractive site for the first town in Roman Britain, in addition to it being chosen as the cult centre.

For most of the first century the governors of Britain were heavily engaged on campaigns. Since the governor headed the civil administration, the provincial 'capital' tended to be where he was, but he would also visit those places which acted as assize centres (*conventus*) for Roman citizens. At first in Britain, few such centres would have been needed since there was no great number of citizens; indeed Colchester may have been the only one, since it probably contained the largest concentration. There would also have been a need for a centre for the more stationary forms of government, such as the procurator's office, but there is no indication that this was ever at Colchester. We know, however, that the veterans at Colchester had to send away to the procurator for aid at the time of the Boudiccan rebellion, an unnecessary request if the treasury had been in the colonia. Moreover, Julius Classicianus, the procurator immediately after the rebellion, died in service and was buried in London.[1] The presumption is that the procurator's office was at London after the rebellion, if not before.

With the situation in Britain becoming more settled by the end of the Flavian
period, the need was probably felt for a permanent residence for the governor
in the south. The choice of a site at London rather than at Colchester for this
building[2] requires some explanation, for it placed the final seal of success on
London as a town and provides the present justification for calling it a provincial
capital.

We know that by AD 60, London was a thriving settlement of merchants, even
if it was not then a chartered town,[3] and it is probable that a number of merchants
were Roman citizens. The latter, perhaps together with a growing number of
citizens in the south and east, might have led to the establishment of another
assize centre at London more conveniently placed than at Colchester.

It is usually claimed that London reached its pre-eminent position by virtue of
its superior geographical situation. To claim this, however, is both to omit a link
in the chain and to ignore other factors. It must be remembered that, immediately
before the conquest, Colchester was the chief trading centre of south-east
England, at a time when London counted for nothing. Basically the geographical
situation of Colchester was not so very inferior to that of London, as Richmond
once pointed out,[4] especially if it is considered as it was before the main network
of Roman roads was laid out and before the Thames bridge was built. London
perhaps enjoyed a rather better approach by water with easier navigation directly
up the Thames; moreover the ships could ultimately tie-up alongside the town.
The approach to Colchester involved crossing the currents of the Thames
estuary to reach the river Colne. Yet today we see east coast ports developing
at the expense of the Port of London, so it is doubtful if geography alone is
enough to explain the emergence of London as the capital. To explain it fully
we must return to a proposition set out in the last chapter (p. 59): that much
depends on the attitude and enthusiasm of a town's inhabitants.

A prosperous and expanding town can attract to itself the organs of provincial
or state government, in the way that most modern European capitals have
developed. But capitals do not become great towns and cities by virtue of being
capitals: Washington, Canberra and Brasilia are but modern examples of such
failure. It might be claimed that legionary veterans, with their rigid military
outlook, living in comfortable retirement and probably controlling most local
affairs at Colchester, would not provide the right atmosphere for a rapid and
vigorous expansion of trade. Such a town would tend to be inward-looking in
its administration, with its commercial ventures largely aimed at satisfying its
own needs. It would lack the diversity in the make-up of its population, in its
trade and in the services it provided, which are necessities for vigorous economic
expansion. Yet London became, as Tacitus said, thronged with merchants,
probably of a less uniform character, and it obviously provided the right atmosphere of encouragement; in something less than twenty years it underwent an
economic explosion. To affect a comparison with Colchester is to compare the
entrepreneurial activity and diverse industries of a Birmingham with the gentility
and uniform habits of a Brighton in the late nineteenth century. By the time

7 Tombstone of Claudia Martina, wife of Anencletus, from London (*Guildhall Museum*)

London became the provincial capital, therefore, it had recovered from the Boudiccan rebellion, and had probably acquired more dignity in addition to prosperity. This prosperity would have been the direct result of the energy and wide-ranging outlook of its inhabitants, who were prepared to use to the full a no more than adequate geographical situation. *That* was what attracted government to London and not to Colchester.✗

Yet one sphere of central government may have remained at Colchester. Frere has pointed out that the reconsecration of the temple there after the Boudiccan rebellion, and the maintenance of the precinct, create an assumption that the cult remained at Colchester,[5] and that there are insufficient grounds for supposing that it was moved to London. It has, however, been suggested that the administration of the cult was removed to London late in the first or early in the second century.[6] Part of an inscription found in St Nicholas Lane, London, is dedicated to the *numini Caesaris Augusti* by the British province,[7] and this has been taken as evidence for the transfer.

A dedication to an emperor's *numen* almost always implies a living emperor as the object, whereas a dedication to the imperial cult would embrace those dead (*divi*) as well. There is also the tombstone[8] (pl. 7) of the wife of Anencletus, a *provincialis*, or servant of the provincial council, which is often taken to mean that the council itself was centred on London. But there are many reasons why a council servant might have been in London, without accepting the necessity for the cult headquarters to be there also. Nevertheless the reading of the numen inscription is far from sure and it is capable of other reconstructions. The mention of *provincia Britannia* does, however, seem reliable, and it is difficult to explain why a dedication by, or on behalf of, the provincial organisation should have taken place at London, unless the town had some special position in relation to the cult. There is evidence from Cyrenaica that the provincial cult need not be centred at the same place as the administration, so that it is possible that London became the headquarters of the provincial council, even though the cult centre remained at Colchester.[9] London would undoubtedly have had its temples✗ L.P. dedicated to both reigning and deified emperors along with most other towns in Britain.

The remaining evidence for believing that London assumed the role of provincial capital can be summarised briefly. In the early second century an 11 acre (4·5ha) fort was being built in what is now the Cripplegate area of the city.[10] An apparently unused wooden writing tablet found near the Walbrook bears the official brand of the imperial procurator's office in Britain,[11] so supporting the suggestion already made with regard to the tombstone of Julius Classicianus. An unused tablet is unlikely to have been thrown away far from the office where they were in use. More important perhaps is the tombstone (pl. 8) of Celsus, a *speculator*, set up by three of his colleagues or friends.[12] A speculator was seconded from his legion for service on the governor's staff, where his duties were largely connected with the law-courts. Mann has noted that speculators are only attested in the praetoria of governors.[13] He has also suggested[14] that a legionary centurion,

8   Tombstone of Celsus, from London (*British Museum*)

Vivius Marcianus, who died in London and who is depicted on his tombstone[15] (pl. 9), carrying a scroll, may have been a *princeps praetorii*. Thus there is no doubt that, at least in the second century, the governor's headquarters lay in London.

The division of Britain into two provinces, Britannia Superior and Britannia Inferior after the recovery of Britain by Severus, would have required yet another capital.[16] The final arrangement, in being by AD 212–13, left London as capital of Britannia Superior, under a consular governor with two legions at his disposal at Caerleon and Chester. Britannia Inferior possessed only a praetorian governor controlling one legion at York, which, we might deduce from the Vieux inscription,[17] was the capital of the new province. York, as the only town of any real consequence at this time in the north, can have had no rivals in the selection. It had been headquarters and the seat of the imperial court during the campaigns of Severus and Caracalla against the Caledonians, and a palace had been provided, although its precise situation is not known.[18] Neither is the situation of the governor's praetorium known, although part of a large building found in 1929 under the Old Station Yard and inside the colonia may be part of it.[19] However, it is more likely that he continued to occupy the praetorium of the fortress.

The reorganisation of the Empire by Diocletian led to further and more fundamental changes. Britain now became one of the dioceses into which the Empire was divided. Overall supervision was exercised by the *vicarius Britanniarum*, who was a deputy of the Praetorian Prefect of Gaul. The diocese of Britain contained four provinces, which are named in the Verona List as Britannia Prima, Britannia Secunda, Maxima Caesariensis and Flavia Caesariensis. At first these were governed by *praesides*, all of equal rank from the equestrian order. The Notitia, however, implies that Maxima Caesariensis had been promoted at a later date since it states that it had a consular governor.[20]

London undoubtedly became the seat of the *vicarius* and the *praepositus thesaurorum*.[21] There also presumably were the offices of the *rationalis summarum Britanniarum* and the *rationalis rei privatae per Britannias*,[22] which between them had taken over many of the duties of the now obsolete procurator's office. The later seniority of Maxima Caesariensis over the other three provinces might also suggest that London acted as its capital in addition to being the diocesan capital. It is not possible to say where the boundaries of these provinces lay, but it is now usually accepted that Britannia Prima and Maxima Caesariensis were formed from the Severan Britannia Superior, while Britannia Inferior was divided into Britannia Secunda and Flavia Caesariensis. If London was capital of the first and York remained as capital for either Secunda or Flavia, two more provincial centres have still to be found. Mann has argued[23] that the identities of these four provincial capitals are provided by the list of British bishops attending the Council of Arles in AD 314.[24] By analogy with Gaul the four delegations from Britain should have included the Metropolitans of each province or their deputies, and he therefore concludes that York and Lincoln became the capitals of the two northern provinces, while Cirencester, although not specifically mentioned,

9 Tombstone of Vivius Marcianus, from London (*Ashmolean Museum*)

probably became the capital of Britannia Prima. In support of the latter there is the implication contained in an inscription from Cirencester recording a dedication made by one of the praesides of Britannia Prima. [25] A. R. Birley, however, put forward the alternative opinion that the inscription is more likely to be of third century than fourth century date, which would, if correct, invalidate the previous suggestion, [26] although such a view is not entirely acceptable on other grounds. There were also the changes (discussed more fully below, p. 304) which took place in the forum and basilica at Cirencester, and which may have arisen from a desire to separate provincial from local business.

It is worth considering the choice of Cirencester and Lincoln as provincial capitals. That they were selected tells us something of their success as towns; a comparison can be made with others, which we might consider appear superficially to be equally successful, but which were not so chosen. It also emphasises what has already been said above (p. 80) about the way in which towns can become capitals, and the contrast which has been drawn between the coloniae of Lincoln and Gloucester (p. 59). The first question which might be asked is why Cirencester and not Gloucester should have been selected as capital of Britannia Prima, when the corresponding choice of Lincoln shows that in Flavia a colonia was selected. That a town was a colonia was obviously not enough to commend it, since in any case, by the fourth century, the distinction between coloniae and other sites had become blurred. Indeed it is worth recording that, of the three military coloniae in Britain, Colchester early forfeited its chance of being a capital, Gloucester does not seem to have been in the running and only Lincoln was successful. On this reckoning therefore the military coloniae of Britain did not score well in the 'capital stakes'.

Two further points are worth attention. Lincoln was the only one to double its enclosed area, and was perhaps also the only one which did not attract many new veterans after Legio IX had left Britain in the early second century. [27] It is probably right to assume that Colchester was founded for a discharge of veterans from Legio XX and Gloucester for one from Legio II Augusta. These legions served in Britain without a break for almost the whole duration of the Roman occupation, and it is likely that any veterans who were later discharged, would have tended to migrate to foundations already associated with their particular legion. A continuing bond of this nature between colonia and legionary fortress could have given rise to a correspondingly higher proportion of retired soldiers among the populations at Colchester and Gloucester. As a result, these towns, although undoubtedly comfortable and prosperous, may have lacked the diversified, extrovert character required to make a successful capital, a factor in their make-up which has already been referred to in describing the selection of London rather than Colchester as the earliest provincial capital (p. 80). A comparison between them and some of our modern 'retirement' towns on the south coast is probably valid. In these circumstances it is not difficult to see why Cirencester was chosen in place of Gloucester. Lincoln, however, appears to have overcome the apparently constricting image of a veteran settlement, which might be considered, in time, to have allowed a greater degree of expansion.

Later still, probably about 370, a fifth province, Valentia was created with a *consularis* as governor. It is not known precisely where it lay, but Mann has suggested that it was the product of the division of Flavia Caesariensis, and that it fell within the area of the command of the *dux Britanniarum*.[28] Carlisle may well have become its capital but too little is known about the town to be certain.

LONDON (*Londinium Augusta*)

What little is known of pre-Boudiccan London is derived mainly from commercial excavations in the city. It has been suggested that the earliest settlements would have grown as the civilian counterpart to a military base, probably a stores-depot. Although London undoubtedly presented an excellent position for a military stores-depot, it is difficult to assess its importance alongside the known continuation, until at least AD 85, of the large depot at Richborough.[29] One might suspect that the chief advantage of a depot at London over one at Richborough would have been the ability to ship stores direct by sea to a point closer to the sphere of actual military operations. If London therefore had been the main depot, it is difficult to see how Richborough could have survived and maintained its usefulness. Since it did survive, even though, apparently, its capacity for storing grain was reduced, it is reasonable to suppose that London was at best short-lived. The advantage of its situation at this early date therefore was either not appreciated, or it was considered not to be superior to Richborough. Perhaps the more immediate political problems, centering on the native capital at Camulodunum, caused it to be overlooked. An early fort at London is, however, almost a certainty, although it is not known where it lay,[30] and unfortunately, in view of the later history of the town, the catalogue of military equipment compiled by Dr Webster,[31] does not help much to establish its position. But there is no good reason to assume that a military presence at London need have been protracted. The fort at Verulamium had been abandoned by AD 50, if not before,[32] and Legio XX had left Camulodunum by AD 49. Indeed one of the reasons for the foundation of the colonia there was to fill the void left by the departure of garrisons from the south-east. It is difficult therefore to accept the survival of a fort at London after *c.* AD 50. Short though this occupation was it seems in this instance to have been sufficient for a large vicus to have been established, with the traders probably attracted as much by the fort as by the geographical situation. Merrifield has suggested that this vicus may have been from the first an ordered settlement,[33] a suggestion supported by recent observations of similar planning in the early vicus at Cirencester (p. 294).

Tacitus refers to early London as an important centre for businessmen and merchants,[34] and there is the implication, already referred to (p. 82), that the

LONDON   (Londinivm)

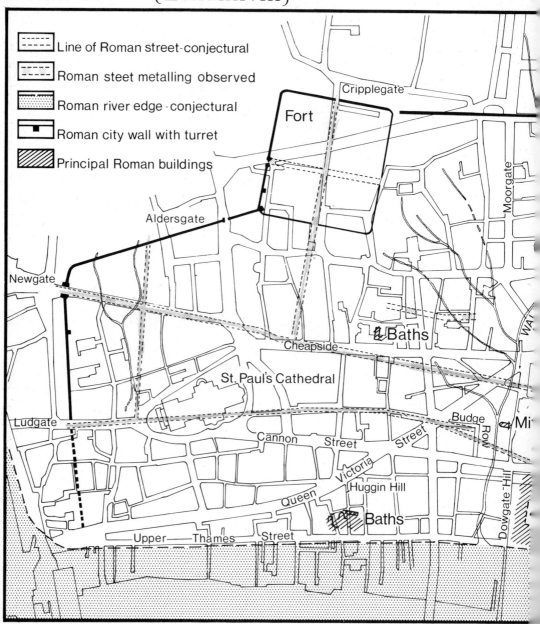

22   Plan of London (*after R. Merrifield*)

procurator's office was here before the rebellion. Certainly London should be considered as the financial centre of the province from the time of the rebellion onwards. A major building constructed of masonry[35] is known to have occupied part of the site of the later forum, in the years immediately after the rebellion. It is a large building, occupying a space 360ft (109m) by 200ft (61m), and it appears

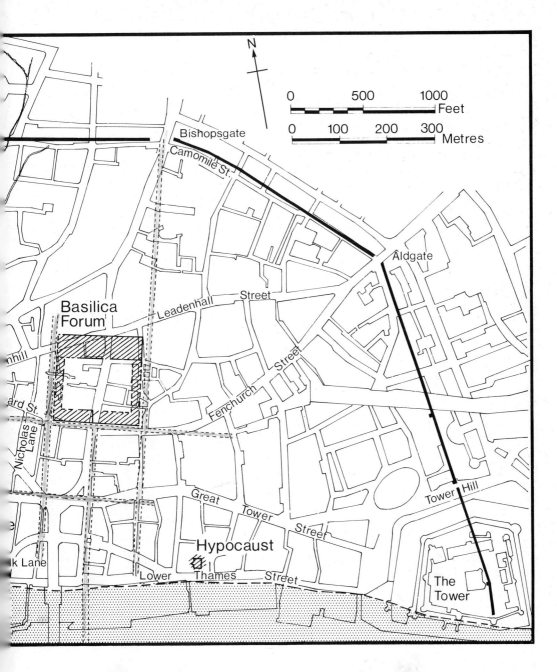

to have been built round a central courtyard (fig. 23). At the north end there is a large hall-like structure, with a basement, or deep room, running almost the full length of, and behind, the hall. The east, and possibly south, ranges appear to have been made up of small rooms, and the outside wall was buttressed on its exterior face.[36] Various explanations have been put forward to account for the

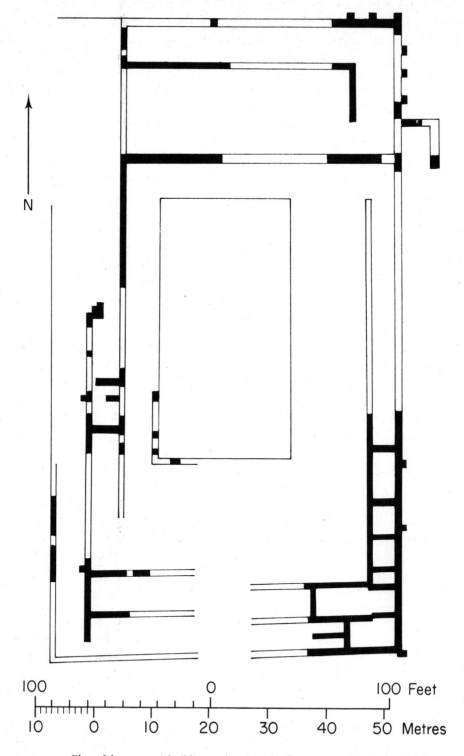

N

100   0   100 Feet

10   0   10   20   30   40   50 Metres

23   Plan of the masonry building earlier than the forum at London (*Brian Philp*)

building's plan: that it was the praetorium of the governor, or the first forum for London, or the *tabularium Caesaris* of the procurator. Lack of refinement would seem to rule out the idea of a praetorium, although if London early became an assize centre, a suitable building would have been required for the court. To suggest that it was a forum implies a municipal status for London which, in all probability, it did not possess so early. The most sensible suggestion, therefore, on present evidence, would be to link it with the imperial procurator. Of great interest, therefore, is the evidence for a pre-Boudiccan masonry building on the same site, for, if the later building was the tabularium, then the earlier is likely to have been also, and the case for the procurator and his staff being at London before the rebellion becomes stronger.

The disaster suffered by London at the hands of Boudicca's followers in AD 60 is well attested by the evidence of burnt layers, in places a foot or more thick, which have been found from time to time in excavations and which can be dated to the mid-first century. The distribution of these sites was first plotted by Dr G. C. Dunning,[37] and it shows the main concentration to be in the area around Cornhill. London is not likely to have been fortified at the time of the rebellion; Colchester was not, and there is no reason why London should have been treated differently.[38]

The gradual recovery of the town after Boudicca must have gone hand-in-hand with the consolidation of its position as a major commercial centre, and with the expansion of its boundaries. We cannot say when precisely the last departments of provincial government were set up there, or when the town was first dignified by the award of a 'charter', but by studying certain buildings it is possible to indicate approximately when these events occurred.

The large buildings north of Lombard Street, already referred to as the possible office of the procurator, and some other buildings immediately adjacent to it, seem to have been demolished during the Flavian period, and on the cleared site, work was started on a forum and basilica for the town. That being so we might argue that sometime in the Flavian period, probably about AD 80–90, London received a municipal charter, perhaps in recognition rather of the prosperity of the inhabitants and their progress towards romanisation, than of its status as provincial capital.[39] The basilica (fig. 24), known to stretch from under Cornhill in the west to Leadenhall Market in the east, was apparently started first, and a number of alterations were introduced before it, and also the forum to its south, were finished, perhaps not before the principate of Hadrian. When complete, the whole complex covered nearly 8 acres (3·2ha) of ground, and was the largest forum in Britain.

At about the same time as work started on the basilica it also began on another large building further south (fig. 25), which has been interpreted as the praetorium of the governor.

It lay immediately overlooking the Thames and in the area now occupied by Cannon Street station and its neighbourhood; the sloping ground running down to the river was terraced to receive it. The central courtyard was probably laid

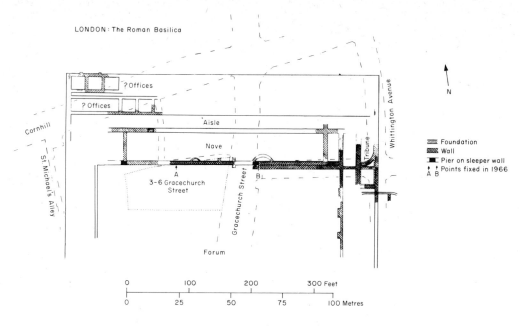

24   The London Basilica (*R. Merrifield*)

out as a garden with fountains and a large ornamental pool. On the east side there was a double range of small rooms with a central corridor running between them, which could perhaps have been offices, or alternatively, accommodation for staff officers or travelling officials: the arrangement is not unlike that sometimes to be seen in *mansiones*, and in the guest wings at the Fishbourne and Carnuntum palaces. This wing also extended east of Suffolk Lane where traces of a patterned mosaic were found. The south wing also had a number of grouped small rooms, as well as some that were larger. Both south and east wings were in the main plainly furnished. Projecting southwards from the north wing into the central court was a large hall-like structure, with massive walls, and 8oft (24·4m) by 42ft (12·8m) in size. East of this hall and possibly connected with the main east wing is part of a circular structure, either an apse or a rotunda. The hall overlay pits containing material dating to the mid-Flavian period; the south wing produced a group of late first-century sherds from beneath one floor, and the east wing had been built over a goldsmith's shop, dated AD 60–80. However it is fairly clear from the plan that more than one period of construction must be represented. So far no part sufficiently sumptuous has been found to be called the residential quarters of the governor. It is possible that they lay in the west and north wings now inaccessible under Cannon Street station, where mosaics and ornate wall-plaster have been recorded although such a situation would be unusual if a comparison is made with other riverside palaces. These normally have the principal wing fronting the river, to create an impressive architectural perspective; those at Aquincum, Cologne and Dura-Europos are notable

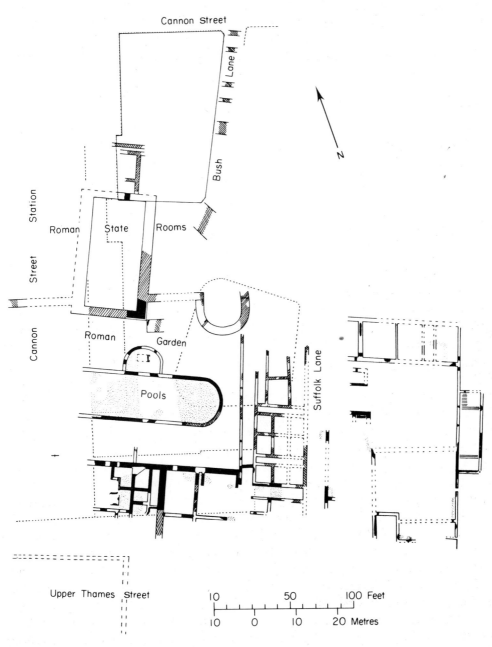

25 The London praetorium (*P. V. R. Marsden*)

examples from different periods, and it is probably right to include the Fishbourne palace in this list, chiefly on the grounds that it was built at about the same time as that at London. It may be, therefore, that this particular building in London was devoted to some other public use, and that the praetorium is to be sought elsewhere.

The next stage in the establishment of London as a provincial capital took place early in the second century, when a fort of 11 acres (4·5ha) was constructed in what is now the Cripplegate area of the city. The line of its defences, and the positions of the west gate and some internal buildings have been established by Grimes.[40] Frere has suggested[41] that in part it provided accommodation for an urban cohort, but this is unlikely as only Lyons (Lugdunum) and Carthage are known to have had them outside Rome itself, and they were cohorts originally withdrawn from Rome. Although it is large for the purpose, it more probably housed soldiers who were attached to the governor's staff, and who were required for ceremonial and guard duties in the capital. We cannot say, however, where they were accommodated before the fort was built.

By the early second century also, London was beginning to expand eastwards, and to a lesser extent, west beyond the Walbrook. That much seems clear from the extent of a serious fire which took place early in Hadrian's principate and which affected buildings in those areas.

As yet there is no evidence to suggest that London was fortified before the end of the second century; neither is there evidence for earthwork defences of the type associated with many Romano-British towns. Changes in the alignments of some east-west streets, especially of that leading to the later Newgate, might however imply successive and different town boundaries in the west. One of these bends occurred just east of the Walbrook which might have formed a natural boundary for a time; the other lay south of the south-western corner of the Cripplegate fort. While these lines may well have represented legal boundaries there is nothing to suggest the presence of fortifications on either of them (fig. 22).

The 2 miles (3·2km) of stone wall which ultimately enclosed London on the landward side cannot have been built until some years after AD 183–4, as a worn coin of Commodus minted then was found by Grimes in a deposit of soil which antedated the construction.[42] More recently Marsden has excavated an internal tower contemporary with the wall near Newgate, in which was found a scatter of coins and two coin moulds for the manufacture of forgeries. The deposition of the layer containing these coins, which took place after the tower had been constructed, must be placed at about AD 225–30, so that the fortifications on the west side at least must have been erected before that date.[43] It is necessary, therefore, to try to place the provision of fortifications for London in an historical context bracketed by these two dates, bearing in mind that the city seems never to have possessed the intermediate stage of earthwork defences. Merrifield has suggested that London as the seat of the governor was given priority during the Albinian rebellion, so that, where other towns had to make do with earthworks, it received stone walls.[44] This is by no means impossible, especially if, as seems likely, work on stone fortifications had already started elsewhere, implying the existence, at least, of masons trained in this type of work, who could have been transferred to London in emergency. Nevertheless, much has still to be learnt, not only of London's fortifications, but also of all others; not all may be homogeneous and Cirencester is worth remembering in this respect.[45] Where defences are not homogeneous in character, the difficulties of dating become greater, as the evidence from a single section will no longer apply to the complete circuit.

The construction of the wall was carried out so as to incorporate the Cripplegate fort into the new defences. By joining the town wall to the north-east and south-west corners, the fort's north and west sides effectively became part of the new circuit. But the fort wall was only 4ft (1·2m) thick, whereas the town wall varied from 7–9ft (2·1–2·7m). A thickening was therefore inserted into the top of the rampart on the inside of the fort wall, where it had become part of the new circuit, to make it up to the required width. On the east and south sides of the fort, where strong fortifications were no longer required, the wall was left as before and the ditch beyond it was filled.

The line of the wall round London on the landward side is well established, except for a short stretch on the west side, south of Ludgate Hill. It is usually concluded, however, that no continuous defensive line was ever constructed along the river in Roman times.[46] Lengths of a massive wall have been found from time-to-time along Thames Street, which Grimes has attempted to show belongs either to the riverside defences, or to wharves.[47] But this wall, recorded as being 9–10ft (2·7–3·0m) thick, is known to turn northwards up Lambeth Hill, so that it is unlikely to be part of a defensive curtain wall, unless one postulates an earlier alignment for the west side of the city.

The shore-line has also been identified in several places. It is likely that most of it would have been occupied either by open beaches or, more probably, by quays and wharves, and indeed it is possible that some of the walls which have been observed in Thames Street belonged to the latter. Yet it would be strange if the whole river frontage, nearly a mile in length, had been left entirely undefended, and quite out of keeping with what is known of other riverside towns in Britain and the Empire. If the walls already mentioned were quays, one might expect to find fortifications behind them, but buildings appear to lie too close for there to be room. There seem to be two possible solutions. Either the riverside buildings themselves formed a united, continuous frontage which was capable of being defended, or else the wall was placed further south than has hitherto been thought. In all the discussions about its position one factor seems seldom to have been considered: the probable marine transgression during the last half of the fourth century and after, which is known to have affected other coastal sites in Britain,[48] and which would have caused the backing-up of water in rivers and streams. Observations have shown in places the existence of a possible gravel shore, from which pottery of first and second centuries has been recovered. Overlying this is

10   Life-size bronze head, supposedly of Hadrian from the Thames, London (*British Museum*)

another layer of gravel and mud, together with some third and fourth century pottery, which probably represents a submerged beach, of a type recently identified on the Humber at Brough. Indeed, there is a marked similarity in the stratified sequences of the foreshores of the two rivers.[49] If, therefore, the riverside wall of London was placed further south than hitherto thought, it is not impossible for the foundations to have been undermined and for it to have been destroyed by flood water in the immediate post-Roman period. A layer of transgressive mud up to 8ft (2·4m) thick has been observed in the Dowgate area, south of Upper Thames Street, which apparently contained Pingsdorf ware. Unfortunately it is here that the Walbrook joined the Thames, so perhaps creating exceptional conditions. But if such a layer of mud was to be seen elsewhere, it might be rightly assumed that transgressive influences came as far as the known Roman buildings under Thames Street, and that the riverside defences had been wholly or in part swept away in the process, as happened at Brough and possibly also at York (p. 176). Perhaps William Fitzstephen, who, in 1174, quoted[50] a tradition that the south wall with its towers had been destroyed by the Thames, was not so far wrong after all.

London is somewhat exceptional among Roman towns in having at least one, and possibly more, sizeable streams flowing through its centre. The largest of these was the Walbrook, which was in places up to 14ft (4·3m) wide and which was initially retained between stout timber revetments. As, however, the ground level rose on either side the banks tended to give way and ultimately the stream became much reduced in size and depth.[51] The presence of these streams must have raised problems during the construction of fortifications and it is unfortunate that so little is known of how they were overcome, especially along the south side of the circuit where they flowed into the Thames. On the north side, however, brick culverts carried three of the Walbrook's tributaries through the city wall, and similar channels carrying other streams are also known elsewhere on the circuit. It is not known if any structure existed which would enable these culverts to be defended, such as a grille across them, or a sluice-gate of the type known at Silchester (p. 266).

There is little information about the gates leading into London. Apart from those serving the fort, there were probably six on the landward side. In addition, another must have led to the bridge over the Thames, and it is not unlikely that the entrance to the Walbrook would have been guarded by a water gate. The best known is Newgate (fig. 18), consisting of twin portals flanked by square towers, which projected in front of the line of the curtain wall, so resembling the west gate of the fort. Aldersgate is thought also to have had projecting towers and to have been inserted after the curtain wall had been built.

The gates which carried the principal roads out of London were: from Newgate a road ran to the vicinity of Marble Arch, from where Watling Street diverged north-west to Verulamium, with the westward road continuing on to Silchester. Ermine Street, the main road north, left the city at Bishopsgate, while the road to Colchester and East Anglia left by Aldgate. The precise position of

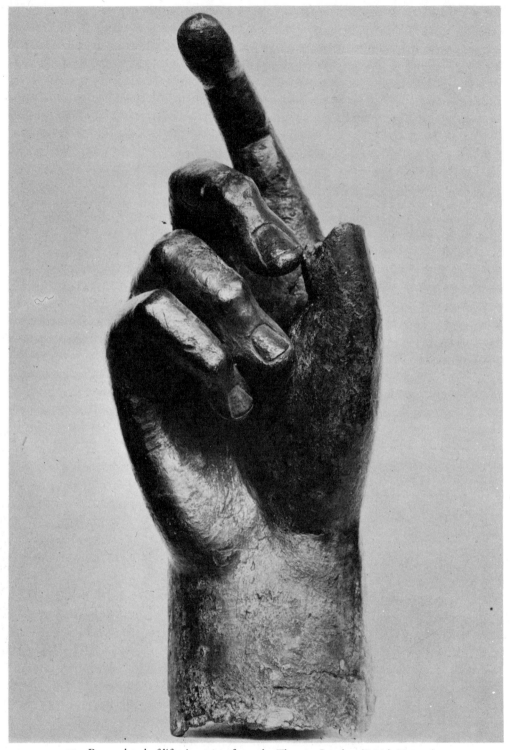

11 Bronze hand of life-size statue from the Thames, London (*British Museum*)

the Roman bridge across the Thames to the extensive Southwark suburb is not
known. Merrifield has argued that it lay slightly downstream from the present
London Bridge.[52] Over it would have passed the road which, after branching
south of the river, would have led, as Watling Street, to the south-east and as
Stane Street to the south and as far west as Chichester.

Two types of external semi-circular towers, attached to the city wall, have
been identified at London: some are solid from the foundations, others are hollow.
Most of the solid bastions are situated on the east side, although one is known not
far west of Aldersgate. Hollow bastions occur on the north and west sides and
include additions made to the wall of the fort. Grimes has recently shown that
one of the latter must be medieval in date,[53] with the strong likelihood that all
hollow bastions are of similar date. The solid bastions are known to have contained reused Roman masonry, including tombstones, in their foundations and
therefore are more likely perhaps to be of Roman date. But both Merrifield and
Grimes have raised doubts on this conclusion, as they have drawn attention to a
piece of green-glazed pottery found beneath the masonry of the Camomile
Street bastion.[54] Merrifield points out that such ware was common in the
medieval period but rare in the Roman. It is worth emphasising, however, as
Grimes has done, that its apparent rarity in the Roman period is due precisely
to its often inaccurate identification as medieval ware. Apart from imports,
kilns manufacturing such wares are known to have existed near Derby,[55] and

12   Bronze arm of a life-size statue from Seething Lane, London (*Guildhall Museum*)

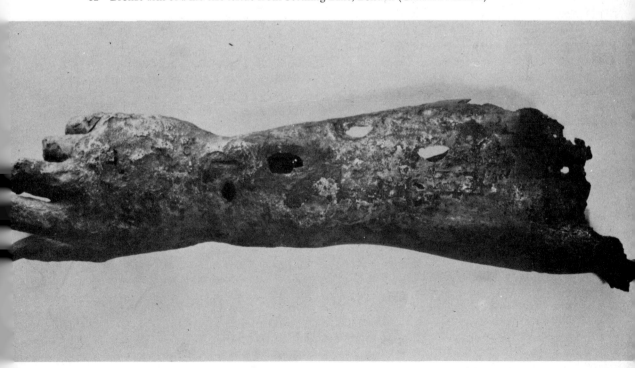

probably also in Hampshire,[56] in Wiltshire,[57] and near Chichester,[58] and others may possibly be found in due course.

Few buildings in London have ever been completely excavated. Parts of a number of houses have been found, however, in the central area and beside the Walbrook, where the land was artificially raised and levelled. It is clear from the hypocausts, mosaics and painted plaster which many possessed that these were houses with some degree of comfort. Some, such as a house in Billingsgate, even seem to have had private bath-wings. There is also much evidence for humbler buildings with timber frames and wattle and daub walls, which may have been shops and workshops. The activities of their occupants is well attested by the wide variety of manufactured goods found in London.

Part of an exceptionally large Flavian bath-house has recently come to light on Huggin Hill. It contained a heated room greater in size than any yet found in Britain and the building was probably a public baths.[59] It was terraced into the hillside, like so many other structures fronting the river. In so doing the builders appear to have tapped some natural springs which drained from the north along the interfacial surface where gravel overlies clay. Large storage tanks were constructed along the exposed embankment at the back of the terrace, into which this water was fed, and from there to supply the baths. This building appears to have been deliberately demolished in the middle of the second century, to be succeeded by one of poorer quality, and not associated with its previous use. Another, smaller bath-house is known just north of Cheapside.

Although much of the water supply of London came from numerous wells, it would be strange if there had been no properly surveyed and constructed aqueduct, bringing unpolluted water from outside the city. This was considered an important amenity in the Roman world, to be adopted even in quite small towns and villages in Britain. Moreover, even towns with many wells, such as Cirencester, were supplied with fresh running water from an aqueduct. It has been argued that the wells and natural springs of London sufficed and that no aqueduct was needed.[60] Yet wooden water-pipes with iron junctions have been found beneath the Bank of England and near the Temple of Mithras, and clearly imply some form of distributive system for running water. Apparently the former were found lying in a north-west and south-east direction,[61] suggesting perhaps a *castellum aquae* near Cornhill. These pipes have been interpreted as drains to remove surplus surface water. But the ease with which this could have been done by using other, simpler materials and without the arduous labour involved in the manufacture of such pipes, does not encourage this explanation. It is of course possible that they were water-pipes being reused as drains in the positions in which they were found. Such pipes, however, were rarely, if ever, first used for anything but the distribution of fresh water.

Although many Romano-British deities were worshipped in London, few temples are known. An inscription from Budge Row[62] records the restoration of a temple or shrine dedicated to the Mother Goddesses. Another, scratched on a jug, is evidence for the existence of a temple in the suburb at Southwark,

13 Bronze left hand of a life-size statue from Gracechurch Street, London (*Guildhall Museum*)

14 Two bronze fingers from a life-size statue from Fenchurch Street, London (*Guildhall Museum*)

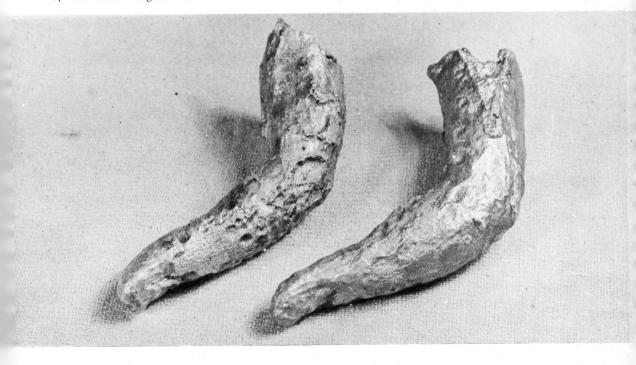

15   Bronze head, supposedly of Claudius, from the river Alde in Suffolk (*British Museum*)

dedicated to the Egyptian goddess Isis.[63] The only fully identified temple in London is that dedicated to Mithras, which was excavated by Grimes in 1954 on the Bucklersbury House site north of Cannon Street.[64] In 1889 a marble relief showing Mithras slaying the bull was found in this area, together with the head of a river god, and it is probable that both came originally from the temple. Grimes has tentatively suggested that it was built towards the end of the second century, at a time when the cult was beginning to be diffused in the western Empire. The building had an unusual basilican plan with an apse at the west end, supported on either side by two roughly quadrant-shaped buttresses with a third rectangular one at the head of the apse. There was a narthex at the east end, which could not be fully excavated as it ran out under the Walbrook street. No less than three further changes of the internal arrangements took place after its construction, prolonging the life of the temple well into the fourth century, although the later stages suggest a decline in its affairs. At one stage in its life, however, possibly early in the fourth century, a crisis induced the burial of some of its major cult objects below the floor of the nave. There, in two separate places, were found the heads from statues of Mithras, Minerva and Serapis, a small statue of Mercury, and a more-than-lifesize hand clasping the handle of a dagger. It is possible that they were buried at a time when there was danger of desecration by Christians. Nevertheless the temple was not apparently abandoned then and appears to have continued in use without a break until the middle of the fourth century.

As in most towns in Britain, evidence for the survival of civilised life after the collapse of the central administration is scarce. Although London has produced some metalwork of the type associated with late Roman military uniforms, the total number of such finds is not high when compared with some other towns or villages. Of interest, therefore, in this context of survival, are the recent discoveries made in a large house in the Billingsgate area. This house, which had its own bath-suite, was built about AD 200, and a large number of coins, dated to the end of the fourth century and scattered on the floor of one of the hypocaust stokeholes, strongly suggests use after AD 400. The baths were, however, ruinous by the end of the fifth century as an Anglo-Saxon saucer brooch was found among fallen roofing material.[65] Part of the east wing of the house was heated by a hypocaust and in the ash filling its stokehole was found part of an amphora, dated to the fifth century and imported from the eastern Mediterranean.[66] There can be little doubt therefore that this house was still occupied during the fifth century. It is hardly likely to be an isolated example and it is to be hoped that others will come to light in due course.

4

<hr>

The Coloniae

<hr>

A quarter of a century has now passed since Richmond published his paper on the coloniae of Roman Britain.[1] Much of what he wrote stands as firmly now as it did then, but he would have been first to have acknowledged the need for revision. Insofar as Colchester is concerned we have his later account in the Victoria County History,[2] but almost a decade has passed since even that was written, and more since Hull's *Roman Colchester* appeared. Richmond's authoritative survey of York in the Royal Commission's series[3] required revision almost before it appeared in print, so slow are the organs of official publication, but it retains much of its great value.

   Certain aspects of the British coloniae relating to the reasons for their foundation, the choice of sites and their administration, have already been discussed in preceding chapters. Apart from emphasising again the difference between the veteran foundations at Colchester, Lincoln and Gloucester and the different circumstances in which York received promotion, it remains only to describe the individual sites.

COLCHESTER (*Colonia Claudia(?) Victricensis Camulodunensium*)

The British oppidum of Camulodunum covered a very large area inside its boundary dykes, although the main centre was concentrated within these dykes in a much smaller enclosure near Sheepen Farm. When the colonia was founded a new site, slightly south-east of the native centre, was selected on a reasonably level promontory enfolded in a loop of the river Colne (fig. 27). It is normally assumed that the boundaries of the first colonia corresponded with those later marked by the town wall, which enclosed an area of 108 acres (44ha). But a fresh examination of the representative material from the first colonia has recently shown a distribution which was restricted largely to the western end of the walled enclosure, with the greatest concentration in the North Hill area.[4] It would appear that some of the burnt layers and other material from the eastern half, on which the original assumption was based, belonged not to the Boudiccan fire but to one which seems to have swept through much of the town in the mid-second century. This distribution might imply that the area of the first foundation was not as great as that of the later town, and also carries with it the possibility that the land on which the legionary fortress stood was used for the colonia when it was abandoned in AD 48–9. Although the situation of this fortress has never been satisfactorily established, Miss Dunnett (now Mrs Niblett) has found in the North Hill area pits and gullies which were earlier than buildings burnt by Boudicca's rebels, and which she attributed generally to a military occupation. In particular, a pre-colonia timber building, associated with military equipment, was excavated in 1966 in Insula 11.[5] She has also repeated an earlier suggestion that such a position for the colonia, relative to the temple of Claudius, could be matched by the arrangement at Lugdunum, where the temple to Rome and Augustus was situated outside the town, a possibility which did not escape Richmond. But the situation is very confusing; a number of ditches of Boudiccan or earlier date have been discovered in recent years, and it is difficult to see yet how these will fit the general pattern.

There are points worthy of further consideration. The insulae in the North Hill area seem to show more variation in size than those further east, and the lines of the streets bounding them are more irregular than the street grid of the later town, as though laid out to respect existing buildings (fig. 26). But as only one has so far been shown to follow a definite pre-Boudiccan alignment, this aspect should not be stressed too far. Even in this area the street plan seems to have been altered extensively during the rebuilding after the fire. Much argument has taken place whenever the position of the forum at Colchester is discussed. It is usually assumed to have been in the neighbourhood of the Temple of Claudius, with preference given to Insula 30, although some doubts have always been voiced as to whether it actually included the temple and its precinct.[6] Certainly, Insula 30 is known to contain five large parallel walls, which were observed during building work. They seem to be of second-century date, but little else is known about them. Nevertheless no other insula near the temple precinct has produced building remains which could be interpreted as a forum or basilica. Indeed Richmond has even gone so far as to suggest that, to begin with, the insulae around the temple would have been more likely occupied by buildings devoted to provincial business, with the principal public buildings of the colonia lying further west.[7] Certainly if the first colonia underlies only the western part of the later town, then there would be more likelihood for the forum to be in, for instance, Insula 18. Very little is known of the buildings in this insula, but its position in a corner formed by the principal north-south and east-west streets, is one often considered favourable for the forum of a town. Mrs Niblett's excavations in the north-east corner of this insula revealed part of a building, of possibly Neronian or early Flavian date, with massive walls 5ft (1·5m) thick.[8] This building, although rebuilt once, lasted without further major structural alterations until at least the early fourth century, in strong contrast with the

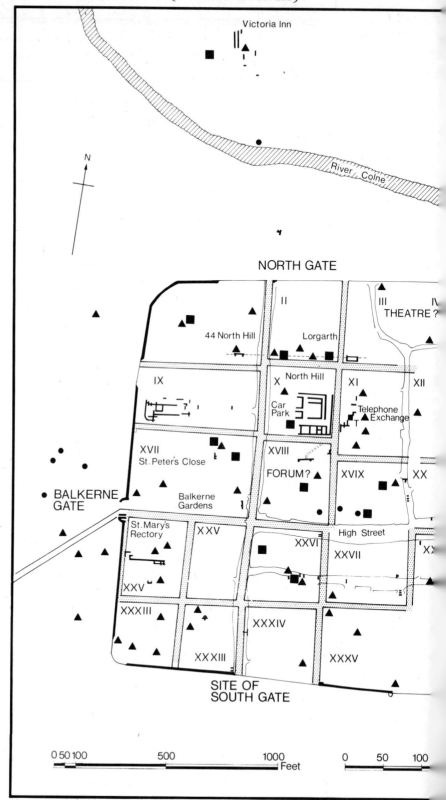

26 Plan of Colchester (*after Rosalind Niblett*)

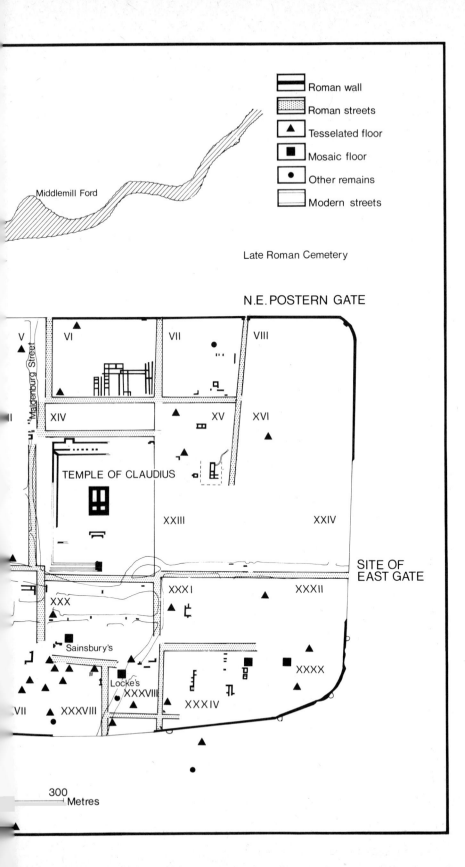

Roman wall
Roman streets
Tesselated floor
Mosaic floor
Other remains
Modern streets

Middlemill Ford

Late Roman Cemetery

N.E. POSTERN GATE

V
VI
VII
VIII

Maidenburg Street

XIV
XV
XVI

TEMPLE OF CLAUDIUS

XXIII
XXIV

SITE OF
EAST GATE

XXXI
XXXII

XXX

Sainsbury's

Locke's
XXXVIII
XXXX

XXXVIII
XXXIV

VII

300
Metres

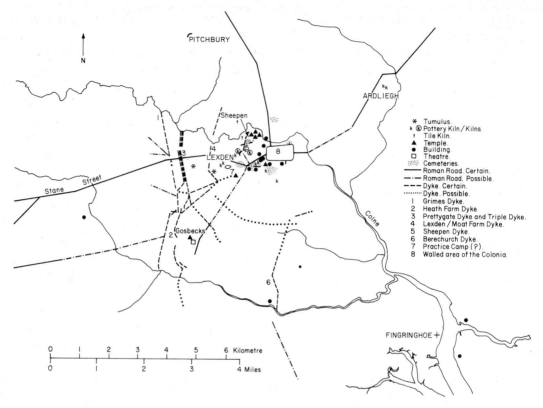

27   The Colchester area (*Rosalind Niblett*)

usual, rapidly-changing structural history of more normal town houses. For the pre-Boudiccan colonia, it might be suggested that, following Tacitus, only a curia, or council-chamber, was built and that the 'forum' at this time was simply an open space. Certainly there is no basilica at the Claudian colonia at *Aequum*, and an open raised area apparently served instead, behind which were situated the civic offices and curia.[9]

The town sacked in the Boudiccan rebellion was in its infancy. Much time and money had nevertheless been spent on its public buildings, which included, according to Tacitus, a council chamber, a theatre and the great temple. The site of the theatre has never been satisfactorily established, although the lay-out of the medieval buildings in Insulae 3 and 4 is reminiscent of the dwellings built round the theatre at Vieil Évreux, and may indicate its presence. A massive wall foundation was found in the area and the position would have had the added advantage for a theatre of a sloping hill against which the cavea, or seating bank, could have been placed. An alternative site lies in Insula 13, where a massive curving foundation has been found below Maidenburgh Street.[10] If not the theatre then one or other might possibly be an amphitheatre, recalling the local interest which there must have been in its shows, and which expressed itself in the decoration on local pottery types and on a terracotta plaque,[11] displaying scenes of gladiatorial combat.

Undoubtedly the eye-catching focus of the colonia would have been the Temple of Claudius, raised on its podium above the surrounding buildings. The podium measured 105ft (32m) by 80ft (24·4m) and, so as to conserve stone in a region where good material was scarce, was constructed over earth-filled vaults, which still survive below the Norman castle. The width of the podium would have allowed for a portico with either six or eight columns across the front, rising to a height of about 30ft (9m). The front wall of the cella is probably marked by the position of the cross wall in the foundations which separates the longer vaults at the rear of the podium from the shorter at the front. A sloping masonry apron at the front of the podium implies the steps by which the front of the temple was approached. Some 90ft (27m) in front of the temple stood the sacrificial altar. Flanking the altar and set slightly to its rear were two pedestals, which probably carried statues. The temple and its court were flanked by an asymmetric portico on its north side,[12] and on the south side by a massive screen-wall which appears to have incorporated at its centre a monumental entrance to the court. The exterior of the screen was possibly clad in an ornamental sheath of coloured marbles imported from many distant parts of the Empire. The whole work, with its bays and niches, would have provided an impressive architectural introduction to the temple.

The temple is invariably known as the Temple of Claudius and there is some reason to believe that it was so dedicated in his lifetime. However, Frere considers it unlikely, not only because it was theologically incorrect, but also because it would have been directly contrary to the emperor's wishes.[13] He suggests further that a rededication to the *Divus Claudius* after the Boudiccan rebellion would have corrected the earlier lapse into bad taste. Nevertheless there would appear to be some substance in believing that it was originally dedicated to Claudius. The policy of Augustus and Tiberius with regard to official dedications had been to refuse them, especially in Rome, where senatorial opinion at the time made it expedient to do so. Even so, Augustus sanctioned a cult to himself in some western provinces on condition that it was combined with Roma. Private dedications both to the living Augustus and to the living Claudius are prolific in eastern provinces, but also come from Italy and the west. To cite Claudius' letter to the Alexandrians as proof that he also refused the request from Britain, is to compare two superficially similar requests. But closer examination suggests marked differences in the way that Claudius might have reacted to each. There was little to be gained politically by sanctioning the request from Alexandria. Indeed, by acceding to it Claudius would possibly have antagonised further the Jewish part of the population, who were still simmering from the anti-Semitic policies of Gaius, and whom he was trying to placate. The situation in Alexandria was therefore very different from Britain. Here, we might feel, politics would over-ride his personal feelings in the matter, which were probably much the same as other members of the ruling class. A dedication to Rome or Augustus would have little meaning to the Britons, and moreover the same dedication had failed to be attractive in Germany. But by sanctioning a cult to himself as a living god, he would have involved them in something tangible, which they could have understood, rather than in an abstraction. Claudius had himself been to Camulodunum. What better way could have been found to strike awe into the people than by making out that he was a god? In the context of something unusual happening at Colchester, Seneca's satirical gibe has most meaning. Despite this explanation, another possibility has been explored by Fishwick,[14] who has suggested that the temple was most probably voted by the Roman Senate after Claudius' death and deification, and that it may not have been completed by AD 60.

Apart from areas of burning related to the Boudiccan fire, which have been found in a number of places, little is known of the private houses built by the first veterans, and the shops which supplied their needs. One of the most interesting discoveries, however, was the burnt ruins of a fully-stocked pottery and glass-ware shop in the south-west corner of Insula 19. There were found nests of samian pots stacked on the floor of the shop, over which molten glass had flowed from vessels presumably stored on shelves above. A similar shop has been identified on the opposite side of the same street but further east in Insula 28. Yet another building possibly used as a store or warehouse has been explored recently in Insula 10. In one room large quantities of wheat had been burnt in the fire, in another over thirty mortaria were found, while a third contained more than eighty flagons.

Some of the problems associated with the early colonia appear also in the post-Boudiccan town; this applies particularly to the whereabouts of the forum. If, indeed, the early foundation took place west of the temple, we still cannot say precisely at what stage the town was extended to the east, although it is clear from the greater concentration of mosaics in the former area that the greater wealth and urbanisation always remained here. But two private houses and part of a third excavated in Insula 6, would seem to have been built during the last decades of the first century, implying an eastward expansion soon after the rebellion, and probably *c.* AD 75–80. The plans of these houses are not unlike a mid second-century house recently excavated at Gloucester (p. 147). Together they show a closer relationship to the compact peristyled houses of the Mediterranean world than to the more normal, rather sprawling Romano-British town house; such plans proclaim the identity of the owners as descendants of legionary veterans and Roman citizens.

But besides a preponderance of legionary veterans among the inhabitants, it is likely that *incolae*, or native members, were also included in the community. Indeed Tacitus explicitly refers to them in his passage describing the events leading up to the Boudiccan rebellion,[15] and the presence of a *censitor*[16] of Roman citizens in the second century might imply, by contrast, their presence too (pl. 16). The stories of hardship inflicted on some natives by the veterans, as told by Tacitus, may have exceeded the truth. It is possible that much of the land-

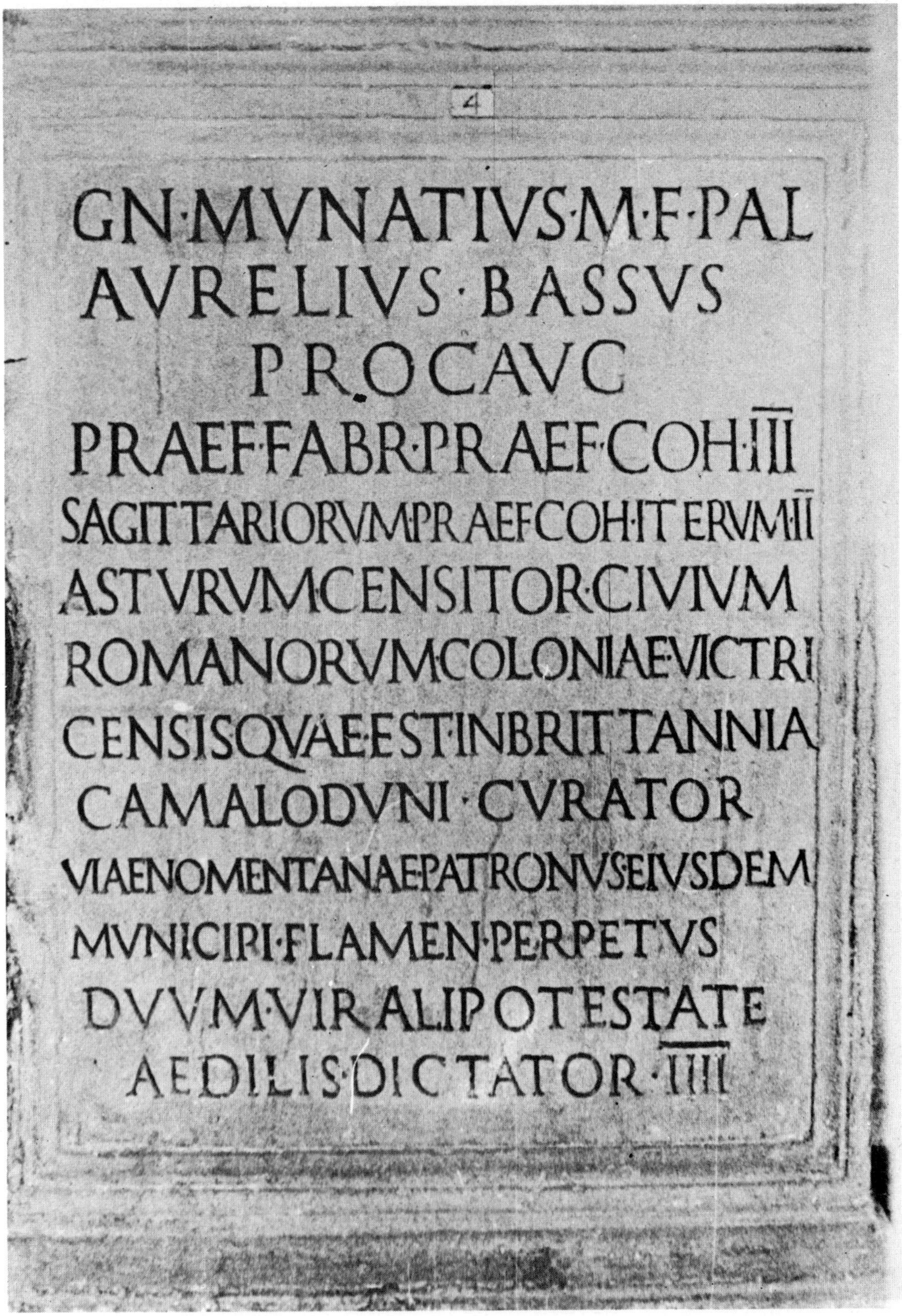

GN·MVNATIVS·M·F·PAL
AVRELIVS·BASSVS
PRO·CAVG
PRAEF·FABR·PRAEF·COH·ĪĪĪ
SAGITTARIORVM·PRAEF·COH·IT·ERVM·ĪĪ
ASTVRVM·CENSITOR·CIVIVM
ROMANORVM·COLONIAE·VICTRI
CENSIS·QVAE·EST·IN·BRITTANNIA
CAMALODVNI·CVRATOR
VIAE·NOMENTANAE·PATRONVS·EIVSDEM
MVNICIPI·FLAMEN·PERPETVS
DVVMVIR·ALI·POTESTATE
AEDILIS·DICTATOR·ĪĪĪĪ

16 Honorific inscription from Nomentum to Gn. Munatius Aurelius Bassus, *censitor civium Romanorum Camaloduni* (*Vatican Museum*)

grabbing may have been restricted to that belonging to the outright enemies of Rome, such as the estates of Cunobelin's sons. Indeed Tacitus' use of the imperfect tense, remarked by Richmond to describe the continuing nature of the sequestrations, sounds more like an extensive political purge being carried out against their followers. We may reason so, for later manifestations clearly show a degree of tolerance towards the natives and their customs, which may be only in part due to the repercussions of the rebellion. This tolerance is best represented by a number of Romano-Celtic temples and other shrines probably built by native inhabitants, which are known outside the town, especially in the areas towards Sheepen Farm, and also by the extensive religious centre at Gosbecks Farm, about 2 miles (3·2km) south-west of the colonia.

The temple at Gosbecks stands in the south-east corner of a ditched enclosure of undoubted pre-Roman origin, presumably to leave room for some prominent cult object such as a grove of trees nearer its centre (fig. 28). The ditch, although it was open until the later second century, was itself surrounded by a large double portico, which stood within one of a pair of walled enclosures. About 500ft (150m) south of the temple, a theatre, which is the largest yet known in Britain, was erected late in the first or early in the second century (fig. 12). At first the earthen seat banks were retained by wooden walls, but by the middle of the second century the outside walls had been rebuilt in stone.[17] Yet for some unknown reason it was demolished about AD 200. The conjunction of temple and theatre was comparatively common in the Graeco-Roman world, but here it probably represents a Romano-Celtic synthesis and the romanisation of a site of obvious native sanctity. Moreover, the theatre and the enclosures are evidence for attendance by large crowds, and it is possible that the site may have acted as some central gathering place for the Trinovantes, where fairs and markets were held in addition to the celebration of religious rites.

These temples and their situations illustrate two contrasting attitudes of the Roman citizens of the colonia towards the local inhabitants. On the one side there is the tolerance which allowed native-style shrines and gathering places to flourish, if not in the town, then at least in the territorium attached to it. Clearly not all the land was distributed among the veterans. On the other side there is the distinction between the citizens with their own markets, shops and temples in the colonia and the native Trinovantians, possibly living in the town, possibly in the territorium, who appear to have had their own commercial and religious centre at Gosbecks Farm. Not only were there differences between Roman and non-Roman but probably also differences between the treatment of *intramurani* and *extramurani*.

In spite of the Boudiccan rebellion, no immediate attempt was apparently made to fortify the town. Mrs Niblett has suggested that a ditch which she found in the North Hill area, 300ft (91m) inside the stone wall, belonged to the fortifications erected towards the end of the first century.[18] But she relies wholly on Tacitus' statement[19] that the colonia had no walls at the time of the rebellion, a statement, which, incidentally, need not imply that no emergency measures

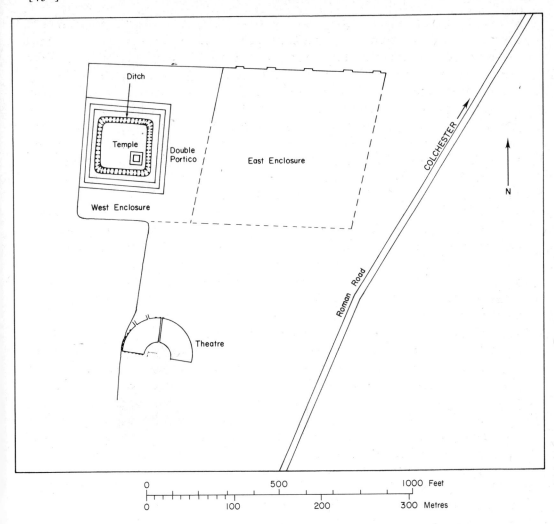

28   Colchester; Gosbeck's Farm temple and theatre site (*after M. R. Hull*)

were taken. It would have been surprising if nothing whatever had been done, and we might envisage an attempt to throw an earthwork round the major part of the built-up area. Nothing less should be expected as the reaction of ex-soldiers to an immediate threat.

For some time it has been thought that the curtain wall, with a contemporary rampart, was erected during the middle or later second century.[20] Recently, however, Mrs Niblett has been able to cut two sections behind the wall, south of the Balkerne Gate, in Insula 25, with surprising results.[21] She found that, originally, a free-standing wall had been constructed, with a street occupying the place normally taken by the rampart. The street itself overlay the edge of the wall-trench and had been resurfaced at least once. The date of construction has not yet been fixed precisely, but would seem to lie in the early second century.

There would appear to be a strong resemblance here to Gloucester (p. 143), but it is doubtful if this free-standing wall ever enclosed the whole colonia at Colchester, and it would seem to have been part of an unfinished fortification. A rampart was added behind the wall in the early third century, when the street was completely obliterated. But a date later than the second century for some of the wall circuit can be argued on the grounds that the gates, with the exception of the Balkerne Gate, seem to be of the single portal variety set between inturns in the town wall and with but a single tower surmounting them. Gates of this type, which can be seen at Canterbury and Caerwent, are usually indicative of a late third-century date. The north-east gate at Colchester has been excavated and conforms to this pattern (fig. 20). A fallen fragment of masonry from the tower gives some indication of its superstructure, which would appear to have had at least a pair of windows set in the inner face at first-floor level.

The most imposing gate at Colchester was the Balkerne Gate through which ran the road to London and the west.[22] The plan of this gate was unusual for Britain (fig. 17). It was set wholly in front of the line of the curtain wall and contained two main portals flanked by foot passages, which were in turn flanked by quadrant-shaped guard chambers. It is normally assumed that the guard-rooms cannot have risen as towers above the central portion and that the gate was of uniform height all over. The size and style of this gate, as compared with what is known of the others at Colchester, might be explained by its position astride the main road to London, in which place it would undoubtedly be considered the principal gate of the town. Yet its architectural style is redolent of earlier forms and it should rightly take its place with the Verulamium Gate at Cirencester, the Chester and London Gates at Verulamium and the East Gate at Lincoln. All have the same archaic pattern when compared with the gates of later years, while the Verulamium and Cirencester gates are also known to antedate the town walls. This should have raised questions as to the contemporaneity of the Balkerne Gate with the curtain wall as a whole and with the other gates at Colchester. In the past it has done so, only for the questions to be dismissed, in spite of structural and other details which must continue to raise doubts in this direction.

Yet there are discrepancies which have never been satisfactorily explained by this assumption, and a careful re-examination is an urgent need. The gate as first constructed possessed carriageways with an abnormal width of 17ft (5·2m). For these to have been vaulted a height of at least 27ft (8·2m) is required for the floor of the room above the gate. But such an arrangement seems excessively clumsy, creating a 'hump' which, if the gate was contemporary with the walls, would have had to be crossed by anyone proceeding from one to other of the parapet walks on either side. A far better arrangement would have been for the upper floor of the gate to be level with the parapet walks. It is interesting therefore to observe that the first major alterations of the gate reduced the width of the carriageways to little more than 10ft (3m), so effectively lowering the height of the floor above by nearly 4ft (1·2m). These alterations were dated rather vaguely to the third or fourth centuries, which takes no account of more recent discoveries. It would seem that the Balkerne Gate belonged to the phase of fortification which included the free-standing wall, but that it was altered during later modifications to the defences.[23] Colchester may therefore prove to be another example of a town where fortifications were begun in stone during the second century, but where the work was discontinued, only to be resumed after an interval, when newer architectural ideas were employed. However, unlike at other towns where this happened, no earthworks seem to have been built in the interval. Clarity about the defences is certainly not aided by a recent authoritative statement which says that the wall cannot have been built before AD 140–50, that the Balkerne Gate cannot have been constructed after AD 70–90 and that the two structures are of identical build.[24] Little is known of the other principal gates, of which there were at least three in addition to the two already mentioned, as well as a small postern, only 2ft 7½in (800mm) wide, in the west wall, south of the Balkerne Gate (fig. 21). The curtain wall itself appears to have been of uniform thickness throughout the circuit, and is known to have been penetrated by at least three large, brick-vaulted drains. One runs northwards through the north-east gate, another runs out a few feet south of the east gate, and the third southwards in Vineyard Street out of Insula 37. Six rectangular, solid, internal towers are also known, which appear to be bonded with the inner face of the curtain wall, but spacing is too irregular to suggest the positions of others. Although six external, semi-circular bastions are also known along the south-eastern part of the circuit, they are almost certainly medieval in date; no convincing evidence for bastions of the Roman period has ever been found.

Brief mention has already been made of some private houses in the town. Unfortunately, owing to the presence of modern Colchester, it is exceedingly difficult to recover complete house plans by excavation. Most are indicated only by fragmentary remains, often observed in commercial excavation. It is surprising therefore in these circumstances that about 50 mosaic pavements have been recorded. No town of equivalent size in Britain has produced so many, and this can only point to a considerable density of buildings of quality. Nevertheless, as Richmond pointed out,[25] most of them are found to lie in the area west of the Temple of Claudius. This distribution might be taken as a further indication that the centre of gravity of the town remained in that quarter after the Boudiccan sack, and even after the official boundaries of the colonia had been expanded to include the area round the Temple of Claudius. Most of the mosaics, however, although often large in size, were somewhat restrained in their designs, exhibiting a wealth of geometric patterns, but rarely large scenic or pictorial devices. None with human figures and only one with animals are known so far. Dr Smith has suggested that some second-century mosaics at both Verulamium and Colchester were the work of the same 'school'.[26] One indication of greater opulence was found by Miss Richardson in cutting a section through the eastern defences in the area now occupied by the Technical College.[27]

It was a fragment of painted plaster which had been embellished with gold-leaf decoration, normally only rarely used; the fragment need not have come from a private house.

A substantial town house is known in Insula 9 beneath what is now the Technical College. Unfortunately, the excavation was carried out mainly in 1865, and no precise information is available apart from the plan. More recently parts of other houses have been excavated in Insulae 10, 25 and 39. A surprising feature of the town is the apparent absence of evidence for light industrial work, such as might be carried on by coppersmiths or blacksmiths, and which is usually so abundant in other towns; one example is a possible coppersmith's workshop in Insula 10. Yet Colchester is one of the few places in Britain where a coppersmith is actually known by name, for Cintusmus dedicated a plaque to the god Silvanus Callirios, probably at a shrine just outside the town.[28] Perhaps such work was more commonly carried out extramurally and a considerable industrial site is known from the early period in the Sheepen area. Richmond attributed the absence to accident of discovery, but it should not be forgotten that industry was sometimes controlled in chartered towns.[29]

One other building in Insula 15 must be mentioned. It is commonly identified a Mithraeum, but Richmond has pointed out that it contains neither the structural features nor the associated objects to support this interpretation.[30] The building is divided into four main parts, and the principal room, which had a floor sunk below the level of the other rooms, showed indications of wooden partitions. But these wooden structures do not follow the regular pattern expected at a Mithraeum; moreover the heavy concrete floor was not properly rendered and the walls were devoid of plaster or decoration except in the doorway leading to the main room. During its construction the builders had tapped a spring, which ran into the lower room and from there the flow of water was conducted out through the east wall along a tiled and vaulted drain to emerge from the town under the north-east gate. The drain was large by any standards and the flow of water must have been quite considerable. The south face of the building, where possibly the entrance was placed, appears to have been adorned with half-engaged pilaster columns made of brick and probably plastered. The building would also appear to lie in its own enclosure. Many other suggestions have been made about its function, varying from the religious to the industrial, and none is entirely satisfactory. But one explanation that does not seem to have been made is that the spring may have been invested with curative or magical properties, the building being in fact a nymphaeum. This would account for most of the structural features including the external architecture, and also for the smallness and self-contained nature of the building, but not for the absence of embellishment. However, it would have been quite sufficient for people to come to take the waters. Such a conclusion is supported by the evidence provided by the excavators who recorded a hard, calcified layer over much of the floor in the main room. The water obviously has a high mineral content, and an analysis might prove informative.

In the absence of specific evidence, it is difficult to define the limits of the territorium of the colonia. Richmond has suggested[31] that it should be sought in the Colne valley. In this region there are certainly a number of well-furnished villas, which may have belonged to the descendants of the original veterans or to the richer incolae. There are also numerous records of buildings immediately outside the town. It seems abundantly clear that the territorium also included places connected only with natives living on it, such as near the Gosbecks temple site and the old capital at Sheepen Farm. In the aftermath of the conquest many buildings on the latter site, no doubt belonging to hostile natives, were destroyed and its defences were levelled. That done, the remaining population seem to have been herded nearer the fortress site and used to manufacture military equipment. This activity continued after the foundation of the colonia, when the site became a larger works-depot, run by the natives under Roman supervision, where clay, sand and gravel were dug, brick and tile was baked and metal fittings manufactured for the new town. This activity was abruptly terminated by the Boudiccan rebellion.[32] With a return to normal after the rebellion, the need for an industrial site can hardly have lessened, yet the Sheepen area seems then not to have been used, except for quarrying.[33] There is a slight suggestion that the works were moved nearer the town. In later years, however, the site of the old capital and much of the area surrounding it on Warren Field appears to have been used for the chief industrial area of the town, as well as for providing living space for many people. So it would seem that the site was never fully deserted, but was probably used principally by the native population, although many of these appear to have moved into the colonia during the late first century.[34] There is slight evidence in this later period for metal working, and we may suspect that more is still to be found. The principal industry, judged by the extant remains, was the manufacture of pottery, brick and tile, and glass. A square glass bottle found in one of the Bartlow Hills tumuli had the letters CCV moulded on the base, and it has been suggested that this may refer to a municipal glassworks,[35] although it could equally be an abbreviation of the *tria nomina* of a citizen manufacturer. The manufacture of pottery at Colchester seems to have been carried out on a large scale, and it is clear that the products were widely traded. Some two dozen kilns have already been explored and these probably represent only a fraction of those in use. A wide variety of wares was manufactured, the most interesting of which was samian pottery, and a series of colour-coated vessels. Among the latter are a number of beakers decorated in barbotine style with a surprising miscellany of running animals, gladiators, hooded figures and vegetation.[36] The samian pottery was the result of an attempt by an East Gaulish firm to start production in Britain in the late second century. The special illite-bearing clay required for its successful manufacture is not found in this country and therefore presumably had to be imported. Although large numbers of vessels must have been produced in the special kilns needed for the firing, and although about twenty individual potters are known by the names stamped on their wares, it is doubtful if the venture was completely successful. The quality seems to have been uniformly poor, even though the repertoire included numerous decorated forms, and they enjoyed only a very limited local market.[37]

The extramural temples at Colchester have already been mentioned. The largest group, consisting of at least four of Romano-Celtic type, lay north-west of the colonia and towards the river. One was very large and was enclosed within a roughly trapezoidal temenos; it seems to have been built towards the end of the first century and certainly survived until the late fourth century. Another smaller temple or shrine has been found in the playing fields of the Royal Grammar School, slightly south-west by south of the town. It seems to have contained a square cella with a portico on one side only. Originally the temple was surrounded by a roughly oval ditch. Later, when a walled temenos was added, one of its walls was curved outwards so as to respect the ditch. Another building within the temenos may have been an assembly hall. In the course of excavation, two dedications to Silvanus were found in a pit in the temenos; these settle the question of this temple's ascription.

Mention of Colchester would not be complete without some description of its cemeteries. Two of the principal surviving funerary monuments are the tombstones of serving soldiers, who must have died and been buried at Colchester in

17   Fragmentary tombstone of a Roman knight from Colchester (*Colchester and Essex Museum*)

18   An engraving of the objects found in a child's grave at Colchester (*Colchester and Essex Museum*)

the years immediately following the invasion.[38] Another must refer to a veteran centurion,[39] and a fourth to the only member of the equestrian order attested as originating in Britain (pl. 17).[40] All these were recovered from what must have been the most important cemetery west of the town, with the graves lining the main road to London. At least one walled mausoleum has been found in this same area near the Royal Grammar School. Many of the burials were richly furnished. One of the most interesting was that of a child, who had been buried with a wooden box containing nearly two dozen pipeclay figurines of humans and animals (pl. 18). Some of the human figures seem to recline in the attitude adopted in the classical world at a polite dinner party; one figure (not so politely!) scratches the back of his head while apparently conversing with his neighbour, and another his cheek. Others appear to read from scrolls. All are seemingly caricatures, and although lifelike do not present an altogether attractive appearance.[41] If indeed they were toys then they are certainly representative of that strong vein of 'black' humour which often runs in nurseries! Included with the figures in the grave were also a number of fine quality vessels of glass, samian and green-glazed ware, including three miniature vessels normally called 'tettines'. All told it is something of a strange collection and one cannot help but wonder if here was the equivalent of a Roman child's dolls' tea-party. We might also wonder whether, if the contents of the wooden box had been excavated more carefully, evidence for miniature tables and even couches might not have been found, on which some of the figures so obviously were made to recline. An examination of the carved bone inlays found with the figures might provide some information.

There remains one last question to put. What happened to the Trinovantes? Did they become attributi and so lose their independence in the territorium of the colonia; were they considered as a separate unit but with their administration based on the colonia; or were they provided with their own administrative centre entirely separate from the colonia? The first seems most unlikely since Ptolemy refers to Colchester as a town of the Trinovantes.[42] Opinion is divided between the other two possibilities. Stevens has suggested that *Caesaromagus* (Chelmsford) may have been the capital of an independent civitas, although on balance he is inclined against it.[43] Richmond supported the same possibility,[44] perhaps slightly more emphatically than Stevens. Joyce Reynolds was inclined to suggest that the tribal institutions survived within the framework of the colonia.[45] Such is the nature of the problem. But, since a solution is inextricably linked with the history of Chelmsford, it has been left until that town is considered in its turn (p. 195).

LINCOLN (*Colonia [Domitiana] Lindensium*)

The foundation of a colonia at Lincoln appears to have taken place towards the end of the principate of Domitian (pl. 19),[46] and was probably part of a plan which also embraced the sister colonia at Gloucester, founded in the next principate. That being so, and if we are to deduce the official name, it is better to draw an analogy with Gloucester than with Colchester.[47] Therefore the official name would possibly have been *colonia Domitiana Lindensium*[48] and the reason for its not surviving in full would have been the *damnatio memoriae* pronounced on Domitian after his death. Presumably the colonia was not renamed.

The foundation of a colonia at Lincoln, like that at Gloucester, and possibly also at Colchester, was designed to make use of land which was already, in part at least, imperial property. This is what happened at *Aequum* in Dalmatia under Claudius or Nero, where a colonia replaced the fortress of Legio VII C.p.f. on its transfer to Moesia. The legionary fortress at Lincoln, built by Legio IX Hispana and used later by Legio II Adjutrix, seems to have been evacuated in the late seventies. Even then the defences were left intact, presumably to delimit land still in government ownership. Or was there still rife a feeling that it might be needed again as a fortress?

It is usually assumed that this colonia was founded for a discharge of veterans

19 Dedication to Fortune from Mainz, giving the name Lindum (*Mittelrheinisches Landesmuseum, Mainz*)

from Legio IX Hispana, although there is evidence that veterans from two other legions died at Lincoln[49] and may be presumed to have lived there. But neither of the latter legions was serving in Britain at the time of the foundation, by which time also Legio II Adjutrix had been withdrawn. Moreover, the latter had been newly recruited as late as AD 69, admittedly from serving members of the fleet, and it is unlikely that a major discharge of veterans would have taken place quite so early, especially as the legion was required for service in Moesia just before the date at which the earliest possible discharge could have taken place. So Legio IX was probably the one concerned.

The area enclosed by the legionary defences was approximately 41 acres (16·6ha), and it lay at the southern end of the limestone ridge, where the river Witham breaks through. The selection of such a site for a town, some 200ft (60m) above the valley floor, shows the inaccuracy of the oft-repeated generalisation that Roman towns preferred the plains to hill-tops.[50] So far only slight evidence has come to light for Iron Age occupation of the site, which would have been part of the tribal territory of the Coritani, and which would presumably have been requisitioned or purchased from the tribe by the Roman army. But

Lincolnshire as a whole was by no means devoid of native settlements and one of the major tribal centres lay at Old Sleaford, only a few miles south of Lincoln. There can be little doubt, therefore, that a strong native element must have been included in the colonial territorium.

Until quite recently it was thought that the legionary defences of timber and turf were used for the colonia, possibly being strengthened by the addition of interval towers, set astride the rampart.[51] Nevertheless the legionary defences were still standing when the colonia was founded, with the timber-work of the rampart and the gates still intact.[52] Almost immediately work was started to provide them with a stone cladding, both at the gates, and in front of the rampart, where a wall 4ft (1·2m) thick was built, so lending greater dignity and permanence to the defences. The wall partly overlay a legionary ditch; moreover it had no proper foundations. This combination ultimately caused it to lean outwards away from the rampart. Excavations in East Bight and Chapel Lane have also shown that internal towers of masonry were provided with the wall, possibly to replace earlier timber towers; it is not known if the former coincide with either the positions or spacing of the latter. The four main gates of the fortress remained the principal points of entry to the colonia.

At some time not earlier than the third century, and probably *c.* AD 210–30, the four main gates may have been rebuilt on a more monumental scale. Fortunately, much information has been gathered about their structures from recent excavations. Moreover, fragments of the west gate were exposed in the nineteenth century, while parts of the east and south gates were still visible in the middle of the eighteenth century, even though only the surviving portion of the south gate was reasonably well recorded. The north gate, as represented by the Newport Arch, still partly stands today,[53] although its demolition was nearly caused quite recently by a refrigerated fish lorry.

The principal gate into the colonia seems to have been the east gate, if size and form are any indication (fig. 18). Hence the main road from the south could have made a more oblique and gradual ascent up the hill in place of the steep, direct climb to the south gate. Recent excavations at the east gate have shown that, in the third century, it consisted of two carriageways, each about 15ft (4·6m) wide, with no flanking passages for pedestrians. The carriageways were in turn flanked by external semi-circular towers, 26ft (7·9m) in diameter, each part of a guard-chamber extending 26ft (7·9m) further back. The north tower of this gate has been consolidated and is open to view in front of the Eastgate Hotel. At the same time as the gate was rebuilt, the town wall also seems to have been reconstructed for a stretch on either side, so that the gate appears to have had short wing walls attached to it.

The north gate, of which the Newport Arch formed the rear arch of the single carriageway, is different in plan from the east gate (fig. 18) The carriageway was flanked by foot-passages and the external towers were solid and segmental instead of being hollow and semi-circular. The rear of the gate projected some 18ft (5·5m) behind the rear face of the curtain wall. The south gate, originally thought by Richmond to have a similar plan,[54] now appears to have only a single carriageway with no foot-passages,[55] in spite of the two carriageways attributed by Richmond.[56] This gate was probably of only minor utility and the steep approach up the side of the escarpment would have made use by vehicles almost impossible. The gate was possibly flanked by semi-circular or segmental towers.

Perhaps the most spectacular survival was a major part of the west gate which had been enclosed within the bank of the Norman castle. It was uncovered in 1836, only for the arch to collapse almost immediately (fig. 20). The famous draw‌ Samuel Tuke shows a single arched portal with a tower or upper st‌ ‌e windows are discernible in the front face of the tower as

‌e new town, Lincoln (*Lincoln Archaeological Trust*)

well as one doorway leading in from the parapet walk at the side. Possibly like the south gate, it appears only to have had one carriageway with no foot-passages.[57]

It is probable that, when the rebuilding of the gates took place, the narrow curtain wall was either replaced or added to, to make a more substantial structure, 9ft (2·7m) thick on most of the circuit, while at the same time the rampart was heightened. However, this thickening did not everywhere exist, especially near the east gate and in East Bight. It may have been at this time also that the dimensions of the ditch were greatly increased; its size and line can be appreciated by the depression in the modern ground surface behind the Eastgate Hotel, although its present outline may have been caused by medieval recutting.

An alternative explanation for the sequence of fortifications can nevertheless be made. It is possible that, when the stone defences were reconstructed during the third century, gates with rectangular towers were constructed without projections and flush with the front of the new, wider curtain wall. If so, then the projecting towers represent additions made to the gates at a later period, probably during the first half of the fourth century.[58] Certainly the segmental towers at the north gate are not bonded with the masonry of the curtain wall, but if they are not part of the original scheme, then Lincoln would be the only town in Britain to have added external gate-towers (cf. west gate of the new town, p. 132). Also, if the gate-towers were additions, were they part of a larger series of added external bastions? As yet, there is little evidence in support of such a suggestion. There is a record of a possible external semi-circular tower, 9ft (2·7m) in internal diameter, which might be medieval, at the north-east angle, but nothing more.[59] However, supporting the suggestion of the existence of such towers is the great ditch on the north-east side of the colonia. Single ditches of this size were usually late in date and were often only dug as part of a scheme to reorganise a town's defences. Such a reorganisation often included the provision of towers.[60] Thompson has also suggested that it was during this phase of refortification that the foot-passages of the north gate were blocked by masonry.[61]

Very little is known about the streets or internal buildings of the colonia; what there is has been derived largely from the result of chance discovery and not from proper excavations (fig. 29). It is fairly clear that the north-south and east-west streets intersect in the centre of the town. That being so, we should conclude that one of these streets, which presumably perpetuated the lines of the fortress streets from the four main gates, must have been carried across the site of the demolished principia. In one of the corners formed by the intersection, the forum and basilica of the town should lie, but as yet not enough is known to state in which one. In this respect Lincoln appears to differ from Gloucester (p. 143), where the forum seems to have occupied the same site as the principia. However, the north-south street is known to have been partly lined on both sides with colonnades, which were penetrated by the main east-west street. The positions of some of the columns are marked out on the modern surface of Bailgate. In the north-west angle formed by the junction of the two streets a major building, usually

LINCOLN (Lindvm)

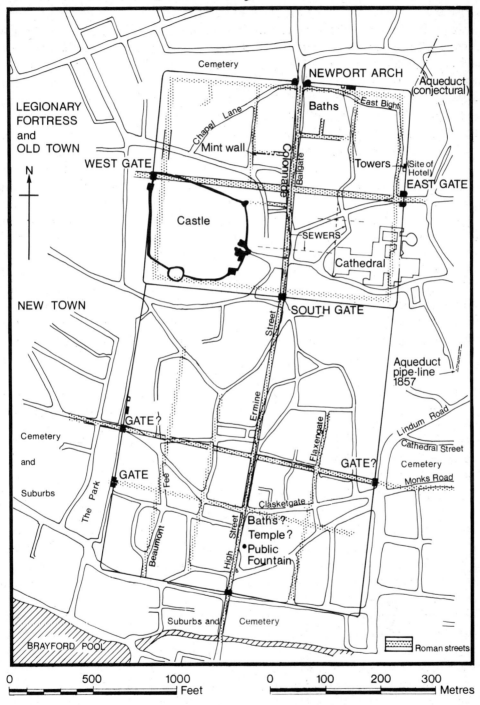

Cemetery

NEWPORT ARCH

Aqueduct (conjectural)

LEGIONARY
FORTRESS
and
OLD TOWN

Baths

East Bight

Chapel Lane

Mint wall

WEST GATE

N

Towers

(Site of Hotel)

EAST GATE

Colonia

Bailgate

Castle

SEWERS

Cathedral

NEW TOWN

Street

SOUTH GATE

Aqueduct
pipe-line
1857

Ermine

Lindum Road

GATE?

Cathedral Street

Cemetery
and

Flaxengate

GATE?

Cemetery

Monks Road

Suburbs

GATE

Fee

The Park

Beaumont

High Street

Claskergate

Baths?
Temple?
•Public
Fountain

Suburbs and

Cemetery

BRAYFORD POOL

Roman streets

0   500   1000
Feet

0   100   200   300
Metres

29   Plan of the old and new towns, Lincoln (*after Christina Colyer*)

assumed not to be the forum, existed behind the colonnade. The thirteen columns appear to represent two different but connected buildings. At the ends were double inosculating columns; the central one is triple and is flanked immediately to its north by another double column. The distance between the two latter is 20ft (6m) as compared with an intercolumniation of 16ft (5m) for the remainder. Three mosaics are known from the area and part of the outside wall of the building still survives as the Mint Wall at its north-west corner. South of the east-west street and in the south-west angle of the road junction the columns make a hexastyle frontage, with double columns of the same type as above, at both ends; they may possibly be the front of a temple (p. 134).

Traces of another public building came to light in Cottesford Place during excavations in 1957–8. Here were found substantial remains of a large building equipped with stokeholes, flues, hypocausts and tessellated pavements, and it may be suggested that it was part of a bath-building. If so, it was conveniently situated just south of a possible *castellum aquae* on the north wall some 300ft east of the north gate. Public open spaces probably contained imperial statuary; the finding in the last century of the life-size foreleg of a horse, cast in bronze (pls. 22a, b), would imply an equestrian statue, although it is not known where it stood.

Little is known of domestic or commercial buildings in the town. Some isolated mosaics, found mainly in the nineteenth century, might suggest the presence of dwelling houses. The mosaics themselves are mainly composed of restrained, conventional patterns, and, in this respect, resemble the mosaics from the colonia at Colchester.[62]

Despite the paucity of the remains of buildings, Lincoln is known to have possessed one of the best developed sewerage systems in any town in Britain. The principal north-south sewer, which ran beneath the street, was found in the Bailgate. At its maximum it was 5ft (1·5m) high and 4ft (1·2m) wide, built in stone and roofed with stone slabs. Smaller sewers and house drains were found to flow into it, and manholes were placed at intervals, so that the interior could be inspected for disrepair and, if necessary, for cleaning. Traces of other parts of the system have been found north-west of the Cathedral, and also outside the town just north of the east gate. High-capacity sewers of this type point to a very large volume of water being used in the town, with a considerable effluent from both public and private users, and this should be borne in mind when considering the difficult problems of the aqueduct.

The aqueduct at Lincoln has always had many puzzling features. It was discovered in part as early as 1700 but not properly excavated until 1950–2 by F. H. Thompson.[63] Despite Mr Thompson's excavations and his ingenious solution to the problem of raising water to the town through a height of about 70ft (21m), many points are still not satisfactorily explained. The aqueduct pipe-line approaches the town from a north-easterly direction, appearing to come from a stream called Roaring Meg, a little over 2000yds (1·8km) away. According to Thompson's projected line it should strike the east wall of the town, about 80yds (73m) north of the east gate, quite close to where observation in 1971 of a

21 Tombstone of Volusia Faustina, wife of Aurelius Senecio, decurion of Lincoln (*British Museum*)

commercial excavation behind the Eastgate Hotel recorded a very solid and massive masonry foundation just behind the wall and embedded in the rampart. This would be more than adequate as the base for a large cistern. What then of the vaulted reservoir, or castellum, which exists on the north wall, about 100yds (91m) east of the north gate? Did the pipeline branch in several directions before reaching the town, as might be suggested by a section found much further south near Lindum Road in 1857, or is there perhaps another source to be found which was led to the north reservoir?[64]

The pipeline was made up of earthenware pipes, each 3ft (914mm) long with a maximum internal diameter of $5\frac{1}{2}$in (140mm) and a wall thickness of 1in

22   Bronze foreleg of horse from a life-size equestrian statue from Lincoln (*Society of Antiquaries of London*)

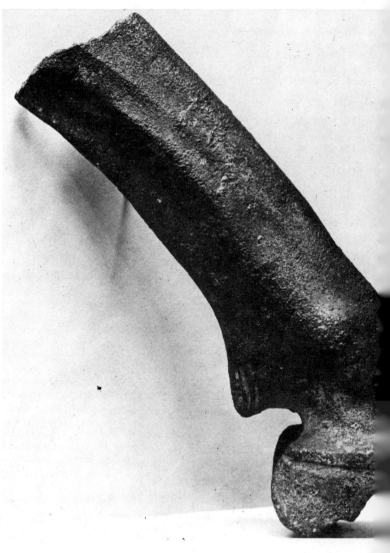

(25mm). At one end of each pipe the diameter was reduced to $3\frac{1}{2}$in (88mm) for a distance of 4in (101mm), so that this narrow end would fit into the wide end of the next pipe. The whole pipeline was encased in waterproof pink concrete to form a pressure jacket approximately 15in (381mm) square in cross section. For most of its recorded distance it ran below ground, but at a point about 160ft (48m) from the modern city boundary it had probably emerged to run along the top of an embankment, which no longer survived at the time of the excavations. The embankment seems to have given way to a series of individual masonry piers at a point which roughly coincides with the same boundary. There were seven piers, which varied slightly in individual dimensions, but which measured approximately 5ft (1·5m) by 6ft (1·8m) with about 9ft (2·7m) between each. An eighth pier, which appeared to terminate the series at the north end was considerably larger, 16ft (4·9mm) long by between 9ft (2·7m) and 10ft (3m) wide. It is to be supposed that these piers, with arches between them, supported the pipe and its concrete jacket across an area of lower ground, so reducing the gradient.

Thompson argued that the Roaring Meg stream was the source of the aqueduct. From the stream the water could have been raised by endless bucket-chain to a tower at least 70ft (21m) high, from which it could then flow by gravity into the town, or alternatively it could have been pumped along the pipe to the same ultimate height by means of a force pump of a kind known to Roman hydraulic engineers. Thompson discounted a tower, probably correctly, on the grounds that the larger terminal pier was too slight a structure to act as a base even for a timber superstructure, and he concluded that a pump was used. There are however serious objections to this conclusion, over and above those already considered by him. He suggested that a double-barrelled reciprocating pump of the type found at Silchester with a bore of 3in (76mm), a maximum stroke of 10in (254mm), and 9in (229mm) between barrel centres would be suitable,[65] and that it would be placed on the large terminal pier acting as a platform. Under these conditions he considered that $\frac{1}{2}$ gallon (2·3l) of water could be displaced for each double stroke or, allowing for a 50 per cent leakage rate and 20 strokes a minute, 5 gallons (23l) of water a minute could be pumped to the colonia. This would be hardly sufficient to satisfy the drinking water needs of the population, let alone such buildings as the public baths, and if this was the only source of running water, why the large sewers? Thompson therefore suggested that a larger and more efficient pump might have been employed, but in neither case does he consider the work load of the wretched men manning the pump handles! Roman engineers knew nothing about crank-shafts, so that a rotary system such as a treadmill could not have been employed to work the pump, which must, instead, have depended on a simple system of reciprocating levers pivoting on a central fulcrum. With a pump of the Silchester dimensions a ratio of 2:1 is about the maximum that could have been employed on the system of levers (see fig. 30), so as not to give an inconveniently big swing at the handle end. It should be remembered that the pressure at the pump would be about 30lb per

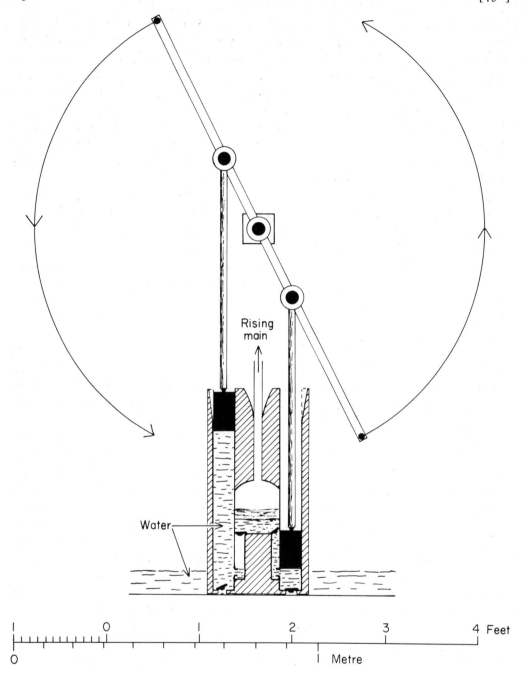

Rising
main

Water

| | 0 | | 2 | 3 | 4 Feet |

0 | Metre

30   A suggested working arrangement for a force-pump of the type found at Silchester

square inch (2·1kgf/cm^2) and, with the equipment arranged as described above,
the work done in forcing 5 gallons (23l) of water up to the town would equal
3500ft lb (480kgf-m) per minute which takes no account of work wasted by

leakage of water, or in overcoming friction. The latter, owing to the low velocity of the water acting against the internal surface of the pipe, would have been small and would have added only the equivalent of one or two feet to the height over which the water had to be pumped. But if the output had been doubled, then this factor would have increased four times; treble the output and the factor would have increased nine times.[66] With two men working the handles each would have been required at a minimum to do the equivalent of lifting a $\frac{3}{4}$cwt (38kg) weight one foot (305mm) off the ground at the rate of 20 times per minute. We cannot help but feel that a more efficient method would have been to employ a wagon, a pair of horses and a number of barrels! Admittedly the work load on pumping could have been reduced by introducing intermediate pumping stations, but this must also have increased the wastage, and no evidence has been found for such stations. Pumping would also have been made easier by reducing the length of the stroke and increasing the diameter of the bore, and by increasing the distance between cylinders, for by so doing, a more efficient system of levers could have been employed; but there is no evidence of pumps of these dimensions in the Roman world and most of those known have about the same ratio between bore and length. Lastly, pumps of this type have to be immersed in the water they were designed to lift. A platform raised above the water level as Thompson postulated would defeat the whole scheme. The raising of the pipeline on piers above the ground would not have increased the efficiency to any great extent and the system would probably have worked as well with the pipes set on or just below the surface for the whole distance.

If pumps were not used, what was the alternative? It might be suggested that the piers formed part of a conventional bridged aqueduct which was used to carry the pipeline over an area of low-lying ground, with the water flowing by gravity from a source higher than the colonia. But the piers were not substantial enough to carry a massive weight. Therefore we might visualise perhaps a low masonry substructure of a kind which was used on the Hürth–Hermülheim section of the Cologne aqueduct.[67] There the spaces under the arches were filled with loam, reminiscent of the rubble filling found between piers on the uphill end at Lincoln (fig. 31). Certainly the sizes of the piers and the distances between them are very similar. The nearest source of suitable height would be east of Market Rasen, perhaps on the spring line near North Willingham, where the Lincolnshire Wolds rise to a height of over 500ft (150m). The northward swing of the aqueduct channel near the Roaring Meg stream might then be explained if a circuitous route was followed to take advantage of the slightly higher ground of the ridge which divides the Ancholme valley from that of the river Witham. The overall distance by this route would have been in the region of 20 miles (32km), quite within the capacity of Roman engineers.[68] The only doubt must be whether the pipeline, as constructed, could have withstood the pressure of a head of water which may have exceeded 100ft (30m) (about 43lb per square inch or 3kgf/cm^2). But certainly there is considerable room for fresh investigations.

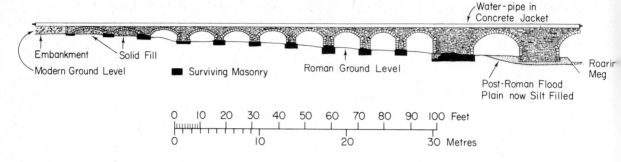

31   Restoration of the Lincoln aqueduct bridge on the south approach to Roaring Meg

It would seem that canabae grew on the hillside south of the legionary fortress and that an extra-mural settlement developed from these origins and continued to grow after the colonia had been founded. Ultimately it became enclosed as part of the town, being surrounded first by a bank and later by a wall which joined the earlier circuit at its south-west and south-east corners, and which ran south almost as far as the river Witham. In this way the size of the fortified area was more than doubled from the original 43 acres (17·4ha) to about 100 acres (40ha).

Although stretches of the curtain wall of the new town have been exposed from time to time in building work, it was not until 1948 that excavations could be carried out on the bank behind the wall, at Beaumont Fee, on the west side of the circuit. Since 1968, however, a long stretch of wall, in places still standing to a height of 14ft (4·3m), has been cleared at The Park just north of the previous section.[69] Further sections on the east and south sides were cut in 1973.

The new town was first enclosed by a bank, 30ft (9m) wide, with no sign of revetment, except for a thick wedge of clay tipped at the back. However, on the east side of the circuit, evidence was found in 1973 for a substantial fence on the crest of the bank, some 10ft (3m) behind the surviving front face. This is the first time in Britain that an urban earth rampart has survived to a sufficient height to yield information of what existed on top. A construction date in the late second century can be envisaged. Shortly afterwards a masonry wall, 5ft (1·5m) thick, was inserted into the front of the bank. It is probable that no gate existed at The Park in either of these phases. However, after the wall had been built, a hole was knocked through it for the insertion of a gate, 16ft (4·9m) wide. Inturns, 9ft (2·7m) wide, were added either side of the entrance to retain the rampart, which had been heightened when the wall was built. These inturns projected inwards for 15ft (4·6m) from the back face of the wall. A thresh-hold of stone slabs was added in the gate, and had been much worn. Sometime during the middle of the fourth century, gate-towers were constructed forward of either side of the entrance on solid foundations, measuring approximately 20ft (6m) across by 25ft (7·6m) from front to rear; they projected 10ft (3m) from the front face of the wall (fig. 21). In the south tower was a guard-chamber 9ft (2·7m) wide,

while that in the north tower was 10ft (3m). Both would have been approximately
15ft (4·6m) long.[70] The guard-chambers were probably set at first floor level,
as there did not appear to be direct access to them from within the gate. Both
towers also contained much reused masonry from the entablature of elaborate
and substantial buildings (pl. 20). Towards the end of the fourth century the
curtain wall was strengthened by the addition, at its back, of a massive buttress-
like work which extended for about 30ft (9m) south of the gate. However, north
of the gate and on the southern part of the circuit it had been completely rebuilt
to a width of 10ft (3·5m). The buttress to the south was 16ft 9in (5m) wide at the
base and it was tapered towards the top in a series of insets, which ultimately
reduced it to a width of 7ft (2·1m) or less. At the same time the rampart was
widened to about 80ft (24·4m), but this may represent no more than the soil
excavated for the foundations of the new wall, tipped at the rear of the existing
rampart. Coins of Theodosius and Arcadius were found associated with the upper
surfaces of the street in the gate.

The contrast represented by the defences of the so-called upper and lower
towns is worth some comment. If the origins of the lower town lie in the legionary
canabae then it is likely to have contained a much higher proportion of Britons,
and perhaps peregrini from other provinces, in its population. If the sequence
of the defences is correct, there is a strong similarity between the lower town and
the native civitas capitals. We cannot doubt, however, that overall control was
exercised by the magistrates and ordo of the colonia, although it is probable that
the lower town was enfranchised at a later date. There would seem to be a basis
for comparison here with some of the towns of other provinces where veteran
settlements were planted in their midst.[71] Control of the whole colonia was
normally in the hands of the veterans, although some existing institutions seem
to have survived in certain cases, and customs varied from place to place, with
little hint of uniformity. But the effect in some places might be likened to a town
within a town, the new organisation making little practical difference to most of
the peregrine inhabitants. At Lincoln we might see the existing peregrine 'town'
in the successor to the legionary canabae, for there is no reason to believe that
the settlement went into liquidation when the army moved out of the fortress.
Indeed such evidence as there is points to a flourishing Flavian community
which may, or may not, have been given the legal rank of a vicus. In time, this
settlement of predominantly peregrine inhabitants, although subject to the
colonia, will have become fully enfranchised, probably under Caracalla, when
it reached parity with, and was able to play a full part in the administration of,
the mother foundation on the hill. In time, too, this advance may have been
sufficient to break down, in turn, the exclusive and rigid social barriers first
erected by the colonists, and no doubt bequeathed to their descendants. Therein
lay the strength of Lincoln, and, in its absence, the weakness of Gloucester. In
these circumstances it might be better to abandon the name 'lower town' in
favour of 'new town', because, although both were part of the same colonia,
they had their origins in very different societies.

No more is known about the buildings in the new town than about those of the old town. Part of a colonnade of a building of some magnitude was found on the east side of Flaxengate in 1946–7. Its walls were decorated with marble veneers imported from the Mediterranean. Another building with flue arches is known on the corner of High Street and Clasketgate and may have been a bath-house. Further south and on the same side of the High Street, a large octagonal stone foundation, measuring 20ft (6m) across, probably formed the base of a public drinking fountain, no doubt fed by the town's aqueduct. Another find of considerable importance was made in 1845 not far from the fountain base, when an inscribed stone, reading VIC HRAPO MERCVRE(N)SIVM,[72] was discovered, associated with column bases and large worked stones. This stone and probably another found in Lindum Road outside the walls, and reading (A)POLLINENSIVM[73] might refer to constituent vici, or wards of the new town (p. 38).

There is some evidence that, within the new town, the steep hillside at its north end was terraced by the construction of massive walls at right angles to the slope. A wall, 15ft (4·6m) thick, is known to exist opposite St Michael's Church-yard, with another, 4ft (1·2m) thick, nine feet (2·7m) further north, and with made ground behind them. Richmond considered that the line marked by this terrace could be followed through, from above Beaumont Fee in the west, to the lower garden of the old Bishop's Palace in the east,[74] but it is possible that the walls could be part of a theatre set into the hillside, with the cavea against the slope.

Various extra-mural buildings are known, especially outside the new town, and Lincoln also seems to have had a thriving pottery industry, with kilns in Cathedral Street, on the racecourse and slightly further away at Swanpool, Boultham, North Hykeham and South Carlton. Stone was probably quarried at Greetwell to the east and northwards along the line of Ermine Street. Apart from this, there is no other specific evidence of industries in the immediate neighbourhood of Lincoln, although smelting of local iron ores was certainly carried out in Lincolnshire,[75] and the coppersmith, Celatus, must have had his workshop nearby, if not in Lincoln itself.[76]

Although the sites of temples in the town cannot be suggested with any degree of certainty, there is nevertheless direct evidence for the practice of the imperial cult. It is contained in the inscription from Bordeaux, which mentions one of the seviri Augustales, M. Aurelius Lunaris[77] who was probably a rich merchant (pl. 31). Lewis makes the suggestion that the temple of the imperial cult was represented by the hexastyle facade in the south-west corner of the intersection of the two main roads in the town centre.[78] Temples to Apollo and Mercury are inferred from the inscriptions referred to above and Lewis has also suggested that the temple to Mercury may be the building in the lower town where that inscription was found.[79]

Dedications to Mars and the Fates are also known on altars. The survival of Celtic religion in what was probably the territorium is shown by an inscription[80] from Nettleham, just north of the town. It is a joint dedication to the numina

Augustorum and Mars Rigonemetos, by Q. Neratius Proxsimus, presumably a citizen of the colonia. There is no evidence for Christianity from Lincoln itself, but symbols which occur on lead tanks from nearby Walesby and Bishop Norton, and on a lead casket from Caistor would imply its practice. Moreover, if Mann is correct in his emendation of the list of bishops attending the Council of Arles,[81] then Lincoln was the seat of a bishopric in the fourth century.

Apart from Lunaris and Proxsimus, other inhabitants of the town are known from tombstones. A decurion, Aurelius Senecio, erected a stone to his young wife Volusia Faustina (pl. 21). A veteran from Legio VI Victrix, G. Julius Calenus, who died there, and another from Legio XIV seem to have been citizens of the colonia, as was a nameless, retired decurion of the cavalry regiment, Ala II Asturum. The cosmopolitan nature of the population is illustrated best by the tombstones, one of a Greek, Flavius Helius, the other of a non-citizen called Sacer who came with his wife and son from the civitas Senonum in central Gaul. Both were probably merchants who had settled in Lincoln. Of interest also is the tombstone of Claudia Crysis, who died at the quite exceptional age of 90.[82] Lincoln is also noted for elaborate tombs. One, from the cemetery near Monks Road and probably outside the east gate of the new town, produced a remarkable stone relief of a figure with turreted crown and cornucopia. North of the old town is recorded a narrow trench bordered by rows of *loculi*, or compartments, each of which contained a stone coffin, and which Richmond likened to the guild tomb-chambers of Rome.[83] Into such a context would fit the dedication of an altar to the Fates made by Antistius Frontinus, who is described as a guild treasurer, probably of a burial club.[84]

As at all the British coloniae it is difficult to suggest the area occupied by the territorium. We might suggest that the river Trent lay within its western boundary, a deduction perhaps confirmed by the milestone of Victorinus found at the intersection of the two main roads of the old town.[85] This gives the distance to *Segelocum* (Littleborough) as 14 miles (22·5km). Not much is known about the Roman site at Littleborough, but by the third century it would undoubtedly have been the next place of any size after Lincoln on the most important route to York. It could well have been a vicus in the territorium. Another milestone, found in Sibthorp Street, probably marked the first mile (1·6km) on the road to Leicester and was set up by the Respublica Lindensis.[86] The Bailgate milestone was made from stone derived from near Ancaster, which has led Whitwell to suggest that this vicus may also have been in the territorium.[87] Another early fourth-century milestone, possibly supports this implication on the basis of figures often quoted for it. In the *Roman Inscriptions of Britain*, it is stated to have been found $\frac{1}{4}$ mile (400m) north of Ancaster, but 20 miles (32·1km) south of Lincoln and showing ostensibly that the distance had been most likely measured from Lincoln.[88] But the distance from Lincoln to Ancaster along Ermine Street is only just 18 miles (30km) so that the stone has little value in the context in which it was found. In addition no mention of the municipal authority or the actual distance is recorded on it. But the evidence of milestones in this respect is not entirely reliable and should always be supported by other evidence, although Mommsen was able to apply the principle to parts of Italy and Africa.

The chief roads which ran through Lincoln were, from the south, Ermine Street and its alternative route, King Street, which diverged from it at Water Newton and was reunited just south of Lincoln and then continued northwards to the Humber at Winteringham, the Fosse Way which ran south-west to Leicester from a junction with Ermine Street south of the town and Till Bridge Lane which left Ermine Street about 6 miles (9·7km) north of the town to run to Littleborough and then on to York. A road also ran north-eastwards to the coast. There is evidence of an embankment leading probably to a bridge, where Ermine Street crossed the river Witham. Lincoln was also fortunate in its communications in having the Car Dyke, which united the river systems of the Wash with the river Witham, and the Fossdyke which ran on from the Witham to the Trent. This artificial system of inland waterways was probably constructed during the early part of the second century, perhaps under Hadrian, partly to help drain the Fens and partly to serve for the transport of goods.[89] It would appear also that this canal system remained in use until the end of the fourth century, contrary to what has previously been thought. It was used to carry heavy and bulky goods, such as pottery, building materials and agricultural produce. That Lincoln was a recipient of some of these goods need not be doubted, while convenient links could have been formed, via the Humber and Wash, with continental ports.[90] It is surprising, therefore, that Lincoln has produced a much lower proportion of East Gaulish samian potters' stamps than either York or the Fens.[91] This may have been caused, as Hartley suggests, by the fact that goods destined for Lincoln would have had to be transferred to barges, either in the Humber or the Wash, whereas they could have reached York and the Fens direct. But this difficulty was obviously overcome when dealing with other imported goods, whether wine, foreign stone or goods of which no trace survives, and it may be that the samian markets at Lincoln were already monopolised by merchants from Central Gaul, and their more discerning patrons showed little desire for the poorer quality East Gaulish vessels. This system of waterways was probably also responsible for the fact that stamped mortaria, manufactured at Lincoln, are found as far north as Newstead and the Antonine Wall. To cope with this waterborne trade, wharves or quays would be required on the banks of the river Witham, and a 20-foot (6m) long stretch of large, dressed blocks of stone, sitting on what appeared to be an old river bed, has been observed near the south-east corner of the new town in St Rumbold Street. Alternatively, it might have been part of the structure of a mill-stream, used for grinding corn or even sawing wood or stone. Fragments from the stone hubs of two wooden water wheels have been found in the river south of the new town,[92] and they may have formed part of a fairly extensive system. But such activities would have to be separated from the main navigable channel of the river.

We cannot say what happened to Lincoln, once the provincial administration had broken down in the early fifth century. There are remarkably few of the zoomorphic buckles and fittings, attributed by S. C. Hawkes and G. C. Dunning to the late Roman army in Lincolnshire and only one has been recorded from Lincoln itself. In addition, most of the earliest Anglo-Saxon settlement comes from the south of the county, although Caistor has two early cemeteries.[93] We might wonder if the colonial territorium became one of the protected reserves which seem to have occurred in parts of Britain during the earliest part of the Anglo-Saxon period, when an equilibrium was reached between the Romano-British inhabitants of the area and the incoming settlers.[94] If so, then a study of the distribution of these early Saxon settlements might indicate better than anything else, the boundaries of the territorium. It is interesting though that an Anglian *praefectus Lindocolinae civitatis* was present in the later seventh century, suggesting, if not continuity, at least a return to ordered life.[95]

GLOUCESTER (*Colonia Nervia Glevensium*)

A comparison once made between the coloniae at Gloucester and Lincoln suggested that they were so similar in foundation and early plan that they might both have been built by the same public works contractor. But recent excavations in both places have shown that this comparison was misconceived, for the planning at Gloucester appears to be very different from that of Lincoln.

The official name and probable date of foundation of the colonia at Gloucester can, however, be fixed with greater accuracy than that of Lincoln. A tombstone[96] found in Rome of a *frumentarius* of Legio VI (pl. 23), which describes him as being *Ner(via) Glevi*, gives the official name as *colonia Nervia* (or *Nerviana*, as Richmond pointed out) *Glevensium*.[97] Founded presumably therefore in the principate of Nerva, the date must fall between AD 96–8. The reason for the choice of site would seem to be the same as for that of Lincoln. Recent excavations by H. R. Hurst and others have shown that certainly from *c*. AD 67 a legionary fortress existed on the site of the colonia at Gloucester. Earlier theories relating to the legionary fortress have suggested a date *c*. AD 49 for the initial foundation, which is usually placed at Kingsholm, just north of the later site. Excavations in 1972 have tended to confirm the conclusion that the first fortress lay in that area. Be that as it may, the second fortress at Gloucester, now known to have covered an area slightly over 43 acres (17·4ha), was occupied from *c*. AD 67 first perhaps by Legio XX, later probably by Legio II Augusta.[98] The land chosen for the new colonia was therefore, as at Lincoln, already imperial property. It would seem that expediency played as much part in the choice of sites for both coloniae as the fact that they were not far from potentially hostile tribes.

It has always been assumed that Legio II Augusta was transferred to Caerleon under the governorship of Julius Frontinus in AD 74–5. Hurst's excavations on a number of sites[99] have shown, however, that continuity probably existed between the legionary occupation and the first colinia. The latest coin of the legionary period to be found so far is dated AD 77–8, and Hurst's interpretation would imply

23   Tombstone from Rome of M. Vlpius Quintus (*Soprintendenza alle Antichita di Roma*)

that the first buildings of the colonia were erected immediately after the demolition of legionary structures. The simplest explanation envisages the fortress being left intact, on a care and maintenance arrangement, after the bulk of the legion had moved, and it should be remembered that this was the normal situation for any legionary fortress during periods of extended military activity. The evacuation of Gloucester, linked as it is with the date of the foundation of the fortress at Caerleon, depends chiefly on what Tacitus tells us of the activities of Julius Frontinus in south Wales.[100] But Legio II Augusta could have campaigned in Silurian territory quite as effectively from a base at Gloucester as from one at Caerleon and to have made a legion undertake a strenuous campaign at the same time as it had to build a new fortress, seems a strange combination. Far better to have finished the campaign first and then to have built the fortress, as Agricola was later to do at Inchtuthil. Moreover, unlike Chester, which was built in territory pacified nearly two decades before, Caerleon was built in the territory of an extremely hostile tribe who were also a wiley and resourceful enemy, and who had already administered serious rebuffs to Roman arms. Far safer then to have left the legionary base at Gloucester until a proper appreciation could have been made of the Silurian conquest. If we can therefore shift the foundation date of the legionary fortress at Caerleon beyond Frontinus' governorship we can more easily accommodate Hurst's evidence from Gloucester. His *terminus post quem* of AD 87 for the construction of a colonia building is provided by two coins. We might therefore envisage a stage during the construction of Caerleon when Gloucester was held too, and only on completion of the former would the latter be evacuated.[101] This suggestion is supported by recent results from Caerleon where it was found that some barrack blocks in the retentura had not been built in the Flavian period.[102]

Evidence (figs. 32–3) from four sites has shown that, as legionary barrack blocks were demolished, their places were taken by buildings which closely resembled them in plan, the only distinguishable differences being that, in some examples, the buildings were extended to include the verandah, so that they were then the width of the centurions' quarters, and that, in all, a different form of construction was used. Instead of being timber-framed throughout, as in the legionary period, they were now probably half-timbered structures based on low masonry walls. Some of these blocks were, however, subdivided by party-walls to create what seem to have been lines of terrace houses. Here we can see coordinated planning extended to the domestic buildings of the colonia, each veteran being given his

24   Fragmentary tombstone from Bath of a Gloucester decurion (R. G. Collingwood and R. P. Wright, *The Roman Inscriptions of Britain*, Vol. I; the Clarendon Press, Oxford)

GLOUCESTER (Glevvm) LEGIONARY FORTRESS c. A.D. 70

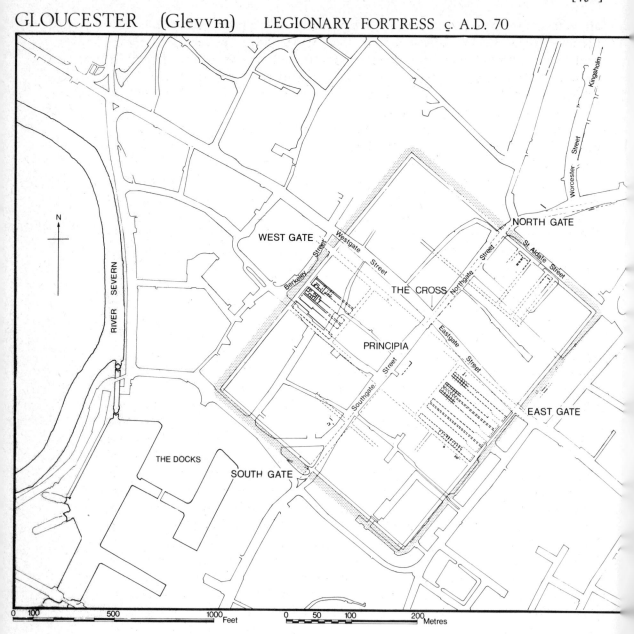

32　Plan of the legionary fortress, Gloucester, *c.* AD 70 (*after H. Hurst*)

plot of land with its house, and it will be interesting to see, when opportunity arises, how much of the new town was taken up by this type of development,[103] and whether, when suitable excavations take place, the first colonia at Lincoln was similarly planned. However, despite the regularity of outline, some, if not

all, veterans seem to have been allowed a degree of latitude in the planning of
the internal rooms, for here there is greater variety. There is a certain similarity
with some types of estate development today, where the basic house plans differ
only in detail from one another. At this stage, many of the streets and alleys
which had divided the blocks of the fortress were perpetuated, although some on
the south-east side were built over.

Unlike Lincoln, the forum and basilica at Gloucester appear to have been built
on the site of the legionary principia. The basilica is known to lie across the south-
west side of the forum and, if it has a normal plan, the whole complex, which
probably measures 320ft (97·5m) by 225ft (68·6m), was larger than the principia,
and extended over the legionary streets to the north-west and south-east. The
forum is thus in the unusual position of interrupting the street grid to cut across
the line of the principal north-east to south-west street, which followed the lines
of the legionary viae praetoria and decumana (fig. 33). The first forum, presumably of Trajanic date, had a gravelled court flanked by ranges suggesting part-
timber construction, with wooden columns. Later, possibly when the wood
decayed, it was replaced by masonry and the piazza was provided with a floor of
sandstone flags. On the south-east side, where excavations have taken place (pl.
25), there seems to have been no more than a double portico. A gutter ran round
the piazza close to the stylobate. Near the south corner of the piazza a base for a
monumental statue had stood. This had been rebuilt at a later date when the
surrounding floor had been resurfaced with broken tile and crushed limestone.
On top of this new surface, fragments of cast bronze were found (pl. 26), suggesting that an equestrian statue had once stood on the base.[104]

So far no conclusive evidence has been found to show that the colonia was
walled from its foundation. There are, however, indications that, as at Lincoln,
a narrow-gauge wall was inserted into the front of the legionary rampart, which
has now been proved everywhere to coincide with the line of the later and more
substantial wall. The later wall has unfortunately masked evidence for an earlier
one, but at one point near Eastgate Street, a masonry and half-timbered building
had been inserted into the back of the legionary rampart, which had been partly
levelled to receive it. The building was occupied during the second century, so
must belong to the colonia. It would be surprising therefore, as Hurst points out,
if the surviving fragment of legionary rampart was left in isolation against the
outer wall of the building, unless some form of revetment still kept it in place
at the front. On analogy with Lincoln, the revetment may have been a narrow-
gauge wall. The hypothetical existence of a wall at this period would also help
to explain problems relating to the later construction. Had an early wall existed
here, it would have to have been free-standing, as the presence of the building
behind it precludes the existence of a rampart, so it might more closely resemble
the wall at Colchester, rather than that at Lincoln.

The first houses of the veterans early began to take on a more individual
appearance (figs. 33–4). Partial demolition and rebuilding of separate houses in
the terraces, on both the Telephone Exchange (Berkeley Street) and New Market

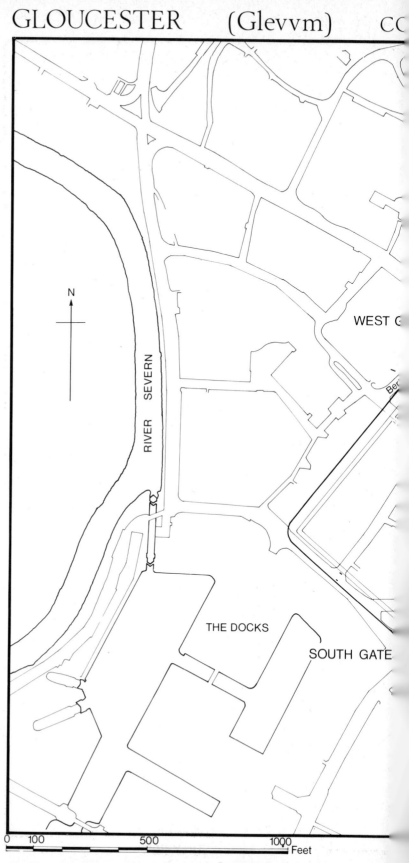

33   Plan of the colonia, Gloucester, *c*. AD 100 (*after H. Hurst*)

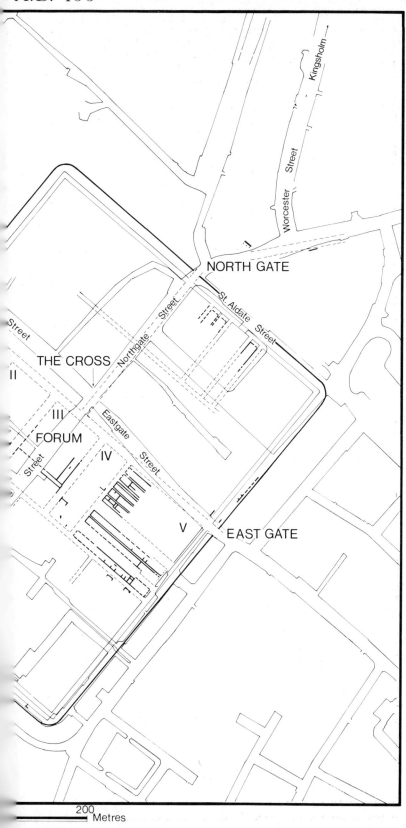

NORTH GATE

Kingsholm

Worcester Street

St. Aldate Street

THE CROSS

Northgate Street

Street

II

III

FORUM

Eastgate Street

IV

Street

V

EAST GATE

200 Metres

25 Forum courtyard at Gloucester in the mid second century, with the statue base in the centre of the photograph (*Gloucester City Museum*)

26 Fragments of bronze from an equestrian statue, which stood in the forum at Gloucester (*Gloucester City Museum*)

Hall sites seems to have occurred within a few years of the initial construction, giving rise to modifications which embraced more substantial and better quality foundations and floors. These alterations were followed by more radical changes which continued seemingly down into the Antonine period. Some of the terrace houses now disappeared, their places being taken by small detached houses, which were by no means always as spacious as the originals. There does, however, still seem to be some continuity of plots, although not all appear to have been built on. This undoubtedly represents changing social conditions, to be explained in a number of ways. By AD 125, when the first changes were taking place, few of the original veterans could still have been alive, so that if there was continuity

GLOUCESTER   (Glevvm)   COLONIA ç. A.D. 150

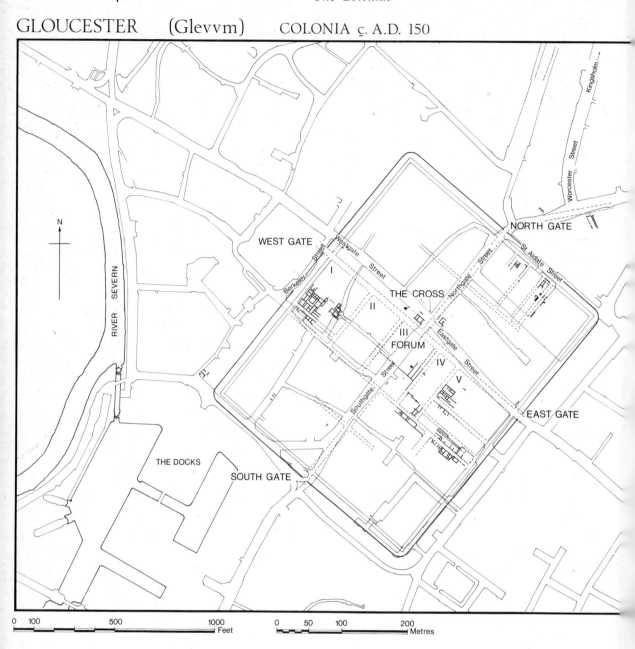

34   Plan of Gloucester, *c.* AD 150 *(after H. Hurst)*

of ownership, these new houses might have been occupied by their families, but possibly in rather reduced circumstances. Perhaps the life of a veteran in his declining years, with his savings partly or completely gone, and having to rely on his wits, was not the sinecure modern writers often make it out to be.

In some cases, however, we might envisage a veteran who had prospered sufficiently to move to a villa in the territorium, in which case he might have set up commercial premises on his town site and put a slave or freedman in charge. Certainly there is evidence of small-scale industrial processes, with both iron-working and pottery manufacture being carried on in different premises. The essential clue to this period seems, however, to be partly provided by the next, for on the Telephone Exchange site, by the middle of the second century a number of plots had been amalgamated and a single house built upon them. Moreover, at least part of what must have been a public right-of-way had been extinguished, though the Lex Ursonensis[105] emphasises that all such roads belong to the colonia and were to remain so. We need not doubt therefore that the owner of the house was not only a man of substance who had succeeded where others appear to have failed, but also that he must have had considerable influence in the public affairs of the town. The compact style and plan (fig. 36) of the new house is reminiscent of the peristyled courtyard houses of Italy, of which similar examples are known at Colchester, and surprisingly also at Caerwent (p. 388). A mosaic had been laid in what may have been the principal room, and at least one other room had another. There was provision in the courtyard for a cistern which may have fed an ornamental fountain. Another, larger cistern was found outside the east corner of the building. The house was demolished either towards the end of the second century or during the third, and thereafter the site seems to have remained vacant, although a building nearby, slightly further from the defences, continued in use until the late Roman period (fig. 35). The same sequence was observed on the New Market Hall site in Insula v south-east of the forum. Here the terrace houses appeared in the same first building phase, but underwent less change later; they apparently remained in existence until the end, two dispersed coin hoards of Theodosian date being found in the ruins. At some stage mosaics had been inserted in many houses, and one had a leopard portrayed in the centre.[106] A somewhat similar type of building was also found on the Bon Marché site, near the north wall in St Aldates Street, where the intervallum street met one from the south. This house possessed a colonnade on its north side, and a mosaic had been inserted in one room, c. AD 200.[107]

The end of the second century saw modifications to the fortifications. If the town had already been ringed by a narrow-gauge wall, it would seem that it had perhaps become unstable, for the building, which had been let into the back of the legionary rampart near the site of the east gate, was demolished and the foundations were sealed by a new rampart. Rectangular towers of masonry, measuring $16\frac{1}{2}$ft (5m) by 10ft (3m) externally, were built at the same time, one being identified near the gate, and these would have been attached to the inner face of the original narrow wall, if this indeed existed. Another similar tower was excavated in 1932 at the south corner of the town.[108] It is, of course, possible but probably unlikely, that this rampart and its towers represent the first attempt at erecting colonial defences at Gloucester, in which case the town would have

GLOUCESTER   (Glevvm)   COLONIA ç. A.D. 250

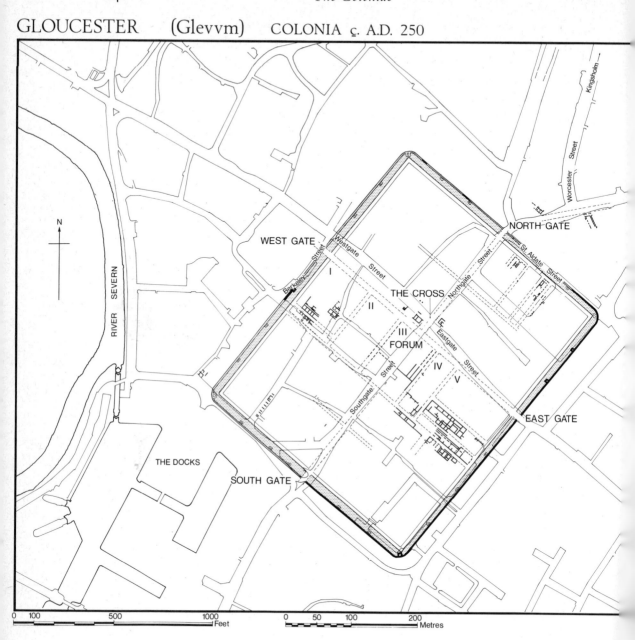

35   Plan of Gloucester, *c.* AD 250 (*after H. Hurst*)

been a close analogy to nearby Cirencester, where masonry towers and gates coexisted with an earth rampart (p. 302). Further modifications took place apparently during the third century, when a masonry wall, $6\frac{1}{2}$ft (2m) thick, with a chamfered plinth, was constructed in front of the rampart, and joined on to the earlier towers. Some small distance north-east of the gate, the inside face was found to curve towards the front (pl. 27), as though the new wall was here being bonded with an existing narrower wall, whose front face nevertheless coincided with that of the new wall. Unfortunately the narrow wall, a stretch of which can thus be shown to have been left intact near the gate, did not survive in situ, for that section itself had also been rebuilt, probably during the fourth century, in order to bring it to the greater standard width of the remainder, so obscuring any earlier structure. The lower courses of the latest work had been built of large oolite blocks, suggesting the reuse of masonry from a substantial building which had been demolished. It would seem most likely that Mrs O'Neil came across a section of this fourth-century rebuild when she exposed the inner face of the south-west wall in the Technical College grounds in 1961.[109] Fragments of an external tower, found on the Eastgate Street side, were constructed from similar stones set on timber piles, so that it may be contemporary with the rebuilt wall. Other external towers are known elsewhere on the circuit.

Nothing is known of the gates of the Roman town, except that they lie approximately in the same positions as the medieval north, south, east and west gates. The greatest discrepancy probably occurs at the west gate, where the line of the Roman street, as deduced from the positions of known remains of building, demands that the Roman gate should be about 50ft (15·3m) south-west of the medieval gate.

Persistent water-logging also prevented an attempt to locate the Roman ditches near Eastgate Street, if indeed they had survived the deep medieval recutting which had taken place.

Apart from the forum, the sites of other possible public buildings are known from Westgate Street where a colonnade with Corinthian capitals was found just north of the modern street.[110] Its position led Richmond to suggest that it represented a street frontage,[111] but now that the street is known to be further south, we must conclude that it forms an internal feature of a large building. Fragments of another massive building are known near the Cross in the centre of the modern town.[112] Originally interpreted as the forum it would now appear to belong to the next insula north-east. As recently as 1971 a column, 3ft 6in (1·7m) in diameter and still standing to a height of 6ft 6in (2m), was discovered during commercial excavations below the basement of 4, Westgate Street. It could be part of the same, or a neighbouring, building. A bath-house is suggested by an apsidal hypocaust dated to c. AD 120, on the site of the Westminster Bank in Westgate Street.[113] In its massive colonnades, Gloucester closely resembles the upper town at Lincoln and both testify to the aspirations of the government and the inhabitants to create towns worthy of the Roman model. There is also a close correspondence between their mosaics, and in this respect all three military coloniae exhibit singularly constant tastes. Of other public works, an aqueduct is implied from iron junctions for wooden water-pipes which have been found in the town, and some form of continuous supply would appear to have been needed for the mid second-century house on the Telephone Exchange site in Insula I (p. 147). Another possible cistern, measuring 6ft (1·8m) by $3\frac{1}{2}$ft (1·1m) was found on the premises of the National Provincial Bank in Eastgate Street. Its water supply had been carried in lead pipes.[114] Two other tanks are known, which had been built in to the back of the town bank just south of St Aldate's Street.[115] Unlike at Lincoln there would have been little difficulty in finding a convenient nearby source on the Cotswold escarpment and in conducting the water to the town.

In spite of the nearness of the Forest of Dean and its mineral deposits, Gloucester has produced little evidence of industry within the town. A pottery kiln and iron working furnace have already been referred to (p. 147). Three other first-century kilns are known outside the east gate,[116] but may belong to the legionary period. There is also some evidence of possible bone-working contained in two pits outside the east wall of the town. A public brick works must have existed somewhere in the territorium for a series of tiles and bricks stamped RPG standing for *Rei Publicae Glevensium* has been found, not only in the town itself but also as far afield as Cheltenham. The tiles are sometimes stamped with the names of the aediles, the magistrates responsible for controlling public works, and one example is known where the quinquennales are named,[117] although it is not easy to understand why this should be so. The region of Gloucestershire as a whole has

36   An Antonine house in Insula I, Gloucester (*H. Hurst*)

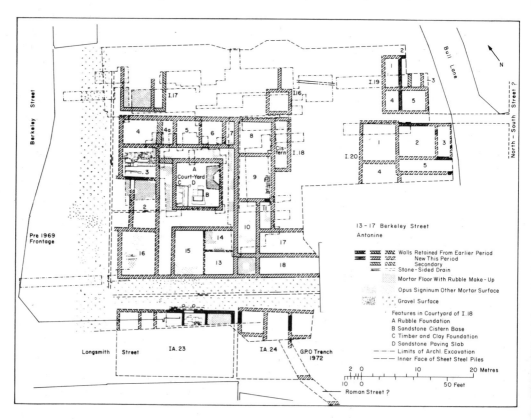

produced far more tiles stamped with non-military marks than any other part of Britain. Another series is known beginning TPF, followed by a further letter in a series of which A to P have so far been recorded.[118] The first three letters probably refer to the name of the manufacturer, the fourth may be a batch letter. Apart from a small number, most of these tiles have been found outside Gloucester and chiefly at Cirencester, but they are known as far away as Wanborough (*Durocornovium*). So it would seem from the distribution that this particular firm was not connected with the colonia, despite Richmond's view that, as a means of control, stamping the products of a privately-owned concern would fit with regulations known to have been in force in the brickworks of at least one colonia in Spain.[119] Other stamps, presumably of private companies or manufacturers, known from the region are VLA, LLH, TCM, LLQ, TPL and LHS.[120]

Not much is yet known about the cemeteries. Military tombstones from Wotton would suggest the site of one during the military occupation. Other burials are known from outside the south and east gates, and beyond the latter has been found an inhumation cemetery which included burials of the very end of the fourth or even of the early fifth century. Another cemetery seems to have existed at Barnwood, which lies between the town and the villa at Hucclecote. In the absence of a collection of tombstones such as those at Lincoln and York, we can say little about individual inhabitants. A nameless decurion of the colonia died at Bath at the age of 80;[121] presumably he had gone to take the waters as a cure, but to no avail (pl. 24). One of the quinquennales, Julius Florus, is named on the tile-stamp mentioned above, but the aediles are only known by their initials. An opthalmic practitioner, Q. Julius Muranus, who produced for his patients an ointment called *Melinum*, made from the blossoms of quince or apple trees, seems to have practised in Gloucester.[122]

Neither do we know much about the religious beliefs and practices. We should assume temples to the main imperial and Roman cults. A small fragment of an altar to Mars[123] has been found in the Kingsholm area, north of the town, where perhaps an extra-mural shrine existed, and is a reminder of the shrine to Mars Medocius which may have existed outside the south wall of Camulodunum.[124] The Kingsholm altar was found with another, dedicated *Deo Genio Chogunci* by a man called Orivendus, together with three uninscribed altars.[125] Another deity is attested on a jet plaque, possibly depicting a Celtic god, which was found in a medieval rubbish pit on the Market Hall site.[126] Recently an altar was found on the Bon Marche site carved to represent Attis playing pan-pipes: he was consort of Cybele.[127]

There is evidence of other extra-mural structures in the form of two mosaics belonging to different buildings which must have fronted the main road leading out of the north gate. Another building just outside the same gate produced column bases and capitals and may be an extra-mural shrine or temple, while a second, monumental structure slightly more distant may have been part of an extra-mural market.[128] Buildings are also known in the area between the town and the river Severn. Moreover a wide, metalled area seems to have existed beyond the defences on the north-east and south-east sides. All told, there is a marked impression of an extensive and prosperous built-up area outside the walls.

As might be expected the river Severn provided one of the chief links with other places. Part of a quay, composed of massive masonry has been found on a line set back from the old course of the river. Certainly there is evidence of an earlier, late first-century harbour in a creek of the river, which had timber wharves or landing-stages. Observations by C. Green in 1936–7 would seem to confirm the suggestion of a later and more massively-built harbour wall situated in a creek or bay away from the main current. There is, however, no definite evidence for the date of these various works. In view of the nature of the tides and the Severn bore, a sheltered harbour off the main river should be expected. If provision had not been made, this might well be one of the reasons why Gloucester never developed as an important trading centre like Lincoln.[129] The four principal roads out of the town led to: Cirencester and Worcester through the north gate; the Forest of Dean and south Wales through the west gate; a reputed settlement at Painswick through the east gate; Sea Mills at the mouth of the Avon through the south gate.

As at Lincoln and Colchester, various attempts have been made to define the extent of the territorium at Gloucester. Most recently, Richmond concluded that it lay on the river terraces, around Gloucester and Cheltenham, adducing the distribution of RPG tile-stamps in evidence,[130] although he was careful to add the rider that they are so few as perhaps not to indicate the full extent of the territorium. Nevertheless, they have been found at the villas at Hucclecote,[131] about 3 miles (4·8km) south-east of the town: at Ifold,[132] about 6 miles (9·7km) due south, at Dryhill,[133] about 4 miles (6·4km) beyond Hucclecote, and Frocester. A note of caution should be sounded here; it is surprising how far building material can travel, and it would be as well not to accept these tiles as evidence for buildings in the territorium without further proof, especially as tiles with other stamps, notably the TPF series, also occur at Hucclecote.

On the other hand some facts may be recorded, without comment, with regard to the alignments of roads and the spacing of some villas in the area round Gloucester, which may reflect on the territorium and possibly also on centuriation. It should also be remembered that, in laying out the territorium of the new colonia, recourse would have had to be made to roads which were already in existence, and that there was no obvious intersection of main roads in the town itself from which to start measurements. But a road intersection in the town centre was not always the starting point, and at *Salona* (Dalmatia) the principal grid directions appear to have been aligned on parts of the west and south walls of the old town, which were already in being when centuriation was imposed.[134] It has often been pointed out that two of the main roads approaching Gloucester are aligned on Kingsholm, where the early military site may be suspected.[135] What is not so often realised is that, if the main alignment of the Gloucester–Sea Mills Road, as apparently represented by the stretch of modern road from Whitminster to Hornshill, is produced north-eastwards it strikes Ermin Street

27 Eastern wall of Gloucester, showing junction between Periods 4 and 5 (*J. S. Wacher, with permission*)

at precisely the point where the latter changes direction towards the north gate of the colonia. Moreover, it strikes it at an angle which is only two degrees more than a right angle. This coincidence can be pursued further. The Sea Mills line passes the south-east side of the town, which is not quite parallel with it, at a distance of about 800yds (730m) from the east gate and 775yds (708m) from the edge of the metalled area outside the defences (p. 151). On the north side, the continuation of Ermin Street westwards, again not quite parallel with the curtain wall, passes the north gate at a distance of a little over 800yds (730m). The territorium perhaps ended on the south-east against the steep scarp of the Cotswolds, except possibly where this projected abruptly into the valley below or formed isolated hills. Therefore it is interesting, that, on the lower ground, from about Cheltenham south-west to Aust, there survives a skeletal pattern of modern roads, tracks, footpaths and parish boundaries, which conform with a grid of 20-actus squares[136] laid out with respect to the two coordinate roads. The lines of roads and paths have been much warped in later years, but it is significant that the grid lines cannot be satisfactorily extended either north-west of the river Severn, or much above the 200ft (61m) contour of the Cotswolds. The area so covered by the grid is about 200sq. miles (500sq. km).

We do not yet know what happened to Gloucester in the fifth century. In some areas of the town, including the forum, a layer of uniform grey loam up to 2ft (600mm) thick has been found. That overlying the forum courtyard is largely stone and debris free and clearly points to disuse under wet or even flooded conditions. Since the forum floor had remained at the same level, while those all around rose, local flooding may have occurred. In Saxon times, an alder tree was growing there, so that even then marshy conditions still existed.[137] Elsewhere the loam contains much stone, late Roman pottery and bones, suggesting the dumping of rubbish in unoccupied areas. But with the rise in sea-level during the late fourth century causing the backing up of streams and the possible re-activating of springs, local flooding of the town may have taken place from time to time. York was similarly affected (p. 176). A coin of Valens has been found beneath a mosaic in Southgate Street, and fragments of imported north African amphorae have been dated to the fourth or fifth centuries. Life must therefore have continued in a normal manner into the fifth century. But we do not yet know if the plague which may have reached Cirencester at some time in the middle of the fifth century (p. 313) or that of a century later, also affected Gloucester. The final episode in the history of the town is, however, better recorded. According to the Anglo-Saxon Chronicle, in AD 577 Cuthwine and Ceawlin fought against the Britons at Dyrham, some 35 miles south of Gloucester and killed three kings, Conmail, Condidan and Farinmail, and captured three cities, Gloucester, Cirencester and Bath. If the order in which the cities are given applies equally to the kings then Conmail may have been 'king' of Gloucester. The name is of Celtic derivation, which might suggest that by the end of the sixth century Gloucester had already passed under the domination of Celtic immigrants, probably from Wales or Ireland.

It is impossible to discuss Gloucester without making some comparison with Cirencester, which lay only 17 miles (27km) to the south-east. The essential difference between the two towns has been most adequately summed up by Richmond: 'All the evidence suggests that the colonia remained an efficient going concern, but did not grow and did not attract to itself expensive enterprise or expensive art. This is symptomatic and the cause is not far to seek. It has already been observed that the capital of the Dobunni, out of whose territory the colonia was carved, lay only 17 miles away across the Cotswolds. Of all the Romano-British tribal capitals Corinium Dobunnorum was quite the most successful.'[138] Recent evidence from both towns has tended to confirm this analysis. Gloucester may now perhaps be seen as more prosperous and larger in area than was thought, but we cannot altogether escape the image implied by those early houses of the colonia found on the Telephone Exchange and New Market Hall sites. Even in the better class houses of the mid second-century which replaced them the effect is still one of constraint: good taste instead of ostentation: present comfort rather than gambles on future wealth. All this may have provided the cause for the difference between the two towns, but it does not, unless taken further, explain why the cause should have operated. Here we must hark back to an argument already used to explain why Cirencester and not Gloucester became a provincial capital in the fourth century (p. 86). It all depends on the character of the people concerned. Even today we can make some surprisingly accurate estimates of what people are like by examining the type of house they inhabit. At Gloucester we can detect prople who were anxious to be independent even if, thereby, they sacrificed other advantages: semi-detached versus detached. Their military origins would make them a tightly-knit community with rigid social strata according to their army rank. Snobbery was no doubt rife, especially with regard to non-citizens in the community. Such people tend to be introverted and ultra-conservative, while their army background would give them a respect for, and obedience to, regulations. These were not the people to make great sums of money out of commercial enterprise. The entrepreneurial spirit, often sailing close to the law, might in most cases, have been almost entirely lacking. If, as has already been suggested in an earlier chapter (p. 86), connexions were maintained between Gloucester and the legionary fortress at Caerleon, then it is possible that the veteran class was constantly replenished, so perpetuating the character of the town, as derived originally from the character of its inhabitants. No wonder, then, that the bolder spirits may have departed from this constricting atmosphere, and that traders, given the choice, settled in neighbouring Cirencester. There was nothing potentially wrong with Gloucester as a town or as a site, and it was no doubt a comfortable and civilised place in which to live. The fault, if fault it was, lay with the inhabitants, and, unlike Lincoln, they do not seem to have been able in later years to divest themselves of their original image. Here then lies the real distinction between Gloucester and Cirencester, although we can probably conclude that the inhabitants of Gloucester were quite happy as they were.

YORK (*Colonia Eboracensium*)

Even during the early Empire it had often happened that an existing town was promoted to the status of a municipium and sometimes later to that of a colonia. This practice became commoner from the late first century onwards, and by the third and fourth centuries was virtually normal for towns which had reached any degree of size and importance. In this respect therefore York differs from the three other known British coloniae in that the status was conferred on an existing settlement, which had grown on the opposite bank of the river Ouse to the legionary fortress, and which may have been separate from the canabae. There is, however, no archaeological evidence for separation.

The promotion of York to colonial status probably occurred under Caracalla. It is known that extensive replanning took place during the early third century (see p. 161 below), which would equate well with a complete reorganisation of the town (fig. 37). It is also known that a substantial settlement already existed when this happened, which might suggest that it had earlier received municipal status. This would be in accordance with common practice in other provinces, where promotion to municipium usually preceded later promotion to colonia.[139] The earliest date at which it is known to have been a colonia is provided by the Bordeaux altar, dated to AD 237.[140] Aurelius Victor in his account of the death of Severus in AD 211 refers to it as a municipium,[141] but this may not be entirely reliable, although Mann and Jarrett accept the description.[142] It should be remembered also that, from the early third century, York was a provincial capital. Moreover, during the three-year visit of Severus,[143] and, probably again later under Constantius I and Constantine I, it was for short times, a major centre of the Empire. Both these factors are likely to have affected the town, not least by the existence of an imperial palace. A *domus Palatina* is mentioned in the biography of Severus,[144] and, if it had survived, it would surely have been used again by Constantius I, who died at York, and by Constantine I who was there proclaimed Augustus. The analogy between York under Severus, and Carnuntum under Marcus Aurelius during the Marcomannic Wars, has already been drawn by Richmond.[145] At Carnuntum an imperial palace, built by Marcus Aurelius, was maintained for a considerable time after its first use. The site of the imperial palace at York is not known with any certainty. However, some tentative suggestions may be made as to its position. When the old Railway Station was being constructed in 1839–40, and again in 1939 during excavations for an air-raid shelter, several fragments of very large buildings were found in the area.[146] Part (fig. 38) was obviously a bath-house of some size, with a caldarium (34d) 30ft (9m) wide and over 35ft (10·5m) long; except for the bath-house on Huggin Hill, London, none other so large is yet known from Britain. The most noticeable point about these buildings is that, with one exception, they all appear to be slightly off line from those of the colonia, as though they were in existence before, and were left untouched, when the town was replanned in the early third century. Other parts of this complex which have been found included three

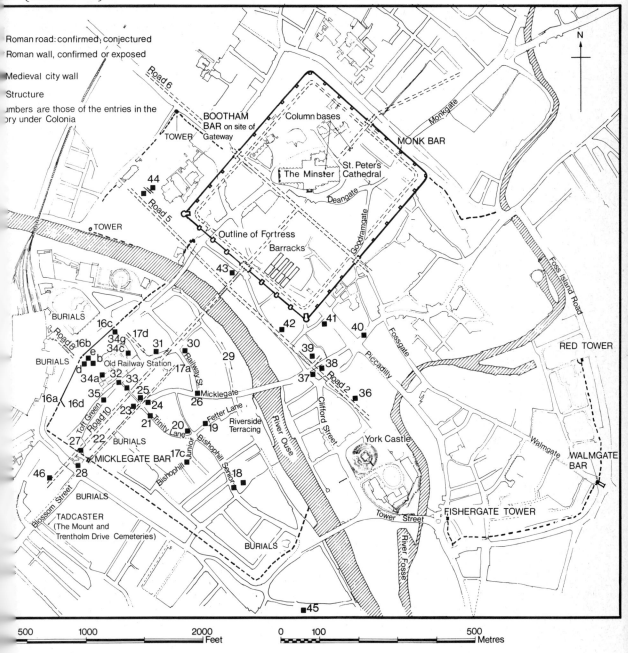

K (Ebvracvm)

Roman road: confirmed; conjectured

Roman wall, confirmed or exposed

Medieval city wall

Structure

umbers are those of the entries in the
ory under Colonia

37 Plan of the colonia at York (*after the Royal Commission of Historical Monuments (England), Crown Copyright—reproduced with permission of the Controller of Her Majesty's Stationery Office*)

separate cold plunge baths (34b, c). At a short distance from the bath (35b) a
small room only 5ft (1·5m) square was discovered in which the altar to Fortune,
once set up by Sosia Iuncina, wife of the imperial legate, Q. Antonius Isauricus,[147]
was found to have been reused as a building stone (pl. 29). South-west of these
bath fragments was another isolated find, consisting of a room (34a), 39ft (12m)
by 24½ft (7·5m), with a semi-circular apse at the north-west end; one surviving
wall fragment was 5ft (1·5m) thick. Slightly further to the south-east was a
smaller, apsidal room with an external buttress at the head of the apse (32). From
below its foundations came the early third-century dedication (pl. 30) to Serapis
by Claudius Hieronymianus, legate of Legio VI,[148] but the building which was
erected over it aligns with other colonia buildings and not with the baths. The
latter seem to have been bounded on the north-east side by a massive wall which
was traced for about 100yds (90m) and by perhaps another parallel with, and
about 40ft (12m) south-west, of it. These walls may, however, represent terraced

38   The bath building under the old railway station, York (*Royal Commission of Historical Monuments
(England), Crown Copyright—reproduced with permission of the Controller of Her Majesty's Stationery Office*)

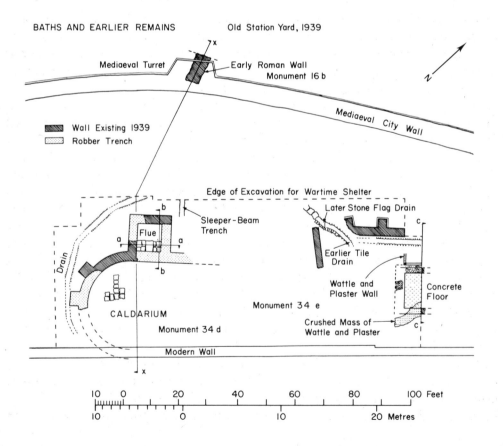

buildings. Traces of earlier buildings, including late first-century timber structures, have also been observed near the caldarium to be on the same alignments
as those of later years. So continuity had been observed, which probably shows
that the alignment was earlier than the colonia.

These fragmentary remains are obviously not enough for an imperial palace
to be created round them, even if all belong to one complex, and there is nothing
to prove that they did. The date of most of the fragments must remain in doubt,
and, moreover, excavations on the caldarium showed a complicated history of
development. Yet, there are features about the buildings, together with other
finds, which seem to distinguish this quarter of the colonia from other parts.
It is curious that the alignment first taken by the early timber buildings should
have been perpetuated by such large and massive successors, which ignore
subsequent development in the colonia. This would, by itself, set the buildings
apart from the general run, and would show that they were of sufficient importance not to have been demolished and brought into line with the rest. It is also
noteworthy that the area should have produced two inscriptions testifying to
imperial legates. As reused building stone they might have travelled some distance
from where they were originally placed, but altars to Fortune are sometimes
found in baths, while the size of the stone dedication to Serapis might suggest
that it had not moved far. There are, in addition, the two bronze plates set up by
Demetrius, which were found in the same area. One is a dedication to the deities
of the governor's residence, the other to Ocean and Tethys.[149] Demetrius has
been identified as the schoolmaster whom Plutarch met in AD 83–4 and who is
mentioned in *de defectu Oraculorum*. Whether the identification is correct or not,
Demetrius was clearly attached to the governor's staff. The deities of the residence
could presumably be invoked anywhere, and, if Agricola was the governor in
question, they could have been placed as easily in a building in which he resided
at York, as in an official residence anywhere else. Moreover, since Agricola spent
much time on active service in the north, and because the *praetorium* in London
does not seem to have been fully finished much before the end of his governorship, he may well have had campaign headquarters at York. It could be argued
that small objects such as bronze plates could have been carried as rubbish to the
site where they were found, although as rubbish they would more likely have
been melted down. But this would add to the coincidence. We might conclude
therefore that the area in question seems from the first to have been used for an
official dwelling connected with the imperial administration. It could equally
have been the site of a different type of praetorium, of the sort suspected at
Brough-on-Humber and at *Praetorium Agrippina* in Holland, where important
imperial officials were accommodated on tours of duty;[150] what better nucleus
for an imperial palace?

When York became the capital of Britannia Inferior, probably under Severus,
the governor of the new province would also have required a residence. Since,
however, the governor was also legate of Legio VI, it is more than probable that
he continued to occupy the legionary praetorium in the fortress across the river

28   Head of the Emperor Constantine from the legionary fortress, York (*The Yorkshire Museum*)

from the colonia. With the reorganisation of the Empire in the late third and
early fourth centuries, the civil and military commands were separated. Then
York became military headquarters for the whole northern region under the
command of the Dux Britanniarum, in addition to being the base for Legio VI,
which was by then probably smaller in size and commanded by a prefect.
Britannia Inferior was also sub-divided into two provinces and York was the
capital of either Flavia Caesariensis or Britannia Secunda. By analogy with what
happened to Britannia Superior, and also with other provinces where similar
sub-divisions took place, it is probable that York was in Flavia Caesariensis.
There would have been the seat of the governor of the new and minor province,
which would have been located in the colonia. Richmond has suggested that a
riverside site would have been selected, like those at London, Cologne and
Aquincum.[251] So far, little is known of the buildings which flanked the river
Ouse, but evidence for early third-century terraces, some distance back from the
river, in the grounds of Bishophill Senior,[152] possibly points to provision having
been made for them. These terraces, of which at least four may be inferred, were
much slighter than those at Lincoln (p. 134) and were retained by walls about
$3\frac{1}{2}$ft (1m) thick, which may have stood originally to a height of about 10ft (3m).

At present, only a small amount is known of the fortifications which enclosed
the colonia. It might be assumed that they were constructed soon after the
promotion, when much of the town seems to have been replanned. The defences
of the legionary fortress over the river are partly followed by the later medieval
wall.[153] That being so, it is probably also right to assume that the colonia walls
will likewise have been followed by parts of the medieval circuit on the other
bank. Nevertheless, but for the north-west section, some caution must be
exercised with regard to the remainder. Sections of the wall have been shown to
be embedded in the medieval mound in the area of the old Railway Station. In
making a tunnel to the air-raid shelter (p. 156) a wall, about 6ft (1·8m) thick, of
roughly-coursed rubble masonry was encountered. It was there slightly in
advance of the medieval wall and appeared to be diverging outwards, presumably
towards the point where Road 8 entered the town,[154] and where presumably
there was a gate. Some 300ft (91m) further south, two other sections of wall
were uncovered again during work on the railway. Their respective alignments,
if correct, would suggest an angle, with a turn being made towards the south-
east. This would bring the Roman wall inside the medieval circuit, at least until
after it had passed Micklegate. A gate would almost certainly have been provided
where the wall met the main road from Tadcaster,[155] which approached from
the south-west, and which formed one of the axes of the town, leading to the
Ouse bridge and the legionary fortress beyond. If the wall takes this line, then
the section of Roman street found just inside Micklegate Bar,[156] must have lain
outside the fortified area of the colonia. Is York, therefore, one of the towns,
such as Silchester, where the construction of defences interrupted the street
system and enclosed a smaller area? If so, then this would appear to be conclusive
evidence for a pre-colonial street grid, showing earlier town-planning, perhaps

29   Altar to Fortune, erected by Sosia Juncina, wife of Q. Antonius Isauricus, imperial legate: from Building
34b, York (*The Yorkshire Museum*)

in connexion with a municipium. It is highly unlikely that this section of apparently extra-mural street would have come from another gate placed so close to the
Tadcaster Gate.

Nothing else is known of the defences, and apart from the two streets mentioned above, there are few other indications of the town plan. The Royal
Commission's Inventory has suggested that the lines of other streets may be
presumed in a warped form in the medieval street plan, but this idea should be
treated with caution, bearing in mind the comparative plans of Roman and
medieval Canterbury and Winchester. Another street at York is, however,
known with a street fountain beside it, which was found in Bishophill Junior.[157]
Its direction ran parallel with that represented by 17a. It should be mentioned here
that Street 17a does not cross the full width of the colonia from south-west to
north-east, but is interrupted by a large, colonnaded building,[158] north-east of
Railway Street.

Some of the principal buildings inside the colonia have already been discussed.
Another worthy of individual mention is the colonnaded building (Building 30)
referred to at the end of the preceding paragraph. Two parallel lines of column
bases were found 40ft (12m) apart. The bases were 3ft (0·9m) in diameter and
were placed 6ft (1·8m) apart; seven were found in the row nearest to Railway
Street, four in the other. Another base apparently occupied an odd position
equidistant between the two terminal columns at the north-west end. We might
wonder if indeed it was intended to support a column, as the distance to be
spanned on either side would have been of the order of 20ft (6m). Perhaps it was
not an 'architectural solecism' as Richmond called it, but the base for a statue,
or it could have belonged to an earlier building. No specific date can be ascribed
to the building, although a coin hoard found in the same area, but not necessarily
connected with it, contained coins as late as Geta. Richmond has suggested that
it may have been a basilica,[159] and certainly it must be a building of some importance since it interrupted the street grid. An altar, dedicated to the *numen
Augusti* and the *genius Eboraci*,[160] was found in the same modern street. Other
colonnaded buildings are known under Trinity Lane and at the junction of
Micklegate with Railway Street,[161] but neither building had columns of significant size. Since it is not yet possible to say which was the principal north-
west to south-east street, it is difficult to assign the forum even to a tentative
position. Building 30 must obviously be a candidate, with its colonnaded
'basilica'. If the 'basilica' was placed symmetrically at the end of street 17a, it
would then have occupied a double insula and would have had an overall length
of about 240ft (73m). However, there would have been little room between it
and the river for the forum, unless terracing had been employed. Neither does it
occupy a very central position, although it would flank the south-east side of the
main street from the bridge over the Ouse. Another possibility, in a better
position, is Building 25 in the Royal Commission's Inventory,[162] which is
described as being 'divided into compartments', a description reminiscent of
the wings of some fora.

DEO·SANCTO
SERAPI
TEMPLVMA·SO
LO·FECIT
CL·HIERONY
MIANVS·LEG
LEG·VI·VIC

30   Dedication tablet from a temple of Serapis, found at Toft Green, York (Building 32) (*The Yorkshire Museum*)

A possible site for a public bath-house, if we exclude Buildings 34d, e, is in Fetter Lane, where a building (Building 19) with an exterior (?) wall 4ft (1·2m) thick suggests more than a domestic bath suite. A cold plunge, 9ft (2·7m) wide and over 20ft (6m) long was flanked by two other large rooms. Interestingly, in one of the latter the floor was made of tiles stamped LEG IX HISP. Some timbers, measuring 1ft (305mm) square and 30ft (9m) long, were also found and suggest roof beams, presumably from the unheated part of the baths.[163] A running water supply is indicated by the street fountain referred to above (p. 163), and by lead

pipes connected to the baths in Building 34, and there would have been little
difficulty in providing the colonia with a continuous flow from an aqueduct. A
possible line for an aqueduct may be indicated by a clay and cobble channel
found on the site of the Railway Offices (RCHM 17d). Terracotta pipes, almost
identical with those from Lincoln (p. 128), have been found on the other side of
the river, leading towards the west angle of the fortress. It was concluded that they
represented the supply for St Mary's Abbey,[164] but their similarity with known
Roman pipes must raise doubts, and it is possible that they supplied water from
the Bur Dike further north-west.

Other public buildings still to be sought and as yet entirely unknown, are a
theatre, or amphitheatre, the temple of the imperial cult,[165] and the temples of
the official religion. The lifesize statue of Mars found in Blossom Street, with an
altar dedicated to the same god, are supposed to have been dumped there in
post-Roman times.[166] There is no way of saying if they came from the colonia
or the fortress, although they are much nearer the former, and therefore might
be slight evidence in favour of a temple there.

Despite the dearth of temple structures, the religious life of the town is well
represented by a series of inscriptions. In addition to those already mentioned,
Mithraism is represented by a Tauroctony found in Micklegate, opposite St
Martin's Church, which might suggest the site of a Mithraeum,[167] and by a
rare dedication to Arimanes, a Mithraic god, found near Building 34g.[168] Other
stones record dedications to Jupiter Optimus Maximus, Britannia Sancta,
Genius loci and Deae Matres in the colonia.[169] Another shrine or temple is
known across the river, probably in the legionary canabae, and outside the
southern angle of the fortress. A dedication to Hercules was found beneath the
Midland Bank in High Ousegate (Building 37), while another inscription,
dedicated to the deities of the Emperors, and found on the same site, would
suggest joint dedications on the same building.[170] The temple, despite its
position near the fortress, appears to have been connected also with the colonia,
as the main dedication was made by a group of people who probably had official
connexions with the latter. Yet another fragmentary inscription refers possibly
to work being done by a primus pilus together with two other men, who,
Wright has pointed out, may be joint magistri of the canabae.[171] Finally, it
should be remembered that, in the fourth century, York was the seat of a bishopric, and a prelate whose name was, appropriately, Eborius attended the Council
of Arles in AD 314. Somewhere a church of equivalent dignity should be situated
in the colonia.

York has no domestic buildings which have been fully excavated. But the
fragments, which have been found from time to time, both within the defences
and outside them, show the veneer of opulence over-lying the comfortable
houses, which is to a large extent lacking in the three military coloniae. The reason
for this difference is not hard to seek. The origins of the town lay in the wealth
accumulated by merchants and traders. Only secondarily would veterans have
been attracted to it, in contrast to the opposite state of affairs in the military

foundations. The population would therefore have the diversity of make-up which is desirable for a flourishing settlement. A house with three mosaics is known below Toft Green (Building 35). In one room, a mosaic depicted the four Seasons with a central panel containing a Medusa head; in another, the mosaic was entirely geometrical in design. Another house (Building 27), perhaps lying just outside the Tadcaster Gate, contained a room with a mosaic, which depicted two stags in a central, octagonal panel and with four corner panels showing joints of venison, so displaying an excellent association of ideas. It would seem to be in the same vein as some much earlier mosaics, and also wall-paintings, which include a mosaic of an unswept room, and paintings depicting articles of food. Both styles are mentioned by Pliny.[172]

Evidence for trade and industry at York is not so difficult to find as at Lincoln or Gloucester. The trading connexions between York and Bordeaux have been stressed ever since the altar of M. Aurelius Lunaris was found. The altar (pl. 31) was recently exhibited for the first time in Britain at York, at an exhibition organised to commemorate the foundation of the legionary fortress. It is a very substantial piece of stone, weighing almost a ton, and the standard of the carving is good.[173] The inscription records that the altar was set up in accordance with a vow made by Lunaris 'on starting from York'. Courteault suggests that Lunaris made this flamboyant gesture to commemorate the successful expedition of Maximianus into Germany in AD 236. This is a possible reason, but other more mundane causes should be considered. If he was, as is usually suggested, a merchant, he would surely have made many trips to Bordeaux, in his life-time. The altar might therefore suggest the carriage of an especially valuable cargo from York to Bordeaux. Other occasions demanding the fulfilment of a similar vow might have been after a first trip, or after the completion of a life-time of trips. More likely the latter, as, by the time the altar was erected, Lunaris was a rich and successful man of business, holding prominent positions at both York and Lincoln (p. 134). Why then was the altar erected at Bordeaux and not at York, or is there a companion altar still waiting to be found at York? Perhaps Lunaris was retiring in his old age to the warmer climate of Southern France. He undoubtedly started his journey from York, for, not only does the inscription say so, but also the altar is carved in millstone grit, a stone commonly used in the colonia and unknown in the Bordeaux region. It would seem, therefore, either that the altar was cut before Lunaris left York, or that the stone was part of the ship's ballast, or even a cargo of stone, and the altar made from it on arrival at Bordeaux. This point does not seem to have occurred to Courteault. On the right side of the altar is a bas-relief of a boar, the badge, or emblem, of York derived from its name. Logically, we might expect to find on the other side, the badge of Bordeaux, but instead there is depicted a river god holding an anchor. Courteault described this as a representation of the river Garonne, but, in view of the identification of the other badge, it is difficult to see why it should not be the river Ouse or Humber.

Another man, possibly in the same line of business as Lunaris, was M. Verecun-

31   Altar erected in Bordeaux by M. Aurelius Lunaris, *sevir Augustalis* of York and Lincoln (*Royal Commission on Historical Monuments for England and Musée d'Aquitaine, Bordeaux*)

dius Diogenes, a native of the *Bituriges Cubi*, a civitas which was centred on Bourges. His coffin (pl. 32), together with that of his wife, a Sardinian lady, Julia Fortunata, was found near Scarborough Bridge.[174] Diogenes, like Lunaris, was a sevir Augustalis of York.

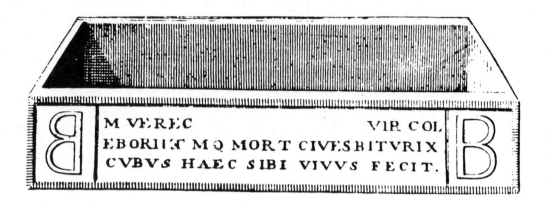

32   Sarcophagus of M. Verecundius Diogenes, *sevir Augustalis* of York: probably found near Scarborough Bridge, York (R. G. Collingwood and R. P. Wright, *The Roman Inscriptions of Britain*, Vol I; the Clarendon Press, Oxford)

Another reminder of York's overseas connexions is contained in the altar (pl. 33) to the African, Italian and Gallic Mother Goddesses erected by M. Minucius Audens, a *gubernator* of Legio VI.[175] He is normally interpreted as having been a river pilot, who would have been most necessary on the Ouse and Humber, where considerable navigational difficulties occur.[176] Evidence for direct trade links with the Rhineland is contained in the jet articles found at Cologne and discussed below, while the Rhenish pipeclay figurine of a bald-headed man, found in a burial near Fishergate, illustrates the reciprocal nature of the trade.[177] Mention might also be made of the massive structure found in Hungate, on a quay beside the old bed of the river Foss, south-east of the fortress (Building 52). It is usually interpreted as the base of a derrick or crane for loading and unloading heavy goods from ships. Although nearer to the fortress than to the colonia, there is no reason to believe that it would have been solely used on behalf of the former.

York was the centre of a lively industry engaged in carving Whitby jet. This material was especially esteemed in the Roman world for its supposed magical properties. In addition to an extensive series of pins, rings, beads and bracelets, the workshops also produced a number of portrait medallions in the form of pendants. They depict sometimes single heads, sometimes those obviously of a husband and wife and sometimes of a family; others are ornamented with a Medusa head, and yet others are shaped as birds or animals. Debris from the manufacture, raw material and also unfinished objects were found on the site of

33 Altar erected by M. Minucius Audens, *gubernator*. Found in Micklegate, York (*The Yorkshire Museum*)

the present Railway Station.[178] It has been suggested that the objects, apart from travelling widely in Britain, were also exported to the Rhineland, where they are especially common in Cologne.[179] Richmond has also drawn attention to the fact that, unlike York, manufacturing waste is so far unknown in Cologne. Neither do the finished products occur in Free Germany, as do other materials, such as glass and enamel work, which were manufactured in the Rhineland.[180] A note in the Royal Commission's Inventory[181] refers to the rarity of the circular discs cut from the centres of rings and bracelets, which were such a common feature of the Dorset shale industry,[182] and suggests that these cores were mainly reused. But some cores have been found, as might be expected, near Whitby. Indeed, it seems most likely that they provided the raw material for the pendants and medallions, most of which were circular or roughly oval in shape.

Another major industry, which may have flourished in York and the area around, was the growing of flax and the production of linen. The Vale of York and the region round Humberhead would provide the suitable rich, moist soil which the plant needs, and certainly both flax and hemp were grown in the Vale as recently as the nineteenth century.[183] Linen was used in Eboracum for wrap-

34 Sarcophagus of Flavius Bellator, decurion of York: found, having been reused, near Scarborough Bridge, York (*The Yorkshire Museum*)

ping bodies before burial, as shows most clearly in the gypsum burials.[184] A useful corroborative piece of evidence comes from excavations at Bishophill Senior, which produced a bone spindle and pottery whorl from a deposit which is later than AD 350 and probably of fifth-century date. Mr R. Patterson of York Castle Museum has said that, in his opinion, the spindle is too fine to have spun anything other than a linen or silk thread.[185]

The same site at Bishophill Senior also produced evidence for pre-colonial bronze and iron working. The former was provided by remains of a waste tub, 18in (457mm) square, of a type recognised at Verulamium and Catterick;[186] the latter from hammer scale. Evidence for a blacksmith connected with the colonia, who was wealthy enough to pay for a tombstone (pl. 37) portraying a smith at work with hammer and anvil, came from Dringhouses.[187]

A mason's yard seems to have existed in the area of the Mount before it was taken over for a cemetery. When this happened, the debris was buried in pits. In addition to coins of Severus and Gordian, worked stone, stone chippings and lead dross were found. The latter implies work of considerable magnitude, where stones were held together with iron cramps set in lead. The coins suggest perhaps a connexion with the rebuilding which occurred in the early third century.[188]

There is little evidence for the local manufacture of pottery. With a flourishing industry in east Yorkshire, the town might have been expected to draw most of its supplies from there. Some certainly reached York, but other vessels found in and around the town have little in common with them, and imply a local industry. Before York became a colonia, an attempt seems to have been made by a samian potter from central Gaul to set up a factory, as a mould for a samian bowl, form 37, was found on the site of the present Railway Station.[189] No pottery kilns or workshops have yet been found. A tilery and legionary pottery connected with the fortress may be suggested by stacked tiles, with legionary stamps, and a pottery store found near St Cuthbert's Church.[190]

As at Colchester, the cemeteries at York have provided much information about the population. We have already met some of its members, but before looking at the activities which were followed by others, we can note the cemeteries themselves. The principal burial grounds of the colonia lay in the area of the present Railway Station, and along the road to Tadcaster as far as Dringhouses. Others are known outside the south-eastern quarter at Clementhorpe and beyond, while single burials have been found as far away as Nunthorpe. Several cemeteries were destroyed when the colonia was developed in the early third century, so as to make room for new buildings. The authorities seem to have displayed a certain callousness, which was matched in the late third century by funeral monuments being used in the construction of defences. A reaction ensued, perhaps from the amount of desecration which was taking place and eventually harsh penalties were imposed by imperial edict on those who destroyed tombs or these monuments.[191] Tomb-robbing had become rife, and the plundering of Diocletian's tomb near Salona (at modern Split)[192] was but one better-known example.

35   Sarcophagus of Aelia Severa, wife of Caecilius Rufus, who was probably a decurion of York: found, having been reused, in Dalton Terrace, York (*The Yorkshire Museum*)

It is not possible to consider all these cemeteries in detail. They cover many gradations of the social scale, and the whole period of Roman occupation. They contain cremation and inhumation burials, including excellent examples of the latter where the corpse was encased in liquid gypsum, which not only preserved impressions of the shape of the body, but also of grave goods which have since perished.[193] Burials of this type have been attributed to Christian rites and the process appears to have been derived from pagan customs in North Africa.[194] Part of an *ustrina*, or cremation area, was found at Trentholme Drive,[195] while there are many fragments from elaborate, ornamented tomb chambers.

Among the burials which might be considered individually as throwing light on the inhabitants, and to which no reference has yet been made, are the following. A tombstone, from near the Mount, erected over the ashes of a 13-year-old child, Corellia Optata, included lines of verse which revealed not only the distress of her father, Q. Corellius Fortis, but also some educational pretensions.[196] Some, like the tombstone of Eglecta and her son Crescens,[197] and that (pl. 36) of Flavia Augustina, her son Augustinus and her daughter,[198] were obviously from family tombs. C. Aeresius Saenus, the husband of Flavia, was a veteran of Legio VI, who had retired to the colonia. The tombstone also records that it was set up for his wife and himself, so implying that he intended to occupy the same grave. Above the inscription is a portrayal of the family. Cresces, another veteran of Legio VI, is recorded on a fragmentary stone, but his name has been partly lost.[199] Stone coffins were frequently used for inhumations in the later period. In one (pl. 35) was buried Aelia Severa, the 27-year-old wife of Caecilius Rufus. She is described as *honesta femina*, a title normally reserved for wives and daughters of decurions.[200] Her coffin was later reused by an unknown man embalmed in gypsum, and the tombstone of Flavia Augustina, mentioned above, had been used as a cover. Another decurion, Flavius Bellator, is mentioned on a stone

36   Tombstone of the family of G. Aeresius Saenus: from The Mount, York (*The Yorkshire Museum*)

coffin (pl. 34) from near the Scarborough railway bridge. He had reached his distinguished position at an early age, for he was only 29 when he died.[201] His heavily-weathered coffin had been reused for a younger woman, who had been buried with a gold finger ring mounted with a ruby. Another coffin found in 1956 near the Castle recalls that a detachment of the Praetorian Guard would have accompanied Severus to Britain. Septimius Lupianus having served his full time as a soldier in the Guard, but not necessarily in Britain, was promoted *centurio ex evocato* to a legion. The coffin belonged to his wife and son.[202]

Gladiatorial shows are perhaps implied by a capital from an ornamental tomb, found near the Royal Station Hotel. Carved on the capital is a somewhat crude portrait of a *retiarius*, with his net and trident.[203] A similar implication is contained on a small bone plaque, found with a burial on the railway site, which is inscribed *Domine Victor vincas felix*.[204] A tile from a cemetery north-west of the fortress inscribed by a workman's finger while the clay was still plastic, suggests the existence of burial clubs (*collegia*) of a type already described in connexion with Lincoln (p. oo),[205] although in this instance it might equally apply to a trade guild, or to a religious or peregrine group.

All the above burials represent the richer classes. In the main they were placed nearer the town, while the poorer people had to make do with burial sites further away. For instance, along the Tadcaster Road the better class monuments are nearly all found between Micklegate Bar and West Mount, while beyond, at Trentholme Drive, almost all the burials, numbering approximately 350, belonged to the poorer classes. Probably the most interesting information from the Trentholme Drive cemetery was obtained by Warwick, Cooke and Rowbotham from a study of the skeletal material.[206] There the people were buried, mostly without coffins, and seldom with grave-markers. Consequently, later graves frequently cut through earlier ones, often only a short time after burial, which led to half-decomposed limbs, heads and torsos being scattered in all directions. The cemetery appears to have been used continuously from the middle of the second century until the end of the fourth. Warwick was able to estimate that 15 per cent of the social class represented by this cemetery died before they were 20, while most deaths (about 50 per cent) occurred between the ages of 20 and 40. Only a small proportion lived beyond 45.[207] In stature the women averaged 5ft 1in (1·549m), and the men 5ft 7in (1·699m), in height, while both sexes appeared to have been involved in a hard physical life. Racially, the males represented a more heterogeneous group than the females, with suggestions of inhabitants whose birth-places were as far away as the eastern Mediterranean. These are interesting, albeit tentative, conclusions, as they confirm evidence from other sources, which show the cosmopolitan nature of many towns in Roman Britain. They would represent not only retired members of the army, but also the numerous small traders, and the slaves and freedmen, who came with their masters from other provinces. At York alone, there are people attested from Sardinia (Julia Fortunata), possibly from Greece or the eastern Empire (Nikomedes), Raetia (L. Bebius Crescens), Gallia Narbonensis

37 Uninscribed tombstone of a blacksmith from Dringhouses, York (*The Yorkshire Museum*)

(L. Duccius Rufinus), Aquitania (M. Verecundius Diogenes),[208] Italy (Gaius. . .). They must all have lived for some time at York and it is easy to see just how mixed the population would become over the years.

Argument has always arisen whenever a territorium is mentioned in connexion with the *colonia Eboracensis*. Forty years ago, Collingwood made the suggestion[209] that the colonial territorium had been carved out of Brigantian lands as a reprisal for a mid second-century revolt. His suggestion was mainly based on an unreliable and obscure reference by the Greek topographer Pausanias.[210] Richmond considered this to be an unwise deduction, and pointed out that a new land settlement was not always made when an existing settlement was promoted.[211] Although no land settlement, of a type associated with the military coloniae, need have taken place on its promotion, it would be surprising if some area was not attributed to it, if only for administrative convenience. This would involve little or no expropriation or confiscation, or even compulsory purchase of land, but simply a change in its ruling authority, which probably affected very little the mass of the population. It is possible that some of the land allocated had previously been part of the legionary prata, and it is probable that the land attributed to the colonia lay in the Vale of York, where land divisions, *per strigas*, have been identified near Tadcaster.[212] There is, however, another possibility that should be considered. At about the same time as York was promoted to a colonia, the neighbouring tribe of the Parisi in east Yorkshire were having some difficulty in maintaining their civitas capital at Brough-on-Humber (*Petuaria*) (p. 393). Indeed, it is likely that the town proved a complete failure through lack of support by the local population.[213] If the town failed, it is probable that the organs of local government failed too. That being so, what was to stop the provincial administration, as an easy solution, from attributing the whole civitas to the colonia?

The end of the colonia has already been the subject of a recent essay by Ramm.[214] There is evidence that standards were being maintained during the last half of the fourth century, but by then a general rise in sea level was beginning to be felt. By soon after AD 350, Brough-on-Humber had been abandoned as a naval base (p. 397). At York, the trouble would take longer to materialise and would be caused more by the backing-up of water in rivers and streams, which, Ramm has suggested, caused flooding up to the 35ft (10·7m) contour at York. Although much of the colonia lay above this mark, it would have had a disastrous effect on the riverside defences, leading, perhaps as at London and Brough (p. 95), to their partial destruction. It would have destroyed or rendered unusable the wharves and harbour facilities, so severing one of the chief lines of communication, by which, in past years, York had grown fat. There is a tenuous suggestion of fifth-century civilian occupation in the legionary fortress. What other evidence there is of the period is one of change: hypocausts and baths disused and a deterioration in building techniques. There is also some evidence, in the form of late fourth and early fifth-century cremation burials, of foederati employed to guard the town after the official garrison had been withdrawn. The closeness to

York of other early Anglo-Saxon cremation cemeteries has led Myres to suggest that in Yorkshire there are traces of settlement by Alamannic *laeti* in the fourth century.[215] But we cannot say if this increased the speed of the dissolution of established order in the colonia. It would be surprising if it did not, and it is probable that, at York, there was no extended survival of Romano-British civilisation as happened in some other towns in central and western Britain, such as Verulamiun and Cirencester.

5

The First
Civitas Capitals

CANTERBURY, CHELMSFORD, VERULAMIUM

With the passing of the Roman army to areas beyond south-eastern Britain and the early release of these parts from military occupation, three tribal regions would have required constitution as self-governing civitates peregrinae, outside the areas of the two client kingdoms of the Iceni and the Regnenses. The three civitates to emerge, probably late in Claudius' principate, were those formed from the Cantiaci, the Trinovantes and the Catuvellauni. The former were made up of a number of smaller tribes welded together. The Trinovantes appear to have continued a corporate existence, despite the colonia at Colchester being founded in their territory. At this early stage, it is likely that the self-governing *civitas Catuvellaunorum* only included the south-eastern part of the tribe, with the remainder in the west and north-west still under military occupation. At this same stage, we might therefore look for three civitas capitals, which we may conclude were founded respectively at Canterbury, Chelmsford and Verulamium. The reasons for the selection of the first and last sites have already been considered (p. 26). Chelmsford is considered below.

CANTERBURY (*Durovernum Cantiacorum*)

Canterbury must have been one of the first civitas capitals to emerge in Britain, and the reasons for its selection, as opposed to other Kentish Iron Age sites such as Rochester, have already been discussed. So far no indication of a military occupation has been found, but a very short period under such control is possible.[1]

Much of the information about Roman Canterbury was recovered in the decades after the last war, when a protracted series of excavations was carried out on bombed areas, and later on development sites, first by Mrs Audrey Williams (now Mrs Grimes) and later by Professor Frere and others. To these sources can be added the information compiled by James Pilbrow, City Engineer in the 1860s, from trenches dug to lay a main system of sewers.[2]

The immediate pre-conquest Iron Age settlement at Canterbury was extensive, and evidence for huts and occupation have been found from as far south as Watling Street and St George's Street to beyond the river Stour in Whitehall.[3] Whether there was a fortified Belgic oppidum here of the type known at Colchester and Verulamium is not yet certain, but a large and deep ditch was encountered during pipe-laying operations north of Whitehall Gardens. It would seem that by the time of the Roman invasion in AD 43, the fortified site at nearby Bigbury had been largely abandoned in favour of the valley site nearer the crossing of the river Stour. Frere has shown that this site was occupied from about AD 10–43, and that it had remained comparatively undisturbed by the political events which affected so much of the Belgic area of Britain during that time.[4] There is also evidence, which reflects on what happened after the conquest, that the area around Canterbury was studded with native-style farms, so confirming the remarks made by Caesar,[5] who among other things, noted that the Kentish people were also the most civilised among the Britons.

Evidence for the early Claudian occupation of Canterbury has been difficult to find, and much of it is very fragmentary. Some changes must have been felt at once, others were slower to materialise and one Belgic hut in Whitehall Gardens (pl. 38) continued to be occupied until about AD 60. Some form of military occupation, either an auxiliary fort or a supply base, might be expected, since Canterbury lay on the direct route westwards from the port and stores depot at Richborough. Alternatively, these early military installations may have been situated a little further downstream on the Stour, which was probably then navigable up to Fordwich, and supplies could have been landed directly. Nevertheless some sort of staging centre would seem to have been required at Canterbury for no other reason than that it afforded the first easy opportunity of crossing the river.

Abundant quantities of pottery have been recovered from occupation layers and rubbish pits of the Claudian period in most parts of the town, but evidence of structures is tantalisingly slight. The first domestic, and also possibly commercial, buildings of the town seem to have been universally constructed with timber frames, as was the habit in the majority of native towns in Britain, with walls of clay or wattle and daub, and floors of clay, or perhaps boards. The elusiveness of buildings representing the early town perhaps shows that no great effort was made at first to construct a town after the Roman manner. The earliest streets almost everywhere are known to overly a layer of greyish-brown loam containing Belgic and possibly some Claudian material,[6] suggesting that work on laying out a regular street system started under Claudius or early in the principate of Nero, although there is some evidence to show that the alignments were not always the same as the streets of later years (fig. 39). To the years of the middle of the first century would seem, therefore, to belong the first attempt at coordinated town-planning, which in turn implies the existence of an authority competent to

38   Excavation of a Belgic hut in Whitehall, Canterbury (Entwhistle)

make decisions. We might so date the emergence of the *civitas Cantiacorum*. But like so many other native towns in Britain, development in earnest did not really start much before the Flavian period. Not enough is yet known about the true position, the precise boundaries or the history of the forum, for it to be dated. It is always assumed to have lain under the centre of the medieval town in the area around the County Hotel. An extent of rammed gravel was found below the cellars of the hotel during alteration work, and this gravel extended westwards under Stour Street. Part of an elaborate and sumptuous building was also found not far away to the rear of what was once the Fleur de Lys Hotel (now a Wimpy Bar). It had been decorated with marble veneers imported from many parts of the Empire.[7] It was noted that little early occupation underlay it, which might point either to a comparatively early date or else to considerable site clearance before building work began. Architectural fragments have also been found in the same general area under the High Street. One difficulty in accepting the

Fleur de Lys building as part of the forum complex arises from the presence of a flue arch leading probably to a hypocaust, which would be unusual in a forum or basilica.[8] Another arises in trying to relate these building fragments to the known street plan. The insulae at Canterbury measure approximately 300ft (91m) by 450ft (122m). One insula would accommodate the forum and basilica, yet there is a slight suggestion that the buildings under discussion cut across two adjoining insulae, although, if a forum, it may not have occupied both to the full, as happened at Silchester (p. 262). Moreover, although centrally placed in the town, it was not so well placed with regard to the two principal streets, one of which would have connected Northgate with Worth Gate, the other Riding Gate with the London Gate (in Westgate Gardens). Unfortunately, trial trenching in the relevant insula north of the intersection has revealed little of any value.

Of other public buildings at Canterbury, pride of place must go to the theatre. This was discovered in 1950 in a small bombed site at the south end of St Margaret's Street. Fortunately, parts of its massive walls have survived in the basements of nearby shops and houses, while others were recorded by Pilbrow beneath St Margaret's Street and Watling Street. Two successive buildings, each with different plans, were identified.[9] The first (fig. 12) was constructed *c*. AD 80–90 and would appear to have been the result of encouragement given to local authorities for civic enterprises by the early Flavian governors, notably Frontinus and Agricola. It is not easy to restore the whole plan from the surviving fragments. The outer wall, 4ft (1·2m) thick, which retained a gravel bank for the seating, traced a shallow curve which, if circular, would have a diameter of 329ft (100m). However, four walls apparently radiating inwards towards a point under St Margaret's Street suggest a more complicated structure. Frere has suggested that the two most southerly walls flanked an entrance passage. Another wall, however, under 5, St Margaret's Street, although attributed by him to the early theatre, makes an exact radius for the curve of the later building, and would help to fill an awkward gap in its sequence of radial walls. Another entrance seems to have existed roughly on an east–west axis, which, if produced to cut the presumed continuation of the outer curve, would give a centre point for the building under the front of the Queen's Head Hotel at the end of St Margaret's Street where it is joined by Watling Street. The sector of the circle so cut off by this chord would measure approximately 280ft (85m) across, and the outer wall at the head of its curve would only be about 75ft (23m) from the centre of the chord. A wall found in 1950 under St Margaret's Street might suggest the boundary of an orchestra, but, if this building was, as seems possible, an amphitheatre, it might have belonged to an arena. The entrance on the St Margaret's Street axis is funnel-shaped, not unlike the arena entrance at Trier.[10] If the orchestra, or arena, was symmetrically placed with respect to the outer wall, it would measure approximately 120ft (36m) across the long axis. However, the dimensions given above preclude the orchestra from being concentric with the outer wall and an elliptical shape might be considered. Circles of differing radii were used in the outer and orchestra walls in the theatre at Vieux,[11] and possibly also at Paris.[12]

CANTERBURY (Dvrovernvm)

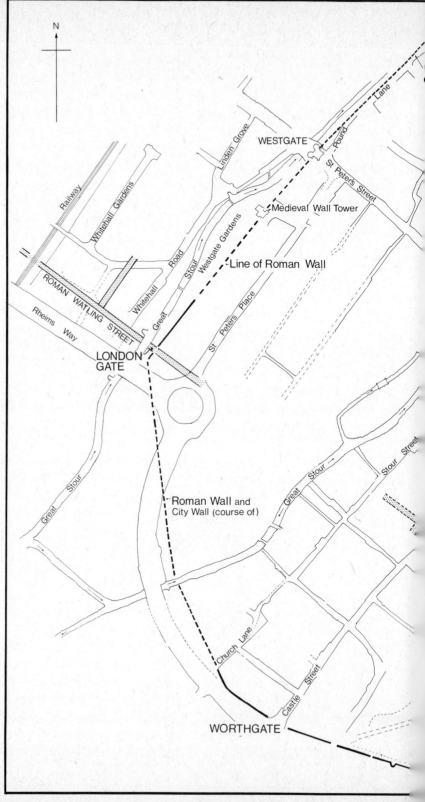

39 Plan of Canterbury (*after S. S. Frere*)

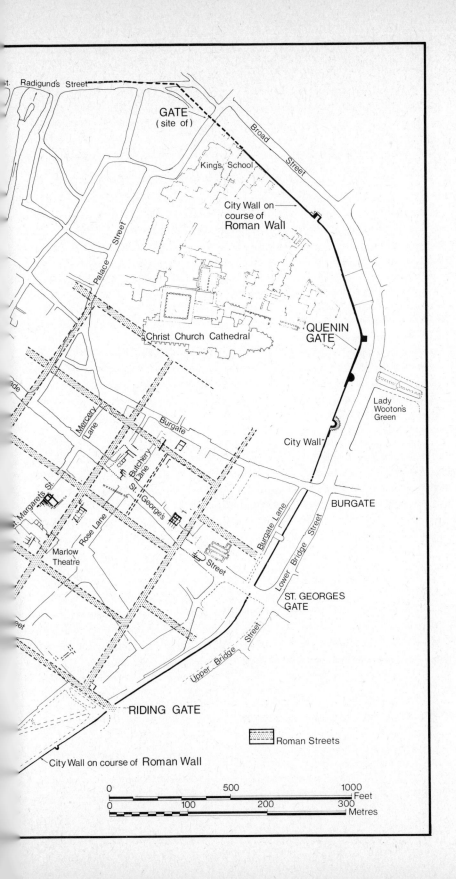

St. Radigund's Street

GATE
(site of)

Broad Street

King's School

City Wall on
course of
Roman Wall

Palace Street

Christ Church Cathedral

QUENIN
GATE

City Wall

Lady
Wooton's
Green

Mercery Lane

Burgate

Butchery Lane

St. Margaret's St.

St. Georges

Rose Lane

Marlow
Theatre

Street

BURGATE

Burgate Lane

Lower Bridge Street

ST. GEORGES
GATE

Upper Bridge Street

RIDING GATE

Roman Streets

City Wall on course of Roman Wall

| 0 | | 500 | | 1000 |
Feet

| 0 | 100 | 200 | 300 |
Metres

In spite of the apparent asymmetry of the building, it is interesting to note that the probable width of the cavea along the St Margaret's Street axis is almost identical with the distance from the centre of that axis to the outer wall at its nearest point. All things considered, it is most likely to have been a theatre of Romano-Celtic type, with a somewhat irregular outline, for which the closest parallels are probably those at Paris and Vieux.

This Flavian theatre was completely rebuilt to a new plan (fig. 12) in the early decades of the third century. As at Verulamium, where the early fourth-century rebuilding tended to make the Romano-Celtic theatre nearer to a classical plan (p. 219), so at Canterbury the result was to turn it into one which closely resembled the great classical theatres of Gaul and Spain. The new theatre was now enclosed on the south side by two massive, concentric curving walls, 12ft (3·7m) and 8ft (2·4m) thick respectively, with an ambulatory 9ft (2·7m) wide between them, to give it a diameter of 232ft (71m). Part of the old theatre was therefore included within the new structure, although it would seem to have been almost completely obscured by the later work, while part at the west end must have been excluded and reduced to ground level. A pair of parallel walls projecting inwards from the inner circumference wall stopped abruptly on an oblique line after penetrating a short distance into the gravel bank of the old theatre. The distance between these walls was 4ft 6in (1·4m) and it may be that they formed the supports for a stair-case leading up to the new cavea. Two radial walls are known: one below St Margaret's Street and the other in a cellar below a house in Watling Street. Between the latter and the staircase walls mentioned above were at least two internal buttresses in the form of flattened apses with their convex sides facing towards the stage. Buttresses of this sort were normally employed in some earth-bank theatres and amphitheatres to relieve the main walls of the weight of soil. That being so, we might wonder if the original intention at Canterbury had been to supplement the earlier gravel bank. But there is enough evidence to show that the space between the outer wall of the old theatre and the new outer walls had not been filled with earth or gravel, which should suggest the presence of masonry vaulting to carry the seats. Yet this would seem to be ruled out in turn by the lack of either sufficient, continuous radial walls, or walls concentric with the outer plan. One possible solution might have involved the partial reuse of the gravel bank of the old theatre. As the cavea descended towards the level of the orchestra, the weight carried by the radial walls would correspondingly decrease, so perhaps making possible the use of shallower foundations. A useful economy could therefore be made by stepping the foundations up and over the surviving gravel bank, and all traces of them would have disappeared long before excavation took place. A lateral entrance leading to the orchestra is implied by the northern termination of the exterior wall, while another massive wall running from this point towards the centre would suggest the end wall of the cavea. As yet the buildings forming the stage are little known, but may have extended back some distance.

One interesting feature of both old and new theatres is their relationship to the neighbouring streets. Neither aligns with the street grid, and, indeed, one street to the east seems to have been diverted round the corner of the new theatre, although it might just possibly have skirted the old. This would suggest that both were related to some other feature, not only earlier than the street plan, but also of sufficient importance for it to be maintained long after the streets had been laid out. A possible suggestion would be an associated temple, perhaps built on the site of a pre-conquest religious enclosure, but so far there is no information to say where it lay in relation to the successive theatres.

One public bath-house may exist in the next insula north of the theatre (fig. 40), and the building with a flue arch behind the Fleur de Lys Hotel would be a likely candidate for a second if the forum was shown to be elsewhere.[13] But the bath-house which was found on the site of the bombed Fountain Hotel (now the Marlowe Car Park) in St Margaret's Street contained rooms large enough to qualify as a public building. One hot room was about 30ft (9m) square with an outside wall 5ft 6in (1·7m) thick, beyond which ran a deep, substantial drain, and a further but less massive wall. West of the hot room was a cold plunge measuring approximately 15ft (4·6m) by 20ft (6·1m), and other rooms were observed to run out under St Margaret's Street. Yet another hot room with a hypocaust was found north of the cold bath. The drain carried away water to the west, which was the same direction followed by another conduit or drain[14] found to cross Rose Lane near its junction with St George's Street. This bath-house would

40   The bath building, St Margaret's Street, Canterbury (*S. S. Frere*)

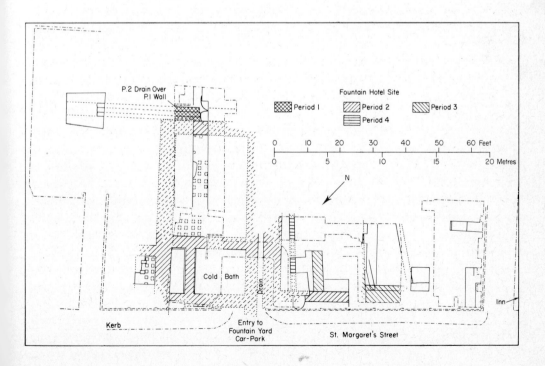

appear to date originally from the late first century, but considerable modifications were carried out towards the end of the second century.[15]

A bath-house of this magnitude, whether the main public baths or not, together with knowledge of other, smaller bath suites attached to private houses, implies the provision of an ample source of running water. As yet there is no indication of an aqueduct which may have fed this system, but, with hills surrounding Canterbury on almost every side, little difficulty would have been encountered in finding a suitable source. The most likely area would have been to the east or south-east, where springs are well known, and are responsible for the name Spring Lane just below St Martin's Hill.

A number of private houses were encountered during the post-war excavations, while others are perhaps indicated by earlier finds of mosaics. One house, which had replaced earlier timber buildings, was situated below Butchery Lane and probably extended out beneath the Parade. It seems to have had a front wing not quite parallel with the Roman street to its west, while other wings projected roughly eastwards from its ends. The earliest construction dates to the end of the first century. In the corner formed by the junction of the south and west wings, and against the internal corridor of the latter, a small room with a hypocaust had been constructed during alterations to the house, probably early in the second century; it may have been a part of a small bath suite. At a later date still, probably at the end of the third century, further alterations took place and it is possible that they then included the laying of tessellated floors in the internal corridor and in the large room of the north wing. The floor in the latter room contained three conventional mosaic panels.[16]

Other private houses have been found behind Martin's Bank in Rose Lane,[17] both north and south of the Marlowe Theatre, in the old Simon Langton School yard,[18] St George's Street opposite the church tower. None show much greater degree of sophistication than the Butchery Lane house. That by St George's Church had one wing terminated by a large room with an apse;[19] that south of the Marlowe Theatre had a room with a conventional mosaic.[20] Possibly the house attached to the bath suite (fig. 41) which now partly underlies Woolworths in St George's Street would have been larger and better furnished. The baths themselves consisted of a series of small rooms, arranged in a block, with small plunge baths attached. One larger room on the east side may have served as a changing room.[21] Although by the end of the first or early in the second century most of these houses had been built in masonry, some houses remained timber-framed throughout the Roman period, while others made use of solid clay walls, which were usually plastered and often painted. Walls of this type have also been observed in other towns, especially in the south-east, where there is a lack of good building stone. One timber-framed house is known to have existed just south of Burgate.[22] Constructed at first in the second century as two separate houses with an 8ft (2·4m) wide lane between them, it was later merged into a single building by extensions constructed across the lane. Occupation was here continuous throughout the Roman period. North of this building lay one of the

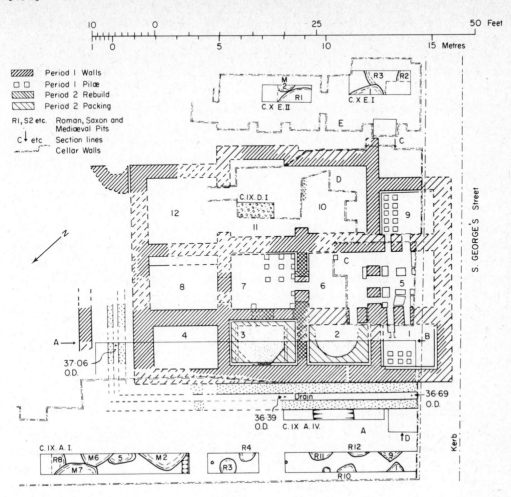

Period I Walls
Period I Pilœ
Period 2 Rebuild
Period 2 Packing
R1, S2 etc.   Roman, Saxon and Mediaeval Pits
C↓ etc   Section lines
Cellar Walls

41   The bath building, St George's Street, Canterbury (*S. S. Frere*)

main streets of the town, while north again an interesting masonry building was found.[23] In the late second century, this substantial building took the place of an earlier, demolished structure. The foundations of the walls suggest a width of at least 2ft 6in (762mm) to 3ft (914mm) and in one place a wall still stood to a height of 5ft (1·5m) where it had been masked by a later cellar wall. The two north corners had been provided with clasping buttresses. The foundations enclosed an area 35ft (10·6m) by 22ft (6·7m) and a slighter internal partition wall divided it, on an east-west line, approximately into two equal halves. A doorway existed in the southern external wall, and what may have been a portico, or walls flanking a flight of steps, appeared between this wall and the street, some 20ft (6m) further south. The building appears to have been completely isolated from any others. It could, of course, be a shop; but its substantial construction, which was matched by part of a thick concrete floor-foundation only surviving in the north-west corner, its isolated situation and its small size would suggest otherwise. For the same reason it is unlikely to have been a warehouse or a store. The excavator, Mrs Williams, tentatively suggested some type of public building, but it is difficult to see what purpose it could have fulfilled. One possibility might be a temple,[24] and the general form of the building can be matched elsewhere; other suggestions might include a *schola*, or guild-room. In either case a projecting apse could be envisaged on the north side where the building disappears under Burgate.

Apart from the building just discussed, no certain temples or churches have yet been found in Canterbury, although parts of a large altar were recovered from Mercery Lane. There is the possibility that St Martin's Church, outside the walled town, lies on the site of an earlier church mentioned by Bede[25] as being of Roman origin. A recent examination of some new evidence, however, suggests that Bede's church is more likely to have lain elsewhere.[26] The practice of Christianity at Canterbury is, nevertheless, implied by the small hoard of silver objects found near the town wall in Westgate Gardens. It contained spoons decorated with ☧ monograms.[27]

No attempt seems to have been made to erect fortifications around Canterbury until the later third century. A number of sections have now been cut on widely separated parts of the circuit and in all the bank was shown to be contemporary with the masonry wall in front. It is not yet clear why there should be a difference near the Castle, but it seems unlikely to have been connected with an earlier, free-standing rampart on a different alignment, as no sign of one has been found elsewhere. If the circuit of the wall and bank is entirely homogeneous, then the date of erection is provided by a coin of Tetricus I and supporting pottery from a section in Burgate Lane. A *terminus ante quem* for the construction is provided by a small hoard of coins, of early fourth century date, found in a pit cut through the tail of the rampart near St George's Street.[28] Elsewhere the line has been examined on both sides of the Riding Gate and in the Westgate Gardens.[29] It would seem that, when the wall was built, a fairly extensive suburb of the town on the west bank of the river Stour was excluded. Excavations in Whitehall Gardens have shown that, at one stage during the second century, the street grid extended over the river.[30] The erection of defences led to the virtual abandonment of the area for the safety provided by the new walls.

The walls enclosed an area of about 120 acres (48ha) in the form of a rather irregular octagon. The wall itself was about 7ft 6in (2·3m) thick, built of coursed flints and mortar, but with no tile bonding courses. The bank close to the Riding Gate was about 25ft (7·6m) wide and 7ft (2·1m) high, with a capping of gravel, which might suggest a rampart walk, although here we might expect the rampart top to be sloping downwards towards street level at the gate. The ditch system had been completely destroyed by the medieval recutting, as the late thirteenth century wall everywhere follows the line of the Roman defences. So far four gates leading into the Roman town have been identified: the London Gate in the Westgate Gardens at one end of Watling Street (fig. 21), the Riding Gate at the other end carrying the road to Dover (fig. 20), Worth Gate at the south end of Castle Street leading to Stone Street, and so to Lympne, and the Queningate carrying the Richborough Road from the area of the Cathedral precincts (fig. 21). Both the London Gate and the Queningate were blocked in the middle ages and replaced by medieval gates at Burgate, Newingate and Westgate. Two other possible gates should be considered. A Roman gate in the same position as the medieval Northgate would be needed to carry the road to Reculver. The medieval Westgate is often considered to overly the site of a Roman predecessor, chiefly on the grounds that a gate was known to exist before the Norman conquest. The inference that a masonry gate, just because it existed in late Saxon times, must have been built during the Roman period, is not perhaps quite so strong as it was. A masonry gate of late Saxon date has been found at South Cadbury,[31] and it is possible that the Westgate at Canterbury is so dated. Admittedly burials are known in the St Dunstan's area, as if a street ran out of the town in that direction. But most of them predate the construction of defences, and there seems no good reason to have an extra gate, in addition to the London Gate in this sector of the wall.

All the known gates, with the exception of the Riding Gate, appear to have been single, arched openings in the wall. The London Gate[32] was only 8ft (2·4m) wide. The rear approach was flanked by walls to retain the bank and these walls may also have supported a single tower above the entrance, as in similar gates at Brough-on-Humber, Silchester, Colchester and Caerwent. A large drain ran through the wall just north of the gate. The Riding Gate[33] had double carriage-ways set between flanking towers (pl. 39), each roughly 20ft (6·1m) square with internal guardrooms entered from the rear. The Worth Gate is shown as a single brick arch in eighteenth-century prints,[34] but excavations in the Castle grounds suggest flanking towers or inturns.[35] Some confirmation was obtained during trenching for a gas main in Castle Street when the trench ran along the east side of the entrance, revealing an inturn $15\frac{1}{2}$ft (4·7m) long. A recess with a tiled floor was situated between the front and back piers of the gate.[36] Part of the north and south jambs and the turn of a brick arch can still be seen embedded in the medieval masonry on the site of the Queningate (pl. 40), which, like the London Gate, appears to have had only a single portal.

Evidence obtained during the construction of the new East Kent Bus Station near St George's Street would imply the existence of a series of square, internal towers constructed with the curtain wall.[37] The tower found measured 16ft (4·8m) across at the rear and the back wall was about 17ft (5·2m) behind the front face of the curtain. External bastions have also been identified at Canterbury and such evidence as there is suggests that, either they were contemporary with the curtain wall, or else they had been carefully bonded with the face at a later date.[38]

An important point to consider, in connexion with the possible existence of an earlier circuit of earthwork fortifications on a different alignment, is the distribution of burials and cemeteries round the town. These tend to come close

39   Doorway in the rear wall of the east tower of the Riding Gate, Canterbury (*Entwhistle*)

to the walled circuit in several places, and in one or two even appear inside it. A cremation cemetery existed near the Castle, and should imply an earlier town boundary within that represented by the wall. The problem of the Dane John Mound arises in this context. It is reputed to be a burial-mound of a type constructed in Gaul and south-eastern Britain during the first and early second centuries, but it could equally be an early motte and bailey castle of Norman date, or even the one built over the other. Three other mounds formerly existed near it, one of which was also inside the wall. The implication is of an earlier boundary taking in a slightly smaller area on the south side of the town. This presumption is to some extent confirmed by the fact that, when the walls were built, an area of vacant ground on the east and south sides was enclosed and subsequently never built over, perhaps to make up for the excluded area on the west bank of the river. The new area was mainly used for the disposal of rubbish in innumerable pits.[39]

Other cemeteries have been identified in Lady Wooton's Green, not far from which was found a fragment of one of the few known Canterbury tombstones;[40] at Oaten Hill, near the Riding Gate; on St Martin's Hill, on the line of the Richborough road; along the Sturry Road beyond the Northgate; near Canterbury East Station, where an inhumation cemetery is known. One of the largest cremation cemeteries existed in the St Dunstans and Whitehall areas. Most of the burials came to light as chance finds and, in the absence of a systematic study, little can be deduced about the people who were buried.

Evidence for industries at Canterbury is fairly extensive. Brick, tile and pottery were manufactured near St Stephen's Road, where three kilns have been found. One pottery kiln was dated to the middle of the first century, the other and the tile kiln to the mid second century.[41] Other kilns making both tile and pottery have been found in Whitehall Gardens, and were in use from the middle second until the early third century.[42] Another pottery kiln was found during the

40   Queningate, Canterbury. The jambs and the turn of a brick arch are visible embedded in later masonry
(*J. S. Wacher*)

construction of an air-raid shelter near Dane John Gardens.[43] Chalk quarrying was carried out in an area near Stuppington Lane outside the town walls, and may have been connected with the provision of lime and flints for the construction of the latter, as an early fourth-century coin hoard had been buried in the quarry debris.[44] Metal-working was also carried on. Iron-smelting furnaces are suggested in Whitehall Gardens, not far from the pottery kilns mentioned above,[45] while traces of bronze-working of mid first-century date were found beneath the early surfaces of the Roman Watling Street not far from Riding Gate. A silversmith is perhaps indicated by the late fourth-century board of objects found near the town wall in Westgate Gardens.[46]

Commerce in the town is indicated by a possible granary or baker's shop near the junction of St Margaret's Street and the High Street, and by part of a large donkey-drive millstone, presumably also from a baker's shop, found near the White Friars Gate, south of St George's Street.[47]

The later history of some of the buildings already described is not without interest. The house behind Martin's Bank in Rose Lane underwent considerable alterations, and during the early fourth century a small bath wing was made in the south end. Use of the hypocausts continued well into the fifth century as one, at least, had been fired without proper maintenance until its pilae collapsed. Late fourth-century coins, including one of Arcadius, were found in the debris.[48] Another house nearby, under Rose Lane, was not so fortunate; it was burnt down in the late third century and not rebuilt.[49] The bath-house attached to a dwelling in St George's Street had continued in use down to *c.* AD 360 and numerous coins dating from 330 onwards had fallen into cracks and repairs in the floor of one of the rooms.[50] The Butchery Lane house bath wing ceased to be used by the middle of the fourth century, although parts of the building were inhabited for a decade or so later before it finally collapsed.[51] The house in the Simon Langton School yard also seems to have survived until the late fourth or early fifth century when some pits were dug through the floors. They contained some unusual late, hand-made, Romano-British pottery. Taken together, the history of these houses simply shows what might be expected: the fluctuating fortunes of individual householders, largely unaffected by external events until the final collapse of civic order in the fifth century. The comparative frequency with which private houses seem to have been provided with bath wings at Canterbury, in contrast to some other towns, points not only to the affluence of its inhabitants, but also to their continuing desire for town life in the later period, when many of the higher social classes were retiring to life in country villas. This contrast between Canterbury and some other towns is emphasised by the almost complete absence of villas in east Kent. Apart from those at Wingham, Margate and Folkestone,[52] slight traces of only three other possible villas are known. Yet farms of Belgic and Roman date were by no means uncommon if the general scatter of pottery over the countryside is taken as a guide. There is no reason why the country should have been any less populous after Claudius than it was in Caesar's day. Moreover, the theatre at Canterbury could probably have seated about 7000 spectators, only about half of whom we might expect to have been living in the town. The lack of villas might suggest, therefore, that much of the land, for a considerable distance around Canterbury, was either in the hands of little-romanised smallholders, or else mainly owned by dwellers in the town. The former seems inconceivable in an area which, for many years before the conquest, had been sampling romanisation, and which was later to become the part of Britain nearest to continental influences. The question was raised in Chapter 1 whether Canterbury had been promoted to a municipium, on the grounds that it lacked the tribal suffix to its name in the Antonine Itinerary. Clearly the suggestion that much of the surrounding countryside was owned by town-dwellers is not sufficient to press the case for a territorium any further. Nevertheless there can be no doubt about the high degree of romanisation in Canterbury. Other towns might have surpassed it in some respects, but in a more ostentatious manner. At Canterbury it would seem to have been accepted as quite normal and therefore nothing about which to make a great fuss and show. Perhaps the need for *aemulatio* was felt not to be quite so pressing, and so was applied more to public buildings than to private demonstrations of excessive romanity. This attitude is reflected in the confidence obviously felt at the end of the second century when Canterbury was almost the only town of any consequence in Britain not to have been given temporary defences. Therefore, it can hardly be argued that later insecurity was the cause behind the absence of villas in east Kent. The four Saxon Shore forts at Reculver, Richborough, Dover and Lympne must have provided ample protection for the Kentish peninsula. We can only conclude that the large majority of local landowners, from the first, preferred to live in the town and continued to do so until the last vestiges of civilised living collapsed about them in the fifth century.

The final decline of Durovernum was rapid compared with some other towns. Being the nearest major town to Gaul it was probably able to benefit from continuing commercial links after more distant towns had been cut off. In this respect it is worth remembering the exceedingly high proportion of coins of the late fourth and early fifth centuries at Richborough.[53] In consequence, when the collapse came, it was all the more sudden, since reasonable standards were probably maintained until the end. Certainly Canterbury seems to have been one of the first towns to have employed foederati for its protection, giving them land in exchange for their services, and forcing on them, at first, a degree of order and discipline. At Canterbury, these years are inextricably mixed up with the tradition of Vortigern, Hengist and Horsa. Vortigern apparently held sway from Wales, which shows that, even after the official Roman administration had broken down, some form of centralised control still existed. It was he who invited the first (?) Saxon settlers into Kent, offering land in return for military service. In so doing he was but continuing a policy which, long before, had been adopted in the Roman Empire for the settling of immigrants from central and northern Europe in frontier lands. Evidence perhaps for the earliest of the mercenaries, probably even earlier than those summoned by Vortigern, was found in excava-

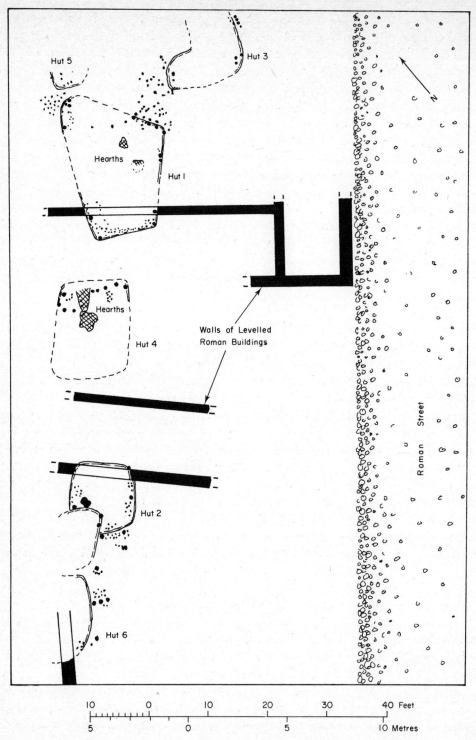

Hut 5

Hut 3

N

Hearths

Hut 1

Hearths

Hut 4

Walls of Levelled
Roman Buildings

Roman Street

Hut 2

Hut 6

10   0   10   20   30   40 Feet
5   0   5   10 Metres

42   Saxon huts in an insula under the old Simon Langton School yard, south-west of Rose Lane, Canterbury
(*after S. S. Frere*)

tions behind Martin's Bank, in Rose Lane, where a sherd of Anglo-Frisian pottery, dated to the early fifth century, turned up in the debris above a Roman house. In spite of this sherd there seems to have been little call for external help at Canterbury until the middle of the fifth century. So far none of the zoomorphic buckles or strap-ends associated with late fourth-century Roman soldiers has been found at Canterbury, although a number are known from Richborough.[54] Myres has also commented on the absence of early fifth-century material.[55] From about the middle of the century, however, Anglo-Frisian settlers were present. So far the huts built by these people have all been found in only one insula of the Roman town, lying to the east of the Marlowe Theatre. One hut was found in excavations for the new stage building of the theatre itself, while at the opposite end of the insula a row of six huts was found, slightly set back from, but nevertheless aligned on, the street which they bordered (fig. 42). The huts were usually sunk about 6 inches (152mm) to a foot (305mm) into the ground and cut through the ruins of an earlier Roman house. They were sub-rectangular in shape and the daub walls were erected on frames of posts and wattles. Some contained rudimentary hearths, and all were filled with the debris of their occupation, which included Roman coins, perhaps used as tokens. The distribution of these huts might suggest that at first these Saxons were given one insula, and that, although they were allowed to live as they pleased, some form of order was enforced, as demonstrated by the neat arrangement of the huts.[56] But this order did not last long and, within a decade or so, mutiny and rebellion had broken out among the foederati who, according to the Anglo-Saxon Chronicle, had, by AD 457, completely taken over the civitas Cantiacorum and its capital at Durovernum. Perhaps in these turbulent years was buried, just outside the town wall, in Westgate Gardens, the silver hoard, containing among other objects, eleven spoons and two silver ingots.[57] They show at least the continuing wealth of the inhabitants until the end, and at least a hope, which proved false, of better times to come, for the owner would hardly have buried them there unless he expected to recover them. At Canterbury, therefore, we can conclude that the end was abrupt, and that no Romano-British civilisation languished on into the fifth or even the sixth century, as may have happened at Verulamium or Cirencester.

CHELMSFORD (*Caesaromagus*)

The Roman settlement at Chelmsford is referred to by Rivet as being at Widford nearby. But the Moulsham suburb of the modern town, south of the rivers Chelmer and Can, is the most likely candidate, which must be distinguished from the imaginary town shown by Stukeley to lie beneath the cathedral and modern High Street.[58] Throughout this chapter, therefore, the Roman site is referred to as Chelmsford, so following the practice of the Victoria County History (*Essex* iii, 63).

The identity of this settlement with the *Caesaromagus* of routes V and IX of the Antonine Itinerary has long been recognised. What is still the subject of considerable argument, however, is the relationship between Caesaromagus and the tribe of the Trinovantes, and it is as well to summarise some of the more recent views here, before attempting to reach conclusions.

Some years ago Stevens drew attention[59] to the fact that the name *Caesaro-magus* is the only example in Britain of a type which, with variations, is not uncommon in Gaul. Usually a Celtic suffix is combined with an imperial name or title, such as Julio-, Caesaro-, Augusto-. He went on to point out that such names were normally given to new imperial foundations and were applied, almost invariably, to tribal capitals. Furthermore, he tentatively suggested that at some time the Trinovantes, or part of them, might have ceased to be attributi of the colonia at Colchester, and that a new town was founded as their capital. But he considered that, on the balance of probability, this possibility was unlikely. However, it should be emphasised that he was only considering a *later* separation of the tribal administration from the colonia. It does not seem to have occurred to him that the reverse may have been possible, with the tribe being attributed only after a period of independence.

Richmond suggested that, from the first, Trinovantians were included in the colonia as incolae.[60] Some incolae there certainly were, but perhaps not as many as Richmond envisaged, for we now know that the early colonia was probably only half the size of the later. Joyce Reynolds, while acknowledging Stevens in a slightly modified form, tentatively suggested that members of the tribe were attributi to the colonia, so retaining their identity but losing their independence. Such then are the views expressed so far.

What can be added? To begin with we must remember that, in Caesar's time, the Trinovantes had thrown in their lot with him against their powerful western neighbours, the Catuvellauni.[61] But to no avail, for Cunobelin later, not only conquered the tribe, but also planted his new capital in their territory. However, we may assume that Cunobelin's capital at Camulodunum did not coincide with the Trinovantian one, which probably lay nearer Gosbecks (p. 112). We might also expect that, by the time of the conquest, the tribal institutions of the Trino-vantes had been largely suppressed under Catuvellaunian domination. It is surprising therefore to find that they re-emerge after the conquest, unlike the four tribes mentioned by Caesar in Kent, who had been so completely submerged that they did not reappear. We might therefore suspect that the reason for the survival of the Trinovantian name and people was due to the remembrance in Rome of Caesar's treaty. In looking for a way in which to undermine the Catuvellaunian power in AD 43, it might have been politic for Claudius to invoke even a century old and out-dated treaty: divide and rule. It would simply have been copying in Essex what was happening in Sussex. The Catuvellauni were the main enemy of both Caesar and Claudius, and the Roman army was out to crush their power for good.[62] In AD 43, Trinovantian people who remembered Cunobelin's conquest only thirty years or so before would still have been alive, and we might suspect a fifth-column acting against Togodumnus and Caratacus

CHELMSFORD   (Caesaromagvs)   LATE FIRST TO THE EARLY FIFTH CENTURY.

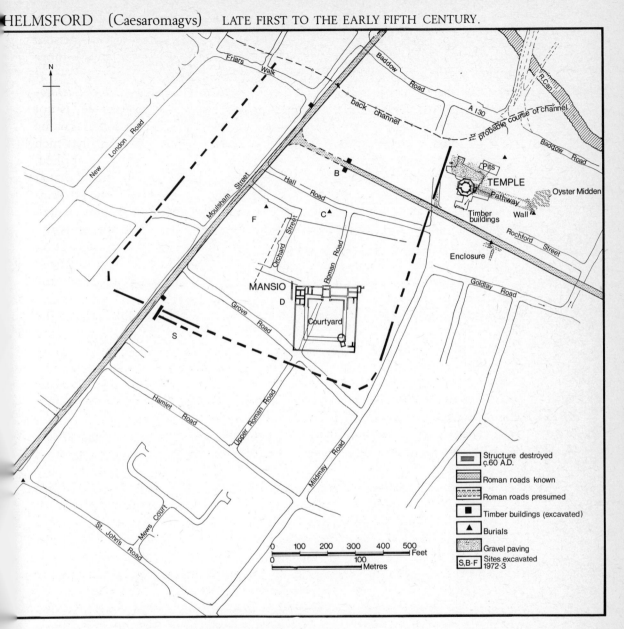

43   Plan of Chelmsford (*after P. J. Drury*)

once the Roman army had landed. A reminder of the part such men might play
is provided by the so-called 'whispering chiefs' on Trajan's column.[63] For the
Trinovantes who remembered their earlier conquest, the Catuvellauni were
probably more hated than the Romans.

In the situation outlined above we might expect that the Trinovantes would have been accorded rather better treatment than the Catuvellauni after the conquest, and the suggestion is strengthened by different treatment accorded to the Catuvellaunian capital of Camulodunum and to the suggested Trinovantian centre at Gosbecks. The former was completely reduced, while the latter emerged under Roman rule as a considerable place of pilgrimage. Then, into the calmed waters of the Trinovantian pond was dropped the stone of the new colonia; we cannot doubt that Gosbecks was included in the territorium. A magnanimous gesture on the part of the Roman administration would be called for to compensate a friendly tribe, and so the Trinovantes may have been provided with a new tribal centre at Chelmsford, with the grandiloquent name of *Caesaromagus*. But as we know, the Trinovantes would have none of it, and ultimately rose in rebellion against the loss of part of their tribal lands. It is more than possible that Gosbecks, at least, was restored to them as their chief religious centre, and that the administration was later centred on the colonia. Ptolemy, using mainly Flavian sources, refers to Colchester as the only town of the Trinovantes.[64] Although it is by no means certainly significant, the Antonine Itinerary refers to *Caesaromagus* instead of to *Caesaromagus Trinovantum*,[65] and in no other source is the tribal suffix added.

What of the site itself at Chelmsford? As will be seen from the description below, occupation was continuous from Claudian times until the end of the Roman period, yet, despite its name, the site never developed along the lines adopted by most civitas capitals. Colchester on one side and London on the other probably exerted so great an economic pull, that its development as a town was seriously hampered from Neronian times onwards. What prosperity it may have possessed probably came from traffic between the two main centres. Once the administrative function had passed from it, there was no real economic need for a major town here. We might count it then as a 'failed' town, with the tribe showing an independence, later to be matched by the Parisi at their capital at *Petuaria* (p. 397).

It will be appreciated that the foregoing explanation rests heavily on Stevens' original suggestion, but postulates an early foundation which failed, rather than a later emergence. As such it would seem to fit the known facts, even those of silence, rather better.

As a 'failed' town, it might be argued that it has no place in this book, in view of our definition in Chapters 1 and 2. But as a conjectural, early civitas capital, unencumbered by subsequent major developments, it is a site which should repay study for what it might tell us of similar early capitals, about which all too little is known.

No evidence for a pre-conquest native settlement of any size has yet been found, although there is one at Little Waltham, about 3 miles (4·8km) north. The main Roman settlement lies between Moulsham Street and Mildmay Road and north-east of St John's Road (fig. 43). Moulsham Street is approximately on the line of the main road from London to Colchester. An early fort has been identi-

fied by Drury in the area south-east of the main London–Colchester road and in
the vicinity of its junction with a minor road. It should not be confused with the
ditch mentioned in V.C.H. as being just north of the 'mansio',[66] which is best
interpreted as a drain. Apart from a general scatter of Claudian coins, pottery
and some military equipment, nothing else is known about the first occupation.
It is unlikely that the fort would have been occupied for any length of time, so it
would not have attracted to itself an extensive vicus. That being so, it is all the
more probable that what came after the abandonment of the fort was a deliberate,
artificial creation. However, the Boudiccan rebellion changed the course of events.
Immediately after it had subsided, another fort was established on a different site,
slightly further south but again south-east of the main road, which remained in
use until well into the Flavian period. Doubtless the rebellion had effectively
removed any members of the tribe who might later have exercised control.

It has been claimed that a raised platform lying roughly between Hall Road
and Hamlet Road and bounded by Moulsham Street on the north-west marks the
site of a walled vicus. But excavation in 1968–72 has shown that there is no substance in the claim. A clay rampart, fronted by a ditch, 10ft (3m) deep, and by a
second, later ditch, has been found some distance north-west of Moulsham

44   Octagonal temple, Chelmsford (*P. J. Drury*)

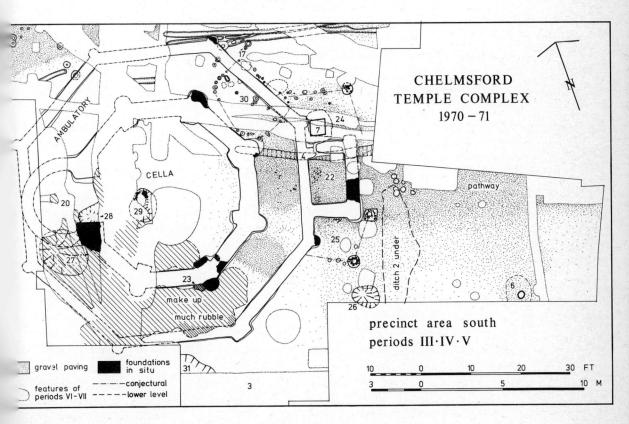

Street, where it runs in a south-westerly direction before turning a corner towards the south-east. Other sections have been revealed close to Moulsham Street and south of the 'mansio'. It appears to date to the late second century, although, not long after its construction, it was levelled and the ditches filled. At no time does a masonry wall seem to have been constructed on the same alignment, and if one existed it must be sought elsewhere. By the time the site was fortified it was probably no longer the civitas capital. Consequently, it is wrong to compare the area enclosed within the defences with the areas of other civitas capitals as has been done in V.C.H. *Essex* iii, as by then it was probably little different from other fortified villages, with which a truer comparison can be made.

Nevertheless, despite its later history, there is slight evidence for more splendid beginnings, which were better in keeping with its prospective status as a new town founded in the Roman manner. A major building, probably part of a baths, lay in the area between Roman Road and Mildmay Road. In 1849, Chancellor uncovered a circular laconicum and part of another heated room of probable pre-Boudiccan date. It is not yet possible to assess the full extent of the building, since it no longer appears to be related to the baths found by Brinson in 1947–9,[67] which were on different alignments. Excavations in 1973 have shown that the earliest baths were probably destroyed by Boudicca, and that they were replaced, first by a more extensive timber building and then by a masonry building, with almost identical plans. Both probably acted as a mansio. The timber building has been provisionally dated to *c.* AD 65–75 and the masonry reconstruction to *c.* AD 125–50. The baths found by Brinson lie at the north-east corner and the whole building appears to measure approximately 214ft (65m) by 217ft (66m), with an internal courtyard.[68] It might be suggested that the pre-Flavian baths were to do with the establishment of the civitas capital. Equally, the building might be explained as the residence of a Trinovantian noble, who had been rewarded for his services to the Romans.

In 1970, excavations just north of Rochford Road uncovered a Romano-Celtic temple with an interesting plan (fig. 44). It was octagonal in shape, not unlike those at Pagan's Hill and Caerwent,[69] with the angles of both cella and portico buttressed by thickenings of the walls. An apse projected from the back wall of the cella outwards across the rear portico, opposite what was presumably the door, and would have provided accommodation for the main cult figures. A porch was situated on the south-east side of the portico. Unfortunately, most of the masonry had been robbed, and little else of the structure survived. A gravel path led towards the temple from the south-east, and there were traces of earlier, flimsier buildings in the temenos. The date of construction was *c.* AD 325 and the coin evidence suggests continuing use into the fifth century if not longer.[70]

Traces of other buildings are known from behind Moulsham Street, with huts and occupation dating from the first to the fourth centuries.[71] Yet others, also of timber construction, and of late first to fifth century date, have been excavated on the frontages of Moulsham Street and the principal side road. A serious fire, from which the settlement did not recover for nearly a hundred years, took place

41 Jet ornaments from a burial, Chelmsford: (a) a Medusa head; (b) a lion devouring a human skull
(*Chelmsford Excavation Committee, Crown Copyright—reproduced with permission of the Controller of Her Majesty's Stationery Office*)

towards the end of the second century.[72] This may have been the reason why no masonry fortifications appear to have been provided.

A fair-sized cemetery is known to have existed along Moulsham Street from about St John's Church to Oaklands Park. Cremation burials have been found, but inhumations appear to have disintegrated in the acid soil. One interesting burial contained a collection of jet objects (pl. 41a, b).

It will be seen from the foregoing account that, apart from the mansio and its bath building, there is little to warrant the conclusion that *Caesaromagus* became a town of any consequence. It may have started as a civitas capital as the result of a piece of deliberate planning, but the plan obviously failed. It might be argued that the Trinovantes, like their northern neighbours, were so impoverished by the Boudiccan rebellion that the development of a capital, even on the modest lines of Caistor-by-Norwich, was beyond their means. Even if it is argued that the administrative centre remained there, there is no justification in seeing either in its name or in the subsequent development anything other than an urban failure.

ST ALBANS (*Verulamium*)

The Belgic site of *Verlamion* covered a large area. It was the sometime capital of Tasciovanus, and, even after about AD 10 when Camulodunum was founded, it remained a principal settlement of the Catuvellauni. Wheeler concluded that its centre was in Prae Wood,[73] after his series of excavations at Wheathampstead and Verulamium between 1930–4. Frere's more recent excavations between 1955–61 have, however, enabled this view to be expanded, and it is now apparent that the Belgic settlement had spilled over the Prae Wood hillside into the valley of the river Ver beneath. Quantities of broken moulds, used in the manufacture of metal flans for coinage, have been found extending almost as far as the river in an area which was later to lie north and west of the forum of the Roman town.[74] Moreover in 1956, a ditch, at least 12ft (3·7m) wide and over 5ft (1·5m) deep, was encountered below Roman buildings during excavations in Insula XXVII.[75] It was running not quite parallel with the north–west side of the later forum and changed direction towards the south–east not far from its west corner. The bottom levels contained only Claudian pottery. Other excavations in the Museum car park and under the Museum itself might suggest continuations of this ditch so as to enclose an area slightly larger than, but approximately in the same position as, the Flavian forum. It is difficult to avoid a conclusion that this ditch had been dug in the pre-conquest period and that it was kept clean until shortly after the conquest, when rubbish began to accumulate in it. Frere has suggested that it may have enclosed a palace area, in view of its close proximity to the mint debris.[76] Another, perhaps more likely, possibility is that the ditch surrounded a sacred enclosure, similar to, but larger than, the one at Gosbecks Farm, Colchester

(p. 112). If so, it would certainly partly explain the later use of this area as the premier insula of the new town. In this respect the Catuvellauni, in spite of being ejected by the Romans from their political capital at Camulodunum, would have been more fortunate than the Trinovantes, if they were able to retain one of their chief religious sanctuaries, whereas the latter lost theirs, for a time, to the colonia at Colchester.

In view of what happened at Verulamium after the conquest, it is probably convenient to consider that it had been the oppidum of Adminius before his expulsion from Britain by his father, Cunobelin, in AD 40. We might conclude that Adminius was expelled either for openly expressed philo-Roman opinions, or for not supporting the hardening anti-Roman outlook of his brothers. Whatever the reason for his expulsion, his travels in Gaul or Italy would have given him experience of romanised provincial towns and buildings. It seems more than likely that he and his followers would have returned to their native lands after the invasion, where they would have been instrumental in initiating the process of romanisation at Verulamium. So we might explain the rapid progress in urban development which then took place, and possibly also the readiness with which military architects were made available to help in the work. Only an ally of some standing would probably have received such benefits, which would have been in the nature of a reward for services rendered to the imperial government. We know more of another returning refugee than we do of Adminius, but there is no reason to believe that the followers of Verica and Cogidubnus were the only ones to be restored to their homelands after the invasion, and such men would have greatly aided the conquest and subsequent pacification. What happened at Catuvellaunian Verulamium is therefore in direct contrast with what happened at Catuvellaunian Camulodunum. The latter was deprived of all political responsibility with typical Roman thoroughness and thereafter was of no consequence, while control of the remainder of the tribe was placed firmly in allied hands. These are, of course, hypothetical arguments, but they provide the best explanation for such facts as we have. They also help to account for the very short military occupation of what was, according to literary accounts, the most hostile and powerful of the south-eastern tribes.

At Verulamium itself, this occupation does not seem to have continued for more than a year or two, judging from the evidence of the first buildings of the town, which were being constructed not later than *c.* AD 49.[77] A small fort had been occupied for a short time close to the river Ver, in the area later to become Insulae XVII and XIX. On the north-west side, its bank had later become buried beneath the town rampart, which was here contemporary with the stone fortifications.[78] A twin-portal gateway of timber has been identified on its north-east side, close to the river Ver, where it was partly cut into by the later town wall.[79] The position of the fort accounts for the course of Watling Street on its approach from London, a line which was perpetuated in the street system of the town. While the military detachment could have been connected with the road works themselves, its placing at Verulamium might also have been deliberate to ensure adequate support for Adminius. Once it had been seen that all was quiet the unit would have been withdrawn.

The first steps in the construction of the Claudian town began shortly after military occupation had ceased. If we are right in assuming the return of Adminius, then the emergence of the civitas Catuvellaunorum will have been one of those cases in Britain where little distinction can be drawn between the pre- and post-military situations, for the military were primarily there to bolster the civil power and not to supercede it. Certainly Verulamium would seem to have started as the civitas capital. Whether it was now, or later, that promotion to municipium came has already been discussed (p. 18): it is not necessary to repeat the arguments. Suffice it to say that the civitas Catuvellaunorum continued a corporate existence as implied by inscriptions found on Hadrian's Wall,[80] and it is likely that Verulamium, whether a municipium or not, will have remained as the tribal capital. If the town was a municipium it might be suggested that its territorium consisted of that part of the tribal area in the south-east which was early released from military occupation, and that the tribal identity was maintained by the northern and north-western parts which were probably not so released until Flavian times.

Contrary to what Wheeler thought[81] and Collingwood embellished,[82] Frere has now shown[83] that many of the streets in the pre-Boudiccan town date back to Claudius' principate and that regular town-planning was then taking place (fig. 45). Moreover the buildings being erected at the same time, although simple in plan and structure were of better quality than Collingwood's 'mud huts'. Wheeler found little more than traces of Claudian occupation in the southern quarter of the town, while further traces have been found by other excavators north of the forum insula. Of considerable importance therefore, for the town's early history, was the uncovering by Frere of the block of timber-framed shops, dating to *c.* AD 49 in the east corner of Insula XIV.[84] He concluded that these shops had been erected, perhaps as a corporate enterprise, by some wealthy Catuvellaunians. Certainly their arrangement means a continuous roof span with the ridge running from south-east to north-west, so implying single or group ownership at the time of building.[85] The starkness of the plan (fig. 49), in spite of the external portico, led Frere to suggest that they were erected with help from military architects and with access to military supply-bases for materials. This would seem to fit the circumstances. Nevertheless a slight degree of individuality in some sections would suggest that local taste and requirements were being consulted and that the whole was not the exclusive work of the army. Most of the shops, possibly leased to tenants, or perhaps sold to worthy retainers, seem to have been engaged in the manufacture of metalwork. Bronzesmiths were active in the shop represented by rooms 24 and 25.

The new town was apparently defended from the beginning by a bank and ditch, which enclosed an area of 119 acres (48ha), although it is probable that the fortifications were not continued along the river frontage. They were first discovered in 1955 below buildings in Insula xx and the line was subsequently traced by excavation and magnetometer survey round the west and north-west

VERULAMIUM.   Julio-Claudian

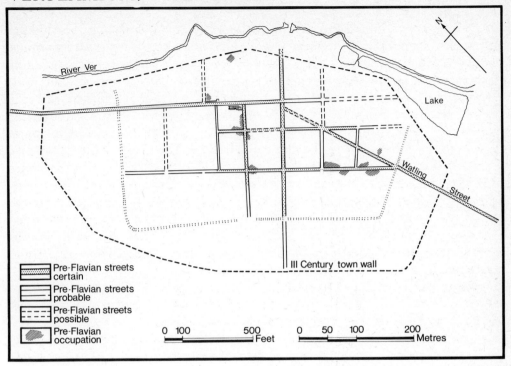

River Ver

Lake

Watling Street

N

Pre-Flavian streets
certain

Pre-Flavian streets
probable

Pre-Flavian streets
possible

Pre-Flavian
occupation

III Century town wall

0 100   500
Feet

0   50   100   200
Metres

45   Plan of Claudian Verulamium (*after S. S. Frere*)

sides and also towards the south. The places where it crossed the line of Watling
Street were marked in the late second or early third century by two triumphal
arches (p. 215 below), which presumably commemorated the earliest town
boundary and showed, on the part of the inhabitants, a keen awareness of their
civic history and legal rights. They provide perhaps the most cogent reason for
belief in a Claudian municipium. It is not easy to explain why a bank and ditch
were needed. The ditch was nearly 9ft (2·7m) deep and 20ft (6·1m) wide and
seems too large to have been simply a boundary delimitation. It is probably best
seen, therefore, as a defensive circuit, and it should not be forgotten that Silchester
was also early provided with defences (p. 256), although this town may have lain
within the kingdom of Cogidubnus. Perhaps it was felt that some sort of protection was needed for those burgeoning centres of romanisation which were situated
not far from frontier regions. It would have been a comparatively easy matter for
small raiding parties to have slipped through the type of frontier then in being,
and created havoc in the principal towns.[86]

One of the main problems relating to the pre-Boudiccan town is the forum or
possible lack of one. Frere has suggested that the insula occupied by the Flavian
forum was sub-divided by a through-street in the Claudian town,[87] and that a

more modest forum and basilica was situated in the north-eastern of the two insulae so formed. Another possibility arises out of excavations conducted by
William Page early this century, when he found masonry foundations below the
Flavian forum near its south-west side.[88] In this context it is important to remember the pre-conquest ditched enclosure which coincided very closely with
the area of the Flavian forum, suggesting that from the first both insulae were
devoted to public use for religious, commercial or administrative purposes. It is
possible also that, by creating an expectation of a Claudian forum and basilica,
we are needlessly complicating the issue. If the site was primarily of religious
significance, priority was presumably given to building a new temple. Moreover
the age of the monumental, unified complex of forum, basilica and sometimes
capitolium had not yet reached Britain, and had by no means spread universally
elsewhere.[89] Most of those in existence by the time of Claudius had been the
result of piecemeal and irregular development. Was there at Verulamium, therefore, a temple, a basilica, or even perhaps only a curia and an open space which
served for a forum? A similar first-century combination may have existed at
Alesia before the unified complex was constructed during the second century.[90]
Although often referred to as Gallic in form, there is an even stronger central
Italian feeling about the Flavian forum at Verulamium, where the curia and
offices of the magistrates were separated from the basilica, so that the comparison is probably only justified for the earliest postulated development. Indeed,
we might go so far as to suggest that at the first stage the forum was based on the
double courtyard type of Gaul, with a street separating one part from the other.
But further speculation is not profitable in the absence of more information.

    The first town perished at the hands of Boudicca's hordes, which even the
defences were powerless to stop. Evidence for the fire has come from numerous
places within the town. It seems likely that the rebellion had far-reaching effects.
One may have been a general disheartening and loss of morale among the survivors, for rebuilding only took place slowly. They had relied on Roman arms
for protection and Rome had failed them. Some may well have lost all their
wealth and possessions, making it difficult to raise funds for new buildings,
especially in view of the pre-Boudiccan hardening financial attitude of Roman
moneylenders. Shortage of capital would be aggravated by loss of profits from
destroyed workshops and business premises. Whole families may have been wiped
out, leaving no heirs, so causing delay and legal disputes over land ownership.
While the governors immediately after the rebellion were concerned with
pacification, they seem to have done little to help mitigate the hardship which
had been caused. But the firmer hand employed by the Flavian governors may
have brought renewed confidence in the province, and, as so often is the case,
capital investment follows confidence, just as it flees from crisis. Certainly at
Verulamium the shops in Insula XIV were rebuilt *c.* AD 75 on similar but less rigid
lines than before and using the same methods of construction. It is interesting,
though, to observe that many of the shops were again inhabited by
metalworkers.[91]

Immediately west of these shops, in Insula XVI, a new Romano-Celtic temple had been constructed by the end of the first century. It was of conventional plan and placed centrally in a rectangular temenos, enclosed during the early second century by a buttressed wall. Entry to the temenos was gained through a gate centrally placed in the north-east wall.[92] It is not known if there was an earlier temple on the site, although it seems probable. Certainly the area north-east of the temenos was an open space at the time of the Boudiccan fire,[93] and its evident association with the temple is marked by the construction there of the theatre in the second century (p. 210). Of about the same date as the temple was the large macellum (fig. 10) constructed on the opposite side of Watling Street. The association of temple and theatre is well known, but the association of temple and market place is less often emphasised, at any rate in towns, even though they are well known in country districts.[94] It may be that the construction of the macellum in this particular place at Verulamium was quite deliberate. If so, we might hazard a guess that the temple, situated on the fringe of the main commercial quarter of the town, was dedicated, either singly or jointly, to Mercury, god of trade and commerce. The sanctity of the site was sufficient to draw large crowds, which later justified the construction of a theatre. The temple seems to have been used after the theatre was derelict.[95]

The principal buildings constructed in the Flavian period were undoubtedly the forum and basilica (fig. 53). It is so far exceptional for Britain in having the curia and magistrates' offices separate from the basilica. As already indicated above, the forum piazza may have contained a temple, but no precise evidence has yet been produced.[96] Various excavations have been carried out from time to time, the earliest being those of Page in 1898–1902, the latest by Frere in 1956. In 1955, fragments of an inscription were found near one of the entrances to the basilica, below St Michael's School yard, which dated its completion to the last six months of AD 79.[97] Construction work on the whole complex, which measures approximately 530ft (161m) by 385ft (117m) overall, was therefore probably started in the early seventies. The site, to begin the description at the north-east end, contained first a range of rooms, about 27ft (8·2m) wide, running the full length of the basilica. Access through them was gained by two entrances placed symmetrically in the frontage on Watling Street. It was outside the northern of the two entrances that the inscription fragments were found. It is not, however, clear from which side these rooms were entered; if they conform to the normal range of offices usually situated behind the basilica, then they were most likely entered from it. There is, nevertheless, an abnormality in the plan at this point, and it would seem that they were separated from the north-east aisle first by a colonnade or portico and then by an open space. It is difficult to explain the arrangement of the known longitudinal walls in any other way. But allowing for this colonnade in front of the rooms and the open space beyond, the remaining parallel walls, if contemporary, which has not yet been proved by excavation, would have formed a basilica of conventional plan, about 120ft (36·5m) wide externally. The main nave would have been approximately 60ft (18·2m) wide

VERULAMIUM.   Late Flavian

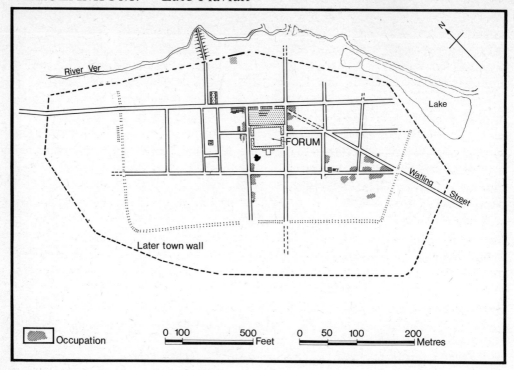

46   Plan of late-Flavian Verulamium (*after S. S. Frere*)

and the side aisles about 30ft (9·1m), so giving roughly the 2:1 ratio between the widths of nave and aisle usually found in these buildings. With dimensions of 385ft (117m) by 120ft (36·5m) the basilica at Verulamium was larger than that at Cirencester and in Britain next only to London in size. The forum was a rectangular piazza about 310ft (94m) by 205ft (62m) enclosed by a single colonnaded ambulatory, 26ft (7·9m) wide, on all four sides including that bounded by the basilica. The two entrances to the court were placed centrally in the short sides, an arrangement rare in Britain, where a single entrance more often occurs in the side opposite the basilica. The south-west side, as first planned, contained only one group of buildings. In the middle was a large hall, 62ft (18·9m) by 40ft (12·2m), flanked on either side by shallower rooms, 15ft (4·6m) by 39ft (11·8m), both of which had been provided with an apse, 15ft (4·6m) in diameter, on the long side. Page considered that the apses were later additions.[98] It is possible that the hall also terminated in an apse, although Page was not able to decide the point. Each of the three rooms had doorways leading on to the forum colonnade, and there were intercommunicating doors between them. Tessellated floors were also found in all three rooms, and the floor of the central hall was about 2ft (610mm) higher than those of the rooms on either side. The walls seem to have been plastered and painted. It is probably correct to conclude that the central hall was the curia or council chamber of Verulamium, and that the flanking rooms were respectively the offices of the duoviri and the aediles, with tribunals being situated in the apses. A somewhat similar arrangement, although on a larger scale, can be seen in the forum of the Dalmatian town of *Asseria*,[99] and seems ultimately to be derived from the central Italian style of forum.[100]

Not a great deal is known about the private houses at this stage of the town's development (fig. 46). Wheeler found three small houses in the west corner of Insula III, and part of another in Insula II.[101] Frere found one in Insula XXVIII.[102] The absence of the large houses of the curial class, which are so easily distinguished by the middle of the second century, is interesting. It tends to show, perhaps, that money was not unlimited, and that what was available was being channelled in public works. If so, it would seem to illustrate a public-spirited attitude on the part of the leading citizens, who put aside personal ostentation for the benefit of their town. Certainly until the Antonine period, the town houses were modest, mainly timber-framed structures, with earth or timber floors, only rarely relieved by concrete or mortar. Nevertheless the walls were usually plastered and painted in simple patterns on the inside, while the roofs were often tiled. Neither is it always possible to distinguish at this early stage between buildings of purely

47   Plan of late-Antonine Verulamium (*after S. S. Frere*)

VERULAMIUM.   Late Antonine

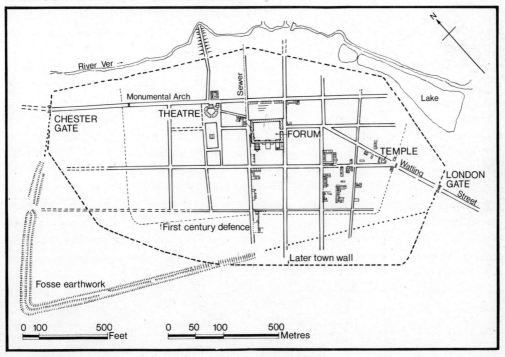

domestic character and those which combined living arrangements with commerce, as both have features in common.

The early second century saw an increase in the number of religious establishments in the town, with an unusually shaped temple built close to the London Gate.[103] The site, in the angle formed by Watling Street and the street separating Insula I from VI, was shaped like a truncated triangle, with the apex facing the gate. A short length of street passed to the rear of the building, so that it was completely isolated. The outer walls were protected from traffic by a row of wooden bollards. The temple itself had a central court which reflected the external shape. The long sides of the court had covered porticoes, while across the base was a range of three compartments, the central one of which probably contained a statue of a deity. The other two contained tanks. Bases for altars or possibly statues were found in the court, and the main entrance, probably with a projecting portico, faced the town gate. A chalk foundation some little distance in front of the entrance may have been for additional altars.[104] Wheeler suggested that the temple was dedicated to Cybele.

This temple lay in an area which saw a good deal of development during the late first and early second centuries. By about AD 100 the town defences were becoming obsolete, the ditch was partly filled with rubbish and the bank slighted into it. Yet its line had probably affected extra-mural development on the London side of the town, where two streets, cutting across Watling Street, were set parallel to the defences and not with the internal street grid. Indeed the second century, once the confines of defences had been broken, was a period of almost uncontrolled development: to the second half of the century belonged the theatre, and the forum temples, while more opulent and better-built houses became commoner. Nevertheless this picture of uniform prosperity was seriously marred by a disastrous fire in the town *c.* AD 155 which, however, may have assisted development by clearing away old buildings. Since almost all private houses and shops were still timber-framed structures, the fire must have spread rapidly and Frere has estimated that at least 52 acres (21ha) were consumed.[105] But circumstances had changed since the Boudiccan fire and the sluggishness which followed it. There must have been sufficient accumulated capital for rebuilding to have started almost at once, and this was apparent not only in the private sector but also in public works. Some slight changes in the town plan can also be discerned such as the new street which was driven obliquely through Insula XIV from the forum to the theatre, and another between Insulae XVII and XIX. Then it was that the theatre and the forum temples were probably constructed. Changes were also made in the methods of construction of private houses, giving rise to a combination of masonry and solid clay walls, which were altogether more fireproof.

The theatre was constructed in an open space immediately north-east of the temple in Insula XVI, referred to above (p. 207). As first constructed it was of Romano-Celtic plan (fig. 13), with a near-circular orchestra, almost 80ft (24·3m) in diameter. The outer wall, which was buttressed to help retain the gravel banks for the seating, inscribed a diameter of about 150ft (46m). Three vaulted entrances, arranged symmetrically about the axes led through the cavea into the orchestra, which could when necessary be used as an arena. The stage building which projected to the rear of the orchestra barely interrupted the curve of its wall, although at one point there were indications of wooden steps leading up to the stage, which was itself floored with planks. It has been suggested that a series of mortar foundations, which lay between the back of the stage-building and Watling Street, were for an arcaded screen along the street.[106] A wooden water-pipe was traced for a short distance, running round the outside wall on the south side, while a vaulted drain led out from the orchestra on the north side of the stage. It is hardly likely that these imply the flooding of the orchestra, or arena, and the staging of ambitious nautical displays, but it is not impossible that some sort of grotto or shrine, with a fountain or running water, was included in the building.[107] In any case the life of these features was short, as they were demolished during the first alterations to the theatre later in the century. Nevertheless, the orchestra contained near its centre an upright pole anchored to a heavy cross-shaped base plate. Its function is not entirely certain, but animals, or even convicts awaiting execution, might have been chained to it.

Within about twenty years the theatre was radically altered. The stage was enlarged by pushing the front wall forwards so that it became a chord of the orchestra. New access to the seating was obtained by timber staircases, rising in the thickness of the banks, from the outer ends of the lateral entrances. The new stage was also provided with a proscaenium of the Corinthian order, although it still had a plank floor. In the orchestra, the whole of the area behind the lateral entrances was covered with a wooden platform for extra seats, presumably for civic dignitaries. Other changes saw the demolition of the arcaded screen along Watling Street and the addition of what may have been a dressing room near the east corner of the stage. In many ways the changes incorporated foreshadowed future alterations, which all tended to make the theatre nearer to the true classical plan (fig. 13), and more suitable for dramatic spectacles.

The two temples which were added at about the same time to the south-west side of the forum, on either side of the curia, gave it an even more archaic, italianate appearance than it had before.[108] The temples were not identical buildings. That near the south corner was excavated by Page and contained a single large room, 64ft (19·4m) by 34ft (10·3m) internally. The walls were massive: 8ft 6in (2·6m) thick. The rear of the temple was marked by a pair of parallel walls 6ft (1·8m) apart and a central, raised apse appears to have been constructed partly within their combined thicknesses. Two plinths projected into the forum ambulatory on either side of the front of the building. Page concluded, from the width of the walls and from curved fragments of painted plaster, that the building had been vaulted. The interior was decorated, over both walls and vault, by frescoes with floral designs, and the floor was tessellated, with a mosaic at its centre. Fragments of statues were also found.[109] Along the south-eastern side of the temple and separated from it by a narrow alley was another building,

VERULAMIUM. Fourth-Century

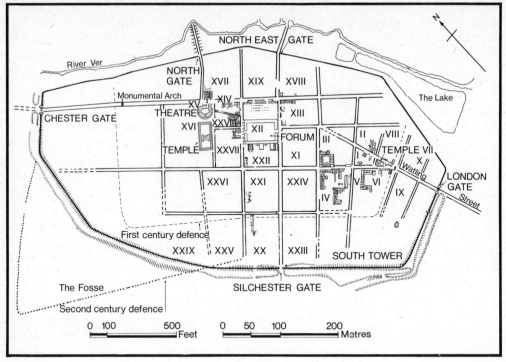

48   Plan of fourth-century Verulamium (*after S. S. Frere*)

but neither its date nor function are known. It was not matched by an equivalent building at the west corner. Perhaps it was the tabularium.

The temple at the west corner was excavated by Wheeler in 1949.[110] Although its internal dimensions were approximately the same it differed in plan at its rear end and in the methods used in its construction. Owing to the ditch of the pre-Roman enclosure running beneath, it was constructed over a series of raised vaults, each cross wall between the vaults being further strengthened by external buttresses. To the rear of the temple, however, in place of an apse, were two rectangular rooms. The first was less wide than the temple and the second, which led from it, was narrower still, and together they probably served as the shrine for the cult statue. It is likely that, when these two temples were built, the colonnade of the forum ambulatory in front of them was extensively modified to provide an elaborate architectural screen in which the front porticoes of the temples and also of the curia were merged. Access from the ambulatories at each end was restricted by doorways placed across them.[111]

Another public building to undergo modifications in the later second century was the market hall opposite the theatre.[112] It was reduced to almost half of its original size and rebuilt in a more massive manner. The front was also given a more impressive facade, perhaps to match the short-lived arcade of the theatre opposite.

It is difficult within the compass of this short account, to do individual justice to each private house in late second-century Verulamium. Most followed the spreading pattern of typical Romano-British town-houses, with two, three or even four wings arranged around a courtyard (or garden?). One large quadrangular house in the west corner of Insula III occupied an area approximately 150ft (46m) by 165ft (49m). Some of the main rooms had hypocausts, which the new methods of construction now allowed, and a high proportion had tessellated or mosaic floors. Another, in the centre of Insula IV, was likewise a house of some refinement and size, with a number of heated rooms in one wing which may have been part of a small bath suite. The rooms contained some fine-quality mosaics, including one with sixteen different geometrical panels and another with a head of Neptune, situated next door to a well-house. This well, however, although sunk to a depth of 38ft (15m), remained unfinished and had shortly afterwards been deliberately filled. The former mosaic can still be viewed in situ; the latter is in the museum.[113] In Insula XXI, Frere found another good-class house with three wings. It was remarkable as being the first house in Britain to provide evidence for a painted and plastered ceiling, as well as having frescoes on its walls. Indeed, its excavation marks one of the first attempts in this country to recover and restore large areas of painted plaster.[114] One room also contained a fine mosaic, now on view in the museum, which had a central panel depicting a lion carrying a stag's head in its mouth.

Nevertheless there were some exceptions to this picture of late second-century prosperity. The timber-framed shops, in the east corner of Insula XIV, had been rebuilt no less than three times after their reconstruction following the Boudiccan fire (p. 204). In each case the sill-beams had probably rotted and had required replacement. The shops themselves had also gradually extended rearwards. In the final phase (fig. 50), only a few years before the Antonine fire, they were still primarily occupied by metalworkers and both bronzesmiths' and a goldsmith's workshops have been identified.[115] After the fire, *c*. AD 155, however, they were not rebuilt and the site was apparently left empty until the late third century. Frere has suggested that it was retained for a public building which never materialised. On the other hand, if these shops had gradually turned from the original tenancies to owner-occupied premises, then it is possible that such men, in a small way of business, would have most of their capital tied up in them, so that rebuilding would have been difficult.

Towards the very end of the second century work was started on new fortifications for the town, in common with many others in Britain (p. 75). It is possible, however, that Verulamium is one of those where the work was begun in stone, with construction of the London and Chester Gates preceding by a short time the erection of the earth rampart.[116] Excavation is still required to prove the point. The Fosse earthwork, which Wheeler originally attributed to the Flavian period, has now been shown to belong to the late second century. Frere has also shown that it remained incomplete,[117] which is the best reason for considering that the two gates mentioned above, if indeed they belonged to the same general period, were constructed before the earthwork, and were not added to it. It would have been senseless to have *added* gates to an incomplete circuit and such gates can have been no part of emergency measures. The Fosse itself has been traced from just west of the Chester Gate, round an acute-angled west corner, and as far as Bluehouse Hill. It might be suspected also of having run beneath the later internal masonry tower, 228ft (70m) west of the London Gate, where Wheeler records a marked depression in the so-called 'natural ground surface'.[118] The full width of the bank was more than 50ft (15·2m), and it stood more than 7ft (2·1m) high. Like most civilian fortifications of this type and date it appears to have been of glacis construction, although a turf wall was embedded in it near its peak. The ditch was about 50ft (15·2m) wide and about 18ft (5·5m) deep. A slight counterscarp bank lay beyond the ditch. It would seem that the very scale of the work defeated the aims of its constructors. As an emergency measure, it is probable that the danger had passed before its circuit was completed.

A few decades later, work on fortifications was resumed, but now a masonry wall, 7ft (2·1m) wide on a 9ft 9in (3m) wide foundation, was constructed with a bank, measuring from 45ft (13·7m) to 50ft (15·2m) wide, behind it. But the line was not the same as that followed by the Fosse. A large section in the west quarter was now left outside the wall, and it is difficult to see why it should have ever

49   Claudian shops (Period I) in Insula XIV, Verulamium (*S. S. Frere*)

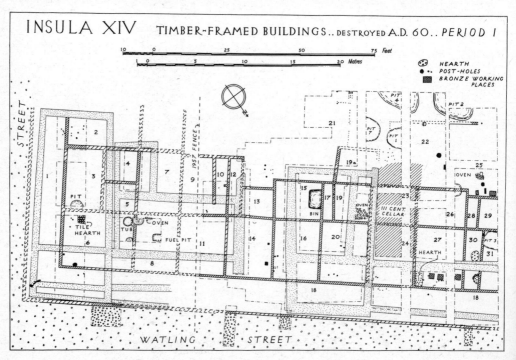

been enclosed by the earlier earthwork. No systematic excavations have taken place within the area, but nothing shows on aerial photographs and neither are there any surface indications of buildings or streets. By contrast, the line of the new wall extended outside the intended line of the Fosse in the south-western part of the circuit. For the first time also, the defences were extended along the river frontage. The wall was fronted by a ditch system, but it is not yet entirely clear whether or not the single, wide ditch which can still be seen on parts of the circuit belonged to the first phase. The new defences took in the existing London and Chester Gates, but a gate of different pattern was constructed in the south-west sector, where the Silchester road left the town. Two other gates probably existed: on the north side, where a causeway can still be seen emerging from the town above the river's flood plain, and on the north-east side where the road to Colchester emerged. The latter matched the position of the Silchester Gate at the opposite end of the town.

The two principal gates on Watling Street were almost identical in plan (fig. 17). Overall, they were 98ft (29·9m) across. Each possessed two roadways, between 8ft (2·4m) and 9ft (2·7m) wide, which were flanked in turn by footways between 3ft (0·9m) and 4ft (1·2m) wide. The depths of the gates were about 20ft (6·1m) from front to back. Both were flanked by drum-shaped towers which projected outwards about 13ft (4m). The ditches were interrupted by causeways beyond the gates. In contrast, the Silchester Gate (fig. 18) possessed only one carriageway, probably about 15ft (4·6m) wide, flanked by footways, while these were flanked in turn by approximately square, projecting towers. The overall dimensions of the gate were about 44ft (13·4m) across by 25ft (7·6m) deep from front to back of the towers.[119]

Frere has suggested that this would have been the most appropriate time, when permanent defences were being constructed, to have commemorated the original boundary of the Claudian town with the triumphal arches placed across Watling Street, at the points where it passed through the earlier defences. The southern arch was represented by a foundation measuring some 15ft (4·6m) by 47ft (14.3m), and Wheeler suggested a double archway.[120] It was completely free-standing in the centre of an important road junction. The northern arch was of slighter construction, 42ft 5in (12·9m) by 9ft 9in (2·7m), and its ends were masked, and later overlapped, by existing buildings. Two tile-lined conduits passed through the south end. One was undoubtedly a sewer, from the direction of flow, but the other might have been part of a water main, carrying water into the town from the higher ground to the north-west. It is not clear whether there were one or two passageways, as the masonry had been robbed to below street level; but since it interrupted traffic on a busy street a double arch might have been more logical.[121]

The mention in the preceding paragraph of a water conduit and a sewer can now be elaborated. It seems clear, from the evidence of pipe-lines within the town, that a source, or sources, of running water was available. The most probable approach line for an aqueduct would have been from the north-west, with a

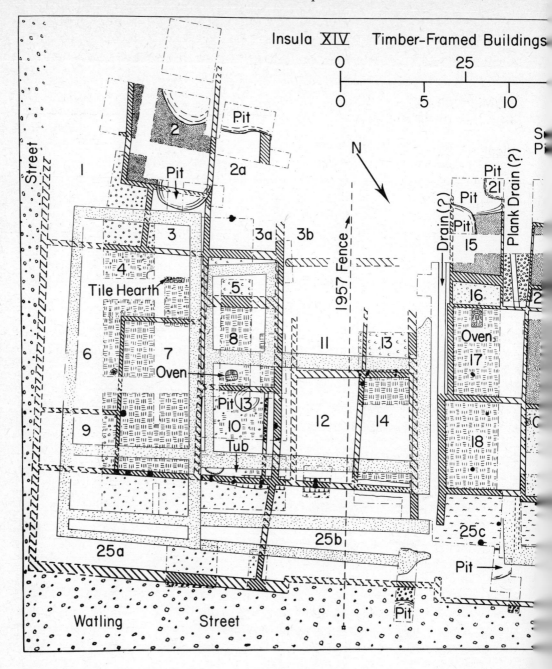

50   Antonine shops (Period IID) in Insula xiv, Verulamium (*S. S. Frere*)

source higher up the valley of the river Ver. A number of buildings seem to have
received supplies of piped water. One noteworthy example is a large late-
Antonine house and shop in Insula xxviii, where, as a sideline, the owner had
built a public lavatory, provided with an attendant, and flushed by two converging

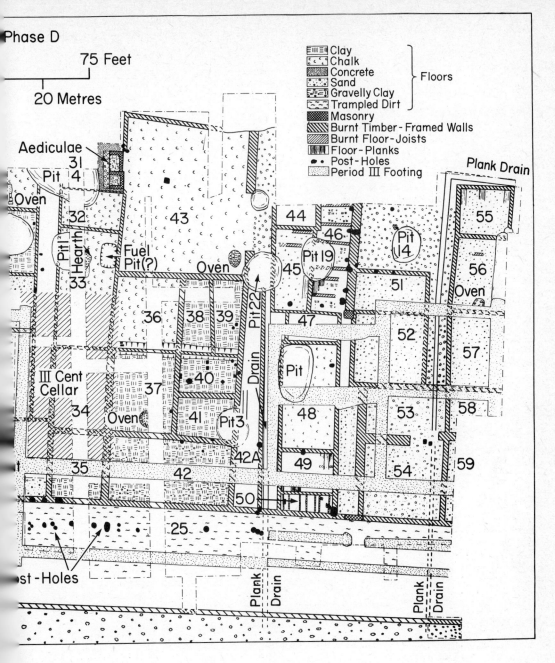

Phase D

75 Feet

20 Metres

Clay
Chalk
Concrete
Sand   } Floors
Gravelly Clay
Trampled Dirt
Masonry
Burnt Timber-Framed Walls
Burnt Floor-Joists
Floor-Planks
Post-Holes
Period III Footing

Aediculae
31
Pit 4
Oven
32
43
44
55
46
Pit 19   Pit 14
Pit Hearth
33   Fuel Pit(?)   Oven   45   56
Oven
51
36   38 39   Drain Pit 22   47   52   57
Pit
III Cent Cellar   40   48   53   58
34   37   Oven
41   Pit 3   49   54   59
42A
35   42   50
25
Post-Holes   Plank Drain   Plank Drain
Plank Drain

water-pipes approaching from the north-west. This lavatory discharged into one of the main sewers, which ran downhill from the south-west part of the town, passing the north-west forum entrance before crossing under the street to resume its course along the edges of Insulae xxviii and xiv.[122] It might be mentioned

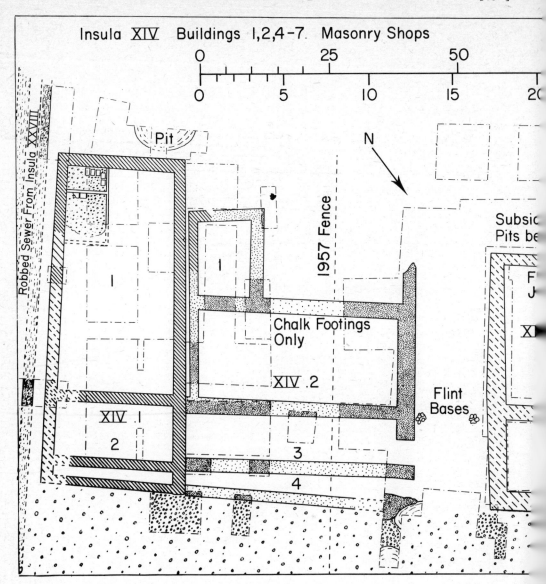

51   Late third-century shops (Period III) in Insula xiv, Verulamium (*S. S. Frere*)

here that no sign is yet forthcoming of a public bath-house, and it is difficult to
suggest a suitable site, although an insula near the river boundary would have
been the most suitable.

By the first decades of the third century, therefore, Verulamium was largely
composed of substantial houses and shops built with flints, bricks and mortar
with tiled roofs; and with more than adequate public buildings and defences.
But new building took place when necessary during the third century, and both
Wheeler's and Collingwood's views on the town's decay require revision.[123]
Even the theatre, despite Miss Kenyon's conclusions, may have continued in

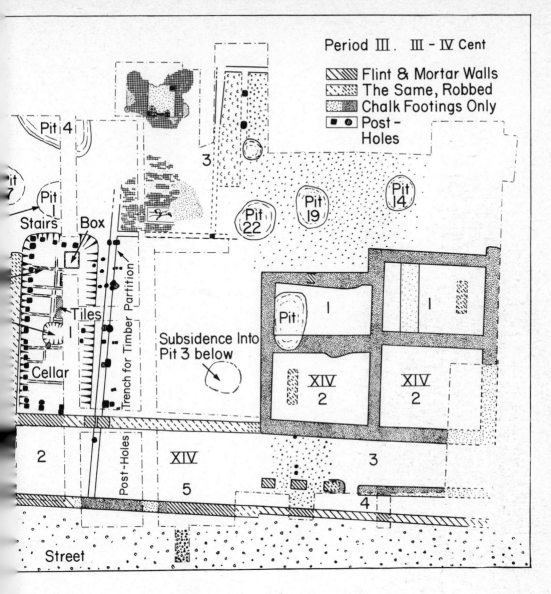

Period III. III – IV Cent

Flint & Mortar Walls
The Same, Robbed
Chalk Footings Only
Post-Holes

Pit 4

Pit 1

Stairs

Box

Tiles

Cellar

Trench for Timber Partition

Pit 7

Pit 3

Pit 22

Pit 19

Pit 14

Subsidence Into Pit 3 below

Pit

I

I

XIV 2

XIV 2

Post-Holes

2

XIV 5

3

4

Street

desultory use. Nevertheless there was perhaps a lack of confidence engendered even in Britain during the third century, while the progressive inflation may have meant that less money was available for anything other than essential repairs. We may so deduce from the return to a spending economy which occurred in the early fourth century, when people once more became interested in erecting new and comparatively useless public monuments, such as the triumphal arch built across Watling Street between the theatre and the macellum.[124] The enlargement of the theatre to take more spectators, and its alteration to bring it yet nearer the classical plan (fig. 13), might also be seen as a revival of interest in pastimes and entertainment as opposed to a more severely practical way of life. Its overall diameter was increased to about 185ft (57m) by means of a new exterior wall, 6ft (1·8m) thick, which enclosed a corridor, 9ft (2·7m) wide, between it and the existing wall, now deprived of its buttresses. The orchestra was reduced in size and made less circular.[125] The alterations to the theatre were extended to other buildings in the complex, and both the temple in Insula XVI[126] and the macellum in Insula XVII were modified in plan.[127]

This process of renewal rather than repair was extended to many of the town houses and shops. The last quarter of the third century saw the long-vacant site on the corner of Insula XIV occupied by masonry shops of entirely different plan from that of their timber forebears. The number was drastically reduced and two separate blocks are clearly distinguishable (fig. 51). One was of particular interest, as it not only contained a deep, timber-lined cellar, but also fragments of a mosaic depicting a lion attacking a stag, not unlike that in Building XXI, 2.[128]

The later fourth century saw continued prosperity at Verulamium, even though some of the larger houses in the peripheral areas show evidence of declining standards (fig. 48). Nevertheless this was not universal to the town, as Wheeler originally conjectured. Frere has shown that the building of palatial courtyard houses with mosaics, painted frescoes and hypocausts was still continuing into the last quarter of the fourth century.[129] Public buildings seem to have remained in use, although the theatre was closed late in the century and seems to have become a rubbish tip for the market hall opposite. But the temple connected with the theatre was still apparently being used at the end of the century, with a re-organisation in the temenos taking place then. Whether or not it was still dedicated to pagan cults, or whether it had been consecrated as a Christian church is not known. A possible church may be represented by an isolated, basilican type build-ing in Insula IX,[130] while another is perhaps indicated by the apsidal building found outside the London Gate in a cemetery area.[131] It is not known if the defences were reorganised during the late fourth century to include external towers. Two such towers are known on the southern part of the circuit, but they appear in part to be bonded with the wall.[132] The ditch system does have some oddities, suggesting more than one attempt at construction, especially in the vicinity of the south corner. Whether this was related to an attempt to provide a full number of bastions cannot yet be decided, but it should be remembered that by no means all towns, even on the continent, were provided with a regular or complete system.

The later history of the town is important for the light it sheds on the fifth century for Britain as a whole. Historically, the item of note is the presumed visit of St Germanus, Bishop of Auxerre, to the town in AD 429. Frere's excavations in the area north-west of the forum have now provided evidence of the town to which he came. The building already referred to above, in Insula XXVII, was not constructed before AD 370 (fig. 53). Subsequently it went through various alterations, which included the addition of first-quality mosaics. One of the latter was in use so long that patching was required, before it was cut through for the

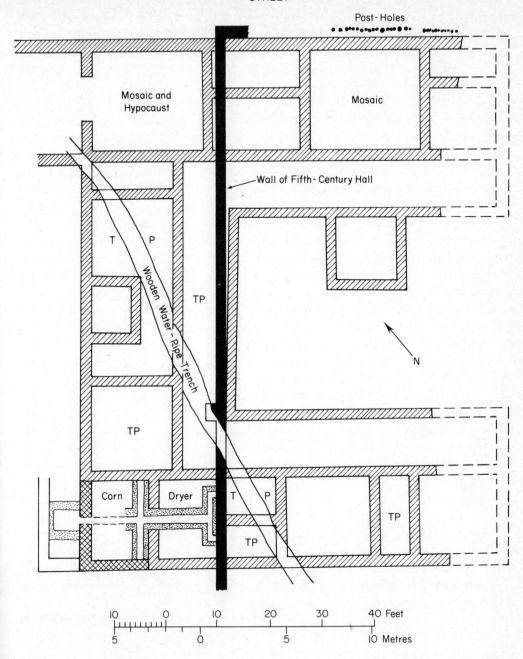

STREET

Post-Holes

Mosaic and
Hypocaust

Mosaic

Wall of Fifth-Century Hall

T   P

TP

Wooden Water-Pipe Trench

TP

N

Corn   Dryer   T   P

TP

TP

| 10 | 0 | 10 | 20 | 30 | 40 Feet |

| 5 | 0 | 5 | 10 Metres |

52   Late fourth-century house in Insula XXVII, Verulamium (*after S. S. Frere*)

insertion of a corn-drying oven. This oven saw sufficient use for the stokehole
to have been rebuilt. Only then was the whole building demolished and a new,
masonry barn or hall erected on the site, with substantial, buttressed walls. The

life of this building is not precisely known, but Frere hazards a guess that the sequence of structural phases which have been described would take it perhaps as late as AD 450. Then, with the barn demolished in turn, a wooden water-pipe was laid across the site.[133] The latter implies the continued functioning of the town's aqueduct, the survival of the skills necessary for its maintenance and the continued demand for fresh running water. It is probable that, like some other towns in Britain, Verulamium relied for its defence at this time on soldiers of Germanic origin, and a bronze buckle from the equipment which they wore has been found in the theatre. As yet though, no trace has been found of the huts which they inhabited, such as are known at Canterbury (p. 195). Perhaps they should be sought in the southern part of the town, which appears to have decayed earliest. In this context it is worth mentioning the rectangular hut, measuring about 15ft (4·6m) by 12ft (3·7m), which Wheeler found had been constructed over the derelict site of a large house in Insula III.[134] Unfortunately it contained no contemporary datable objects. The survival of Verulamium until the end of the fifth century or beyond has led Frere to suggest that it was the centre of a Saxon-free enclave,[135] of the type possibly also established round Silchester. In support, he points to the absence of fifth or sixth-century Saxon cremation cemeteries in the area. Only with renewed Saxon pressure in AD 571 did the area finally fall under their domination, by which time the town itself must have been in an advanced state of decay.

So much for the history of the town. However, there are some aspects which do not fit neatly into an historical narrative, since they cut across several phases of development. Some allusions have already been made to trade and industry, especially in connexion with the shops in Insula XIV, where bronzesmiths, black-smiths and goldsmiths worked. Before the second-century fire, the larger shop on the corner (XIV, 1) appears to have been a wine shop, judging by the large number of broken amphorae associated with it.[136] Another wine shop, or perhaps only a wine cellar, was indicated by scratches on the walls of the cellar of an extra-mural building over the river. The scratches were no doubt formed by the pointed ends of amphorae when they were being rolled along the floor. Wheeler also found evidence of iron working, in the form of slag, below the Triangular Temple. The same temple produced evidence for the import of Italian pine-cones as sacred, aromatic fuel for the deity. A butcher's shop was indicated in an early fourth-century building in Insula III, where dismembered joints from aged horses had been stripped of their flesh before burial.[137] It was considered that the meat was turned into sausages on the spot, and it is worth remembering that various types of salami are still made from horse, donkey or mule flesh. A possible fulling shop may explain the existence of certain cement-lined tanks in a building in Insula V.[138] There is also ample evidence for the carriage of British and foreign stones to Verulamium both for decorative and utilitarian purposes: Carrara marble, Rutland and Oxfordshire oolite, Purbeck marble, Collyweston slates.

Somewhere near at hand there must have been a considerable factory for the manufacture of tile and brick, but except for isolated kilns at St Stephens, Park

Street and Elstree, it remains so far unlocated. The use of yellow bricks during the early second century is noteworthy. Large flint and chalk quarries must likewise have existed on the fringes of the Chilterns. Some pottery kilns have been found close to Verulamium, and pottery manufacture was also carried on at Radlett and Brockley Hill; others will no doubt be found. Pottery was, however, brought in from more distant places and in the fourth century particularly from the Nene Valley and the Thames regions.

Although the sites of no less than four temples are known in the town, little more can usefully be said about the religious practices or beliefs of the inhabitants. A Mithraic token was found in a mid second-century context below Building IV, I. It had been made from a denarius of Augustus.[139] Although unique it helps little in deciding if there was a Mithraeum in the town, as it was undoubtedly a personal possession, but a jar depicting Mithras, Hercules and Mercury found on the site of the market hall[140] might strengthen the possibility. Of interest also on the religious scene was the finding of two domestic shrines or *aediculae* in one of the Antonine shops in Insula XIV.[141] Another interesting aspect of the super-stitious beliefs was afforded by the finding of large numbers of coins and metal objects on the old river bed outside the town, as though they had been thrown in the river to propitiate the water spirits.[142] Christianity is attested by the martyrdom of St Alban, the establishment of a *martyrium* on the place of his execution and the visit of St Germanus to combat the heretical Pelagian sect, if not also by the two buildings which may be churches.

Little is yet known in detail of the cemeteries. A major one existed outside the London Gate, where some tombs were constructed of brick and flint masonry.[143] Others are known to have existed in the area of the lake in the modern park, and outside the Chester Gate. Recently, Dr Stead has been excavating a major cemetery beyond the Silchester Gate, but most of the burials belonged to the pre-Roman period. Nevertheless one Roman burial produced a silver mirror.[144] Another largely unpublished cemetery of the late fourth century existed over the river to the north.

Stead found evidence for ribbon development along the Silchester road until the time when the town was walled.[145] Another large building over the river to the north-east had been burnt in the third century, but had previously possessed a cellar or vault (p. 222 above).

Another extramural work of interest is the artificial river bank which originally flanked a different course a little to the north-west of the present one. It suggests that the river was to some extent guided in its flow by a revetment of wood and clay, and it is possible that this was done in order to harness it for driving mill-wheels.[146] Road widening at the foot of Holywell Hill revealed a masonry foundation close to the present river course, which has not probably changed a great deal just here; the foundation may have belonged to a mill.[147] It is probable that the river was also used for transporting goods, and the existence of a wharf at the Park Street villa, $2\frac{1}{4}$ miles (3·6km) downstream, might suggest that agricultural products were brought up to the town in this way.

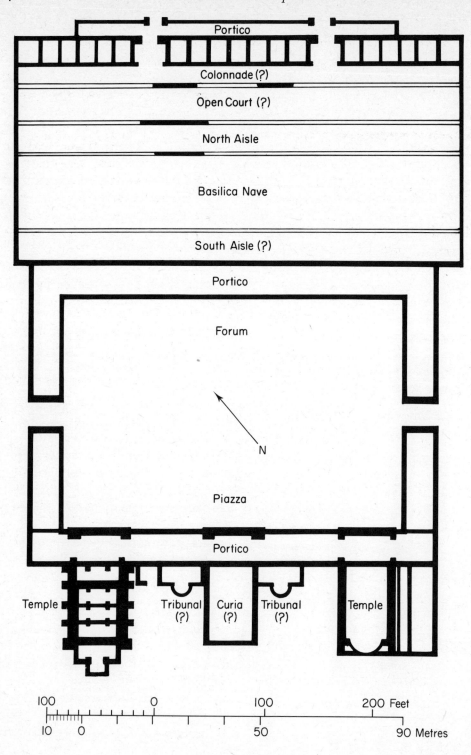

The scarcity of villas in the immediate surrounding countryside has already been noted in an earlier chapter (p. 19), which perhaps, as in the rather similar case of Canterbury, denotes that the majority of landowners lived in the town. Nevertheless, one large villa existed just outside the Chester Gate, near Shepherd's Cottages on the Gorhambury estate. Excavations there in 1956 and 1958 revealed part of a large building, dated to the early or mid second century, which contained a big, apsidal cellar. Later the cellar was deliberately filled; much painted wall plaster and moulded stucco fragments, which included human forms, was found in the filling. In the fourth century, the villa was completely rebuilt to a different plan which included a small bath suite.[148] If the date of the first building is indeed as suggested, then the elaborate nature of its decorative features is very much in advance of the houses in the town. We must conclude therefore, either that it belonged to some person of distinction, who was not afraid of spending money on personal ostentation at this early date, or that it was a building with some public purpose. The other villa at Park Street lies only $2\frac{1}{4}$ miles (3·6km) south of the town. This was an extensive site with a long history of occupation going back before the conquest. It may have been, as Mrs O'Neill suggested, a grain producing centre, with its markets primarily in the nearby town. It certainly achieved a high level of prosperity in the fourth century, when it reached its maximum extent with numerous ancillary buildings in the area.[149]

6

From Client Kingdom to Civitas

CAISTOR-BY-NORWICH, CHICHESTER, SILCHESTER, WINCHESTER

The system whereby Rome encouraged friendly contact, and made treaties, with neighbouring kings had its roots in the Republic. There grew from this system a series of 'special relationships' with local rulers outside and sometimes even within the provinces, so that Roman influence was often extended beyond occupied areas. There grew also a tendency to view these rulers as clients of the Roman state, from which protection could be obtained, but to which obedience was due, although much depended on the strength of individual rulers. Under the principate, the policies followed by different Emperors varied considerably. For instance, a client kingdom could be maintained for administrative convenience and the acceptance, by Claudius, of two British tribal states, the Iceni and the southern Atrebates, as client kingdoms is probably best seen in this light. The possible acceptance of a third, the Brigantes, would have been partly for the same reason, but more to help strengthen and stabilise the northern frontier. Manpower economy was therefore a desirable secondary benefit. The establishment of more formal frontiers under the principate usually led to the suppression of kingdoms inside the provinces, while those outside were sometimes maintained for security reasons. In the latter class, outside the province, we may put the Brigantes and much later, perhaps the Votadini. It is difficult, however, to classify the Iceni, but from a passage in Tacitus, it would appear that they were first treated as a kingdom outside the province.[1] The Atrebates must surely have been within it.

A strong contrast therefore exists in the different ways that the imperial government first coped with the problems of civil administration in Britain. The contrast admirably demonstrates the versatility of the Roman approach, which often accepted and maintained what was workable in local affairs, and adapted what was not. So we find only a few years after the invasion, a client kingdom within the province and two more outside it, existing alongside the three newly-constituted civitates. Although subject to military intervention by the governor, usually as a last resort in cases of open defiance, the kingdoms probably suffered much less interference in their internal affairs than the civitates. An example of direct intervention by the governor seems to have been the disarming of suspects by Ostorius Scapula and the 'reduction' of territory as far as the rivers Trent and Severn, which started a minor revolt among the Iceni.[2] The 'reduction of territory' might be seen as the bringing of the Iceni inside the province, a step which they resented, as they clearly considered that it infringed the independence which they thought still belonged to them. Another example was the military intervention in Brigantia in support of Cartimandua. Ultimately all internal kingdoms in Britain were suppressed: the Iceni after the death of Prasutagus in AD 59 or 60, the Atrebates after the death of Cogidubnus in the Flavian period, when his kingdom was split into two or possibly three civitates, and the Brigantes after their occupation during the governorship of Agricola.

Considered in historical order, however, the civitas Icenorum, with its capital at Caistor-by-Norwich must first claim our attention.

CAISTOR-BY-NORWICH (also *Caistor St Edmund*) (*Venta Icenorum*)

The site selected for the civitas capital of the Iceni seems to bear little relationship to any pre-Roman settlements. Allen's work on the native coinage has shown that the main concentration lies in the Breckland area, around Bury St Edmunds and Thetford, although three hoards are known from the Norwich region.[3] Moreover he has concluded that, at the time of the Roman invasion, the main part of the tribe was ruled by a man whose name, derived from his coins, was probably Antedios, although at least three separate regional organisations can be distinguished within his kingdom. The Iceni seem to have led a somewhat isolated existence. Few of their coins from the pre-conquest period travelled outside the Norfolk region. This perhaps reflects their resistance to Catuvellaunian aggression. On the arrival of Claudius, they surrendered, and according to Tacitus regarded themselves as the allies of Rome.[4] In return they were acknowledged as a client state. It might be argued from subsequent events that no clear understanding of their obligations to Rome was impressed upon them, from which we might draw the conclusion that no formal treaty was drawn up. The Iceni clearly thought that, in return for tribute and the supply of army recruits, they had retained their full independence. Such was not the case, as they were soon to learn. The arbitrary action of Ostorius Scapula, as it must have seemed to them, provided a rude awakening as to the true state of affairs. The abortive revolt was crushed and it is probable that Antedios was removed in favour of Prasutagus. He was a man of renowned wealth and obvious philo-Roman outlook. To what extent he owed his command over the whole tribe to his wife Boudicca we cannot say, but her later behaviour would point to a considerable power behind the throne. Apart from the ever present possibility of the intervention of the governor, the administration of the tribe seems to have been left entirely in the hands of Prasutagus and his advisors. They were allowed to continue minting their own coins, although none appear with Prasutagus' name on them. There is little sign of a Roman military presence and very little indication of romanisation. As yet, no new tribal centre seems to have been considered.

Prasutagus seems to have been successful in controlling the tribe. He also seems partly to have appreciated the external political situation, since he included Nero in his will, although he showed less realisation of the changing views in Rome with regard to client kings. In consequence his death, in AD 59 or 60, started a chain of events in which Rome nearly lost the British province.

The general course of the Boudiccan rebellion is well known.[5] What is not quite so well understood is the reason why the Romans behaved as they did, even allowing for their natural arrogance in such a situation. It is equally obvious that not all the arrogance was on their side. It is important to remember also the attitude of Nero, who, if Suetonius is to be believed,[6] often seized the entire estates of those who had been 'so ungrateful' as not to leave enough to him in their wills. In another comment Suetonius makes it appear that even half an estate was considered insufficient. Can we therefore blame, even if we cannot excuse, the wretched Catus Decianus, always branded as the villain of the piece, or his officers who were simply following his example, if they were only carrying out the instructions of their imperial master?

In the aftermath of the rebellion, Decianus was replaced as procurator by Julius Classicianus. We need not dwell too long on his supposed liberality towards the rebels, as it was undoubtedly coloured by self-interest. Apart from his personal animosity to Suetonius Paullinus, of which Tacitus speaks, his motives in attempting to have the governor recalled, were otherwise entirely practical. He saw future imperial revenues dwindling to vanishing point in the punitive campaign which followed the rebellion, at a time when Nero was becoming most demanding. Paullinus was doing no more than many other generals did in similar circumstances. In victory the rebels had given no quarter; they should have expected none in defeat. If this had been no part of Paullinus' duty, it would have been unnecessary to create a trumped up charge for his recall.

It is worthwhile pondering the unenviable position in which Classicianus must have found himself when he arrived in Britain. He probably faced two main tasks: to secure the revenues normally paid as taxes, and to recover what was left of Nero's share of Prasutagus' will. Land would no doubt have been included in the terms, but Nero needed cash, if slightly later references are to be believed.[7] We shall never know how much of the original share was rescued from the wreck, but it must be doubtful if Nero immediately profited to any great extent. Allen has suggested that the large number of coins, which ended the Icenian series and which were often struck from broken dies, either were made in part to pay reparations to Rome, or in part to pay Boudicca's troops.[8] The latter would seem most likely, as the former operation would surely have been most strictly controlled and few coins would have escaped into general circulation.

The after-effects of the rebellion will have been twofold. Almost a complete generation of men of marriageable and procreative age would have been wiped out in battle while poverty, starvation and slavery will have reduced the number of survivors. It seems doubtful whether the population could have been restored to its original level within a generation, if indeed it ever was. It is interesting to compare the similarity between Caistor-by-Norwich and Caerwent, the capital of the Silures (p. 00). Unlike the rebellious Iceni in their previous history under Roman rule, the Silures had from the first dissipated their strength by continuous hostility, until finally conquered by Frontinus. The two capitals were very similar in their later size and plan. It might be said that both towns, as the result of earlier vicissitudes and due to the impoverishment of their aristocracies, missed the great period of Flavian development and never fully made up the lost ground.

This is the background to the foundation of the civitas capital at Caistor-by-Norwich. No permanent military occupation seems to have been imposed on the tribe after the rebellion, although garrisons were no doubt kept in their territory for a time. Yet it is difficult to see how a properly-constituted civitas can

42   Aerial photograph of Caistor-by-Norwich from the south-west (*J. K. St. Joseph, Cambridge University Collection—copyright reserved*)

have emerged immediately. There would have been few suitable surviving candidates for magistracies or council. In the circumstances, the appointment of a praefectus civitatis to rule the tribe during the next critical years would have been a wise choice by Petronius Turpilianius. It is possible that such an officer, had one been appointed, would have chosen for his headquarters a tribal centre other than that associated with Boudicca. It has been mentioned above (p. 227) that one of the tribal districts may have had a centre in the Norwich area. So far, no indication of a pre-conquest occupation has come to light at Caistor-by-Norwich, in which case we might assume that the actual choice of site was completely arbitrary and made simply for administrative convenience. Certainly we can conclude that something which was probably not a fort, must have attracted to the site the agglomeration of native dwellings which appear in the early Flavian period. We might hazard a guess that it was the residence of the praefectus.

Aerial photographs (pl. 42) have shown that a widespread network of streets extended beyond the later defences on the north, east and south sides. Some are obvious extensions of the rectangular street grid. There is, however, a remarkable concentration of streets which appear to radiate from a point outside the north-east corner and not all of which conform to the grid. It is also in this area that early pottery and coins have been found. Here, we might suspect, lay the nucleus of the earliest town, and here possibly also lay the earliest administrative buildings. The site is now occupied by the grounds of Caistor Hall. Excavations there during the last century revealed part of a late third or early fourth-century house, but unfortunately little else.[9] The main street grid has been dated to *c.* AD 70, but no evidence has yet been produced for the streets in the north-east quarter, which might possibly be slightly earlier.

To judge by the extent of the street grid, the early town was intended to be of considerable size, covering an area more than twice as great as that which was later included within the walls (fig. 54). However, it is not yet known if all the peripheral streets belong to the same early period. The provision of streets seems to have been the only major development during the Flavian period, presumably because the Iceni were still too impoverished to pay for large public buildings. The only buildings so far known to have existed at this stage were simple timber structures, but only slight traces of buildings were found on the site of the forum, and none on that of the baths, suggesting that the sites were from the first largely reserved. An open space would have served quite adequately as a market place and gathering ground during the preliminary years, and it was not until the principate of Hadrian, when, perhaps spurred on by a visit of the emperor in person, a more substantial building appeared on the forum site, although there is nothing to show that it was itself a forum.[10] Excavations carried out by the late Professor Donald Atkinson between 1930–3 uncovered both the forum and the baths, although no full account was ever published by him. Recently, however, Frere, working from Atkinson's notes, has produced as sensible an account as is ever likely to appear in print.[11]

CAISTOR, NORFOLK   (Venta Icenorvm)

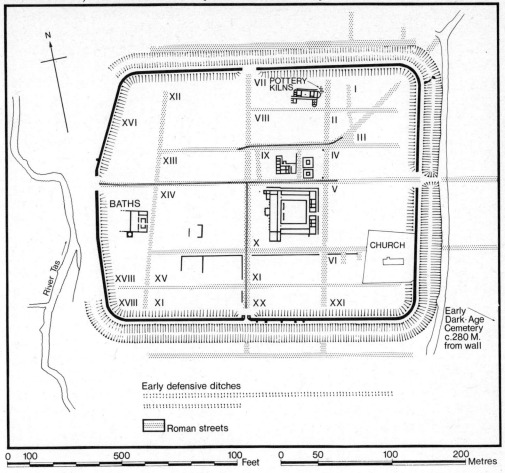

N

XII

XVI

XIII

BATHS

XIV

VII POTTERY KILNS

VIII

IX

I

II

III

IV

V

X

VI

CHURCH

XVIII   XV   XI

XVIII   XI   XX   XXI

Early Dark-Age Cemetery c.280 M. from wall

River Tas

Early defensive ditches

Roman streets

0 100   500   100 Feet

0   50   100   200 Metres

54   Plan of Caistor-by-Norwich (*after* S. S. Frere)

The forum lay in, but did not occupy the whole of, Insula X, which itself was near the centre of the later walled town (fig. 55). It seems to have been built in the Antonine period, and possibly replaced an earlier, Hadrianic building. It was not entirely symmetrical in shape. The basilica was on the west side of the forum and had only one aisle along its eastern length. It was situated at a higher level than the piazza and was approached by three flights of steps. Behind the aisle, just over 12ft (3·7m) wide, was the main hall, 30ft (9·1m) wide and 177ft (54m) long. At the south end of the hall was a room, perhaps the curia, of the same width, which added another 32½ft (9·8m) to the overall length, and which appears to have projected beyond the south forum wing. A wall, 16ft (4·9m) from the north end, demarcated a space which was probably a tribunal. Two small, heated rooms had been built against the west wall of the basilica at this point, and were probably offices. Yet another room, probably a shrine, approximately 20ft (6·1m) by 24ft (7·3m) projected from the west wall and had been placed almost symmetrically opposite the central flight of steps from the forum piazza. The west wall of the basilica was provided with external buttresses, which probably correspond with the intercolumniation inside.

The forum piazza was approximately 100ft (30m) square and was surrounded

55   The forum insula, Caistor-by-Norwich (*S. S. Frere*)

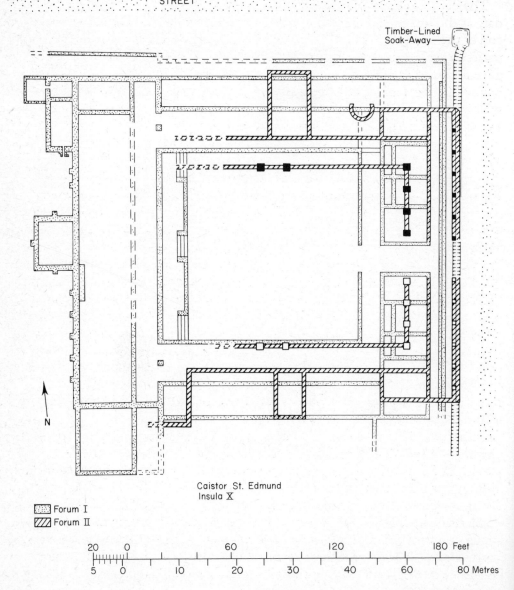

STREET

Timber-Lined
Soak-Away

Caistor St. Edmund
Insula X

Forum I
Forum II

20   0   60   120   180 Feet

5   0   10   20   30   40   60   80 Metres

N

on the three sides away from the basilica, by an internal colonnade, which was rather wider on the north and south sides than on the east. Behind the two wider colonnades were single, long halls, although on the east side a range of eight rooms was divided in half by the main entrance. Evidence for an external portico was found on the north and east sides, but a single wall projecting southwards near the south-east corner might suggest that the plan in this area was incomplete. The cost of the building seems to have been reduced by using brick and flint only for the main walls of the basilica and the north wall of the forum. Elsewhere a combination of chalk blocks and unfired clay bricks was used, with the latter being layed on flint sleeper walls.

The baths, in Insula XVII, not far from the west gate, appear to be of the same date as the forum, being built in the Antonine period.[12] So far only the eastern end of the building has been excavated (fig. 9), which contained a partly covered palaestra with a single entrance from the street to the east. From it, three doors gave access to the frigidarium, which ran the full width of the building, while beyond lay the tepidarium. A circular laconicum, enclosed within a square outer wall was situated on the south side of the building at the junction of the tepidarium and frigidarium. The frigidarium had a tessellated floor. North of the palaestra was yet another rectangular room which may have served as a dressing room or a latrine.

So far there is no indication of other obvious public buildings. However, three Romano-Celtic temples are known. Two lie in Insula IX immediately north of the forum.[13] Although nearly identical in size they were by no means identical in superstructure, as that nearer the forum had much thicker walls than the other. Both seem to have been built during the last half of the second century, although they need not have been strictly contemporary. There was no indication of a temenos, but the northernmost temple was approached over a gravel yard from the street to the east. Another temple, somewhat later in date and situated in its own precinct, is known outside the walled area, east of Caistor Hall.[14] Near it was found a small bronze bust, reputedly of Geta.[15] The latter seems to belong to a similarly-inspired series of small bronze busts from the Fens.[16] They are normally identified as emperors but may represent gods. A miniature votive axe, like those from Woodeaton, Oxon.,[17] has also come from the town. A more recent discovery made near the east gate was a bronze saucepan handle carrying a boldly executed figure of Mercury.

There is some evidence of a water supply and sewerage system. Part of the channel of a wooden water-pipe was found in 1938 outside the walled area in the paddock of Caistor Hall,[18] but it is not yet known if it was fed from an aqueduct, although the existence of the baths might imply one. If one examines carefully the most recent aerial photographs (pl. 42) of Dr St Joseph,[19] it is possible to distinguish a number of clear-cut dark lines, sometimes running down the centres of streets, like that heading for the west gate, or sometimes nearer the verges. It seems likely that these represent a system of sewers, perhaps originally constructed of timber and similar to one known at Cirencester (p. 310). An indication of their size and depth is given by the discovery of one such drain east of the forum, which was 6ft (1·8m) wide at the top, had a depth of nearly 4ft (1·2m), and which drained into a timber-lined sump at the north-east corner of the building.[20] A well-organised system of sewers of this type, especially on a quick draining site such as Caistor, might add to the suspicion, already voiced above, that there was a supply of running water from an aqueduct.

In the same aerial photographs, referred to above, two parallel ditches can be seen, apparently enclosing the street grid south of the walled town. It is generally supposed that these ditches belonged to a phase of the town defences earlier than the masonry wall and enclosing a larger area. As yet they have not been examined by excavation, a study which is overdue, but if they indeed represent earthwork defences of the town, then it is probable that they belong to the period at the end of the second century when such fortifications were being constructed for towns over a wide area.[21] Yet there is some slight reason for disquiet over this explanation. There are only very few instances where civil earthwork fortifications had more than one ditch, and where there were two or more they were normally placed close together. The fact that at Caistor they are at least 25ft (7·6m) apart and that the inner appears to follow a dead straight line for a distance of more than 1300ft (400m) might suggest, alternatively, a military origin. If so, then the dimensions would suggest something of legionary size. Against this, we might argue that there is no sign of a break in the ditches for an entrance, although this difficulty could have been overcome by the use of bridges, which were in fact used on the later defences at the south gate. Against it also is the fact that the ditches appear to cut a street which runs not far from the river Tas (see p. 238 below for further discussion of this street). There is also a possible change of alignment of the outer ditch to be explained.

The construction of more permanent fortifications does not seem to have been undertaken at least until the third century, when a much smaller area of 35 acres (14ha) was enclosed. A similar reduction in the size of the town can be observed at Canterbury and Silchester (pp. 188, 264). Atkinson excavated sections on both the north and south walls and identified the site of the south gate (pl. 43), as well as a number of bastions on the south and west sides.[22] On the north side the wall was found to be 11ft (3·4m) wide at the base and still stood to a height of 19ft (5·8m), while on the south side the foundations were 12ft (3·7m) wide. The bank was found to be contemporary with the wall in both cases. Beyond the wall was a berm about 15ft (4·6m) wide and a single ditch about 80ft (24m) wide and 17ft (5·2m) deep.

The south gate consisted of a single opening 13ft (4m) wide set between curved inturns of the curtain wall. The entrance passage was 13ft (4m) deep with arches $2\frac{1}{2}$ft (762mm) wide at each end. Socket-holes for double doors were observed in the masonry. It seems likely that there would have been a single tower over the entrance, similar to that over the north-east gate at Colchester (p. 114).[23] The passage was flanked by square guardrooms which were entered from the rampart sides, while a small arched culvert ran out through the curtain wall beside the

43 The south defences of Caistor-by-Norwich, looking east. The modern ramp in the right foreground
masks the position of the south gate.

east guardroom. Entrance to the guardrooms ultimately became blocked by
accumulating earth and rubbish. Nothing is yet known of the structures of the
other gates, of which there seems to have been one set in each wall. Unlike the
south gate the east gate was approached by a causeway across the ditch.

Some problems still remain to be resolved about the external bastions. Where
bastions exist at other towns, they are normally additions made to the fortifications during the fourth century. There is, however, a photograph in Atkinson's
unpublished records which shows one of the bastions apparently bonded with
the curtain wall, which might imply that they were contemporary. But Mr
Stephen Johnson, in a reappraisal of the photograph, considers a bond unlikely.
Nevertheless it should be remembered that it is easier to create a bond between
new and old masonry when the materials used are flint and brick, as they are here,
than it is with good quality ashlars. An alternative solution might, however, be
considered. Two shapes of bastion have been identified: rectangular alternating

with semi-circular. Venta Icenorum is therefore the only town so far known in Britain to have been fitted out with two types of bastions. It might therefore be suggested that the one series of bastions belongs to the first phase of masonry fortifications, while the second series were additions. Unfortunately, even now this does not finally solve the problems relating to the date of construction, and the answer is only to be sought in fresh, careful excavation.

Late in the second, or early in the third century, a serious fire seems to have destroyed the baths and the forum, which had earlier been damaged by fire. The latter was not immediately rebuilt and the site was left in a derelict state; most building remains had been obliterated by the end of the third century. Only then did rebuilding take place. A contrast exists here with the forum at Wroxeter (p. 373), ruinous at the end of the third century and never rebuilt. As yet, it is difficult to see why the Caistor site should have been left derelict for so long, even if its rebuilding implies an ultimate return of civic pride, backed up, presumably, by adequate financial resources. When rebuilt the plan (fig. 55) was noticeably different from the earlier, and rarely did the two coincide. The size of the piazza was a little reduced on the north side, but internal ambulatories were retained. The east wing, now robbed of its external colonnade, seems to have consisted of a long hall-like structure, bisected by the main entrance into the piazza. Additional rooms extended westwards from this wing for short distances at each end. Approximately in the middle of the north and south wings were single rooms projecting back from the ambulatories; that on the north side was slightly larger, and that on the south contained an oven. The steps leading up to the basilica from the piazza were now covered by a gravel ramp. Unfortunately, the higher level on which the basilica was placed had resulted in the foundations being entirely removed by ploughing, so that Atkinson was unable to trace its plan. It would seem also that other parts of the later forum were not entirely recorded, as isolated remnants of walls feature on the plan.

Only three domestic buildings other than the wattle and daub structures referred to above, have so far been excavated within the walls. Two of these lay north of the forum in Insula IX and were separated by only a narrow space.[24] Both were probably built in the early years of the third century. At some later date, possibly about AD 300, both houses seem to have been united, and in the area occupied originally by the north end of Building I, a number of furnaces, hearths, rough floors and walls were constructed. This part of the premises was used for the manufacture of glass, apparently on a fairly large scale,[25] at least until the middle of the fourth century.

Other industrial remains are scarce. Evidence for a bronze-working furnace was found in the paddock of Caistor Hall,[26] but there was no indication of the type of goods manufactured. At least four pottery kilns were found beneath the third-century house in Insula VII. They were active from the Trajanic to the early Antonine period.

It is possible that Caistor lay on the fringe of a notable sheep-grazing area and that a principle industry was the preparation and sale of woollen goods. A large iron wool-comb comes from the site itself, while others are known at Worlington and Ixworth to the south. Manning has suggested that these combs were of a type to be associated with manufacture on a scale larger than the purely domestic and that they should be considered in the same context as the great cloth-knapping shears from Great Chesterford. He further makes the suggestion[27] that Caistor may be the Venta of the Notitia Dignitatum,[28] with its *procurator gynaecii*, or manager of a state weaving-works. While an attractive suggestion, it is still far from being proved, despite other slight evidence adduced by Manning to support it. More recently, however, Wild has pointed out that, of the three towns in Britain with the name Venta, Caistor has the weakest claim to be that mentioned in the Notitia,[29] chiefly on the grounds of name survival. Both Winchester and Caerwent carry elements of Venta in their modern names, whereas Caistor does not, and there is reason to believe that by the fourth century the town was simply called Icini,[30] a development which can be observed in other towns of the western Empire.[31] Wild has also claimed that, apart from the Breckland, much of the land around Caistor would probably have been unsuitable for sheep in the Roman period, despite its exploitation in the Middle Ages.

The house which overlay the kilns in Insula VII was comparatively substantial[32] although much of the construction was still of wattle and daub. The part excavated consisted of a range of rooms set between external corridors and terminating in an apse at the east end. Two small wings projected southwards, one of which also ended in an apse. A small bath suite was incorporated. The house seems to have remained largely unaltered until the early fifth century, when it may have been burnt to the ground. The implications which this fire has for the final fate of Venta Icenorum have been much discussed and are again referred to below (p. 238).

Traces of other buildings, constructed of timber, have been found as far distant as 300yds (274m) east of the walled town. They were encountered during the excavation of an Anglo-Saxon cemetery (see p. 238), but unfortunately the records were scanty,[33] no proper plans survive, and little is known about their date. It would be reasonable to suppose that the majority belonged to the phase of the town's development before the stone walls were built, and probably therefore date to the second or third centuries. Many hearths and ovens were also encountered in the same area, but no indication of their use was recorded. There is some evidence, however, that many of the structures had been destroyed by fire.

In the absence of inscriptions, little can be said of the inhabitants of Venta Icenorum, or of their occupations. A stone oculist's stamp, mentioning P. ANICUS SEDATUS is recorded as having been found on the site.[34] At least one gold ring set with an engraved onyx implies some degree of individual wealth, while another in Norwich Museum is of less certain provenance. A fragment of a blue glass chariot-race beaker inscribed EVA MVSCLO might imply a passing interest in that sport on the part of an inhabitant.

One of the problems of Caistor concerns the approach roads. Apart from the road from the south, there is little indication on the ground of roads coming in from other quarters, although, according to the Antonine Itinerary, some did exist, including a road running almost due west to Camboricum.[35] The road running north-east from the town has been traced for a short distance, but its general objective is not known: it seems to be making in the same general direction towards the coast as another road which passes some miles north of Caistor. It was probably aimed, at first, at a crossing of the river Yare at Trowse Millgate.

The road from the south approaches on the left bank of the river Tas opposite to the town, and is then usually assumed to have crossed the river to enter by the west gate. This arrangement may not always have been so, as the town street nearest to the right bank of the river appears to run further south than the remainder, and, as already noted above (p. 234), is probably cut by the earlier defensive ditches. It is therefore possible that the construction of the first fortifications led to the realignment of the roads.

The ultimate fate of the town has for some time excited interest, in view of the apparent evidence for a massacre of the inhabitants which Atkinson found, and also because of an early Germanic cremation cemetery some 400yds (366m) east of the town. Caistor is also one of the towns which have produced metalwork usually associated with the equipment of the late Roman army. In 1930 Atkinson excavated Building 4 in Insula VII. He found the skeletal remains of at least 35 men, women and children, apparently covered by the debris of the house which he thought had been burnt over their heads. He dated this occurrence to the first decade of the fifth century. In consequence, ideas of a revolt among a federate garrison became generally accepted. Yet there are factors about this evidence which render it not quite so easily explicable. In the first place, examination[36] of the bones revealed no trace of burning, while the limb bones of only six individuals could be distinguished. There was evidence of violent blows made to some of the male skulls, but usually of a kind associated with blunt rather than sharp weapons. Moreover the layer of burning which Atkinson viewed as the destruction debris of the house, may have been no more than the ash in a suspected hypocaust, the top floor of which had probably been removed before the bones were deposited. A photograph shows that the lower floor was only 12–18in (300–450mm) below the surface of the field.[37] It is difficult to reconcile all these points with Atkinson's interpretation, although some act of violence would seem to have been committed. The same house produced over 30 coins dating to AD 390 or later, implying that it must have been occupied well into the fifth century.

The cemetery to the east of the town contained many burials inserted through earlier Roman layers (see p. 237 above) and Myres has suggested that the earliest were deposited during the fourth century and that use of the cemetery continued throughout the fifth.[38] Such then is the evidence for the decline of Venta Icenorum, which seems to repeat much of the pattern already described in connexion with Canterbury (p. 195). As a town near the east coast it must have been one of the first to fall completely under Anglo-Saxon domination.

CHICHESTER (*Noviomagus Regnensium*)

The extent of the kingdom of Verica just before the conquest naturally has an immediate bearing on that of Cogidubnus afterwards, even though the latter was enlarged. The distribution of Verica's coins (fig. 57) has shown that his kingdom was centred on Sussex and east Hampshire with a probable capital at Selsey,[39] or possibly even near Fishbourne.[40] But the Catuvellauni had been whittling away this kingdom and probably by AD 42, when Verica was expelled, it had been reduced to little more than the coastal plain north of Selsey. It seems likely that the Chichester entrenchments (fig. 58) formed part of a defended perimeter for this area.[41]

The southern Atrebatic kingdom had for many years practised good relations with Rome. Verica, like some of his predecessors, had styled himself Rex on his coins, and it is likely that the title had been granted by the Romans who looked upon him as an ally and an essential counter-balance to the powerful Catuvellauni. His expulsion marked not only the peak of Catuvellaunian expansion, but also the removal of the balancing factor from Britain. It is hardly surprising that Roman military intervention followed, ostensibly perhaps, to redress wrongs to an ally, but mainly to deal with the threat of the Catuvellauni, now poised beyond the north-west frontier of the Empire.

It is not known if Verica, by then an old man, was restored to his kingdom after the invasion. It is possible, as both Hawkes and Cunliffe have most recently suggested,[42] that a small force landed directly in the Selsey region either to restore Verica, or perhaps more likely to install Cogidubnus as his successor. Frere has argued[43] that Verica's return was necessary, for without him the reason for perpetuating his kingdom disappears. After a short time he could then have been replaced by the younger Cogidubnus. But this is not the only explanation. Augustus had shown earlier, when exercising a preference for Verica after the expulsion of Tincommius, that it was dynasties and not individuals that were important to Roman diplomacy. Once Claudius and his advisors had decided to perpetuate the Atrebatic kingdom, the most eligible dynast available would have been chosen as king. One view of Cogidubnus would see him as an Atrebatic refugee of an earlier period, who was brought up in Rome from his childhood, gained his citizenship under Claudius, and who was most likely in his twenties or early thirties when he succeeded Verica. Such an upbringing would help to explain the highly romanised buildings which early appeared in his realm. However, Richmond and Ogilvie argue that the phrasing of Tacitus[44] implies that he was already king when the Romans arrived. But this argument fails if the other states given to Cogidubnus were transferred some time after the conquest. A third alternative[45] might envisage him as already king of the northern Atrebates, but if he then inherited the southern kingdom, he would have been more likely to have kept his capital in the north.

His kingdom certainly included the southern Atrebatic region. It has been pointed out[46] that pottery typical of the area is not found east of the river Adur,

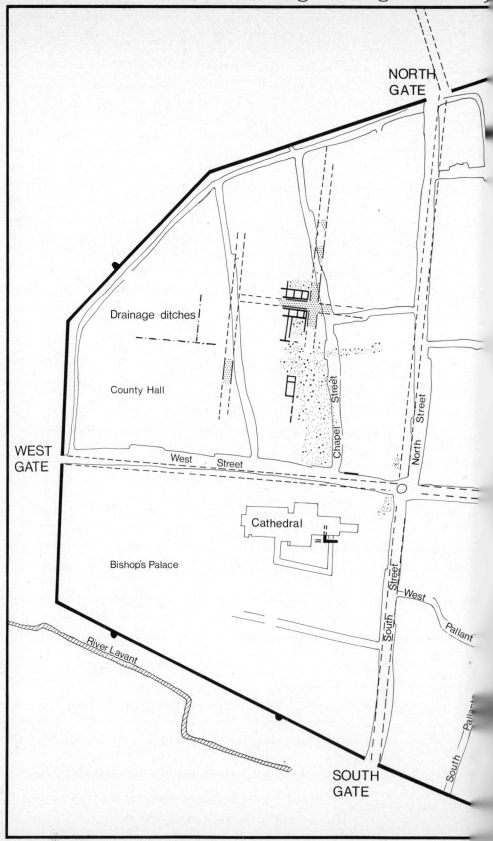

56 Plan of Chichester (*after A. Down*)

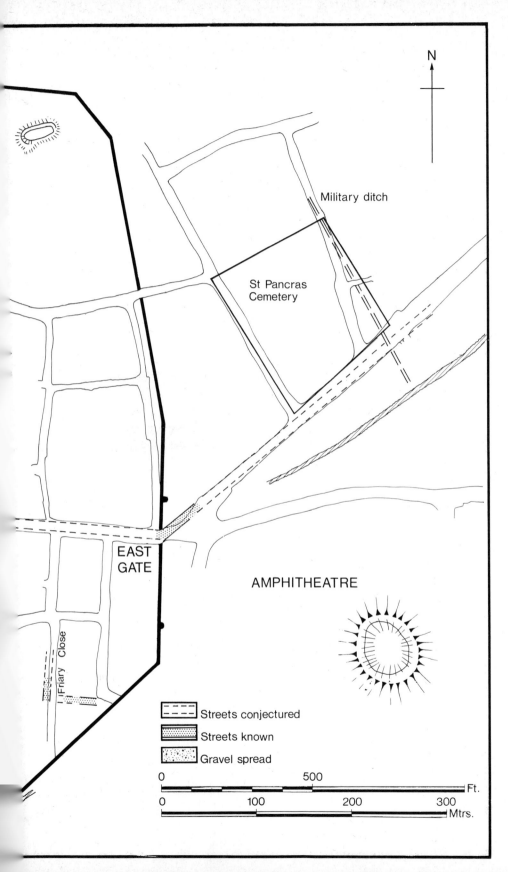

N

Military ditch

St Pancras
Cemetery

EAST
GATE

Friary Close

AMPHITHEATRE

- - - - Streets conjectured
▓▓▓▓ Streets known
∴∴∴∴ Gravel spread

| 0 | | 500 | | Ft. |
| 0 | 100 | 200 | 300 | Mtrs. |

nor west of the river Test (fig. 57). Little is to be observed north of the South Downs. Attention has also been drawn to the condition of the hill forts in this area just before the invasion. Almost without exception all remained abandoned, with their fortifications in disrepair, through to the conquest, so portraying the apparently pro-Roman attitude of the inhabitants. By contrast, in east Sussex and also north and west of the Test, many hill-forts were re-commissioned against the Roman advance.

So much for the southern Atrebatic kingdom which Cogidubnus inherited. But Tacitus mentions that he was also given certain other states to rule over.[47] We cannot be absolutely certain at what stage this happened, whether at the conquest or at some later date, although the former would seem most likely. Which were the states given to him? Cunliffe has argued[48] against one of them being the northern Atrebatic kingdom, which had been occupied by the Catuvellauni before the invasion, and instead, has suggested that it was the unknown tribes in east Sussex and west Kent. There is certainly no reason why the latter should not have been included, although the early constitution of the civitas Cantiacorum would have taken care of the administration of much of that part.

57 Distribution of Atrebatic coins and pottery (*after B. Cunliffe*)

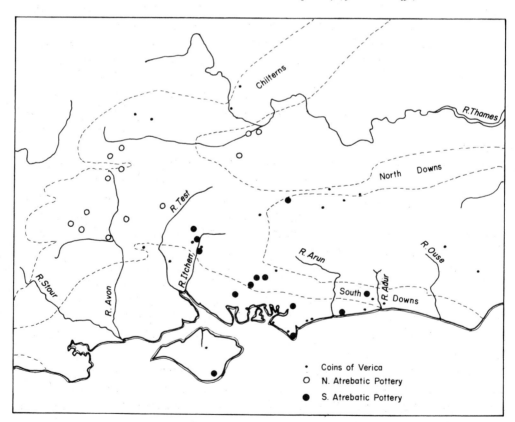

But his other argument carries less conviction. Much of the area which he ascribes to the northern Atrebates later became divided between the administrative areas of the civitas Belgarum and the civitas Atrebatum. Yet according to Cunliffe's own definition the capital of the former virtually lay on southern Atrebatic territory at Winchester. Unless, therefore, Cogidubnus' kingdom was *reduced* in size at the outset, we can only conclude that the civitas Belgarum was created after his death from part of his original kingdom, part of the northern Atrebatic area and the southern part, possibly, of the Dobunni, so that its full extent may have stretched from just east of Winchester as far as the river Severn.[49] This overlap between the original kingdom and a later civitas surely indicates what states were given to Cogidubnus. The inclusion of the northern Atrebates will therefore have extended his frontier, certainly as far as the river Kennett, and possibly even to the Thames, and would have included also the oppidum at Silchester.[50] Only on his death would the three new civitates have been constituted, the core of his old kingdom becoming the civitas Regnensium.

Newly-established king or not, where did Cogidubnus' earliest capital lie? It is possible that, after the invasion, it remained at Selsey, if it had ever been there; the subsequent erosion of the site has made it impossible to prove. However, the earliest history of Fishbourne should be remembered; Chichester would appear to have been a less likely candidate. Nevertheless, at both, the first buildings were of military character. Fishbourne seems to have been a coastal stores depot, either connected with the initial landings or with the southern campaigns of Vespasian and Legio II Augusta, but this use may not have lasted more than a year or so, after which the store buildings were replaced by a series of other timber buildings. Cunliffe has interpreted the largest of these as the first residence of Cogidubnus,[51] but there are reasons for rejecting his view.[52] If, however, his interpretation is right, then it is probably right also to see Fishbourne as the 'capital' of his kingdom: the 'capital' at this stage comprising mainly the residence of the king.

In Chichester, recent excavations, especially those by Alec Down in Chapel Street, have shown a series of pre-Flavian timber-framed buildings, of which the earliest are undoubtedly of military origin. No less than five phases have been uncovered, the first three following one another without a break, but separated from the fourth by a time when part of the site was used for making pottery. Doubt must remain about the military or civilian nature of the two later phases, until excavations have been carried out elsewhere. Nevertheless, it is worth noting that none have much relationship with the planning of the Flavian town, and a military origin is highly likely. It is becoming increasingly clear that the street grid at Chichester and possibly also the principal public buildings were not constructed before *c.* AD 75–85,[53] by which time we should assume the demise of Cogidubnus and the break-up of his kingdom.

Many authorities have claimed, on all too little evidence, that Chichester saw a process of rapid romanisation. There is indeed the dedication to Nero, dated to AD 57–8, found in 1740 on the corner of St Martin's Lane and East Street, but now lost.[54] It would imply the presence of some grandiose structure, and we might wonder if it came from a palace at Chichester before Cogidubnus retired to his new one at Fishbourne in his declining years. Certainly if Chichester is to be seen as his capital at this time, then one would expect to find his official residence on the spot. Apart from this inscription, there is as yet little indication of advanced romanisation in the Claudio-Neronian period, for the famous Cogidubnus inscription[55] is perhaps best ascribed on present evidence to the early years of Vespasian's principate (pl. 44). Such romanisation as there was would seem no more than a veneer restricted to Cogidubnus and his entourage and which penetrated to no great depth in society.

We are left therefore with three possible sites for Cogidubnus' early capital: Selsey, Fishbourne or Chichester, and at present it is impossible to say which it was. It is probable though that towards the end of his reign Chichester was developing at the expense of the other sites, while Fishbourne increasingly became his country retreat.

As mentioned above, the first proper attempt at major town planning seems to have taken place at Chichester during the early or mid-Flavian period. This possibly represents the change-over from client kingdom to civitas, following

44   Dedication plaque of a temple of Neptune and Minerva, Chichester (*Chichester Photographic Service Ltd*)

the death of Cogidubnus, or alternatively his retirement from active affairs and their placing in younger hands. It is probably to this period that the Cogidubnus inscription,[56] which was found in 1723 near the junction of St Martin's Lane (Lion Street) and North Street, belongs. It records the dedication of a temple jointly to Neptune and Minerva made on the authority of Cogidubnus, who is described as an imperial legate and king (pl. 44). The implications of this title have been discussed at length by other writers[57] and there is no need to repeat the arguments here. Cogidubnus' possible adlection to the Roman senate, which honour might have accompanied his legatine authority, would probably have been made early in Vespasian's principate in return for the services he had rendered to the new emperor at the conquest and possibly also during the civil war of AD 69 (see below p. 257). The temple was erected by a *collegium fabrorum* which is sometimes interpreted as a guild of smiths, and taken to indicate the extent to which Roman customs had become adopted at Chichester.

During the earliest stages of replanning the town, a large area near the centre was spread with a thick layer of gravel (fig. 56). For some time it has been thought that it represented the piazza of the forum, but more recent excavations in 1970–1 have shown that it covered far too great an area. It seems therefore to represent a general levelling-up of the centre, so as to seal remains of earlier destroyed buildings. We might wonder if this large, gravelled open space acted as the forum, or place of general assembly, before the construction of proper buildings. Perhaps it was this that attracted to the site the name of Noviomagus Regnensium, or literally according to Jackson, the 'Newfield' or new *clearing* of the Regnenses.[58] The forum almost certainly occupied part of this area, and is thought to lie in the corner formed by the intersection of North Street and West Street. A massive wall, over 6ft (1·8m) thick was found below the Dolphin and Anchor Hotel, on the north side of West Street, and may be part of the forum or basilica.[59] Further east, and on the west side of North Street, the corner of a large foundation of limestone blocks was seen in a building trench to be set in the gravelled area mentioned above.[60] Since it appears to be an isolated structure it is most likely to have been the base for a large statue, and similar to that situated in the forum piazza at Gloucester (p. 143). The statue of Jupiter, probably of third-century date, and attested by the inscribed plinth (see below p. 253) found on the Post Office site was probably connected with a temple precinct.

Although the forum appears to have lain in an angle formed by the intersection of the two principal streets of the town, the remainder of the street system is imperfectly known. The modern lines of North Street, South Street, East Street and West Street, which meet at the Market Cross, probably follow approximately the lines of earlier Roman streets. Indeed the metalling below South Street has recently been seen in a contractor's trench outside the court house. Further support for this suggestion was found on the site of St Peter the Less in North Street, where the eastern edge of a Roman street was uncovered not far from the edge of the modern street.[61] The metalling revealed there represented a second-century widening of the earlier street. The line of another street, north of, and parallel to,

45 (a) Pedestal of a column base, dedicated to Jupiter Optimus Maximus, from Chichester; (b) Left side
of the pedestal, showing two undraped female figures (*Chichester City Museum*)

that surmised on the line of East Street and West Street is indicated by discoveries
made in 1966 during excavations of part of the grounds of St Mary's Hospital.[62]
Other possible street lines parallel with them are suggested by a gravel surface
found in the Theological College gardens outside the west defences, and south

of the west gate,[63] and by another seen during construction of the County Hall extension.[64] More recent excavations on the latter site have, however, entirely failed to confirm it,[65] although observations in 1972 revealed another north-south street. If that in the Theological College is indeed a street, it would imply that the construction of fortifications in the late second century reduced the area of the town, and that the street grid originally extended beyond these limits.

The suggested positions of these east–west streets have led Holmes to suggest a standard distance of 400ft (122m) between them, but the discovery of the St Mary's Hospital example reduces this distance by nearly half, and certainly complete regularity of insulae can rarely be expected in Romano-British towns.

Apart from the street which underlies North Street and the one found at the County Hall, only one other north-south street has yet been found, just west of Chapel Street and near the Central Girls School.[66] Its exceptional width, 35ft (10·7m) suggested at the time a junction with another street, and this has since been confirmed.

The existence of other public buildings has been indicated during excavations over the past few decades. In 1960 and 1962 excavations undertaken in advance of an extension to Morants shop on the north side of West Street revealed part of what may have been a public bath-house. Part of an apsidal cold bath was found together with walls at least 5ft (1·5m) thick. This building dated to the fourth century but overlay an earlier bath-house, one room of which contained a black and white mosaic.[67] Although a number of wells have been found at Chichester, there is as yet no indication of an aqueduct or its distribution system. But two large sewers, one certainly timber-lined, have been found near the County Hall extension and may represent part of a system which covered the town. The larger of the two ditches was 4ft 6in (1·4m) deep and 9ft (2·7m) wide and was apparently bordered by a fence or hedge to prevent unauthorised access. It probably drained westward into the river Lavant, which in Roman times ran round the west side of the town. In the late fourth or early fifth century the ditch became clogged with large quantities of building debris and rubbish.

In 1930, a commercial excavation brought to light several architectural fragments from the West Pallant area near All Saints' Church. One piece was carved with an elaborate acanthus decoration (pl. 46). All probably came from a public building and it has been suggested that they were part of the proscaenium of a theatre. Alternatively they may once have decorated a temple. Another temple is, of course, indicated by the Cogidubnus inscription, but excavations carried out in 1967 around the area in which it was found proved indeterminate, although a brick foundation seen in a service trench in nearby North Street may belong to it.

Another public building of importance, the amphitheatre, was recognised in 1934 when trial cuttings were made in a suspect area about 500yds (457m) southeast of the east gate (fig. 14). The arena, 185ft (56m) by 150ft (47m) was set 4ft (1·2m) below the contemporary ground level and floored with gravel. The arena wall appears to have been boarded over and then covered with painted plaster,

46   Architectural fragment from West Pallant, Chichester (*Chichester City Museum*)

in a similar fashion to the Cirencester arena, where traces of pink-painted plaster survived on the wall. The date of erection was placed between AD 70 and 90 by the excavator, who also considered that it had ceased to be used by the end of the second century. It was also suggested that this abandonment was caused by the building being left outside the defences of the town, and that the masonry was robbed to supply stone for the walls.[68] Although possibly correct, these conclusions must now be regarded as doubtful as amphitheatres excluded from towns by the construction of defences are not uncommon in Britain and a number are known to have continued in use. Certainly the first earth-bank fortification would have required no stone, and only with the construction of the masonry walls later in the third century would the amphitheatre have been at risk from robbers.

Some fragments of partly-engaged columns were found at St Richard's Hospital, some distance outside the town walls to the north-east. No foundations of buildings were seen, and they would appear to have been dumped in a disused gravel or clay pit of a later date. However, they imply a building of some size with an elaborate facade.

No early civil defences comparable with those at Silchester or Verulamium are yet known at Chichester, and certainly if the Claudio-Neronian period was marked by a continued military use of the site, none should be expected. Suspicions might be aroused by the length of ditch uncovered during excavations of the St Pancras cemetery, east of the town, but it appeared to be defending an area to its east, as a palisade trench was found near its lip on that side, and it probably belongs to the early military phase.

The earliest defensive circuit, an earth bank, was seemingly erected round the town towards the end of the second century. The existence of this bank was not reported until excavations took place in 1959 when a trench was cut through the rampart behind the masonry wall in the grounds of Cawley Priory on the south part of the circuit.[69] The first-phase bank was there found embedded in the core of the rampart, and despite the fact that no less than seven sections had previously been cut through the bank without its being observed, it is probable that the line of the early earthwork closely follows that of the later masonry wall. A trench, dug in 1932 behind the [illegible] Palace bastion, could be re-interpreted to take an early bank into acc[illegible] since 1959 near the north gate clearly show[illegible]k to receive the wall. Although two ditches [illegible]e masonry wall, and are supposedly contempora[illegible] or even both may belong to the earlier phase of fo[illegible]ished sections three ditches are shown, of which at [illegible]een recut during the Roman period, while the middl[illegible]seems to be later than those on either side.[70] There is as yet no [illegible] the gates which existed during this phase, but they presumably occupied the same sites as the later gates, and may even have been built of masonry.

The precise date of construction of the masonry fortifications is not yet known, but along with most other town walls in Britain, it probably took place during the middle decades of the third century. The circuit has been examined at a considerable number of points,[71] especially on the north part of the circuit. The wall was built of coursed flints, 8ft (2·4m) wide at the base, and still standing in places to a height of 8ft (2·4m) or more. It had everywhere been incorporated in the medieval wall. The width was reduced to about 6ft (1·8m) by means of two internal scarcements. Excavation in a garden of Friary Close, at a point where the front face had been protected by a bastion, showed that it had originally been clad with dressed stone. The rampart does not seem to have been augmented to any great extent when the wall was built, but was levelled off to meet the top scarcement on its inside face. The inner ditch appears to have been sacrificed when the wall was built; presumably the second ditch was cleaned out at the same time, and it is probable that this accounts for its recutting. Yet another new ditch, cut between the wall and the surviving outer ditch would seem to be indicated by the published section.

It has always been assumed that the four main Roman gates coincided with the sites of the medieval gates, placed approximately on the four cardinal points of the compass. Excavations just east of the south gate showed the Roman wall and bank, and it was thought that the gate itself lay further west beneath the modern street. A similar situation was observed beside the west gate when excavations took place just north of its probable position in 1964.[72] A woodcut of the Westgate by an eighteenth-century artist shows a central round-headed

47   Westgate, Chichester; eighteenth-century woodcut by Grimm (*Chichester Civic Society Excavations Committee*)

arched opening with a smaller foot passage to one side (pl. 47). The arches lack keystones and the voussoirs of both are massive, as is the masonry of the imposts. It seems likely that this is an illustration of the Roman west gate which had continued in use down to the eighteenth century. The masonry is very similar to that of the Newport Arch, Lincoln (p. 122). The south-east corner of the east tower (?) of the north gate was seen in commercial excavations. It was constructed of large, dressed ashlars, and it is unfortunate that a series of earth falls prevented all but the most cursory examination. The relationship of this masonry to the curtain wall and rampart might suggest that the tower was either a later addition or else represented a rebuild.[73]

58   The Chichester Entrenchments (*after B. Cunliffe*)

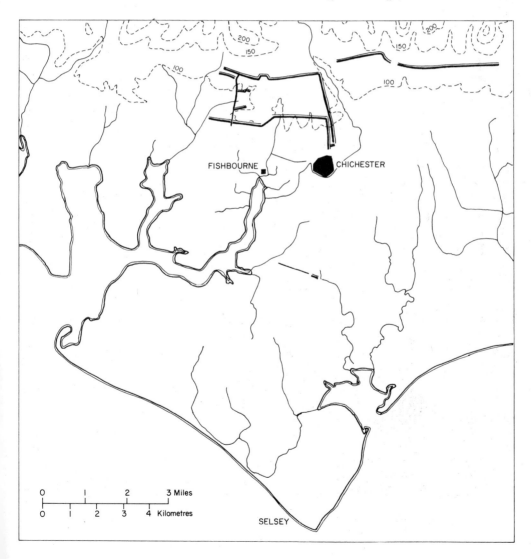

Five external towers are known at Chichester and four lie on the southern part of the walled circuit. All were additions made probably at some time in the middle of the fourth century, and in order to erect them solid foundations which were roughly square in shape, were dug down to the underlying rock. At the front, at ground level, lines of large ashlars were placed to form aprons, on which the towers proper were built. These were nearly horseshoe-shaped in plan and projected some 17ft (5·2m) from the front face of the curtain wall, with the same maximum width. The lowest course consisted of a chamfered plinth; above was a facing of small blockwork, with a core of flint and chalk masonry. They were probably solid to at least the first floor level. Short retaining walls seem to have been built against the sides of each tower.[74] The inner ditch, open before they were constructed, appears to have been filled and a new, wider one excavated on the line of the outer ditch.

No internal building at Chichester has ever been completely excavated, although the sites of a number of houses are known, chiefly from very fragmentary remains. Extensive building remains have been found round the Cathedral. Several of the rooms contained mosaics, while plain tessellated floors have also come to light. One room contained a hypocaust, and the building was dated to the second century.[75] Another house of similar date was discovered during the eighteenth century in the Bishop's Palace garden; one room had a mosaic floor said to have been 30ft (9·1m) square. Recent excavations in Chapel Street on the site of the Central Girls School have revealed two other substantial second-century houses, facing the west side of the street and separated by an east-west street. That to the north had a gravelled courtyard at its centre. Subsequent alterations saw the latter rebuilt on more solid foundations and enlarged to the east and south, so that it encroached on the streets. During the fourth century it contained at least four tessellated pavements (fig. 59). The building was still in use at the end of the century.[76] Two possible shops have been found in the same area. On the east side of North Street another masonry building, possibly a shop of late third-century date, was sampled in the excavations of 1959; one room had possessed a coarse tessellated floor.[77] A house with a hypocaust is known in South Pallant, and another with a tessellated corridor in the grounds of East Pallant House. The latter was built in the late first or early second century and was demolished in the early fourth century.[78] It is likely that it was connected with a fulling establishment, as a mortar-lined pit, 4ft (1·2m) square and 3ft (0·9m) deep, contained a deposit of fuller's earth, with a well nearby. Other building remains have been found in a number of places north of East Street.

The evidence for a fullery mentioned above is one of the few archaeological traces of industrial and commercial activity found in the town. Bronze-working was carried out between the Flavian and Hadrianic periods on the Chapel Street site; enamelled brooches may have been among the products, as crucibles and enamelling frit were found associated with unfinished brooches. Iron-ore smelting is known to have taken place during the Flavian period on the North Street site. The slag found there points to a bloomery in which the ore was smelted

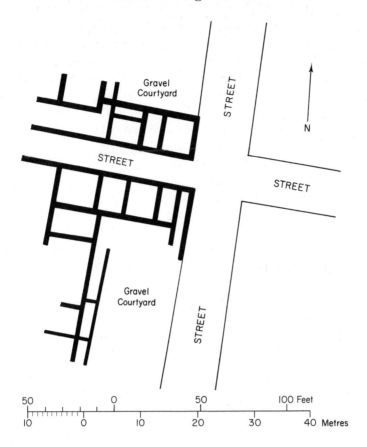

59   Fourth-century houses near Chapel Street, Chichester (*after A. Down*)

without flux, and one small piece of refractory lining from a furnace was identified. Other samples of slag and hammer scale represent the working up of crude
blooms. The same site provided evidence for a possible circular oven, possibly
used for baking, during the first half of the second century. Iron slag has also
been found near the west gate. The Cogidubnus inscription, however, can
probably be taken as providing additional evidence for craftsmen who worked
in the town and who were early organised into a guild in the Roman manner.

Apart from the implied temple dedicated to Neptune and Minerva and the
pedestal of the Jupiter statue or column (pl. 45), there is little other evidence of
religious buildings or beliefs. Yet it is worth recording that both these inscriptions make use of the formulae invoking the *domus divina*,[79] in spite of the fact
that a hundred years or more separated their cutting. The imperial cult, including
that of the divine house, must have been of considerable importance in the town
and would almost certainly have warranted a temple of its own. An altar probably
dating to the late first century and dedicated to an unspecified local genius was
found under North Street close to the town centre,[80] while a small votive
figurine, found outside the town near the south-west corner, probably came

from a domestic shrine. Part of a pipeclay figurine of Venus was found on the St Mary's Hospital site. A small bronze figure of a horse found in East Street might also be a votive object.

As with all sites where few inscriptions have been found, little can be said of the inhabitants. The altar to the local genius mentioned above was erected by Lucullus, son of Amminius. The recurrence of a good Belgic name is interesting and indicates the continuing racial affinities of some of the population. Neither father nor son were seemingly Roman citizens, but it is interesting to note the Latin name of the latter. Three fragmentary tombstones tell us something of other inhabitants. Two, from the area of the south gate, where they had probably been incorporated in the masonry of the defences, refer to Aelia .. Cauva,[81] who was 36 when she died, and to Catia, who was possibly the wife or daughter of Censorinus, and who died at the age of 23 or 24.[82] The third tombstone, found in the south-western sector of the town wall where it had probably been used for the same purpose as the other two, refers to an unknown man who died at the advanced age of 85.[83] The first tombstone appears to be of late first century date, the second is probably mid second century at the earliest, and commemorates a woman of native origin whose Roman citizenship originated under Hadrian; the date of the other is uncertain.

One of the principal cemeteries of the town has been found in the St Pancras district,[84] where it must have been situated alongside Stane Street. It was used from *c.* AD 70 until well into the third century for cremations, and some inhumations took place during the third and possibly early fourth century. The cemetery occupied an estimated area of about 4·3 acres (1·7ha) and had contained an estimated 9,500–10,000 burials. The majority of people buried in the area seem to have been reasonably well-to-do and some interesting grave groups were found. One, perhaps belonging to a minor official, contained items possibly connected with his work and with some form of regalia. Another, probably of a woman, contained a tinned-bronze mirror with a wooden frame and leather case. Several were buried, together with their grave goods, in bottomless wood containers, or tiled cysts. An interesting feature of this cemetery is the lack of burials of the period before AD 70 when the early town of Cogidubnus is reputed to have been founded. Little is known of other cemeteries; they might be expected outside the other gates, and there is some evidence of burials outside Southgate. So far, however, no substantial evidence has come to light, and certainly no early burials have been discovered. Their absence strengthens the suggestion, already made (p. 243), that the earliest centre of the Regnenses after the conquest lay elsewhere.

The main roads running from the town are well known. Stane Street, from London, approaches the east gate from a north-easterly direction. Some miles outside the town a branch road diverges to run along the Sussex coastal plain and presumably served the villas in that area. From the north gate a road runs direct to Silchester, and from the west gate to Bitterne with a branch to Winchester leaving it at Wickham. The road from the south gate presumably ran towards

Selsey, where a considerable settlement continued in use during the Roman period, together with some farms in the neighbourhood.

The countryside around Chichester seems to have been divided between farms of continuing native character and villas. Some of the latter, such as Angmering and Southwick, show a development which is normally earlier than that of other Romano-British villas, and we might see here the romanising influence of Cogidubnus. Others, although starting more modestly, ultimately grew to great size, such as Bignor, which must have been the centre of an estate several thousand acres in extent. Yet the eastern part of the civitas in the Weald of Sussex never attracted much villa settlement and it is to be assumed that it was used principally as an industrial area devoted to the extraction of iron. Only in the coastal area was this activity replaced by farming. The relationship between the villas in the coastal area and the many native farms, which have been identified on the South Downs, is not known; it is interesting, however, that their distributions appear mutually exclusive. Moreover, the native farms are associated with extensive areas of cultivated fields, and some certainly in the fourth century became more elaborate.

Little is known of the end of Roman Chichester. One zoomorphic buckle of late military type was found in the upper filling of the disused sewer near the County Hall, and suggests the presence of a late Roman garrison.[85] Since the sewer contained much late fourth- or early fifth-century pottery, the continued existence of an urban militia into the fifth century is implied. Being so near the coast, the town must have relied heavily on the Saxon Shore defences for protection, and the abandonment of Portchester for Bitterne must have been a serious blow. According to the Anglo-Saxon chronicle Pevensey fell in AD 491, and Saxons were settling at Portsmouth very early in the fifth century. Cunliffe's excavations at Portchester Castle are important in this context, as they show that occupation continued even after the main military garrison had departed and that, early in the fifth century, the site was occupied by a strong Germanic element, perhaps foederati.[86] But despite this evidence from nearby sites, and the indications which they provide, the fate of Chichester remains hidden until excavations there provide the necessary evidence.

SILCHESTER (*Calleva Atrebatum*)

Silchester is probably the best known of all Romano-British towns. The long series of excavations which took place intermittently during the nineteenth century culminated in an all-out effort to uncover the whole town between 1890 and 1909, in excavations which were sponsored by the Society of Antiquaries. The objective was largely achieved, within the standards of the day, and as a result we have a reasonably complete, but all too little understood, plan of Silchester. How much was lost in achieving it will never be known. Since then, most work has been concentrated on the elucidation of the town's history, mainly by studying the four different circuits which, at one time or another, were adopted for the town's defences.

In the pre-conquest period the first indications of an important tribal centre appeared *c.* AD 5, when the Atrebatic prince, Eppillus, rebelled against his brother Tincommius, so causing a split within the Atrebates which was not healed until after the conquest. Eppillus is known to have issued his own coins with the mint mark *Calleva* in an abbreviated form. Silchester therefore became the principal centre of the northern Atrebates, until Catuvellaunian expansion overwhelmed them, after which it seems to have been, in turn, an oppidum of Epaticcus and Caratacus.

The Roman invasion must have seen the arrival of, and possibly a short stay by, an army unit, and both legionary and auxiliary metalwork, together with what may be tent fragments, have been found, although no camp or fort is yet known.[87] Their presence was probably needed to suppress any pro-Catuvellaunian faction, and to see to the smooth transfer of administrative power to Cogidubnus. Cunliffe has argued that the northern Atrebates were not included in Cogidubnus' kingdom, but reasons have already been put forward (see p. 242 above) for rejecting this argument. Indeed, Boon's explanation of the two earliest defended enceintes requires Silchester to be part of the kingdom. Here, we might note a slight similarity with Winchester, which also probably lay within his kingdom, for it too seems to have been provided with earthwork defences at about the same time as Silchester was receiving its second circuit.

Little is known about the earliest development of Silchester as a town in Cogidubnus' kingdom. Boon has argued convincingly that the Inner Earthwork was erected on Cogidubnus' orders soon after AD 43,[88] in order to protect the town from attacks by Caratacus, who was still operating around the Severn valley. Attention has already been drawn (see p. 205 above) to the somewhat similar situation at Verulamium, although this town lay outside the client kingdom.

The Inner Earthwork had three original entrances to coincide with roads from London, from Cirencester, and from Winchester and Chichester; those from the last two towns merged before reaching the south entrance (fig. 60). The rampart and ditch were turned slightly inwards at each entrance and both were built in native style with no indication of Roman workmanship in their construction. The lack of a south-west entrance to carry a road to Salisbury and beyond suggests that such a road did not exist when the fortifications were planned, which surely should be another pointer to their early date.[89]

In 1948, Aileen Fox published an article in which she proposed the existence of a street system earlier than that commonly known,[90] by comparing the alignments of various buildings. She concluded that some of the buildings, which were placed obliquely to the known grid, belonged to an early phase in the town's development. When the article was published the Inner Earthwork was still undiscovered. Its discovery has enabled Boon to look afresh at her suggestions, and he has pointed out that there are some 33 buildings, including the bath-house, which appear to be related to a line joining east and west entrances through the Earthwork.[91] Yet, one at least of these buildings, the bath-house, in part overlies the eastern line of the fortification, showing that, although the Earthwork soon became obsolete, the original alignments within the town were for a time maintained. As at Verulamium, the town seems soon to have outgrown its first boundary.

According to the above account, the bath-house must have been one of the earliest major buildings in the town. It is often given a Neronian date, on the inadequate evidence of a stamped tile[92] found in its ruins. Yet it manifestly belongs to the early plan, for its front was realigned when the later street grid was laid out. If the main part of the street grid was Flavian, then a Neronian date for the bath-house is perhaps not unlikely. This first bath-house had a comparatively simple plan. A Tuscan-style portico fronting the street provided access to an exercise yard, which itself seems to have had porticoes surrounding it. Opening off the north-east corner was a latrine with a drain running round all four sides. A triple entrance led from the exercise yard into the changing room, beyond which was a cold room, equipped with a central basin and flanked by plunge baths of different size. Beyond again lay the tepidarium and caldarium, each with its own furnace and plunge bath. The whole building stretched for about 150ft (45m) back from the street frontage. Later alterations, largely undated, considerably extended the bathing facilities (fig. 8), although some contraction was noted towards the end of the building's life.[93]

Boon's identification of the Outer Earthwork as new defences, erected some time between AD 47 and the end of the first century,[95] raises a number of problems (fig. 60). If, as Boon points out, it most likely falls into the Cogidubnian period, having replaced the outgrown, earlier circuit, then the date bracket can be further restricted. The provision of fortifications for Silchester in the Neronian or early Flavian period is so far unmatched at any other town in Britain, with the probable exception of Winchester (see p. 277 below). But the existence of a late Neronian or early Flavian rampart at Winchester, which may also have lain in Cogidubnus' kingdom could help to provide an explanation. Boon has argued that the kingdom was extra-territorial to the Roman province and outside the governor's control. If he is right, Cogidubnus could presumably do as he pleased with regard to defensive measures taken for his towns. But we should remember the governor's intervention in the affairs of the Iceni over a matter of arms, and it seems unlikely that, despite Cogidubnus' loyalty, fortifications would have been erected unless there was good need for them. Loyal or not, there is no firm evidence that, under Nero, Cogidubnus held his high titles or commanded full Roman confidence. It is possible that the Boudiccan rebellion provided the context for the provision of these town defences, but it is a little early for Winchester, where a date of c. AD 70 is proposed, and it is probable that both towns received their fortifications for the same cause. If, however, we consider the political situation in AD 68–70 we may find a solution.

In AD 68 Nero committed suicide and civil war rent the Empire. In quick

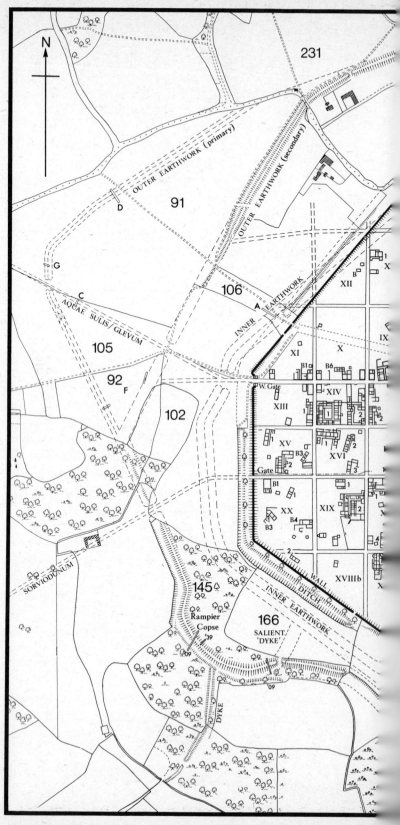

60 Plan of Silchester (*after W. H. St. John Hope and G. C. Boon*)

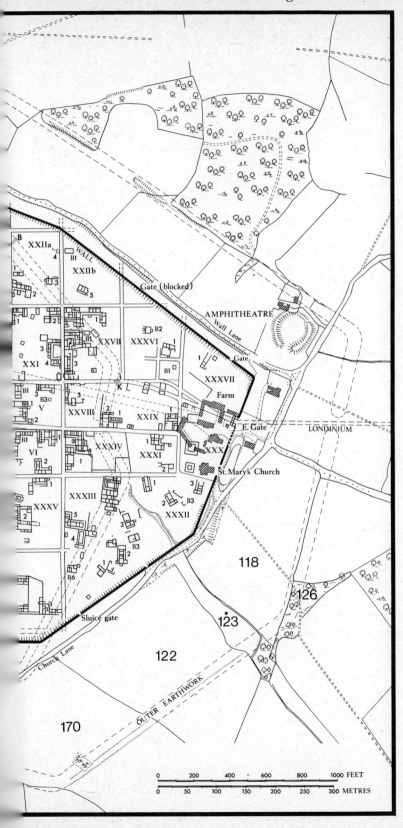

B
XXIIa
B1
4
XXIIb
3
2
5
WALL
Gate (blocked)
AMPHITHEATRE
Wall Lane
1
2
B2
B1
XXVII
XXXVI
1
XXI
4
3
3
B1
Gate
XXXVII
Farm
B1
B1
3
B3
3
K L
V
XXVIII
XXIX
2
1
LONDINIUM
E. Gate
B1
VI
XXXIV
XXXI
2
XXX
2
St.Mary's Church
1
XXXIII
3
XXXV
5
B3
XXXII
118
3
B3
126
123
B6
Sluice gate
122
Church Lane
OUTER EARTHWORK
170

0   200   400   600   800   1000 FEET
0   50   100   150   200   250   300 METRES

succession, first Galba, then Otho and then Vitellius became Emperor, only to be deposed in turn. Finally Vespasian, commanding an army in Judaea, succeeded where the others had failed. He had earlier commanded Legio II Augusta during its campaigns in southern England, when it is possible that he struck a firm friendship with Cogidubnus.

The governor of Britain early in AD 69 was Trebellius Maximus who had for some time been experiencing disciplinary troubles in his dealings with the army. Trebellius was forced by the army to flee for his life and Vitellius replaced him with Vettius Bolanus. The number of legions in Britain had already been reduced to three by the withdrawal of Legio XIV in AD 67. Further reductions were made in AD 69 when the three remaining legions provided vexillations to support Vitellius, although this was to some extent compensated by the return of Legio XIV after the defeat of Otho, whose cause it had supported. The resumption of severe hostilities with the Brigantes threw an additional strain on the province.

This then was the situation in Britain when Vespasian became Emperor: a major war threatened the northern frontier; the garrison was weakened and divided in its loyalty and was commanded by a man who had supported Vitellius, and who, furthermore, did not appear to have full control of his army. The Boudiccan rebellion only a decade earlier must still have been a very real memory. Not for a year was Vespasian able to send a governor on whom he could rely fully to control the British situation. What would have been more natural than for him to have invoked an old friendship, and it seems likely that Cogidubnus supported Vespasian's cause against Vitellius. From what we can infer of the character of Cogidubnus, he could have imparted a steadying influence to an unstable situation, and his hand would undoubtedly have been strengthened by the award of legatine authority. Can we therefore see in the ramparts built to surround Silchester and Winchester at this time the creation of a Vespasianic stronghold in Cogidubnus' kingdom; a protection against a mutinous and unreliable army rather than against a threat from outside the province? The reward for Cogidubnus' loyalty to Vespasian may well have been a 'golden handshake' of massive proportions and quite sufficient to have paid for the Fishbourne palace.[95]

The extension of the town boundary to the Outer Earthwork seemingly enlarged it to too great an extent, for not long afterwards the north-west quarter was reduced by cutting off an awkward salient with a secondary bank and ditch.

Within this boundary, the new civitas capital of Calleva Atrebatum grew after the dissolution of Cogidubnus' kingdom. Although the forum has never been satisfactorily dated, it was probably constructed during the later Flavian period,[96] and certainly seems to have been in existence by AD 100. Boon has pointed out[97] that its construction probably preceded the laying out of the known street grid, with which it does not exactly correspond. The principal axis of the town always appears to have been the east-west alignment. Both the forum and the street leading eastwards from its entrance are virtually parallel with a line joining the east entrance of the Outer Earthwork with the west entrance in its secondary bank. Indeed, this line runs close to the north side of the forum, and, had it been perpetuated, would have placed the latter in the frequently favoured position at the junction of the cardo and decumanus. Boon has also suggested that the direct approach of the London road to the forum was blocked by the temenos of the two temples which were ultimately enclosed in Insula xxx. Indeed, it seems possible that the street which runs from the forum towards the temples and which alone of all the streets appears to have survived the slightly later realignment of the street grid, was deliberately planned to associate the forum with this major religious site, almost as a processional way.

The forum was built round a piazza 142ft (43m) by 130ft (40m). On the north, east and south sides porticoes gave access to ranges of rooms behind them (fig. 7). The main entrance of monumental character lay centrally in the east range. It is difficult to distinguish different periods of structural work from the accounts of the excavation, although there are odd discrepancies in the building lines of the two rooms at the north-east and south-east corners. Neither is it possible to say if the apses which occur in two rooms of the south range and in one of the north were part of the original work, or whether they were additions. The two rooms with apses in the south range may have been public offices or even shrines, but the remainder were most likely shops. A possible exception is the apsidal room in the north range, for hereabouts in 1744 was found a dedication to Hercules Saegon...[98]

All three ranges were surrounded by an external portico, which was only interrupted by the monumental screen wall of the main entrance. The building

61   The Christian church, Silchester (*after W. H. St. John Hope*)

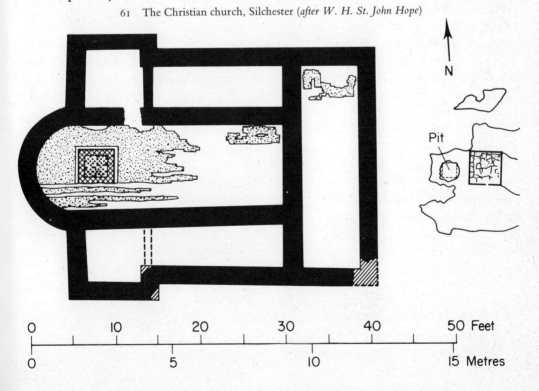

| 0 | 10 | 20 | 30 | 40 | 50 Feet |
| 0 | | 5 | | 10 | 15 Metres |

was constructed using the Tuscan style of architecture, and Bath stone was used extensively for ornamental features. Fragments of a dedicatory inscription cut on Purbeck marble slabs, with some letters about 11in (280mm) high, have been found but unfortunately no fragment was large enough to enable a full reading to be made.[99]

The whole west side of the forum was enclosed by the basilica, with the main hall 233ft (71m) long by 58ft (18m) wide; the nave had a width of 27ft (8·2m). According to Boon there was only one aisle; if so, there is a strong resemblance to the basilica at Caistor (p. 231). At each end of the nave was a semi-circular tribunal, and a range of rooms of varying size extended along the west side of the hall. The central room terminated in an apse and has often been referred to as the curia, but Frere has made the valid comment that it was too small to have comfortably accommodated all members of the ordo.[100] Instead he has proposed that it served as a shrine for the principal deities of the civitas, and that the curia was most likely the large hall at the north end of the range. The bronze eagle found by Joyce in 1866 in the southern room of the range could have come from some composite piece of statuary representing a local *tutela*, or alternatively it may have been an attribute of a statue of Jupiter. The basilica, like the forum, also had an external portico, which was interrupted by the two projecting tribunals. In contrast to the forum, the basilica made use of the Corinthian order, but the fragments of capitals found exhibit a stiffness displayed by much provincial carving.

The forum and basilica at Silchester are often quoted as being typical of such buildings in Britain. Yet it should be remembered that their symmetry is quite untypical, and the majority of Romano-British fora show a good deal of variation. It is possible that the well-known plan of the Silchester building does not represent its full historical development, as later walls, being nearer the surface, could have been more readily robbed, so leaving few traces for mid-nineteenth-century excavators to observe.

Work on laying out the main street grid probably started before the basilica and forum were fully finished. Why the alignment should have been changed, and why the forum was left in an insula far too large for it, are problems which cannot be answered. Perhaps an alignment based on the forum would have required the destruction of too many existing buildings, possibly belonging to influential people. If so, it shows a somewhat piecemeal approach to the problem of town-planning at Silchester and implies that no coordinated plan, covering all stages, probably ever existed. In 1938–9, Mrs Cotton gave a suggested date of AD 90–120 for the street grid, from excavations carried out near the north-western side of the Outer Earthwork, and at the amphitheatre gate (p. 266 below).[101] But these sites lie on the outside edges of the street system and the date may be, as Boon has observed, no more than an indication of the length of time which it took to implement the whole scheme. One of the major buildings affected by the new street-system was the bath-house. There, the front wall of the portico was ruthlessly cut back, and a new wall inserted so that the portico was made much

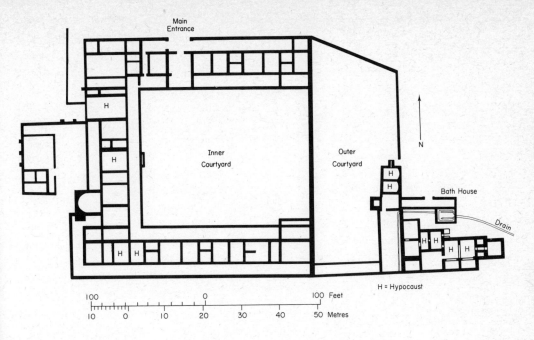

wider at one end than at the other. Elsewhere there are indications that some houses and shops were similarly given new frontages where these cut across projected street lines.

Another public building, which was probably planned at the same time as the street system, is the so-called mansio in Insula VIII (fig. 62). Its alignment is the same as that of the streets and it occupies part of a double insula, close to the south gate. In so doing, it interrupts at the south end the line of the main north-south street east of the forum. This same street, if produced southwards, would coincide with the entrance to the building, and it probably did so in antiquity.[102] It should be emphasised that there is no proof that this building was the mansio, or official inn, for users of the cursus publicus, although there are a number of indications to show that it was no ordinary house. It was a large building, covering almost as much ground as the forum, and larger than any other house at Silchester. At the south-east corner there was a bath-house of considerable size, which adjoined an open courtyard running the whole length of the eastern side, and which was in turn separated from the main building by a substantial wall. The main part of the building was arranged in three wings around a colonnaded courtyard 148ft (45m) by 115ft (35m). The main entrance, with an elaborate external portico, lay towards the west end of the north wing. Apart from the entrance, both north and south wings were almost identically planned, with the rooms mainly arranged in groups of three. Two of each set of rooms ran the full width of the wing, but the third was divided lengthwise by a partition wall into two smaller rooms. The west wing contained what appear to have been reception rooms, three of which were heated by hypocausts. The excavators considered that this wing had been extensively altered, and certainly the published plan contains some pecularities which could only be explained in this way. A westward extension from the centre of the wing may have been part of these alterations, as originally an external portico had existed outside the north, south and west wings, whereas it appeared to terminate against the sides of the extension in the later plan.

Although there is nothing against the building being the residence of some notable citizen, its size alone, when taken with the arrangement of the rooms and the probable early date, would seem to indicate a public use. When it is remembered that Silchester lay on no less than four routes of the Antonine Itinerary, a mansio of considerable size is the most likely interpretation of its use.

It is not easy to ascribe other commercial and residential buildings to this particular phase of the town's development. So far none has yet been found in the area lying between the Outer Earthwork and the line of the later town defences. It is well known that the street grid extends beyond the latter more especially on the north side, so that the discovery of buildings connected solely with the Outer Earthwork phase is by no means improbable. The only building which may possibly belong to it is one of entirely different character: the amphitheatre. It lies close to the north-eastern corner of the Earthwork. Unfortunately it has never been excavated, but one eighteenth-century source records masonry walls, although they were not mentioned by Stukeley. If, however, in common with most other known amphitheatres in Britain, it was built during the late first or early second century, it is one of only two in Britain where construction took place within town fortifications.[103] As far as can be ascertained the area measured about 150ft (46m) by 120ft (36m), with a definite entrance at the south end, and with probably another, less certain, at the north end.

The late second century saw a considerable contraction in the size of the town, brought about by the erection of a new earthwork fortification on a line which more closely approximated to that of the long defunct Inner Earthwork. It is not easy to explain why the Outer Earthwork should have been abandoned in favour of the new line. Even if not fully operative at the time, it would probably have required less work to recommission it than to construct a new bank and ditch, even if the latter was considerably shorter in overall length. Neither is an explanation fully provided by arguing that the Outer Earthwork enclosed an inconveniently large area incapable of adequate defence. What was defensible in the Flavian period was probably defensible also in the late second century. If earthworks were all that were required at this date, the Outer Earthwork would still have been perfectly suitable for use. That a new line was adopted might be taken, therefore, to indicate some different scheme afoot, which required greater economy. It has already been suggested that work on masonry fortifications was started at certain towns in Britain during the late second century (p. 75 above) as a preliminary move by Clodius Albinus. In almost every case where this can be discerned, there is evidence to show that the work was completed in haste by the use of earthwork in place of masonry for the curtain walls. The decision to erect masonry fortifications at Silchester could account for the adoption of a shorter circuit, as this would have produced considerable economies. Only rarely was a stone curtain wall constructed around an area larger than absolutely necessary.

There is some evidence to support the suggestion that the late second-century earthwork was allied to stone structures, although re-excavation is required for final proof. The four principal gates of the town are peculiarly placed with regard to the later curtain wall. All are deeply recessed behind the curtain to which they are joined by inturns. Normally where this structural procedure is followed, as at Colchester and Brough, the gates are an integral part of the inturns, whereas at Silchester they are formed of slighter structures set almost entirely behind the inturns. The fact that the gates may have been of different construction to the curtain wall was mentioned by the excavators without their realising the full implications. At the north gate it was suggested that some change of design may have occurred while the wall was being built,[104] and an apparent difference in construction is also recorded in the account of the east gate.[105]

The bank which formed the linear fortification at this stage was first identified by Mrs Cotton.[106] It everywhere appears to follow the line of the later wall and to be embedded in the later, augmented bank behind it. Since the front had invariably been cut away for the insertion of the wall footings, the full width is unknown, but it probably exceeded 30ft (9m). There seems to have been only a single ditch. It is not possible to say conclusively that entrances existed on the sites of the later north-eastern and south-western gates, but it would be safe to infer one at the latter, since the road to Sorviodunum must have already been in existence for some time. An exit to the north-east, where later the amphitheatre gate stood, is less certain, as, even after the stone wall was built, no street within the town appears to run towards it.

The gates which have been attributed to this period of earthwork fortification were of two main designs. The north and south gates had only single, arched portals, about 12ft 6in (3·8m) wide, which may possibly have had towers over them (fig. 20). The east and west gates (fig. 19) which, as already mentioned above (p. 000), carried the principal road through the town were larger, each having double portals, about 13ft (4m) wide, separated by a central spina of 4ft (1·2m). Both were flanked by guard-chambers, and projecting, rectangular towers.[107]

At some time in the third century, a masonry wall of flint bonded with oolite slabs, about 9ft 6in (2·9m) thick at ground level, was added to the front of the existing bank.[108] The ditch was filled at the same time to provide more stable foundations for the wall, another was dug further out, and the bank behind the wall enlarged. In places on the south-east side, where the wall crossed marshy ground, the foundations were underpinned with wooden piles. At distances of about every 200ft (61m) along its circuit the wall was carried to its height at the full width for lengths of about 12ft (3·7m). Elsewhere the width was reduced to 7½ft (2·3m) by an internal scarcement. The projections, or counterforts, probably acted as bases for stairways leading to the parapet, and are known to exist also at Caerwent (p. 382). Apart from the gates already referred to above, which were incorporated in the new scheme, three additional gates of masonry were planned for the new scheme, perhaps to replace earlier structures of timber: the south-west gate, carrying the main road to Sorviodunum, the amphitheatre gate (fig. 21), and another, smaller postern some 300yds (273m) further north from it. The latter was never completed, and the opening was blocked before the wall had risen to its full height.[109] Both the other gates consisted of simple arched openings in the wall, about 11ft 6in (3·5m) wide, and are typical of the later form of town gates.[110]

Two other openings in the wall merit attention. One was a well-constructed sluice gate (fig. 20) in the south-east sector, through which apparently the waste water from the mansio baths in Insula VIII was carried away.[111] The opening in the wall was slightly over 4ft (1·2m) wide and internally the channel was flanked by brick retaining-walls. Behind the flanking walls were found traces of vertical timbers backed by planking, and it is probable that this represents the sluice gate at the time when only an earth bank existed.[112] The shutter itself was probably of timber and appears to have been raised or lowered in a grooved wooden frame, which was ultimately incorporated in the masonry. The substantial nature of the gate is explained by the fact that a spring rose on the site of the mansio baths. It was probably brought under control for use in the building, surplus and waste water being allowed to drain away through the sluice gate, which could be raised or lowered to accommodate the flow. A smaller channel cut below the frame of the gate probably sufficed for normal use.

The other opening lay in the same section of wall, some 200yds (183m), north-east of the sluice gate. It served to carry the stream which now passes through a break in the wall; only the east side of the original opening was observed in 1902, the other having been destroyed.[113] This stream rises in the area of the public bath-house in Insula XXXIII, and was probably used in the same way as the spring near the mansio baths.

The reference to the water supply and drainage of two bath-houses leads us to consider other comparable arrangements. The geology of the site is such that water could easily be obtained by sinking wells to the clay bed which underlies the surface gravel. The wells varied in depth from 8ft (2·4m) to 30ft (9·1m), and were usually lined with flints, where they passed through the gravel, and below that with timber. Several appear in each insula, and were probably sufficient to supply most domestic needs. Despite their frequency, a need was still felt for piped water, and a wooden pipe-line was traced running from the ditch outside the south-east gate, under the wall and bank and along the north side of the street as far as Insula III, where it possibly served a building on the south side. It is recorded[114] as having terminated against a rough mass of flint masonry situated in the edge of the ditch, from which it was suggested water had been drawn. Yet the pipe runs below the curtain wall and bank which strongly implies an earlier date for its construction, for, if it was later, it would surely have been carried

63   The temple enclosure near the east gate, Silchester (*after W. H. St. John Hope*)

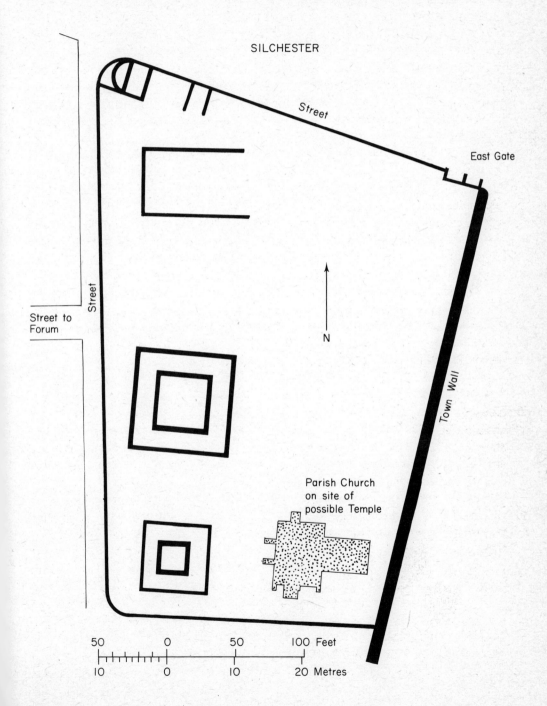

through the gate. If so, then the masonry structure may represent the remains of a castellum which was either partly destroyed when the ditch was dug, or else left standing on its edge. In either case the original source of water almost certainly came from elsewhere, but whether from a nearby spring or from an aqueduct is not known. One of the most interesting finds made at Silchester, which may provide a clue to the way in which an elevated cistern could have been fed, is a reciprocating force pump (fig. 30), found in a pit below a house in Insula XIV.[115] The cylinders, reservoir and rising pipe were made of lead, attached to an oak stock. The cylinders were 22in (559mm) long and of 3in (76mm) bore.

A hint of the religious life observed at Silchester has already been indicated (p. 261). Several temples are known in the town, in addition to other possible shrines. Apparently the main religious site lies near the east gate in Insula XXX.[116] The insula was bounded on the north, south and west sides by a flint wall and by the town wall on the east (fig. 63). We cannot say if the line of the town wall there precisely followed the original east boundary of the temenos, but it probably did so. Two Romano-Celtic temples are known to lie near the west side of the enclosure which occupies a low rise within the town. Both temples are aligned to follow the first town plan. That to the north was the larger, and is indeed the largest in Britain, with a cella 42ft (12·8m) square and an external portico 13ft 6in (4·1m) wide. The cella of the other was 24ft (7·3m) square and the portico approximately 12ft (3·7m) wide. The floors of the first were of concrete, which had been raised considerably above the surrounding ground surface; the smaller had floors of plain red tesserae. Both exteriors had been rendered with red-painted stucco. A small column of Bath stone was found in the Silchester churchyard, which partly overlies the site, and probably came from the smaller of the temples. Fragments of Purbeck marble wall-sheathings and mouldings were also found during the excavations, but the only objects of religious importance were two miniature clay votive lamps.

An apsidal structure in the north-west corner of the insula may be part of a third temple; excavations could not be completed owing to existing farm buildings. A large hall-like building lay between it and the northern temple. The fact that the parish church is parallel to the temples might suggest that its outer walls are in part founded on the remains of a fourth.

Another temple of some importance lies near the west side of Insula XXXV, and was likewise not aligned with the street grid.[117] It was considerably smaller than those in Insula XXX, the cella measuring only 12ft (3·7m) by 14ft (4·3m) with a portico about 7ft (2·1m) wide surrounding it (fig. 64). An entrance about 10ft (3m) wide lay on the east side of the portico, while across the west end of the cella, a platform, 3ft (914mm) high, had been built, presumably to carry statues. The area around the temple produced some interesting finds, which included fragments of three inscribed panels of Purbeck marble, and five fragments from two statues, one of which may have represented Mars. The inscriptions, which are considered below (p. 274), help to throw some light on the institutions of Calleva.

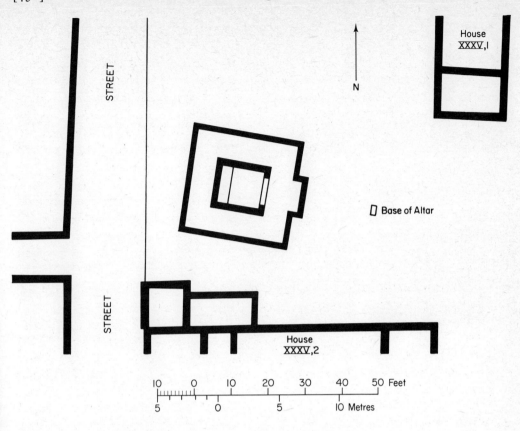

STREET

STREET

House
XXXV,I

N

□ Base of Altar

House
XXXV,2

10   0   10   20   30   40   50 Feet

5   0   5   10 Metres

64   The temple of Mars, Silchester (*after W. H. St. John Hope*)

Yet another temple existed in Insula VII and was of polygonal form with sixteen sides, but with a circular internal face to the wall of the cella. The diameter of the cella was 35ft 7in (10·9m), and the width of the surrounding portico 9ft 6in (2·9m).[118] The building lay in a considerable area of open ground surrounded by a continuous wall on the north, east and south sides which probably formed the boundary of a temenos.

Three other buildings might qualify as pagan shrines or temples, but there is nothing to suggest what cults they represented. There is also some evidence for the existence of aediculae and private shrines in domestic houses. Apart, however, from some small bronze and pipeclay figurines of quite normal type, and some other accessories, there is little else to suggest the religious inclinations of the pagan population, which seem to have been along lines typical for Romano-British towns.

The last building with a religious significance to be considered belongs to a very different category from those already described. It was situated in the south-east corner of the insula in which the forum lay. This building was first excavated

48   Three fragments of inscriptions from around the temple in Insula xxxv at Silchester. They refer to a *collegium peregrinorum* in the town (*Reading Museum*)

in 1892 and re-excavated by Richmond in 1961.[119] It was small, measuring only 42ft (12·8m) by 24ft (7·3m), and the long axis was orientated east-west. At the east end, an ante-room, or narthex, occupied the full width of the building. A circular flint foundation 22in (559mm) in diameter was placed centrally at the north end of the narthex. The rest of the building was divided into a central nave with apsidal west end and two side aisles. The aisles terminated against slightly wider rooms at their west ends resembling transepts, from which they were separated by screen walls (fig. 61). The floor of the nave and narthex had originally been covered with a red tessellated pavement, containing a square of black and white chequerboard mosaic at the base of the apse. Much of the floor had been disturbed at later periods, some of the hollows being attributed by Richmond to the action of squatters. Traces of opus signinum were found adhering to the face of the mosaic. East of the building was a tile base, 4ft (1·2m) square, set in the middle of a mass of pitched flints. The edges of this foundation had been badly robbed, but a straight edge still survived on the south. A pit, carefully constructed in flint and tile, was situated slightly west of the tile base and was an integral part of the whole structure.

Three coins, which had a white deposit still adhering to them, were found with displaced flooring material in the 'squatters' hollows. Richmond claimed that the deposit was the same as the mortar used for the floor matrix, and that therefore the coins must originally have been embedded in it. If so, the floor cannot have been laid before AD 348, which is the earliest date that the latest coin could have been in circulation. However, a recent analysis does not support this theory.

Although there is no absolute proof that the building was a Christian church, its position in the town, its date and its modest plan create a strong presumption. It has been suggested that the isolated structure at the east end was a baptistry with laver and soak-away pit. A baptistry would imply that this was a cathedral, and Silchester, therefore, the seat of a bishop. Probably the strongest argument in favour of it being a church is that relating to its position. The erection of a pagan temple in the second half of the fourth century, so close to the centre of the town, would seem an unlikely possibility at a time when Christianity was in the ascendant. But it should be remembered that even this period saw a short revival of official paganism under Julian and that many of the building's features can be matched in pagan contexts. Yet a lead seal found in the basilica and stamped with a ☧ monogram, flanked by an alpha and omega, might be taken to suggest that the practice of Christianity played some part in the official life of the town.

The consideration of this mid fourth-century building in its correct context as part of the religious life of the town has advanced us beyond that point in time which this narrative had reached, and attention must now return to somewhat earlier commercial and domestic buildings of the town. It is often found in many towns of Roman Britain that the insulae close to the forum are packed along the street frontages with narrow strip-like buildings usually interpreted as shops.[120] One of the most notable features at Silchester is the marked lack of crowded buildings; the number of such premises is few and chiefly confined to the main east-west street. Admittedly, flimsy buildings of this type may have been missed by the excavators, but alternatively we might presume that some others, which on the sole basis of their plans might be called dwellings, incorporated within their structures some provision for commerce or industry, as was done in Building XXXVIII, 1 at Verulamium (p. 216). Certainly House 4 in Insula X at Silchester was partly used as a silver refinery and contained a cupellation furnace.[121] In one or two others it is possible to discern groups of shops united within one block as at Verulamium and Cirencester.

Certainly there is no lack of other evidence to indicate the economic activities of the inhabitants. At an early date, probably before the forum was built, there seems to have been a tannery situated near the north-west corner of Insula VI. A considerable area was found covered with ox-jaws, an indication that skins with only the heads attached had been brought for treatment, as was often customary in the Roman world.[122] Three cobbler's lasts from the ironwork hoards demonstrate the presence of leatherworkers in the town. A number of circular hearths, concentrated especially in Insulae X and XI, were suggested by the excavators to have supported vats used by dyers, although such hearths would have been suitable for a wide variety of purposes, such as brewing, baking or cooking. The rare evidence for silver refining, referred to above, is complemented by more prolific evidence for the activities of bronzesmiths and blacksmiths. The two hoards of ironwork, which were found in 1890 and 1900, contained assortments of smiths' tools, including tongs, anvil, striking hammer and farrier's tools. More recently, in 1955, an iron-smelting furnace was found, in which iron ore, probably from local sources, was reduced to metal. The ironwork hoards also contained a plentiful supply of carpenter's tools, and, of considerable interest, some agricultural implements, which included ploughshares and coulters (pl. 49). Such finds, presumably the stock-in-trade of working town blacksmiths, support the suggestion made in an earlier chapter (p. 65) that many country districts depended on the services provided by towns and villages for repairs and replacements to equipment. Another trade represented was coopering, and it was also found during excavations that parts of barrels were often used to line sections of well-shafts. One of these, however, was found to have been made of silver fir, which is native to southern Europe, and was a container originally used for importing Spanish or French wine.

The houses of Silchester are truly representative of Romano-British urban dwellings. The earliest, insofar as they can be detected, were frequently built of wattle and daub attached to timber frames, similar to those in other early towns. Most also had a simple plan. Some presumably developed as time passed and appeared in a rebuilt, although not necessarily realigned, form at later dates, in which the older alignment was sometimes incorporated into new extensions conforming with the street grid. We do not know precisely at what date masonry foundations and walls began to be used here for private houses, although, as at Verulamium, it might be suspected that such developments did not generally

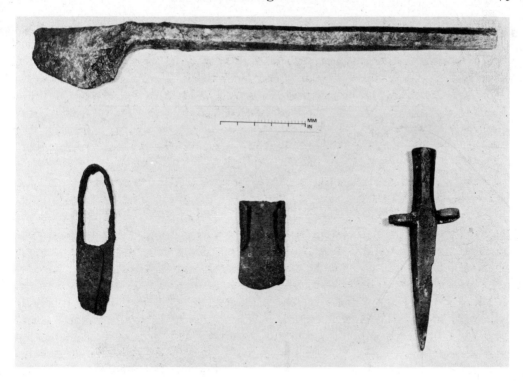

49   Agricultural implements from Silchester (*Reading Museum*)

occur much before the middle of the second century. Some sixteen large court-yard houses are known at Silchester and most conform with the lines of the street grid. The number is hardly enough to accommodate all members of the curial class, even allowing for several members of one family to sit on the ordo at the same time, and we might infer that not all owned houses of the most opulent type. This would be in keeping with evidence elsewhere from which a wide social and economic range of members can be inferred. Although over thirty of the houses are known to have had mosaic floors, they lacked the more ebullient pictorial designs found in mosaics at Cirencester and some other towns. Most are composed of conventional geometric and stylised floral patterns. Only one pavement, which probably came from an earlier version of House xix, 2, contained more animated scenes. Fragments of painted wall-plaster indicate the same types of decoration and the use of standard colours that have been found more recently in other towns.

Many houses had courtyards, or larger areas apparently associated with them, which may have been used as gardens or orchards. One of the most interesting aspects of the earlier investigations at Silchester, in which they were far ahead of their time, was the publication of detailed lists of plant remains. These lists include plants which today would most likely be accounted as weeds, although many, such as Good King Henry, corn salad, nettle, valerian, self-heal, penny cress and

St John's wort, may have been used for culinary or herbal purposes. Other plants possibly were deliberately cultivated in gardens for their appearance, such as mallow, rose, violet and box. Yet others, although also occurring wild, may have been used as vegetables, such as carrot, parsnip and celery; there is also a single example of an edible pea. Both coriander and chervil seem to have been grown as seasonings. Poisonous plants such as hemlock and varieties of nightshade would have been useful for pharmaceutical preparations. Frequent use seems to have been made of wild fruits, such as blackberry, raspberry, wild strawberry, sloe, crab-apple, elder and hazel nuts. Cultivated and improved fruits included a small medlar, bullace, damson, a plum of Orleans type and the mulberry, all of which may have been introduced to this island during the Roman period. Whether grapes and figs should be included in this list is more problematical and the seeds found may have come from imported dried fruit, although both vines and fig-trees will grow readily in Britain. The presence of marsh marigold and water chickweed indicates ponds and marshy areas within the town. Linseed may suggest the preparation of flax for the manufacture of linen, or fodder for cattle.

Other remains found in the course of excavation give a reasonably complete picture of the non-vegetarian diet of a town. Apart from domestic animals and birds kept for food, hunting must have provided the more exotic items on the menu, which included wild boar and several other species of game. Both fresh-water and sea fish were represented and included a variety of shellfish and edible snails.

Boon has suggested[123] that the lack of villas in the country immediately around Silchester indicates that the land was farmed from the town. Further, he has pointed out that certain houses within the town have large yards and out-buildings, which would have been suitable for farm use. Added to the presence of farm implements and a corn-drying oven, it seems a reasonable assumption to make. This raises the interesting question of whether it is, after all, possible to have villas in towns.

So little is known about the burials and cemeteries at Silchester and so few inscriptions have been found, that not much can usefully be said about the in-habitants. One of the principal cemeteries was outside the north gate, but it has never been excavated. Only one tombstone is known,[124] which refers to Flavia Victorina and was set up by her husband Titus Tammonius Victor (pl. 50). The chief interest lies in the name Tammonius, for it also recurs in that of the dedicator, T. Tammonius Vitalis, of the inscription to Hercules found in the forum; his father was Saenius Tammonius and it is probable that the family were prominent in civic life, Roman citizenship having been conferred on the father presumably for service as a magistrate. It is interesting that the later generations preferred to use the more correct form of the name. Despite the fact that so little is known of individuals, we do know that there were sufficient residential non-Callevans in the town to form a guild, *collegium peregrinorum*, which seems to have had connexions with the temple in Insula xxxv (p. 268).[125] The inscriptions (pl. 48) referring to the guild are also important because they have been taken to reflect on the possible status of the town. One inscription refers to [*consistenti*]*um*

50   Tombstone of Flavia Victorina, wife of T. Tammonius Victor (*Museum of Archaeology and Anthropology, Cambridge*)

Callevae, the other simply to C[. . .] C[. . .]. Both Birley and Boon[226] expand
the second to read *civitas Callevensium*, from which they infer that Silchester had
been promoted to a municipium. Frere has rightly rejected this argument, since
it is clear that the second inscription should be expanded to agree with the first.[127]
It is also worth pointing out that the inscriptions, probably of early third century
date, belonged to the period when civic distinctions began to be blurred, and
when a town at the centre of a civitas, and acting as its capital, tended to be
identified with the civitas itself.

The later history of Silchester is difficult to piece together. Shortly after the
construction of its masonry fortifications, it is reputed to have been sacked,
either by the survivors of Allectus' army, or by the successful Romans in AD 296.
It may have been at this time that the basilica was burnt and rebuilt on slightly
different lines; the arrangement of the internal colonnades were altered and
rectangular tribunals replaced the apsidal ones of the earlier period. Silchester is
one of the few towns in Roman Britain which have never produced evidence,
apart from the wide flat ditch, for the addition of external bastions to the curtain
wall, and which might imply that its position was comparatively safe and did
not warrant a garrison of artillerymen. At some unknown date, however, the
southern portal of the west gate, and the sluice gate, were both blocked, while the
width of the south-western gate was reduced by nearly half, presumably to
increase their defensive capacities. There is evidence that the forum and basilica
ended in flames although there is no other indication of widespread destruction.
Five items of military equipment, usually associated with the late Roman army,
have been found in the town,[128] but there is no early Germanic settlement in the
area.

The very latest objects from Silchester have been reviewed by Boon.[129] They
include fragments from glass vessels and beads of the very latest Roman types,
and some bronze pins with western, Celtic affinities. One is tempted to associate
the latter with the Ogham stone from Insula IX, which Professor Jackson, on
stylistic grounds, dated to probably the seventh century or later. However, Sir
Ifor Williams ascribed a provisional date of *c.* AD 450 to the stone while Frere has
also cast doubt on Jackson's conclusions. The inscription on it reads EBICATO[S
MAQ]I MVCO[and it is the most easterly example of this Celtic script yet known.[130]
The Silchester region in the fifth and sixth centuries has also been considered by
O'Neil.[131] He pointed out that a high proportion of coins from the Silchester
excavations can be dated to AD 388–95, and that many of them showed a considerable degree of wear, so indicating continued occupation of the site well into
the fifth century. From Goring up to Dorchester on the north bank of the
Thames, there was an area of intensive early Saxon settlements,[132] which
contrasts strongly with the almost complete lack of similar occupation in and
around the Silchester area. To the north-west and west of Silchester, there are a
number of linear dykes which face away from the town (fig. 88). O'Neil made the
suggestion that these dykes acted for a time as a frontier between Saxon occupied
areas and a surviving British enclave based on Silchester or even London. Further-

more, he considered that they were erected at a time when Saxon expansion had been halted and when a temporary agreement had been reached between both sides leading to a state of equilibrium, such as might have happened after the Saxon defeat at Mount Badon. It is interesting that the alignment of all the major roads from Silchester have been preserved for considerable distances with the sole exception of that to Dorchester, which crossed the implied frontier near Padworth. Presumably it was no longer used beyond that point, for, from there on, almost to Dorchester, the line is altogether lost.

We might conclude therefore that life at Silchester lingered on through the fifth and early sixth centuries until the next phase of Saxon expansion began in the middle of the sixth century, after which it was extinguished for ever.

WINCHESTER (*Venta Belgarum*)

The earliest permanent settlement on the site of Winchester dates to the first and second centuries BC, when a large earthwork was constructed to enclose an area on a promontory partly west of, and partly underlying the western half of, the later Roman town. Recent excavations, however, have shown that this occupation ceased about the middle of the first century BC and was not resumed until *c.* AD 50.[133] There is probably enough evidence from immediately round Winchester for us to be able to attribute the area to the southern Atrebatic kingdom,[134] so that immediately before the conquest it would have been politically under Catuvellaunian domination. Reasons have already been put forward for considering that this part was given to Cogidubnus as an addition to his kingdom after the conquest (p. 242), and a comparison between early Silchester and Winchester has been drawn.

So far nothing has been found to suggest an early Roman military occupation at Winchester. Virtually no samian pottery and only a few brooches of the Claudio-Neronian period have come to light; this is not, however, conclusive proof for the absence of a military occupation.[135] Timber buildings of equivalent date have been identified in the area of St George's Street, but not enough was uncovered to prove either a military or a civilian origin.

However, it is surprising that, despite the extensive excavations, no evidence for either a fort or even for an immediately pre-conquest native centre has yet come to light.[136] In the circumstances, it would be as well if these conclusions were treated with caution, for, if the evidence is not forthcoming, Winchester will be the only town in Britain where the normal criteria governing growth to a civitas capital will be entirely absent.

The first genuine indication of Roman fortifications occurs in the late Neronian or early Flavian period, when an earthwork was constructed. It has been identified in Tower Street, at the south gate, and in the Castle yard where the bank passed across the filled ditch of the native enclosure;[137] the earthwork was also incorporated in the later town defences. A timber-framed gate, with three sets of

WINCHESTER (Venta Belgarvm)

65. Plan of Winchester (*after M. Biddle*)

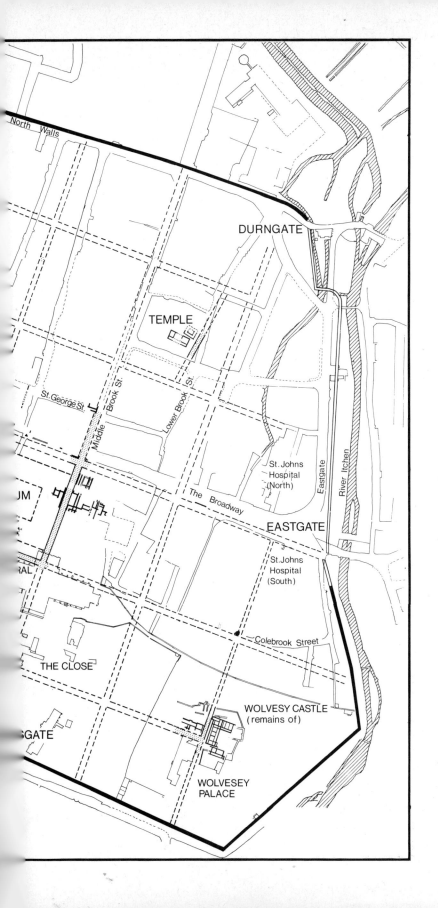

North Walls

DURNGATE

TEMPLE

St.George St.

Middle Brook St.

Lower Brook St.

St.Johns
Hospital
(North)

Eastgate

River Itchen

The Broadway

EASTGATE

St.Johns
Hospital
(South)

RAL

Colebrook Street

THE CLOSE

WOLVESY CASTLE
(remains of)

GATE

WOLVESEY
PALACE

JM

paired ports between the rampart ends, had been erected on the same site as that used for the later south gate. An unworn as of Nero was found in one of the post-holes.[138] Gates of this form are characteristic of the Neronian and early Flavian periods and have been found at the forts at Nanstallon, Baginton and Brough-on-Humber. Reasons have already been put forward (p. 257, SILCHESTER) to explain the construction of fortifications at Winchester *c.* AD 69–70. They may be related to the part Cogidubnus may have played in the civil war, and his possible friendship with Vespasian. However, it is not yet known what line these fortifications took on the eastern side, for no sign of them has been found there. Either they enclosed a different area, or they were never completed. The bank itself was variously composed of clean clay-with-flints or chalk with flints, and was retained at the front by a turf-revetted earth wall; it exceeded 40ft (12m) in width. On the west side there was a curious salient, which was preserved by the later defences.

As at Chichester and Silchester, the death of Cogidubnus brought marked changes at Winchester. It became the capital of a newly-formed administrative area: the civitas Belgarum. The choice of title for the civitas, derived from an ethnic rather than a tribal name, indicates that it was created, as with the Cantiaci, by merging several tribal units, or parts of tribes, each of which was presumably too small for independent status. It certainly seems to have taken in parts of both the old southern and northern Atrebatic kingdoms, and it may have extended westwards beyond Bath.[139] Why this collection of oddments should have been called *Belgae* is obscure. It is also difficult to understand why a site so close to the eastern boundary should have been chosen for its capital.

The change in administrative arrangements brought about considerable development at Winchester. A system of streets was laid out in the Flavian period (fig. 65). So far the lines of the main east-west and north-south streets are reasonably certain, but they do not appear to intersect at right angles. Also known are the streets to the north, south and east of the forum area and another further east. Yet another, found near Lower Brook Street, does not align with any already mentioned, although it is running in an approximately north-south direction.[140] Clearly therefore the street system appears by no means regular and it would be unwise to attempt a full restoration of the plan without more information.

An insula in the centre of the town is known to have contained a large public building complex, which was discovered during excavations underneath the site of the Wessex Hotel and the Cathedral Green.[141] This complex is most probably the forum and basilica, as no other insula contains structures which can be so interpreted. A hypothetical reconstruction by D. Mackreth puts the basilica along the west side of the complex,[142] with overall dimensions of 310ft (94m) by 410ft (125m), but much more information is required before there can be any certainty. What little is known of the plan would imply a forum with a somewhat asymmetric plan, in many ways resembling that at Leicester (p. 340). Construction seems to have taken place at the end of the Flavian period or slightly later. Fragments of Purbeck marble slabs have been found associated with this

51 Altar set up by Antonius Lucretianus, *beneficiarius consularis,* at Winchester (*British Museum*)

building, and a large eye from a more than lifesize statue in limestone (pl. 53) was found in the filling of Saxon graves above. To such a building could also belong the fragment of a building inscription (pl. 52) found in 1957, in Middle Brook Street.[143] It is probably a dedication to one of the Antonine emperors and the letters are the largest known on any inscription in Britain.

It is unfortunate that so little has been discovered of the early history of the town, the explanation being partly that, on the east side of the town, the early levels almost invariably lie at or below the modern water level. However, on the west side there is still a marked absence. As a result, little detailed information is available on its formative years. The Romano-Celtic temple discovered in Lower Brook Street is probably dated to the second century, but, apart from the plan,

52   Fragment of an imperial dedication from Middle Brook Street, Winchester (*Winchester City Museums*)

little more can be said about it. It appears to have been of conventional shape with four projecting pilasters set in the portico wall on the entrance side; the inner pair corresponded with two more at the ends of the front wall of the cella. The overall dimensions were 45ft (13·7m) by 38ft (11·7m), and the cella measured 23ft (7m) by 18ft (5·5m) internally.

Towards the end of the second century, new fortifications were constructed for the town. On the west and south sides, the Flavian bank was embodied in the new work by tipping layers of soil, scraped up from field surfaces, on top of it. The new bank was probably revetted with turf at the front and some turf was also buried in the core.[144] Elsewhere this bank has been identified on the east side of the town in Colebrook Street and on the south side at the south gate. Excavations on the north side have shown the later wall foundations probably cutting through it.

At some time, perhaps fairly early in the third century, a masonry wall was inserted into the front of the existing bank. The excavations in Southgate Street showed that the wall turned inwards for at least 18ft (5·5m) on the east side of the gate. But no actual gate structure connected with this inturn was observed, and it would seem that the gate proper was set well to the rear of the line of the curtain wall to which it was joined by the inturns. If the masonry gate was set back behind the line of the curtain wall, then it would have closely resembled the east and west gates at Silchester (see p. 265 above). Indeed Mr Biddle has pointed out the close similarity of the known dimensions. That being so, we might suggest that at Winchester, as at some other towns, work had started on masonry fortifications before the earthworks were erected.

The construction of the masonry curtain followed closely the line of the earth bank; only on the north side of the town is there perhaps slight doubt. The wall was built of large flints laid in courses between thick layers of mortar, and was about 9–10ft (2·7–3m) thick. It rested on a massive foundation of flints and puddled chalk. No indications of the Roman ditch have yet been found as, on the north, west and south sides it had been replaced by the medieval ditch, while on the east side the presence of the river Itchen might have rendered a ditch unnecessary. The width of the augmented rampart, contemporary with the wall, varied from 40 to 60ft (12 to 18m), the wider dimension being due to a steep downward slope behind the west curtain wall.

The line of the wall has been traced on all sides of the circuit. It forms a slightly irregular trapezoid with a marked salient at the Castle. On the east side it roughly follows the line of the river. It enclosed an area of 144 acres (58ha).[145]

Apart from the south gate little is known of the other Roman gates. It is probable that both the east and west gates lie on or near the same sites as their medieval successors. Massive foundations discovered below the Great Western Hotel and St John's Hospital in 1928[146] are probably part of the structure of the former. The site of the north gate is not definitely known, although the road from Silchester, joined by that from Mildenhall just outside the town, is aimed at precisely the point occupied by the medieval gate. Chalk foundations observed at the north gate in the 1930s may possibly be Roman work. Other possible gate sites are Kingsgate and Durngate, but their Roman origin is entirely unproved.

The evidence for other public works is slight. A conduit, reputedly of Roman date, ran through the wall just south of the Durngate, having been found in 1848. It was 14in (356mm) wide and 9in (229mm) high, and in part was lined with lead. Outside the wall, it ran parallel with it for some distance and was covered with a thick layer of opus signinum. It was argued that the fall, from north to south, indicated an aqueduct bringing water from the river, rather than a drain.[147] If so, it would be contrary to normal procedure, unless the water was drawn off well upstream. A water supply entering the town here is by no means impossible as a line of wooden pipes was found running north-east to south-west in Lower Brook Street. But an aqueduct derived from this quarter must have been of very limited use, as it could hardly have supplied buildings on the rising ground to the west. Indeed, it might be worthwhile to look for an additional line entering the town from the west or north.

The private shops and houses of Venta Belgarum are also little known. Excavations in 1961 revealed parts of buildings in the north-west corner of the insula east of the forum.[148] Building 1 had a small rectangular courtyard fronting the street; a well was situated at the north end of the courtyard. Behind the courtyard, a corridor ran the length of the building and was floored with red tessellation. A fragmentary mosaic was placed centrally in the floor, presumably to correspond with the entrance. At both ends of the corridor, wings projected forward to the edge of the street. The building was occupied in the third century and it seems to have been ruinous by the early fourth century, after which the area was left vacant, but fenced off from the street.

Two other buildings, apparently distinct from Building 1, were identified in the same area in the contractors' excavations, but little can be said about them. Many houses have been indicated solely by the discovery of mosaic pavements. Part of a good-quality mosaic was uncovered in 1878 under the road beyond the west end of the Cathedral burial yard. It was part of a border of a large and elaborate pavement containing interlaced squares with heads, figures and dolphins; it is now in the City Museum.[149] In pattern, it was probably not unlike the better known pavement from the Bramdean villa.[150] Another was found in a house in St George's Street. Such other pavements as are known seem to match the general standard of the British civitas capitals.

One house, or possibly a shop, which has been more fully excavated, is in Lower Brook Street, close to the temple referred to above (p. 282).[151] It was a simple building of three or four rooms with a corridor running down the south side. At the east end of the corridor there appears to have been an entrance porch. A courtyard south of the building directly abutted the street to the east. It is probable that the house was not built until the early fourth century, in which case it is later than the destruction of the temple. In the most easterly room, which itself had a wide doorway opening to the street, there was a large raised rectangular hearth, surrounded on three sides by a trough.[152] Two small ovens opened

53   Eye from a life-size statue in limestone; forum area, Winchester (*Winchester Research Unit*)

off the trough, but had a common stokehole not connected with it. In a later stage the ovens and hearth were removed. Cakes of bronze were found associated with this room, although there was no specific evidence of bronze working, such as moulds, dross or slag. One of several earlier wells in the courtyard produced a small wooden figure (pl. 54), which has been interpreted as a representation of a Celtic goddess.[153] The building appears to have been destroyed in the late fourth century.

Another house or shop, dated to the first half of the second century, has been found at Wolvesey Palace. It was timber-framed, with chalk or mortar floors and with one room decorated with conventional painted plaster. An oven and other hearths were associated with it.[154] After its destruction it was replaced by a more substantial masonry building of Antonine date, but with much the same ground plan as before. Other buildings show extensive second-century development in this area, with both shops and houses represented.

An industry at Winchester is implied by the mention in the *Notitia Dignitatum* of the *procurator gynaecii (in Britannis), Ventensis*.[155] This reference has already been discussed in connexion with Caistor-by-Norwich (p. 237), as it has been claimed that the Venta of the Notitia refers to that town. However, of a number of authorities who have identified it with Winchester, Wild has been the most recent to advance cogent reasons for this choice.[156] He has considered the organisation and character of this institution, but no building has yet been found at Winchester which could be interpreted as a weaving mill. Since it was almost certainly concerned with the manufacture of woollen cloth for official use, it may have been closely associated with a fulling shop. If so, the most likely place to find it would be at the eastern end of the town near the river, and it is worth recalling the aqueduct, mentioned above (p. 284), in this connexion. The Brooks area was certainly the centre of the medieval textile industry.

One of the few inscriptions found at Winchester is on an altar discovered near the south end of Jewry Street and dedicated to Italian, German, Gallic and British mother-goddesses by Antonius Lucretianus (pl. 51), who is described as a *beneficiarius consularis*.[157] The style of the lettering has led to it being dated to the late first or early second century. The duties of these officers seem to have been varied, but they were undoubtedly junior members of the governor's staff, who were often employed in a clerical capacity. Might we therefore suggest that this minor official was stationed at Winchester to help organise the clothing levies then operated by the army? Only with the reorganisation of the government service and the establishment of regular factories in the fourth century would the administration have been placed in civilian rather than in army hands.

In the fourth century, Winchester seems to have been more densely occupied than before. No interruption occurs in the coin sequence and a major late fourth-century cemetery is known at Lankhills. A house at Wolvesey Palace was equipped with tessellated floors and continued to be used until the later part of the century. Unfortunately much of this late evidence has been planed off in the Saxon period and during the Middle Ages, and so little is known of the houses at this time.

There is some evidence that the defences were modified during the fourth century by the addition of bastions. However, two external towers, recorded in the late eighteenth century between the west gate and the north-west angle, are most likely to be of medieval origin.[158] But there is also a projecting tower, probably of horseshoe or semi-circular shape, which had been added to the wall some 17ft (5·2m) east of the south gate, and which is certainly Roman.[159]

The Lankhills School cemetery, lying between the Silchester and Mildenhall roads outside the north gate, is of particular interest because of its entirely fourth-century use.[160] It was in no sense a cemetery used only by the poorer inhabitants, for many of the burials were well and even richly furnished; the majority had their heads approximately to the west, but this alone cannot be taken as a firm indication of Christian burial rites, especially since their alignments seem to be related more to the nearby roads than to the cardinal point. Most were buried in wooden coffins. The most interesting are a number which contain late Roman military equipment in the form of small knives, zoomorphic buckles and belt tags, together with a number of cross-bow brooches and some glass beakers of

54 Wooden image of a Celtic goddess, 7in (180mm) high, from The Brookes, Winchester (*Winchester Research Unit*)

very late date. Apart from the fact that Winchester contained a military garrison in the late fourth century, it is clear that the civilian inhabitants were still reasonably wealthy. Burial did not cease in the area until after AD 400.

Other cemeteries at Winchester are located east, west and south-west of the town. Two isolated burials of Flavian date were found in 1964 in Grange Road, about a mile (1·6km) south of the south gate,[161] during work on a sewer trench. Both bodies had been cremated and the burials contained a range of samian, coarse pottery, glass and bronze vessels. Grave I appears to have had an iron- and bronze-bound wooden box included, while the most interesting object in Grave II was a shale tray or trencher, inscribed with an elaborate geometric pattern. Two joints of pork, a samian cup and platter, and two knives and a spoon had been placed on the tray. There are distinct affinities between these burials and the richer graves of the Belgic period, with perhaps indications of trade with Durotrigian areas, for the shale trays are distributed mainly in the Dorset region, but with outliers at Silchester and London.

Winchester seems to have possessed considerable suburbs outside the fortified area of the town. A house of some substance, with tessellated floors, was cut through when the London and South-Western Railway was constructed in 1838. It lies some 430ft (130m) west of the west gate and close to the road leading to Old Sarum.[162] Another house with tessellated floors was noted when the Great Western Railway was extended to Winchester and lies well outside the south-eastern town boundary. More recently a fourth-century suburb has been noted on the north side of the town and to the east of the main Silchester road. A subsidiary street was found to be running diagonally across the area in a south-easterly direction.

So far there is little evidence for the end of the Roman town. The late military garrison, mentioned above in connexion with the Lankhills cemetery, seems to belong to the late fourth and early fifth century. There is a general scatter of early Anglo-Saxon sherds in later levels in the Lower Brooks Street region but, as yet, no structures to associate with them. Yet over the streets east of the forum was found a layer of rough cobbling separated from the street surface by a layer of black, stony loam.[163] A similar cobbled surface was also found overlying the street to the south of the forum, where it was bounded on the south by post-holes,[164] and again separated from the street surface by a black peaty layer. In both cases the cobbled surfaces were associated with late Roman pottery, with the exception of one coarse, hand-made sherd. Other sherds of similar pottery have been found in later contexts. The implication would seem to be that, after civic discipline broke down, houses were built over the streets, which provided firm, well-drained foundations. At least one similar occurrence has been noted at Canterbury. It is impossible to say precisely when this occurred, but a date in the fifth century might be envisaged. At some stage also the south gate appears to have been blocked first by a ditch and then by a crude masonry wall built across the front between the inturns of the curtain wall, but the exact date of this structure is equally uncertain.

7

Flavian Expansion

CIRENCESTER, DORCHESTER, EXETER, LEICESTER, WROXETER

The considerable expansion of the civilian areas of Britain during the Flavian period has already been discussed in general terms in an earlier chapter (p. 27) and more especially in connexion with the dismemberment of Cogidubnus' kingdom (Chapter 6). But the expansion by no means ended there. The military advances of the early Flavian period caused the release from military government of further considerable areas, so giving rise to the constitution of five more civitates: the Dobunni, Durotriges, Dumnonii, Coritani and Cornovii.

CIRENCESTER (*Corinium Dobunnorum*)

The evolution of the civitas Dobunnorum and its capital at Corinium has already been cited in Chapter 1 as an example of how such developments could occur. Yet the sequence of events there recorded, although in accordance with much modern thought and evidence, leaves several points open to argument.

The most recent, full consideration of the Belgic Dobunni and their initial contact with Rome is by Hawkes in Mrs Clifford's report on her excavations at Bagendon.[1] His views are to some extent bolstered by Allen's work on the Dobunnic coinage, by Mrs Clifford's own interpretation of her excavations and by Miss Fell's report on the pottery. But many points which arise there are open to question. Some of the principal planks in their concerted arguments are the assumptions that Boduocus, as ruler of the eastern part of the tribe, was the leader of the expedition of the Dobunni to Kent, that it was he who surrendered to Rome and was, in turn, made an ally and client king over the whole tribe. Another is that the remainder of the kingdom under Corio[2] was hostile to Rome, allied itself with Caratacus, and built the earthworks in and around Minchinhampton. These suggestions certainly explain many of the facts, but by no means all, and alternatives, in some cases more acceptable, can be put forward.

Allen puts the date for the coins of both Corio and Boduocus as falling between AD 43 and 47. Yet the Roman army had certainly arrived in the Cirencester region

▲ BARTON FARM   SITE OF
                 GLOUCESTER GATE

Thomas Street

Dollar Street

XXX¹₂

Coxwell Street   XXVI

                                  XXVII

Cirencester Park   XXVIII

Castle Street   XXII²

GATE?

+   1967 XXI
1877?

                     Sheep Street

Road   Cemetery

Tetbury   Ashcroft Road

                     1958

+   St. Peter's Road   XX
1969   Querns Road

                                  SITE OF

+   Probable   + 1914
                     line of   Cemetery
+   Fosse
1915   way   + 1971

                                  Querns Hill

                     AMPHITHEATRE

                     Cotswold Avenue

                                  ROMAN △
                                  BUILDING

Chesterton Lane

100   500   1000   1500   100   0
▬▬▬▬▬▬▬▬▬▬▬▬▬▬▬▬▬▬▬▬▬▬ Scale in Feet ▬▬▬▬▬▬▬
0   0

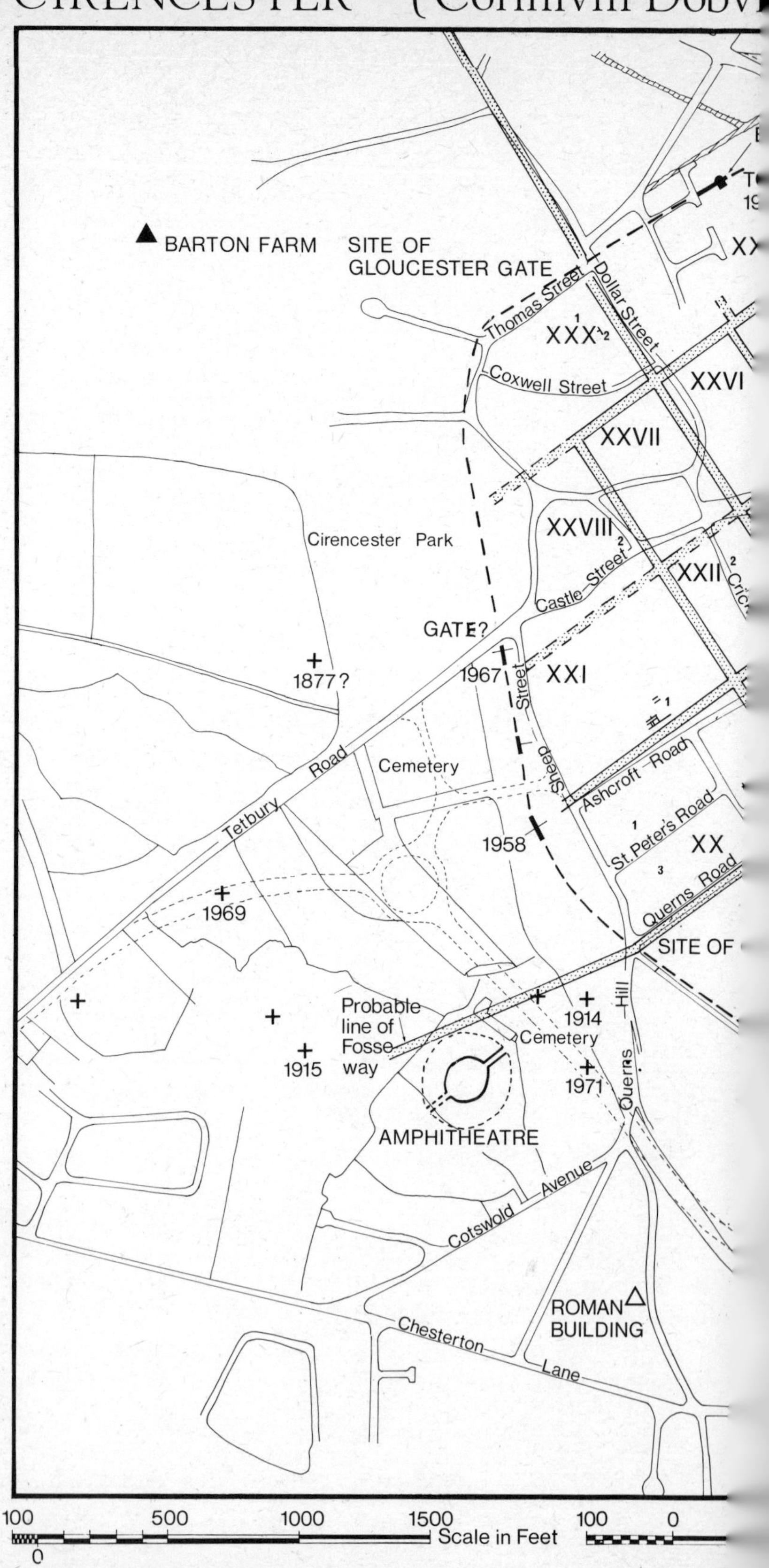

66   Plan of Cirencester (*after A. D. McWhirr*)

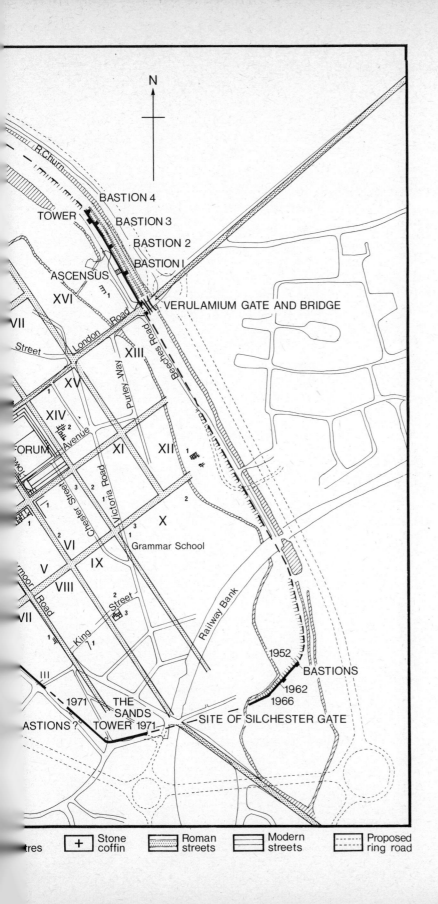

N

BASTION 4
TOWER
BASTION 3
BASTION 2
BASTION 1
ASCENSUS
XVI
VERULAMIUM GATE AND BRIDGE
VII
Street
London Road
Beeches Road
XIII
XV
Purley Way
XIV
FORUM
Avenue
XI
XII
X
Grammar School
Chester Street
Victoria Road
VI
IX
V
VIII
moor Road
Street
VII
King
Railway Bank
1952
BASTIONS
III
1962
1966
1971
THE
SANDS
ASTIONS?
TOWER 1971
SITE OF SILCHESTER GATE

Stone coffin   Roman streets   Modern streets   Proposed ring road by AD 44, if not before, and an initial division of the tribe after occupation would have been meaningless, so that the arrangements then in force can only reflect what had happened before the Roman conquest. Certainly the respective distributions of the coins of Corio and Boduocus are almost mutually exclusive, and that of the latter appears to represent a wedge driven into the Dobunnic heartland, with coins of Corio appearing north, west and south of the area. Moreover the coins of Boduocus are the only Dobunnic coins reflecting a pronounced Roman influence. This noteworthy difference could well throw fresh light on the passage of Dio Cassius which refers to the Dobunni (Bodunni) being subject to the Catuvellauni.[3] Remembering the considerable southward expansion of the Catuvellauni in the early 40s, after the death of Cunobelin, it seems not improbable that they had also penetrated westward into Dobunnic territory by means of the Thames valley, which would have been the easiest and most convenient line of approach. Certainly Boduocus' coins are found predominately in the area of that river's headwaters. Was Boduocus therefore a Catuvellaunian, or even a puppet Dobunnian, king implanted after conquest? We might so believe in view of the noted change in coin styles, which may have been derived more from Catuvellaunian than from direct Roman influence. It is partly because his coins are stylistically the latest in the Dobunnian series and partly because none were found in the two main hoards from Nunney and Sherborne,[4] that Allen gives them a mainly post Roman-conquest date. However, he is careful to point out that it may be wrong to expect them in hoards so far south of his apparent kingdom. Dr Kent on the other hand would tentatively ascribe an entirely pre-conquest date to both series. There seems no good reason therefore to conclude from our present evidence, as Hawkes has done, that the Boduocan coins were issued solely after the Roman conquest, when, by simply placing the larger part of the Boduocan issue into the year or two before the conquest, the way is opened for a complete revision of current theories.

Hawkes has rightly argued that the Bodunni, who surrendered to Aulus Plautius in Kent, were a part of the Dobunni, incorrectly named by scribal error in Dio's narrative. It seems likely also that the detachment concerned would have represented Boduocus' faction, as part of the Catuvellaunian dominions. So far we can follow Hawkes, but at this point we must part company from him. Whether they had surrendered to Rome or not, there seems no reason why Boduocus and his followers should have been treated any differently from other Catuvellaunian invaders of neighbouring territory. They were ejected from Trinovantian, Cantiacan and Atrebatic territory, so why should they have been allowed to remain in possession of Dobunnic land? It often happened that the indigenous tribe, hard pressed by the Catuvellauni before AD 43, actually welcomed Roman intervention. Instead of making out therefore, as Hawkes, Allen and Mrs Clifford have done, that Corio and the remainder of the tribe greeted the Roman army with hostility, the very reverse may have happened. The 'anti-Roman' styles seen by Hawkes on most Dobunnic coinage may be no more than non-Roman. Moreover, if Corio had been hostile, it seems extremely unlikely that he would have been permitted to continue minting his own coins.

Before going further, we must consider next the principal oppida of the Dobunni and their associations. Undoubtedly Bagendon was one of the most important in the decades before the tribe was split. There was the mint of the main ruling dynasty. The absence of Boduocan coins from this site might imply a movement of tribal headquarters under a new 'foreign' king, and in this context we might consider Minchinhampton. Mrs Clifford suggested that these earth-works were a product of an alliance between Caratacus and Corio. But it seems to strain the facts to breaking point, if only because the Roman army would hardly have been guilty of such stupidity as to place a permanent fort at Ciren-cester only 12 miles (19km) from the postulated centre of unbroken hostility. Moreover, Corio would have been unlikely to throw in his lot with his chief enemy, even without the Roman army on his doorstep. Yet the oppidum at Minchinhampton has still to be explained. It undoubtedly belongs to the last Belgic phase in the Cotswolds and has produced not only a coin of Boduocus but also metalwork comparable with pieces from Catuvellaunian homelands. Although Mrs Clifford uses the latter to support her views on the presence of Caratacus, they could equally well have been brought by a Catuvellaunian conqueror, Boduocus, or his followers. With Boduocus eliminated by the Romans, the way would have been open for Corio to have returned to the old dynastic capital of Corinion at Bagendon. This explanation makes allowance for the fact that, while coins of Boduocus have never been found in areas demonstrab-ly under Corio's control, isolated coins of Corio are known from areas under the sometime control of Boduocus. The ultimate choice of Corinium as the civitas capital in the Flavian period also emphasises the importance of Bagendon in tribal politics and the return to that district of the tribal leaders.[5]

We may summarise the foregoing arguments, while at the same time pointing out that they are not necessarily any more acceptable than those put forward by Hawkes. They can only be considered as an alternative, but just as reasonable, explanation of the known facts.

Catuvellaunian expansion westwards led to the conquest of Dobunnic lands in the upper Thames Valley and the division of the tribe. A Catuvellaunian king, Boduocus, ruled over the conquered territory, and at the time of the Roman invasion sent a detachment to Kent to assist the parent tribe. On surrendering to Aulus Plautius, Boduocus was removed from the lands he had conquered and control of the whole Dobunnic tribe returned to the surviving dynast, Corio, who remained as a possible client king until the arrangements were swept away in the reforms of Ostorius Scapula. One last point might be made. The Celtic prefix Corio was by no means uncommon, occurring as a place-name both in Britain and Gaul. Is it only coincidence that the name of the tribal capital of the Dobunni should have incorporated the same prefix, at a time when place-names were being consolidated and Latinised, as that contained in the name of one of its few recorded tribesmen?

Despite uncertainty over the Dobunnic ruler immediately after the Roman conquest, there is less doubt about what happened at Cirencester (fig. 4). A fort, or more probably a 30-acre (12ha) fortress, was established in the area later occupied by the southern end of the town, probably within a year of the invasion.[6] Contemporary occupation at Bagendon continued[7] on a declining scale until the early 60s, by which time a new fort for a cavalry regiment had been established north of the earlier site. North-west of this fort, a civilian settlement started to grow at about the same time as Bagendon was failing. No doubt the fort and its occupants provided the necessary incentive to cause a gradual migration of the inhabitants to a more convenient position immediately outside it. This civilian settlement seems to have been regulated almost from the first, no doubt under legal status of vicus, with streets laid out parallel to the axes of the fort.[8] Unfortunately little is known of its buildings, although excavations near Ashcroft Road beneath Insula XXI and also below the forum showed traces of contemporary timber structures.[9]

The fort at Cirencester was evacuated, probably in company with others in the west Midlands and south-west, during the late 70s, and probably during the first year or so of Agricola's governorship. The constitution of the civitas Dobunnorum must have followed immediately. The selection of Corinium as the site for the capital has already been discussed extensively (pp. 27, 289), and within two or three decades the town had been laid out on a regular grid pattern over an area which included not only the early vicus but also the fort. A forum and basilica, which were larger than those of any other town in Roman Britain except London, had been built; an amphitheatre had been provided for amusements outside the main planned area, and many houses and shops were being erected (fig. 66). Even by this early date, the town was provided with a market, separate from the forum, in Insula II, which may be taken as an indicator of the wealth already concentrated in the neighbourhood.

The site of the town lies almost entirely in the valley of the river Churn, which is floored by a thin layer of clay over gravel. The ground falls away to the south-east, where parts may have been marshy, but rises gently on to the oolite to the north-east, and more sharply to the west. The late Rev. Canon Grensted was of the opinion that stone quarries of Roman date existed alongside the White Way, while others are indicated in the region of the amphitheatre.

The forum stood in the centre of the town and was flanked by Ermin Street on its south-west, by the Fosse Way on its north-west and by the basilica on its south-east sides (fig. 67). Hence the basilica occupied an unusual position with a mainly northerly aspect. Except for the north-east end of the basilica, the whole complex was surrounded by an external colonnade 13ft (4m) wide. It occupied an area measuring 550ft (168m) by 340ft (104m). The piazza floor had been made level with a thick layer of limestone rubble and gravel to counteract the natural slope of the ground to the south-east. No evidence survived to indicate the nature of its surface, but paving-stones of sandstone may have been provided, as in the later periods. The piazza itself measured 350ft (107m) by approximately 275ft (84m). The latter measurement is uncertain as the south-west range has never been

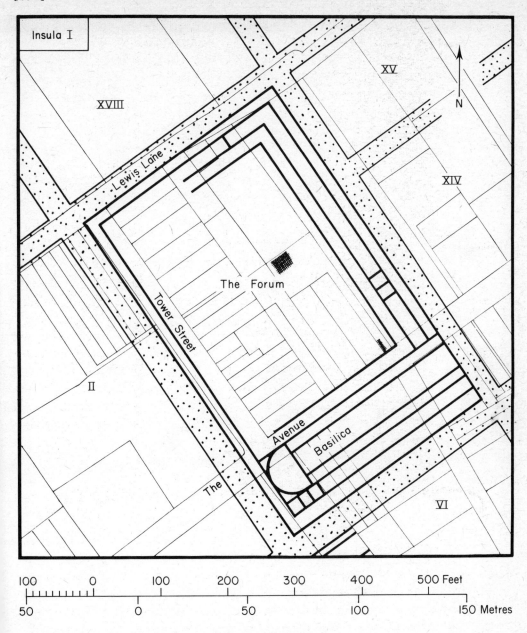

67   The forum insula, Cirencester

excavated. An internal colonnade, about 25ft (7·6m) wide separated the piazza
from the basilica, the north-west and north-east ranges and is to be inferred also
on the south-west side. As far as is known the ranges were divided into shops or
offices in the normal manner.[10] A fragmentary inscription[11] found in Lewis

55   Pedestal base of a column dedicated to Jupiter Optimus Maximus, restored by L. Septimius . . . . . ,

Lane, in the north-west range, includes the word *respublica* and is presumably a reference to the civitas Dobunnorum. It probably belongs, however, to a later period than to the original foundation.

The basilica, which was first identified by Cripps in 1897–8, was partly re-excavated in 1961.[12] It consisted of an aisled hall approximately 80ft (24·4m) wide, running the full width of the insula, but with the south-western end occupied by a paved apse whose diameter was the full width of the hall. The nave was 34ft (10·4m) wide and was separated from the side aisles, each 18ft (5·5m) wide, by sleeper walls carrying columns. The sleeper walls, which had to carry the main weight of the structure, were 4ft 6in (1·4m) wide, but the outer walls were of slighter construction and sometimes did not exceed 2ft 6in (762mm). The apse was not matched by another at the opposite end of the hall, and indeed,

governor of Britannia Prima, at Cirencester (*F. M. B. Cooke; Corinium Museum*)

as Cripps showed, the north-east end was probably covered by a portico forming the main entrance to the building, and giving directly on to the street. Fragments of Corinthian capitals, 2ft 6in (0·76m) in diameter, found in the vicinity probably came from the portico, while part of an even larger capital, 4ft (1·2m) in diameter, may have come from the nave (pl. 57). The precise find-spot of the latter is not recorded, although it is thought to have come from the general area of the basilica.

A range of rooms was incorporated on the south-east side of the basilica, between the hall and the external colonnade. The range was 20ft (6·1m) wide, but to begin with individual rooms appear to have varied in size.

Apart from the architectural fragments mentioned above, other decorative features of the basilica appear to have included mouldings of Purbeck marble and Italian marble wall-veneers. A larger than life-size human eye and lid from a bronze statue came from the apse (pl. 56).

The asymmetry of the basilica as well as the imperfectly known central section makes it difficult to identify individual parts, and it is probably rash to speculate before more is known of the plan.[13]

However, when the basilica was built, the architects failed to take into account the filled ditches of the cavalry fort, over which it had been partly built. Consequently walls sank and cracked, and by the middle of the second century a major rebuilding programme had to be initiated. Some of the original walls, which had been given inadequate foundations, were completely rooted out, and new, deeper foundations inserted. Slight changes in plan were incorporated at the same time and the number of rooms in the south-east range was increased. Parts of the forum were also altered, the internal colonnade was slightly reduced in width and a new floor was laid in the piazza.

The insula immediately south-west of the forum (Insula II) seems to have been laid out from the first, at least in part, as a gravelled open space, with some slight evidence for timber structures. The gravelled surface formed an extension of the street to the south-east which remained unusually wide throughout its life. By

56   Eye from a life-size statue in bronze from the basilica, Cirencester (*J. E. Thawley; Corinium Museum*)

the Hadrianic period, however, a substantial masonry building had been constructed to a plan which closely resembled a wing of a forum. It consisted of a
single range of rooms, each roughly 18ft (5·5m) square, probably with timber
partitions dividing one from another, set between colonnades or arcades and
running parallel to the street (fig. 11). A number of pits were found, both on the
edge of the street and also beneath internal floors, which had been filled almost to
capacity with cut and sawn animal bones, as though from the preparation of
joints of meat. Beyond the range to the north-west, the original open courtyard
was preserved.[14] The combination of open space and probable butchers' shops
would point perhaps to a combined cattle and meat market. Specialist markets and
market halls of this type, while well known in Rome,[15] are rarer in the provinces,
and the existence of one at Cirencester emphasises the agricultural wealth of the
surrounding countryside even as early as the late first and early second centuries.

   Another public building provided in the earlier town was the amphitheatre,
situated about $\frac{1}{2}$ mile (800m) south-west of the town centre. It survives today as
grass-covered banks with the arena entrances easily distinguishable. The first
amphitheatre was constructed with the seating banks raised on mounds of turf
and limestone rubble. In part, the site seems to have been used beforehand as a
quarry, signs of which were observed beneath the north-east arena entrance. The
existence of this quarry was undoubtedly an advantage for the builders as part of
the quarry face was probably used as a backing for the interior bank. The entrances
into the arena were lined with timber and in part revetted with drystone walls,
but there was no indication of similar structures bounding the arena, although
they might be expected.[16]

   Soon after the beginning of the second century the whole amphitheatre was
reinforced with masonry walls (fig. 15). The arena, of elliptical shape, measured
approximately 160ft (49m) by 134ft (41m) after reconstruction and the width of
the seating banks was probably about 96ft (30m).[17] So far, only the north-east
arena entrance has been excavated.[18] It was a passage 15ft (4·6m) wide, and it is
likely that the outer 70ft (21.3m) was vaulted with the seating being carried over
the top. Excavation of part of the seating bank showed a series of shallow terraces
each of which was retained by a narrow drystone wall. These terraces probably
carried the seats of wooden planks.[19]

   Some further rebuilding of the entrance passage and arena wall took place in
the later second century, perhaps necessitated by collapse due to earth pressure.
At this time small chambers were added to flank the entrance at the arena end.
One could be entered from the arena only, while the other could be approached
from either the arena or the passage. One or both may have been prisons or cages
for incarcerating condemned criminals or wild beasts, but it is possible that one
at least contained a small shrine. Dedications to Nemesis were often undertaken
by performers or combatants, and altars erected to the goddess.

   Sites of other major public buildings, which we might expect to have been
provided for the early town, are still unknown. A pair of concentric, curving
walls, with an apparent diameter of 192ft (59m), may represent part of a theatre

57   Part of a Corinthian capital, probably from the basilica, Cirencester (*Corinium Museum*)

in Insula xxx, but too little is yet known for there to be any certainty. No public bath-house has yet been identified, although a building with several large heated rooms, one 50ft (15m) by 40ft (12m), another 32ft (4·7m) by 24ft (7·3m), found in the eighteenth century in the area west of Tower Street, would seem to be the strongest candidate.[20] An aqueduct is implied by the stretch of wooden water-pipe running under the road just inside the Verulamium Gate, on which a castellum aquae may have been placed. Further lengths of pipe were found in Purley Road in 1972. Construction and maintenance of the streets is also worthy of mention as a public work. Webster estimated that a new surface was laid on average every 15 years, although probably localised repairs or patchings occurred more frequently. At first the material used was almost entirely grouted gravel, although later a change was made to limestone rubble, which was well rammed to give a solid surface. It is possible that this change was brought about by the construction of the town's masonry defences, which would have produced large quantities of limestone waste. This almost continuous, if spasmodic, rise in the level of streets, together with the silt generated by them, was undoubtedly the cause of much rebuilding in the town, as houses and shops were gradually submerged by layer after layer of greyish silt which washed off the street surfaces every time it rained.

Temples are of course indicated by the many pieces of religious sculpture which have been found, but no religious buildings have been positively identified. One may, however, exist near Ashcroft Road, in Insula xx, for there was found in 1899 a collection of sculptures and altars associated with the Deae Matres.[21] Although these are somewhat later in date, the site itself could contain an earlier temple.

Construction was not confined to public buildings. Although, as yet, little is known of the early shops and houses of the town, there is enough to show that the most desirable commercial sites near the centre were being developed in the Flavian period. A row of shops in Insula v, across the street from the meat market, appear similar in plan and construction to the Claudian shops in Insula xiv at Verulamium (p. 204). Although built of wattle and daub on timber framework, some had good quality concrete floors and painted plaster in their domestic quarters.[22] Their later development was, however, different from the treatment of the Verulamium shops, partly perhaps because no serious fire ever razed the complete block. Rebuilding, when it was required, took place in a piecemeal fashion, and clearly indicated individual ownership, stone structures taking the place of timber when each proprietor had accumulated sufficient capital.

The use of stone for private buildings seems to have begun at Cirencester well before other towns, such as Verulamium, in the south-east, presumably due to its readier availability. Certainly a masonry house in the south corner of Insula xxiii cannot have been constructed much later than the first decade of the second century, with modifications taking place shortly afterwards.[23]

Towards the end of the second century Cirencester was provided with fortifications. It is, so far, one of the few towns in Britain which shows adequately the complex structural history to be expected in these works. These results have only been achieved by numerous sections being cut at various places on the circuit, and even now there are still points difficult to explain.

The circuit on the east side of the town was largely dictated by the early canalisation of the river Churn, undertaken to remove its course from the centre of the town where it lay on the valley bottom. This operation was carried out by cutting a new course for the river bed and the erection of a 6ft (1·8m) high clay, gravel and stone rubble levee on the downhill side to prevent overflow and flooding of the town.[24]

Subsequent work on the fortifications can be summarised as follows:

1. Preliminary work on masonry fortifications was begun with the construction of at least one, and possibly more, monumental gateways together with square interval towers, of which two are known.[25]

2. Work in masonry must have ceased and the circuit was completed by the erection of an earth rampart, coupled with ditches, which incorporated the existing gates and towers.

3. A stone wall, 4ft (1·2m) wide, was built in front of the existing rampart, which was itself raised in height.

4. The stone wall (pl. 61) was in places entirely rebuilt to a new width of 10ft (3m) by cutting further back into the rampart, which was itself again raised in height. These alterations were probably required by instability or even collapse of the narrower foundation.

5. Disuse of the internal towers was followed by construction of external towers.

6. Sundry repairs and modifications were made to the structures, especially on the east side of the circuit where they were exposed to flood water from the river. These were most noticeable in the vicinity of the Verulamium Gate.

It can be seen from this long sequence of construction, reconstruction and repair, covering a period of some 200 years, that work on the defences must have been nearly continuous.

In earlier discussions of fortifications at London, Verulamium and Silchester, it has already been suggested that the initial work in masonry was undertaken on the orders of Clodius Albinus, who foresaw the day when he might have to leave a defenceless province in order to contest his imperial claims. Perhaps he did not realise that his time for preparation would run out so quickly, and his scheme for massive masonry fortifications had rapidly to be translated into emergency earthworks for the majority of towns. The later consolidation of these earthworks with a stone wall cannot have taken place at Cirencester before about AD 220, but as yet we cannot say precisely when the wider wall was inserted. A date during the late third or early fourth century would seem most likely, while the erection of external towers followed during the second half of the fourth century. These towers were of polygonal form, probably not unlike those at Caerwent (p. 388), and were constructed on solid bases projecting outwards over the inner ditch.

The most impressive part of the fortifications so far excavated is the Verulamium Gate which carried the joint road from both Verulamium and Leicester into the north-east part of the town. Unfortunately only about half of the gate was available for excavation in 1960, and the remainder lies under the modern London Road.[26] Moreover, that part excavated had been heavily robbed, so making difficult the restoration of the full plan. In front of the gate a masonry bridge abutment was found. At the time, it was thought that this was contemporary with the gate, but if the river course was altered before the gate was built, as now seems most probable, an earlier bridge at this point would have been a necessity. It is of course possible that the first bridge was constructed of wood, and that the masonry bridge only replaced it when work was started on the defences, but there was insufficient evidence to decide the point. The masonry abutment had been constructed so that the plan represented adjacent chords of a large arc, and it is necessary to remember this when attempting to restore the gate plan.

The gate itself consisted of two parallel walls 4ft (1·2m) wide, set 4ft (1·2m) apart, through which the portals were constructed. The *spinae* were set at right angles to these walls, which were continuous beneath the carriageways. Although the masonry of the *spinae* had been entirely robbed, the positions of two portals were indicated by sets of wheel ruts. One set approached the inner face of the gate at right angles, while the other ran obliquely and appeared to fan out from the first set. At the north-west end of the gate, a projecting semi-circular tower, 19ft (5·8m) in external diameter was found.

The main problem in restoring the plan of the gate centres on the overall width and consequently on the number of portals which it possessed. There are two possibilities, although the second is more likely. The first envisages only three portals, with that in the centre slightly wider, at 13ft (4m) than the two flanking passages of 10ft (3·1m). The overall width of the gate would then have been about 82ft (24·6m). But there are serious objections to this restoration. In the first place, if both outer portals had been used equally by wheeled traffic, a second oblique set of ruts should have existed to complement those referred to above. None were observed. Moreover, the set which approached the gate at right angles were by no means situated in the centre of the street, but were well on the north side. Lastly, the central apex of the bridge abutment would have lain opposite, not the central carriageway as might be expected if the whole structure was symmetrical, but opposite the southern *spina*. In view of these objections, it is probably best to envisage (fig. 17) a four-portal gate, containing two central carriageways of 13ft (4m) each, flanked by subsidiary carriageways of 10ft (3·1m) each. In these circumstances a similar and complementary set of wheel ruts would have occupied the southern half of the street; the gate would have been placed symmetrically within the bridge abutment and the overall width of the gate would have been about 100ft (30·5m).[27]

Apart from the private shops referred to above, there is a great deal of evidence to illustrate the commercial and domestic life of the town. Already in the second century, houses were being equipped with top-quality mosaics and painted wall plaster. One house below Dyer Street, which was uncovered in 1849 and seen again in 1972, when another mosaic was found, produced two splendid pavements, and painted walls decorated with garlands of leaves. One of the pavements, dated to the late second or early third century, contained a central panel with hunting dogs apparently pursuing a quarry which was set in part of the mosaic that had not survived. Also included were sea animals and heads of Neptune and Medusa. The other pavement, dated to the late second century, incorporated Bacchic figures, and pictorial representations of the story of Actaeon, and of the Four Seasons.[28] Another pavement, probably from the same building but discovered much earlier in 1783, depicted a spirited marine scene, which Professor Toynbee has described as perhaps the best-drawn and most classical in style of all British figured mosaics.[29] But most evidence for this side of town life comes from fourth-century buildings, and consequently more properly belongs to the period of the town's greater distinction.

In 1891, a small rectangular base was found in Victoria Road, which measured 16in (406mm) by 17½in (444mm) high (pl. 55). One face is lost, but the other three faces contain inscriptions referring to the restoration of a Jupiter column by L. Septimius . . ., who is described as the praeses or governor of Britannia Prima.[30] The importance of these inscriptions has already been discussed in Chapter 3 (p. 86), and it need only be repeated here that they are usually taken to imply that Cirencester became the provincial capital of Britannia Prima after the Diocletianic reforms at the end of the third century.

The presence of a provincial governor's court would certainly have enhanced the importance and prosperity of the town, although it is not known if it ever affected the legal status. But it is interesting to observe certain fundamental

58   Fragment of inscription from House XII, 1, Cirencester (*J. E. Thawley, Cirencester Excavation Committee*)

changes which were made in the lay-out of the forum and basilica at about the same time, as these may well have been connected with the separation of provincial from civitas affairs.

The forum was divided in two unequal parts by a wall, perhaps carrying an elaborate architectural screen, built parallel to the north-west range and 130ft (40m) from it. The wings of the forum within the new north-western enclosure were also extensively altered. The internal colonnade was enclosed and a continuous mosaic floor laid within it, the mosaic being made up of a series of panels each containing different geometrical patterns. In the centre of the north-west range a large foundation was built across its full width and was floored with tessellation and mosaic. A projecting plinth, constructed at a later date, adjacent to the inner colonnade wall at this point, gave extra depth and probably provided the base for a portico. The floor level of the piazza also seems to have been raised above that in the south-eastern enclosure.[31] It is possible that this part of the forum had been earmarked for provincial business and perhaps even converted into the governor's praetorium, with the audience hall placed centrally in the north-west side. Such an arrangement would have deprived the town of a considerable area of public open space and also commercial premises. Other alterations which took place south-east of the basilica may have been intended to make good part of this loss.

The street which flanked the outside of the basilica was always rather wider than most. It was now closed at the south-west end by a row of small square rooms, not unlike those in the forum wings, and it is possible that the north-east end was similarly treated. The end room of the basilica was incorporated in this row. It is possible that the external colonnade on the south-west side of the forum was extended across the front of this new wing. Certainly the external colonnade south-east of the basilica seems to have been demolished, and several of the original rooms along this side were amalgamated and turned round so that they opened outwards instead of into the hall.[32]

The enclosure of this wide street would certainly have provided a substitute for some of the lost space in the piazza, and the additional shops or offices in the blocking wings and along the length of the basilica would have helped to remedy the loss of covered premises. It is possible that these new arrangements also affected the building in the west corner of Insula VI, but too little is known about it for there to be any certainty.

A possible alternative explanation might envisage a separate curia being constructed at the north-west end of the forum from the basilica, and not unlike the much earlier arrangement at Verulamium.

In spite of ample evidence to demonstrate the prosperity of the town from the first, there can be little doubt that the wealth contained there in the fourth century far exceeded that of its earlier years. How much of this was due to the town becoming a provincial capital and how much to the rich country estates which abounded in the civitas cannot be apportioned, but it must have owed much to both.

The apparent wealth of a community can often be measured by noting the existence of specialist firms to provide what are nowadays euphemistically called 'luxury consumer products'. At Corinium, two firms can be detected, which respectively supplied mosaics and sculpture, and no doubt there were others in different fields. Mosaics in particular are usually considered as a measure of surplus wealth and as status symbols. This firm has been referred to as the Corinian school by Dr D. J. Smith;[33] he considers that it was certainly the largest in Britain and one of the major mosaic workshops of the western Empire. By analysing various patterns repeated from one mosaic to another on many of those from Cirencester, he has concluded that they were the products of a single workshop, which was in being during the first half of the fourth century. It seems to have laid mosaics in at least six private houses in the town, and considering how few houses have been anywhere near fully excavated, this is a high percentage. Moreover, the firm also did a considerable amount of business with villa owners in the civitas, with examples of their work occurring as far away as Somerset and Oxfordshire. Nearly 50 individual pavements can be attributed to them, and they seem to have been the firm which invented the Orpheus mosaic in which the central figure is surrounded by concentric panels of birds, animals and trees. One of these patterns appears in the house below Dyer Street, which at an earlier stage possessed the Hunting Dogs and Marine Scene pavements (p. 303); another occurs in the house at Barton Farm, just outside the north-west town boundary.

A sculptor's workshop, which produced such pieces as the head of Mercury, the head of a River God and a relief of Deae Matres, has been identified by Professor Toynbee. She suggests that these pieces came from the hands of a first-rate Gaulish sculptor who had set up shop in Cirencester.[34] Compared with other less sophisticated pieces it may indeed be so, but there seems no reason why a British sculptor should not have been responsible for their execution. But these and many other pieces, nearly all of a religious nature, must represent patrons, mostly wealthy, some not so wealthy, who were prepared to pay for the adornment of local shrines and temples. It is interesting to compare the best quality Romano-British sculptures, which betray so much classical influence, with the strong continuing strain of native work. Cirencester and the surrounding district has produced a remarkable number of pieces, usually depicting Deae Matres or nameless local deities, executed in a wooden, two-dimensional manner. A whole range of variants can be detected from the near classical to the purely native in conception. Perhaps the most remarkable native piece is the plaque of a triad of *genii cucullati*, in very low relief, from Cirencester. The execution is so simple that it is little more than a cartoon, yet the figures have a vitality which is difficult to match elsewhere.

In this connexion it is also interesting to be able to record a known sculptor, Sulinus son of Brucetus, who may have had a workshop at Cirencester and possibly also at Bath, for he left altars dedicated to the Suleviae at both places, and he mentions his occupation on that from Bath.[35] It has been suggested that

59   Mosaic with central panel containing a hare, from House XII, 1, Cirencester (*Cirencester Excavation Committee*)

his Cirencester workshop was situated near Ashcroft Road, on the site which produced the collection of sculptures and altars referred to above (p. 301).

The wealth of the inhabitants is also reflected in the metalwork which they purchased. Most notable amongst these pieces is the bronze figure of Cupid, which may have served as part of a table lamp. It is probably the product of a Mediterranean workshop.[36]

Most of our knowledge of private houses has come from examples which could not be completely excavated. Recently, however, two adjacent fourth-century houses in Insulae x and xii have been uncovered close to the tail of the town bank. Both were well-equipped with heated rooms, while that in Insula xii had a small bath suite attached; its principal rooms were furnished with mosaics made by the local firm (pl. 59). The house in Insula x (fig. 68) was approached from the street by means of a projecting portico, and appears to have been planned more like a winged-corridor villa than a conventional town house. A barn-like building lay to its rear, which seems to have served as a general workshop. Smithing was certainly carried on, and nearby was found a neatly-piled stack of sandstone slabs, ready for use either as flooring or roofing material. The workshop seems too large to have served the house alone, and the varied nature of the work practised might suggest that it served a much larger estate. This again raises the question, first elaborated in considering Silchester (p. 274), whether it is possible to have a farm inside a town. Was this house in fact connected with the open land in Insula x, where few buildings are known, and where there are few signs of extension of the street system? The dividing line between villa and town house becomes even more blurred when we consider the house found under Barton Farm in 1825. It was scarcely more than a few hundred feet outside the town boundary as represented by the fortifications, and we have seen before (p. 21) that it is not safe to assume that they always represented earlier boundary lines. The house was demonstrably large and it was furnished in the best manner. The Orpheus pavement, of Corinian school manufacture, dates it at least to the early fourth century, but little is known of its earlier history. A house seems to have been stood there before the mosaic was laid, but no evidence of date was recovered.[37] However, a layer of 'earth' overlay an earlier floor, suggesting a period of disuse. Remembering that the first defences were not constructed until the late second century, was this therefore a town house which was not enclosed within the first circuit of fortifications because it had been temporarily abandoned? Can we therefore say with conviction that rebuilding at a later date turned it into a villa, simply because it then lay outside the town?[38]

Something of the commercial life of the town has been noted above in connexion with the markets, the shops in Insula v and the activities of mosaicists and sculptors. However, it is worth supplementing the information already given about the Insula v shops. By the fourth century all had been reconstructed in masonry (fig. 69), and some five shops were identified in the 1961 excavations.[39] More information will be forthcoming from excavations at Price's Row, off Watermoor Road, in 1972–3, where the continuation of the block will be ob-

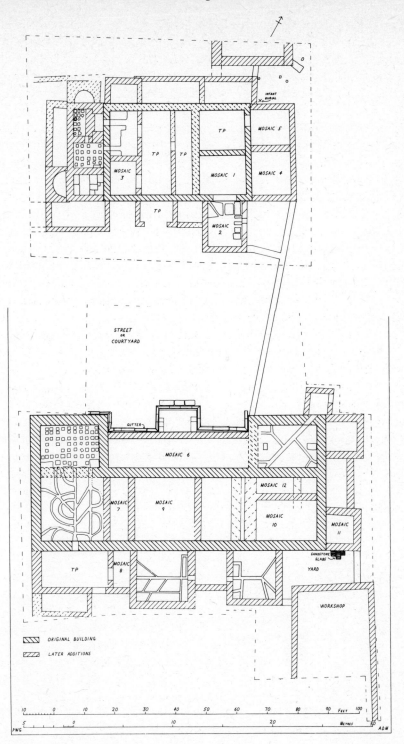

68   Fourth-century houses in Insulae X and XII, Cirencester (*A. D. McWhirr*)

tained. In at least two cases, adjacent shops had been merged, presumably caused by an owner of one shop buying up his neighbour's premises. Almost without exception, all the shops were equipped with ovens of various shapes and sizes, while two at least had wells. With a meat market over the road, it might be suggested that they were concerned with the preparation and sale of cooked meats. Alternatively, the ovens were just as suitable for baking bread, and it would be possible to suggest other uses, although there was no sign of metallurgical refuse or processes. Blacksmiths there were nevertheless, and the triple-chain pot-hanger in the museum is a splendid example of their work. A working goldsmith is attested by the base fragment of a crucible with specks of metal adhering to the surface, and found on the market site in Insula II.

There is no indication of pottery manufacture as yet, although characteristic local wares are abundant, as are colour-coated vessels from Thames Valley potteries near Oxford. It is interesting that almost all the coarse pottery which occurs at Cirencester reached the town from kilns situated south and east of the Cotswolds. Presumably it was found easier to move bulky and fragile goods by water, rather than by carrying them over the Cotswold scarp from the Severn Valley by road. In describing industries round Gloucester (p. 150), it was noted that Cirencester was in the area served by a number of brickworks which stamped their products. The best known firm is probably that which used the initials TPF as its trade-mark.

Classical religions are well represented at Cirencester by statuary and inscriptions. Of greater interest, perhaps, is the obviously widespread devotion to cults associated with the Deae Matres and local Celtic gods, especially that of the *genii cucullati*. Reliefs of the latter, sometimes showing three figures and at other times four, besides occurring at Cirencester, are widespread over the Cotswolds, and

69   Fourth-century shops in Insula v, Cirencester

the deity represented must have been held in high esteem. The assumption made
by Miss Alcock, that these had their origin in the Rhineland and occur frequently
in the Cotswolds because traders or slaves brought them there,[40] is difficult to
accept. The concepts of fertility embodied in the deity would have been widespread throughout the Celtic world, so leading to a degree of parallelism in
development, rather than to a simple diffusion from a single cult centre. The
Cotswold figures have a distinctly local feel, which is not entirely matched by
others.

It is unfortunate that no temple sites have yet been identified in the town. One
has been suggested in Insula xx near Ashcroft Road, where the altar to the
Sulevian Mothers and the reliefs of Deae Matres were found, although the
alternative suggestion that it was Sulinus' workshop (p. 306 above) is just as
likely. Another possible site is to the south-west of Tower Street, under Jefferies'
Nurseries, for there have been found bronze statuettes of Minerva, Diana and
Cupid, and the large Corinthian capital in which native deities have been incorporated in the design. An extensive paved area in the western corner of
Insula xiii, which has not yet been traced to its full extent, might be interpreted
as the temenos of a temple.[41] It was bounded by a single wall on the south-west
side, but the paving itself is of fourth-century date.

An earlier discussion in Chapter 3 (p. 84) referred to Mann's suggestion that
the bishop missing at the Council of Arles and represented by a deacon was from
the see of the Metropolis of Britannia Prima, whose church would have been at
Cirencester. Evidence for the practice of Christianity in the town, before the
Edict of Constantine, may well be contained in the palindrome which had been
carefully scratched on the wall plaster of a house. It was found in 1868, probably
near the southern end of Victoria Road. It reads:

> ROTAS
>
> OPERA
>
> TENET
>
> AREPO
>
> SATOR

and the letters can be rearranged to form a cross made up of the title of the Lord's
Prayer in Latin, PATERNOSTER with a common N. Left over are 2 AS and 2 OS, the
Latin equivalent of the Greek **A Ω** which symbolised for early Christians 'the
beginning and the end' of the Revelation of St John the Divine.[42] Consequently
this inscription may be seen as a hidden reference to Christianity made at a time
when open reference would have invited persecution.

The cemeteries outside the town are as yet imperfectly known. There is
evidence that they existed outside the Verulamium Gate alongside the Fosse
Way; outside the Silchester Gate, which was identified in 1881 when the now
defunct Midland Railway was constructed, and from where a number of tombstones have been recovered; beyond the Gloucester Gate at the north end of
Dollar Street and stretching for some distance towards Stratton; along the Fosse
Way beyond what used to be thought of as the Bath Gate, although the existence

60   A stone eagle from Cirencester (*Colin Shuttleworth; Cirencester Excavation Committee*)

óf this gate is now open to some doubt;[43] and outside the Amphitheatre Gate at the south-western end of Querns Lane, where a large inhumation cemetery of late date is at present being excavated. Preliminary observations on skeletons from this cemetery by Dr Calvin Wells record a high ratio of males to females. Most seem to have been fairly well nourished with a not too abrasive diet. Osteoarthritis was less prevalent than at some other sites, although the proportion of fractures sustained was high. One case of gout was recorded.[44]

No further deductions about the ethnic, social, dietary or medical history of the inhabitants of the town can yet be made. Some information on individuals can, however, be obtained from tombstones, amongst which we can number those of Philus, a Sequanian, who died at Cirencester aged 45;[45] Publia Vicana the deceased wife of Publius Vitalis, who were both Roman citizens;[46] Casta Castrensis;[47] and Julia Casta who died aged 33.[48] Three more tombstones found in 1971 near the Silchester Gate, where they seem to have been intended for use in a bastion, mention Aurelius Igennus (Ingenuus?), who died at the age of 6, Nemomnus (Nemonius?) Verecundus who lived to the age of 75, and Lucius Petronius Comitinus, who died aged 40.[49]

A certain amount of evidence has been accumulated over the past few years about the last decades of the Roman town. It is clear that repairs to the defences were still being carried out in the late fourth or early fifth century, and finds of zoomorphic buckles and boar-tusk ornaments betoken the presence of a detachment of the late Roman army. Certainly at the Verulamium Gate flood prevention work was being undertaken to prevent the river undermining yet again the foundations of the wall and gate.[50] In the forum, the paved floor of the piazza reached a state of wear in which outlines of individual stones could barely be distinguished (pl. 78). Yet the surface appears to have been kept clean until the end, implying that, although civic finances could not pay for replacements, there was still in being a measure of pride or discipline.[51] Moreover, a complete absence of coins on the floor would suggest that cleaning operations continued long enough for all Roman coins to have passed out of circulation. According to Dr Kent this had happened by AD 430.[52] So we can infer continuation of commercial life until nearly the middle of the fifth century.

What happened after that is open to question, but a slight clue is provided by excavations carried out in 1962 on a house flanking Ermin Street at the west corner of Insula XXIII.[53] This house had been provided with a portico on the road side, which, over the years, became filled with silt to a total depth of 8ft (2·4m). The source of this greyish silt could be traced back to the street. In dry weather, passage of traffic would have worn the surface to powder, which, on the first heavy shower of rain, would have been washed off the camber into porticoes of houses flanking the street. In time not only would the portico have required a new floor, but the street also would have needed resurfacing to surmount the quagmire, which, at certain seasons, would have crept from the edges over the whole surface. Each new surface laid would have aggravated the discomfort of the householders and shopkeepers whose premises opened on to the street, as it would have served only to restart the cycle at a higher level. Consequently the formation of silt is to certain extent a measure of traffic flow. But there came a time at Cirencester, when a new ditch, dug between the street and the by then entirely engulfed portico, remained unfilled with road silt and open to collect leaves, grass and weeds (fig. 89). We may conclude that at this point in time, traffic had dwindled to an insignificant level or had ceased altogether. Unfortunately the dark, organic filling of the ditch contained nothing by which the accumulation might be dated. But a companion ditch further south produced human bodies.[54] It would appear then, that at this stage all traces of order had broken down: grass was literally growing in the streets and unburied bodies were left to rot in roadside ditches. It is perhaps placing too great an emphasis on two bodies, but taken in conjunction with the general desertion of the town, we might wonder if this event was connected with one or other of the severe epidemics which occurred in the fifth or sixth centuries. One, attested as having been 'diffused throughout the world' in about AD 443, would fit very well the general chronology which has already been established for the abandonment of the town. Certainly an epidemic would cause many inhabitants to flee, and leave behind inside the town the conditions which we have already envisaged.[55]

But supposing there was a residue of people determined to stay on in the increasingly unsafe conditions. Would they stay in a disease-ridden town, which had suddenly grown too big for them, or look elsewhere? When excavations were carried out at the amphitheatre, it was found that in the final stages, at least one large timber building had been erected in the arena, and the north-east entrance had been considerably reduced in size. These alterations were associated only with small scraps of weathered, late-Roman pottery and a scatter of late Roman coins.[56] Was the amphitheatre turned into a fortified retreat for the survivors, more easily defended than the 2½ miles (4km) of town wall? These are all possibilities, which must await further investigation. But it is worth remembering that amphitheatres on the continent were often incorporated into defensive circuits, and in the Middle Ages very nearly housed complete towns for safety. One last shred of evidence: the element 'chester' appears twice at Cirencester, firstly in the town name itself and secondly in the hundred of Chesterton, which contains the amphitheatre.[57] Finally we are told by the Anglo-Saxon Chronicle that in AD 577 'Cuthwine and Ceawlin fought against the Britons and killed three kings, Conmail, Condidan and Farinmail, at the place which is called Dyrham; and they captured three of their cities, Gloucester, Cirencester and Bath.' If the order is correct, Condidan was king of Cirencester, and he was the only one still to carry a Latinised name, so suggesting at least a surviving Romano-British contingent, whereas the other two were purely Celtic. But had the captured 'city' of Cirencester been reduced only to the amphitheatre, and was the Anglo-

61 Section of the north wall, Cirencester, restored by the Department of the Environment (*D. J. Viner*; *Corinium Museum*)

Saxon warrior buried on the site of the Barton Farm house one of the assailants killed in the battle?[58] Such are the questions still to be answered, but in answering them, we shall probably do much to clear up some of the outstanding problems of the end of Romano-British towns.

DORCHESTER (*Durnovaria*)

The tribe of the Durotriges put up a considerable resistance to the advance of the Roman army. In the account by Suetonius of the campaigns of Legio II Augusta and its commander, the future emperor Vespasian, it is recorded that thirty battles were fought, two warlike tribes were conquered and twenty oppida were captured.[59] But since it is also recorded that at times he served directly under Claudius, presumably not all these victories were in the south-west, as is often assumed.[60] However, one of the warlike tribes was almost certainly the Durotriges, and a number of the captured oppida were in their territory, for excavations at Maiden Castle,[61] Hod Hill,[62] Spettisbury Rings[63] and South Cadbury[64] have all produced evidence of successful assaults, sometimes combined with massacres of the defenders. Roman military equipment has also been found at Ham Hill[65] and we might suggest that it, among many others, should be added to the list.

The defeat of the Durotriges was followed by military occupation and government, with forts placed at intervals throughout their territory. It became as much part of the frontier zone as did that of other tribes in the midlands and south-west. Treatment of individual septs of the tribe, however, varied from place to place. The inhabitants of Hod Hill, for instance, were banished altogether, in spite of having surrendered after only a preliminary bombardment, and a Roman fort was constructed in the north-west corner of the hill-fort. By contrast, at Maiden Castle the survivors of the Roman assault were allowed to remain in residence, although the gates were removed and the ramparts were slighted. The way the inhabitants were treated, therefore, was probably dictated more by military requirements than by a spirit of revenge or punishment.

The Durotriges, although much influenced by Belgic cultures, seem to have retained a good deal of their earlier social structure. This gave rise, as we have seen, to a multiplicity of hill-forts scattered over the whole tribal area. The social implications of these many hill-forts have never yet been satisfactorily resolved, although a number of suggestions and theories have been put forward.[66] Towards the time of the Roman conquest, however, we may suggest that some kind of paramountcy was in being, and that some of the hill-forts exercised control over areas containing others. Chief among them probably was Maiden Castle, the *Dunium* of Ptolemy,[67] for so we may infer from what came after, and possibly also Hengistbury. That the former also happened to be the largest may be coincidental, although the size and scale of the fortifications indicates control over a large population. Probably the most important factor was that it contained the influential people in tribal politics, acceptable to the Romans and to whom they could dictate terms when the time came for clearing up the aftermath of military conquest. Although the neighbouring hill-fort at Poundbury was occupied intermittently during the Belgic period and is nearer to the site of the Roman town than Maiden Castle, it was long ago pointed out by Wheeler that it would be unlikely to carry equivalent prestige.[68] It is probably best seen as an outlying bastion of the main fortifications.

The occurrence of military equipment, a handful of pre-Flavian coins, and some samian and imported ware of similar date is probably an indication that a fort may first have occupied the town site at Dorchester. Certainly if precedent was followed, a fort should be sought in the vicinity of Maiden Castle, close to the newly-laid road system. The most likely spot would be near a river crossing and the low hill, west of the crossing of the river Frome, would seem to be the strongest candidate. The Royal Commission inventory mentions a street, sealed beneath the later town rampart in Bowling Alley Walk on the south part of the circuit near its west corner, which, it was suggested, could have been the inter-vallum road of a fort.[69] More recent excavations, however, in the same area would suggest that it was not a street at all. In view of the discovery of a probable legionary fortress at Lake Farm, near Wimborne, which was occupied during the Claudio-Neronian period, it is unlikely that any fortifications near Dorchester would be greater than auxiliary size.[70]

With a fort near Dorchester, the mechanics of town formation would almost certainly have followed the course already discussed in connexion with Ciren-cester. Inhabitants would have drifted gradually away from Maiden Castle to the greater convenience offered by a vicus outside the fort. Despite contrary opinions put forward by the Royal Commission, there seems no reason why tribal chiefs should not have been among them, but whether they were or not, their presence in the vicinity must be deemed a necessity if we are to explain the choice of the vicus at Dorchester as the civitas capital when military government ceased. Wheeler visualised a ceremonial abandonment of Maiden Castle in favour of the new town on the river Frome, although the sudden migration which he also postulated is probably further from the truth. However, both from Wheeler's evidence from Maiden Castle and from the evidence of the town itself, it would seem that the constitution of the civitas and the development of its capital occurred in the first decades of the Flavian period, a feature which it had in common with the four other capitals considered in this chapter.

But the whole civitas was not always administered from Dorchester. Two inscriptions from Hadrian's Wall refer to a tribal detachment from the *civitas Durotrigum Lendiniensis*.[71] *Lendiniae*, or *Lindinis* (Ilchester), was the vicus which grew in the valley below the native settlement on Ham Hill. Stevens drew attention to the significance of these inscriptions and the likelihood that the tribe had been divided;[72] Richmond suggested that the tribe was divided in its administration from the first owing to the hostility with which they had met the Romans.[73] However it is possible, as Frere considers, that this division took place at a later date and came about by the promotion of a pagus to civitas status.[74] This may have been partly caused by the increase in prosperity of the north-western part of the Durotriges in the fourth century, with a remarkable proliferation of opulent villas in the Ilchester region.[75] Such a concentration was indicative not only of wealth, but also of political power.

70   Plan of Dorchester (*after W. Putnam*)

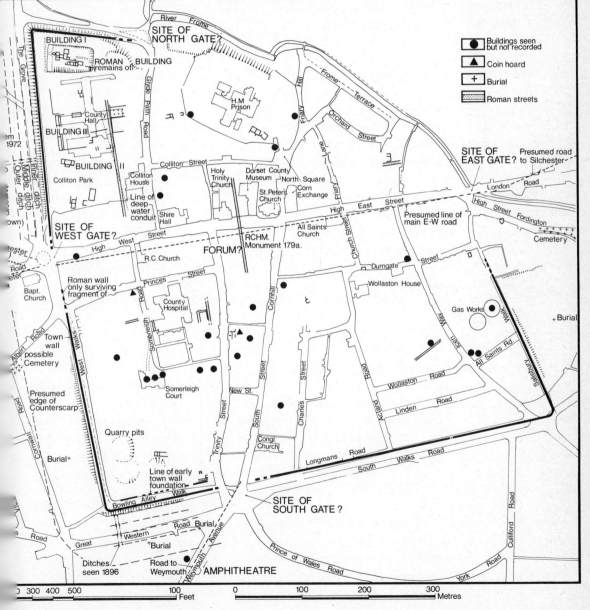

The site on which the town of Durnovaria grew is at the end of a chalk promontory which falls mainly from the west towards the river Frome, flowing past its north and north-east limits. The ground also falls away to the south, so that the main east-west axis forms a spine across the site.

Only in the last few years has there been a consistent excavation policy in the town. Earlier work was somewhat spasmodic; most information has come from the observation of commercial work.[76]

Apart from the amphitheatre, there is as yet little evidence of public buildings, although the position of the forum may be indicated by walls and a gravelled surface observed to the west of Cornhill. Walls seen under Cornhill were aligned with the street grid, and the gravelled area is thought to have extended at least for 125ft (38m) from east to west. Mid first-century pottery was found in several places below the floor, and late fourth-century material was found on it. Such a wide date range is certainly suggestive of a public building, which had been but little altered after its primary construction.[77]

This proposed situation for the forum (fig. 70), while possible, is not usual. It has already been stressed that in Britain the normal position for a forum is in one of the angles formed by the intersection of the decumanus and cardo maximi, and at Dorchester the former is thought to run slightly south of High West Street, while the latter was uncovered in excavations off Trinity Street not far north of the site of the south gate. If the interpretation of Monument No. 179a as a street is correct, this would place the forum one insula distant from the cardo maximus. This section of street has been linked with another, north of High West Street, found at an earlier date, to give a continuous line. The difficulty could be resolved by reinterpreting No. 179a as part of the forum courtyard, with the forum cutting across, but not necessarily wholly occupying, two adjacent insulae.

No site can yet be indicated for a public bath-house, but its existence can be inferred from the aqueduct. The latter probably entered through, or near, the west gate, which is the highest part of the town. No help can therefore be obtained by considering the directional flow of the water supply or drainage, as almost any part of the town would have been equally suitable.

It is also too soon to attempt a reconstruction of the street plan. Apart from the known, or accurately inferred, main axial streets, two others, which are part of a grid system, are known. One ran east-west some 350ft (106m) south of High West Street, the other ran north-south, some 400ft (122m) east of West Walks Road and continued northward towards Colliton Park.[78] It has been suggested that streets were remade rather than repaired with successive deposits of metalling. This policy might well account for the shallower sequence of stratified deposits at Dorchester, as it will have prevented the almost continuous rise in ground level observed in other towns (cf. CIRENCESTER, p. 300 above).

The best known public building is the amphitheatre at Maumbury Rings, situated about ½ mile (800m) outside the south gate (fig. 14). Although long identified as the Roman amphitheatre, excavations carried out by H. St George Gray before the first world war showed that it had been built round a Neolithic

henge monument.[79] The structure is therefore somewhat unusual for an amphitheatre, having a nearly circular external circumference and only one arena
entrance. It measures about 330ft (100m) in diameter externally, and the arena,
slightly more elliptical than the exterior, had internal dimensions of 192ft (58m)
and 156ft (47m). The banks, now grassed over, still stand to a height of up to
30ft (9·1m) above the arena floor, which was originally surfaced with gravel. In
order to construct the arena, an appropriate area had been excavated to a depth of
10ft (3m) below the surface of the undisturbed chalk, so obliterating the depres-
sions over the internal ditch and shafts of the henge. An enclosed gangway, from
3 to 6ft (0·9 to 1·8m) wide, with wooden walls, was constructed round the circumference of the arena, and so helped to retain the exposed chalk of the walls and
the looser material of the seating banks above. Both sides of the gangway were
extended into the entrance for short distances. The arena was closed by a gate,
12ft (3·7m) wide, level with the inner wall of the gangway, and it is possible that
the seating was carried over the 22ft (6·7m) wide entrance passage on timber
staging. Although internal gangways are not unknown in provincial amphitheatres,[80] other examples have yet to be found in Britain. Lacking a second
entrance, the gangway was probably required to allow performers to enter the
arena from the enclosed end, without having to cross the main floor, as might be
required in certain types of shows between opposing combatants or animals.
The illusion would have been improved if the passage had been roofed. Opposite
the entrance a recessed room, 18ft (5·5m) by 14$\frac{1}{2}$ft (4·5m), had been constructed
in the bank at arena level. It could have served either as a cage for wild animals or
possibly as an assembly point for performers, who had entered via the gangways.
A peculiar point in its construction, however, was the rear wall, which seems to
have been only 3$\frac{1}{2}$ft (1·1m) high, as it was cut off by a ramp descending from the
crest of the bank. If the ramp and the room were contemporary, the roof height
would have precluded use by performers. Yet the room seems large for use only
by animals. Similar rooms, diametrically opposed across the short axis, may have
served the same purpose, or perhaps acted as shrines to Nemesis. It is possible,
however, that official boxes were built above the latter.

Despite the Royal Commission's view that it was not used until the second
century,[81] a more recent assessment of the evidence suggests a first-century date
for its adaptation.[82]

Another public work of considerable interest is the aqueduct. First identified
in 1900, sections have been cut across its channel on a number of occassions since,
the most recent in 1968.[83] The supply is normally considered to have been drawn
from the river Frome at Notton Mill, Maiden Newton, although it has never
been confirmed, and an alternative source exists at Steps Farm, Frampton, some
distance nearer the town (fig. 71). The channel seems to have been open and un-
lined; it measured from 3 to 5ft (0·9 to 1·5m) across the bottom, although the
average is about 5ft (1·5m), with an assumed width of 7 to 8ft (2·1 to 2·4m) at the
top, where the lips had been weathered. A maximum depth of about 3ft (0·9m)
is recorded. The excavated chalk and other material had been heaped into a bank

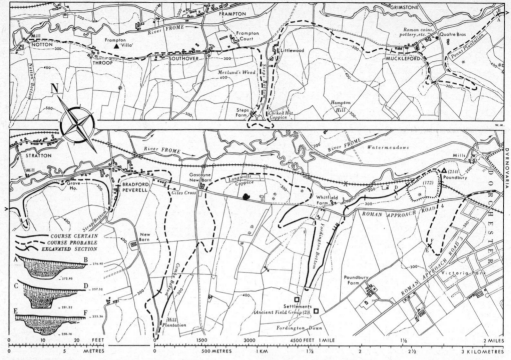

THE ROMAN AQUEDUCT (227a), TO THE NORTH-WEST OF DORCHESTER

71   Line of the Dorchester aqueduct (*Royal Commission of Historical Monuments (England), Crown Copyright
—reproduced with permission of the Controller of Her Majesty's Stationery Office*)

on the downhill side. It roughly followed, and ran somewhat below, the 300ft (91m) contour with a fall of 25ft (7·6m) in a total length of $11\frac{1}{3}$ miles (18·2km). If it had contained 2ft (609mm) of water, the flow is calculated to have been nearly 13,000,000 gallons (6×10^8 litres) per day, which would certainly have supplied most needs of the town, supplemented as they were by wells. The supply entered the town near or at the west gate, and presumably some form of settling and distribution equipment would have been provided. Since this point is higher than any other in the town, a raised castellum aquae would not have been necessary. It has been suggested that surplus water was diverted to the river through the conduit found in Colliton Park: $2\frac{1}{2}$ft (762mm) wide between mortared walls and $1\frac{1}{2}$ft (475mm) high, and set at the bottom of a $10\frac{1}{2}$ft (3·2m) deep V-shaped trench, which must have been 10–12ft (3–3·7m) wide at the top before weathering took place. The conduit was probably roofed, and, where it ran for some distance beneath a street, filled also. It must be admitted that, apart from a capacity almost equal to a quarter of the aqueduct's, it seems a most elaborate way of disposing of surplus water. Some slight clues as to the purpose of the conduit are to be found in the buildings at the north end of Colliton Park, towards which point it is aiming. But the majority of structures there are appreciably later than the probable late first-century date of its construction. However, there are some indications of industrial processes which may have been inherited from earlier buildings, and the outfall pipe set in the concrete floor of room 2 in Building 1 is suggestive of 'wet' processes (see p. 322 below).

The first fortifications were constructed some time in the late second century, presumably in the same spate of Albinian building which affected most other towns. An earth bank was fronted by one and possibly two ditches, with evidence suggesting a timber tower near the south-west corner.

There is, however, an indication of attempts to provide a masonry curtain wall on at least part of the circuit, for, near Bowling Alley Walk, a chalk and flint foundation 10ft (3m) wide, has been observed in two places sealed beneath the tail of the later rampart. This wall would seem never to have been completed, and is additional evidence that work in stone was initially contemplated.

About AD 300 the fortifications were nevertheless strengthened by the addition of a stone wall on a revised alignment. A small part of the core of this wall still stands above ground level in Albert Road. The foundations would appear to have been over 10ft (3m) wide. Owing to the abnormal width of the primary earth rampart, which in places was as much as 50ft (15·2m) across, the wall was sometimes inserted into its brow, in contrast to the more normal practice of cutting back the front of the bank.[84] The wall was built of grouted limestone rubble masonry over a foundation of pitched flints. Bonding courses of flat slabs of stone were incorporated at intervals. Facing was probably with limestone ashlars, but none have survived. The rampart was considerably enlarged when the wall was built, extending the width to as much as 80ft (24m). The full extent of the circuit is reasonably certain on the north, west, south and south-east sectors, but the north-east part is mainly conjectural, although its line is approximately dictated by the course of the river beyond.

There is little apart from road alignments to indicate the positions of gates, and no structural evidence has been recorded. The positions of the east, west and south gates can be approximately inferred at the ends of High Street and of South Street respectively, with a probable north gate or postern at the bottom of Glyde Path Hill. A medieval gate is known at the east end of Durngate Street; it may represent the site of an earlier, Roman gate, and, if so, might explain cemeteries which would otherwise be awkwardly placed near the south-east angle.

Little is known of the early shops and houses. A first-century timber-framed building was found in 1970 at Greenings Court, where it was separated from the neighbouring street by a wooden fence.[85] Most examples of domestic and commercial buildings are much later in date, especially those excavated in Colliton Park near the north corner of the town between 1937–9, which provide the only complete plans. The area seems to have remained open ground during the first two centuries, and was only then developed slowly and with little attention to economy, as the buildings were well spread out. Building 1 (fig. 72) is interesting for its unusual plan and for the presence of mosaics in all the rooms in the main range, which may be identified as the living quarters. An arrangement whereby the floors of four of the rooms were progressively lowered, with communicating drains from each room, is worth noting, as it was undoubtedly intended to ease the washing of the floors. The southern range of this building seems to have been first planned as a separate structure, which was later joined to the main residence. Some of its fittings could be those of a small domestic bath wing, although it lacks certain facilities, such as plunge baths, which were normally considered essential. But the combination of a steam-heated room, rooms with thick concrete floors, one of which was adapted for draining surface water, and a 'drying' room with ovens and hearths, might suggest fulling or dyeing. If so, the well sunk to the north of the range could have replaced water originally supplied by the conduit, perhaps to an earlier structure. The small niche in the wall of room 2 might then be seen as containing the statue of a deity presiding over the activities of the establishment.

The only other houses worthy of individual mention are Buildings II and III. The latter contained an exceptionally long and narrow north-south wing, divided into three main parts and opening on to a courtyard to the east, with some

COLLITON PARK, DORCHESTER
BUILDING I (182)

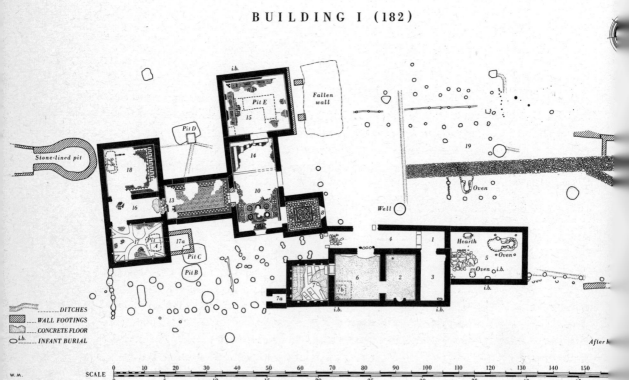

72 Fourth-century house, Colliton Park, Dorchester (*Royal Commission of Historical Monuments (England), Crown Copyright—reproduced with permission of the Controller of Her Majesty's Stationery Office*)

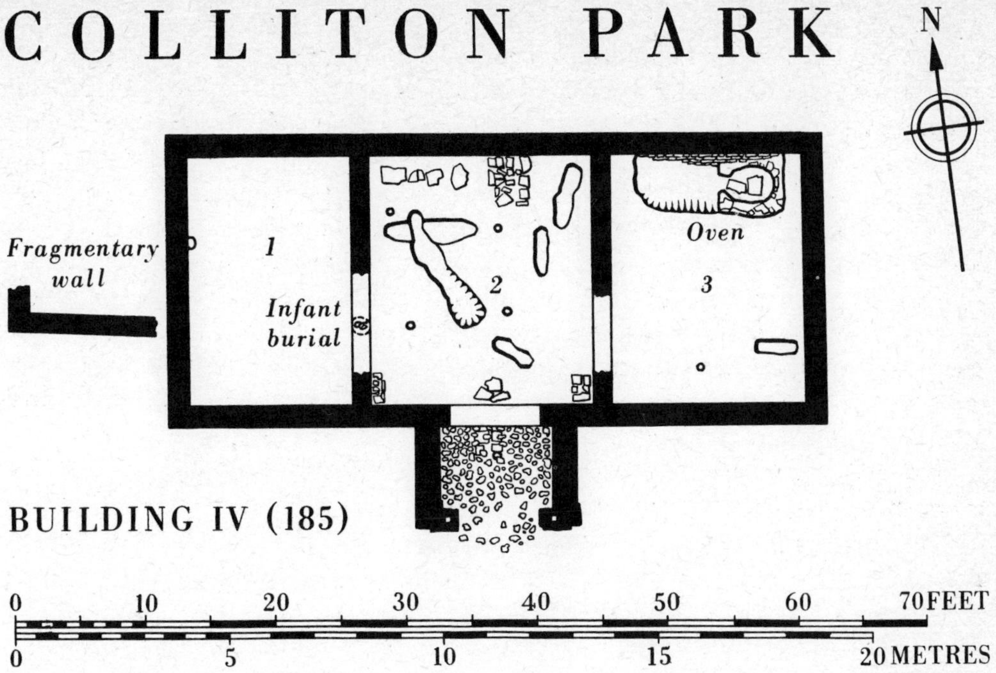

COLLITON PARK

N

Fragmentary
wall

1

Infant
burial

2

Oven

3

BUILDING IV (185)

73   Small house, Colliton Park, Dorchester (*Royal Commission of Historical Monuments (England), Crown Copyright—reproduced with permission of the Controller of Her Majesty's Stationery Office*)

evidence of smaller structures related to it. A number of ovens situated in it might suggest a workshop rather than a dwelling. Building II was little more than a cottage (fig. 73) compact and symmetrical and situated not far from the southern edge of Building III, and possibly represents the domestic quarters of a manager. It contained three rooms in a single rectangular block, with a south-facing portico projecting from the centre.

Some rare structural features were observed in these buildings: a collapsed window embrasure in Building I, and the impression of reeds on the reverse side of wall plaster. The latter were presumably used as an alternative for the more conventional wattle backing,[86] but the plaster may equally have come from a ceiling.

Despite lack of detailed knowledge, the houses of Dorchester were by no means all the residences of poor people, as is shown by the number of good quality mosaics known in the town. Moreover we know that they also possessed excellent items of furniture, for at Dorchester use was made of the local Kimmeridge shale in place of perishable wood, and working in shale may be considered a local industry of the region, even if it was not carried on in the town.

Durnovaria, like Corinium, has been considered by D. J. Smith as the centre of operations of a mosaicist's workshop. Here, however, most examples occur in villas in the civitas, and only two from the town have been positively identified as their work.[87] This may be a point of some significance. Apart from the famous pavements with Christian motifs at Frampton and Hinton St Mary, Smith considers that the Neptune mosaic in the Gloucestershire villa of Withington was also almost certainly the work of the Durnovarian firm. Furthermore, he suggests that they were able to penetrate what was apparently another firm's operational area because that firm had already ceased to function. Moreover at Withington the Neptune mosaic of the Durnovarian firm is later in date than the Corinian workshop's Orpheus pavement. If therefore the Durnovarian firm was operating at a later date than that at Corinium, the presence of only two of the firm's pavements among some fifty known from the town might suggest that there had been a decline in the wealth of the inhabitants. But obviously this recession did not equally affect the countryside, although it is perhaps associated with the shift westwards of the tribal centre of gravity.

There is some evidence for other industrial processes carried on in the town. A hearth associated with lead working was found beneath the gravel thought to represent the forum piazza. It may have been used by a plumber for manufacturing or soldering lead sheet during construction work, and is similar to small plumbers' furnaces found in construction levels of the basilica at Cirencester.[88] Metal-working was also probably carried on in six furnaces located near the south-west corner. A late blacksmith's forge was found at Colliton Park and is a reminder that low-grade iron ores occur locally.

The nearest source of local pottery was probably at Purbeck, but a local brickworks may have produced the characteristic antefixes found in and around Dorchester, which are decorated in relief with bearded faces.[89]

Stone quarries on Purbeck yielded the famed 'marble', which was not only used extensively at Dorchester, but also travelled widely throughout the country. The only tombstone from Dorchester, which was set up in memory of Carinus, is made of it.[90] Other quarries on Portland provided stone for building and for architectural features. With such an abundance of local material, it is surprising that stone for both sarcophagi and buildings was brought from Ham Hill near Ilchester.

There is very little evidence of religious practices at Dorchester; a bronze statuette of Mercury, a pipeclay figurine of Venus, an inscription to Jupiter, possibly removed at a later date from the town to Godmanstone, and three carved heads reused in the eighteenth century and said to represent Cernunnos. In the absence of specific evidence from the town, it is worth including the late fourth-century Romano-Celtic temple built on the long-deserted Maiden Castle.[91] This must have been built at a time when a growing Christian community was being established in the town (see p. 326 below) and was perhaps making life intolerable for adherents to pagan cults. Can we see in this temple, erected in a place which, even three centuries later, must have evoked memories and legends, the general dissatisfaction of part of the population: a reaction perhaps to events which they could not control but only resent? In such circumstances attempts are often made to put the clock back.

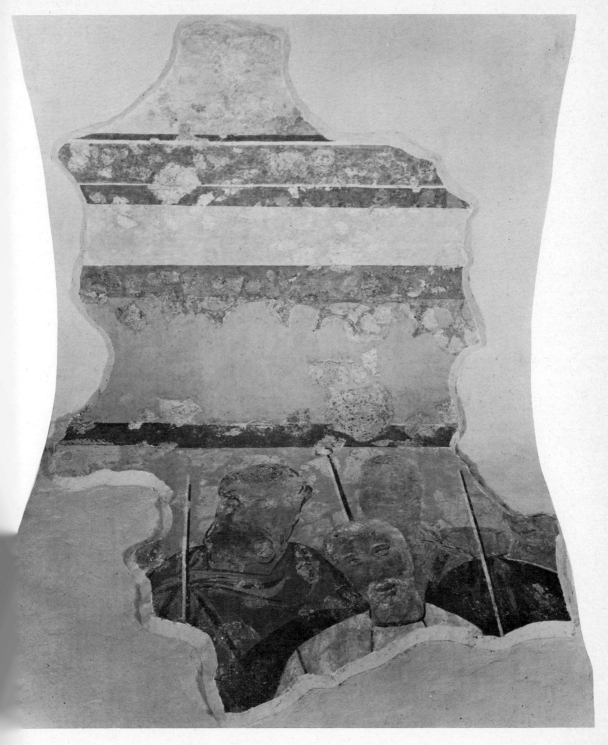

62 Painted wall and roof vault from a mausoleum, Dorchester (*C. J. Green, Crown Copyright—reproduced with permission of the Controller of Her Majesty's Stationery Office*)

More information on burial practices comes, however, from a number of well-furnished cemeteries. Some were obviously alongside main roads, although it should be noted that there were none outside the east gate, where the road crossed marshy ground. Surprisingly, the largest cemetery so far discovered lay between the western defences of the town and Poundbury; another was on Fordington Hill just north of the south-east corner.

Excavations, which are still continuing, on the Poundbury cemetery have revealed an interesting situation.[92] It has been estimated as covering about 5 acres (2ha) with a rate of interment of about 1000 graves per acre. By far the largest number of burials followed a uniform rite: fully extended with head to the west, usually contained in a plain wooden coffin, and normally with no grave goods. Some 'family' groups made up of two adults and one or two children have been identified, with one burial in each group embalmed in gypsum in a lead-lined heavy wooden coffin. A number of rectangular mausolea, two with plastered and painted internal walls and vaulted roofs (pl. 62), contained groups of burials, which were more handsomely interred in lead or stone sarcophagi, often with the body embalmed in gypsum. They seem to be a development of the 'family' group burials noted above. The overall date of the main cemetery would seem to fall mostly within the fourth century. Ramm has pointed out that gypsum burials in Britain probably indicate Christian burial (cf. York, p. 172 above) and at Dorchester this is confirmed by the additional features. Nevertheless, earlier second- and third-century cremations and random-orientated inhumations do occur, in addition to a few of the post-Roman period.

This cemetery seems to represent the development of a considerable Christian community in the town. The existence of such a community is, of course, supported by the Christian symbolism used in some of the mosaics from the Durnovarian workshop. The cemetery is also important for the information it will ultimately provide on the physical characteristics of the inhabitants. Moreover, it is hardly likely to be unique, and other towns should ultimately produce analogies.

The end of Durnovaria is difficult to discern. Recent finds of Anglo-Saxon grübenhauser and zoomorphic buckles are evidence for laeti or gentiles in the town, presumably in the late fourth or fifth centuries. The late Roman coin list is not so very different from towns with attested fifth-century occupation.[93] Desertion rather than destruction, as in most cases, would seem to sum up the closing years.

EXETER (*Isca Dumnoniorum*)

In the foregoing sections and chapters we have considered towns which had been established in districts associated with primary or secondary Belgic culture, even if it was confined to the ruling classes. Such people, although perhaps hostile to Rome at first, were nevertheless more receptive to Roman ideas and the Roman way of life than those living in parts remote from the south-east, who had never been touched by the earlier culture. In these areas the path to romanisation and consequently urbanisation was slower, more difficult and often never fully achieved.

The Dumnonii in the south-west peninsula were locally infiltrated in the later pre-Roman Iron Age by immigrants from north-west France, who were absorbed into the tribe without causing any noticeable political change. Penetrations by the Durotriges of their south-east border country had more effect. But no unified control was exercised over the whole tribe, except in the loosest way. No coins were ever issued in their territory and up to the time of the Roman conquest they seem to have remained a confederation of smaller units. Trade relations were maintained with both the Durotriges and Dobunni.[94]

The arrival of the Roman army in Dumnonian territory after their successful conquest of the Durotriges seems to have resulted in a capitulation, for there are as yet no signs of opposition. The immediate ensuing occupation was little more than a token display with forts at Exeter and possibly near Taunton, and a probable supply base at Topsham just south of Exeter on the estuary of the river Exe. A small fortlet on Stoke Hill, just north of Exeter might be related to this period, as can another overlooking the Bristol Channel at Old Burrow. These arrangements seem to suggest that the Romans feared little from the Dumnonii, which emphasises their lack of unified control and their inability, perhaps, to take concerted action. Strategically, the Romans probably saw the ultimate southwest peninsula as lying beyond the left flank of their new frontier system, which seems to have terminated in the Exeter region, where a legionary fortress was established late in the principate of Claudius.

In the Neronian period, however, the situation changed. There was not only the uncertainty following the Boudiccan rebellion, which led to a tightening of military control, even in some areas not directly involved, but also the continuing hostility of the Silures, who took the offensive against the Province. It was probably to repel the latter, raiding across the Bristol Channel, that the left flank of the frontier was extended into Devon and Cornwall, with a replacement coastal fortlet at Martinhoe, and another fort at Nanstallon in the Camel valley.[95]

The military occupation at Exeter has been the subject of considerable argument. Excavations by Aileen Fox in the postwar years and in 1959 found extensive areas of Claudio-Neronian 'settlement', which she interpreted as being part of the early town.[96] Objections were raised because a town at this date in the southwest would have been an historical improbability, and attempts were made to reinterpret the structures as army buildings. The differences of opinion were partly resolved by the discovery of an early ditch, belonging probably to an auxiliary fort, running beneath the South Gate of the later town.[97] It is probable that this fort was established as a preliminary measure and that it was quite soon replaced by a legionary fortress on a new site further west. So far, no indication has yet been found of the boundaries of the fortress, but barrack blocks and a large spendidly-preserved bath-house have been found on the Guildhall, Goldsmith Street and Pancras Lane sites, and the St Mary Major site respectively. The bath-house may have lain on one of the principal axes of the fortress, since the street which bounded it to the south-west ultimately linked the north-east and south-west gates of the town. The bath-house was considerably reduced in size during the late 60s, perhaps an indication that the main strength of the legion was spending most of its time on active service. The fortress was finally abandoned in the 70s.[98]

The withdrawal of the army and the constitution of the civitas Dumnoniorum, as with the other civitates described in this chapter, therefore took place *c*. AD 80. However, here for the first time in Britain, the Roman administration perhaps came up against the problem of lack of unity. With no obvious pre-conquest tribal capital, the choice of site for a civitas capital would have been even more arbitrary, and we must fall back on a reason already proposed to account for the selection of some others in the Province: that the site chosen represented the greatest concentration of influential natives. We must assume therefore that the fortress at Exeter had acted as a better magnet than an auxiliary fort and had attracted such people from the more widely scattered hill-forts and settlements to its associated vicus. The unequal way in which romanisation penetrated the area shows most clearly how little pressure to conform was put upon the ordinary tribesman, once his basic obligations had been carried out. If a freeman went to live in a town, he went there because he wanted to, and not because he was made to by an unfeeling organisation.

The site of the new capital was therefore placed on a hill, overlooking the lowest, easy crossing point of the river, from which the town took its name, and occupied much of the area of the razed fortress.

Aileen Fox observed that timber buildings and a street near South Street were destroyed and covered with a uniform gravelled layer which she then interpreted as the bed for the floor of the forum piazza. This new area was bounded on the north by a pair of parallel masonry walls, which, she thought, most likely represented a colonnade round the piazza.[99]

It is now clear, however, from Griffiths' more recent excavations, that the basilica and therefore also the forum were constructed during the Flavian period, by converting the legionary bath-house. In this respect there is a strong resemblance to Wroxeter (see p. 360 below). The basilica appears to lie on the south-east side of the forum and was made up of a nave about 33ft (10m) wide with a north-west aisle 13ft (4m) and south-east aisle 20ft (6m) wide. Entrance to the south-west end of the nave was gained by ascending a flight of steps leading from the forum colonnade to a small portico set against the basilica wall (pl. 64). The water-pipes which had originally supplied the baths were relaid, presumably to provide a supply for public drinking fountains.

The public baths were probably in the next insula south-east of the forum, and the piazza found by Aileen Fox perhaps belonged to them, even though it appears to lie in the insula beyond. The cold plunge of the baths, measuring 52ft (15·8m) in length and with a depth of 4ft (1·2m), was found in the Deanery Garden in 1934.

EXETER (Isca)

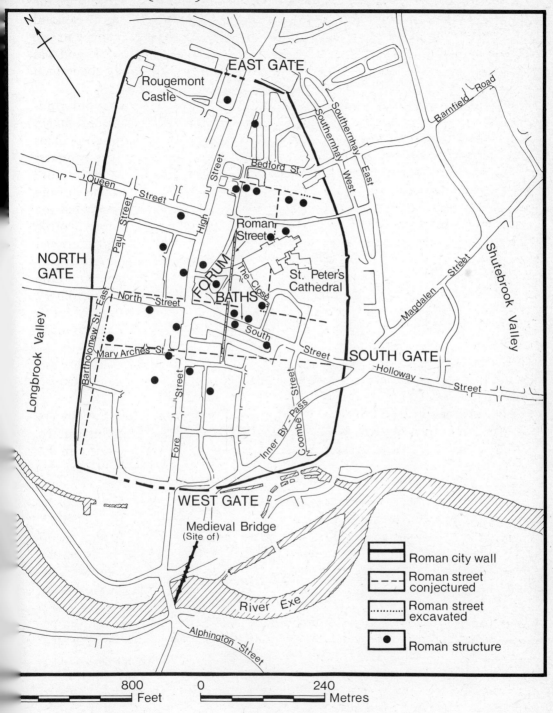

74 Plan of Exeter (*after A. Fox and M. Griffiths*)

The bath was surrounded by a pavement of sandstone blocks, which in turn supported a colonnade. The proximity of the next street to the north-east would, however, have prevented the plunge bath from having a width of more than half its length.[100] It is almost certain that the building extended south-west of South Street; remains of walls and tessellated and concrete floors have been found beneath it, beneath Guinea Street beyond and extending under buildings on either side. However, it is possible that these remains belong to another building next to the baths,[101] but in the same insula.

It is not yet known from which quarter the town aqueduct was fed and it would probably have perpetuated the fortress line. The water-pipes in the forum and the size of a drain, found in excavations in Bear Street and used to carry waste water from the baths, would imply its existence.[102]

The internal streets of the town are gradually becoming better known, and it is now possible to see the main outlines of a regular system, which probably owed

63 Nineteenth-century engraving of the south gate, Exeter (*Exeter City Library*)

much to the earlier fortress (fig. 74). The street connecting East and West Gates has recently been uncovered by Griffiths on the St Mary Major site, and it is probable that the 'light metalling' mentioned by Aileen Fox as disappearing under Kalendarhay was the edge of this same street. The next street to the south-east is known and, to the north-west, another could be inferred as running approximately on the line of Fore Street. There is then room for one more between the latter and the street found near Bartholomew Street, which also appears to have been repaired and retained as part of the town plan. The line of the road from South Gate is established, although the next street north-east and leading to North Gate is not quite parallel with it. The staggered position of these two gates was presumably to avoid exit from North Gate into the steep-sided Longbrook Valley. Only one other parallel street on this line is known so far, from excavations north-east of the Cathedral,[103] but there would be space for another between these two, and yet another south-west of the South Gate line. The town, therefore, seems to have been made up of some 25 insulae, measuring approximately 250ft (76m) by 300ft (91m).

Little is known of other public buildings and there is no indication yet of either a theatre or an amphitheatre.

The first fortifications to be constructed followed the normal pattern of late second-century works and were certainly later than AD 160. The rampart, of interlaced layers of clean clay and gravel obtained from the ditch, was 25ft (7·6m) wide at the base. Excavations at South Gate in 1964–5 showed that the masonry gate was possibly contemporary with the earth rampart.[104] If so, Exeter should join the handful of towns, such as Cirencester and Verulamium (pp. 213, 302) where preliminary work in stone had been carried out before the linear circuit was completed with earthworks. Only a small part of the gate could be excavated, as the remainder lies beneath South Street, and it appears to be a square or rectangular guardroom probably in the base of a tower, flanking the south-west side of the entrance. A modern wall and basement had unfortunately destroyed the front of the tower, so there is no way of knowing whether it was semicircular or flat.

However, the overall width of the gate is provided by the position of the butt-end of the town wall which is known to lie under the pavement on the opposite side of the street; there is a gap of 55ft (16·8m) between the wall ends. If allowance is made for a companion tower on that side of the gate, then the gap is reduced to 23ft (7m). Aileen Fox has therefore postulated a single main carriageway with flanking foot passages, after the manner of the Silchester Gate at Verulamium (p. 215). Nevertheless, it should be remembered that a later date has been suggested for gates with this type of plan,[105] and on these grounds it could belong to the second phase of fortification. But a nineteenth century print shows, on the inside of the medieval gate, a round-headed arch with no keystone (pl. 63), which is almost certainly a Roman survival, and not unlike the Newport Arch at Lincoln (p. 122). The opening portrayed can be little more than 9–10ft (2·7–3m) wide, even if ample allowance is made for the effects of perspective. Twin

64   Steps leading to the basilica, Exeter (*Robert Turner; Exeter Archaeological Field Unit*)

carriageways of 9ft (2·7m), with a central spina of 3ft 6in (1·1m) (the width of the other walls of the gate) and 9in (229mm) rebates against the towers for the doors (fig. 19) would therefore seem not impossible.[106]

No records have survived of the other gates; their probable positions have already been discussed above.

The construction of the stone wall in front of the existing bank took place some time during the third century. Unfortunately more accurate dating is not yet possible. The wall was constructed on an unmortared rubble base, 11ft (3·4m) wide. Above this, from the level of the external chamfered plinth, the method of construction used a grouted rubble core behind large squared ashlars. The inside face was left rough up to the level of the top of the rampart, above which it was faced. Most of the masonry was constructed of Trap, a volcanic stone out-cropping locally on the Rougemont hill and used extensively in the Roman period, but sandstone and chert were also used. Three scarcements on the internal face reduced the width of the wall to 6ft 3in (1·9m) at a height of 8ft 6in (2·6m). In places the wall still stands 14ft (4·3m) high.[107]

Knowledge of the private houses and shops of Isca is fragmentary, and, as in most cases where a modern town occupies the same site, is derived mainly from observation of commercial excavations. A summary of such finds was compiled by Goodchild and published in 1952.[108] References are normally to lengths of wall and fragments of tessellated floor. The occasional hypocaust was noted. Such controlled excavations as have taken place show that wooden structures continued to be built until the end of the second century, in spite of a plentiful supply of local stone. One recently-found house was very reminiscent of some Antonine houses at Verulamium (p. 209). The frame was of light timber construction, and there were opus signinum floors in two rooms, with an earth floor in a third room possibly intended for a mosaic, as a sackfull of tesserae were found with it.[109] Later, and probably not much before the third century, increasing use was made of masonry for private buildings, which, in turn, allowed the incorporation of heating systems. Even then, however, the general standard was not very good, and the fact that so few tessellated or mosaic pavements have been recorded from Exeter is a measure of either the comparative poverty of the inhabitants or their lack of *aemulatio*.

There is, however, slight evidence from which some of the industrial life of the town can be made out. In excavations at South Gate, a thick rubbish layer was found below the Roman civil defences and dating from the late first to mid second centuries. Set in this layer was a probable cupellation furnace 2ft 3in (685mm) long and 1ft 6in (457mm) wide. The base and sides had been lined with crushed, calcined animal bones. Another flat hearth was found nearby, while some 30yds (27m) to the south-west the same waste layer was encountered, and these contained fragments of tuyères.[110]

The religious life of the town is poorly represented so far by surviving remains. A possible temple site is thought to have existed in Broadgate, and four small bronze statuettes of Apollo, Mars, Mercury and Ceres (or Fortune) were found nearby. The post-war excavations produced a sherd of pottery on which a small ☧ monogram had been scratched, indicating perhaps a small but poor Christian community in the mid fourth century.[111]

The relationship between the civitas Dumnoniorum and its capital town has always excited considerable speculation, some of which was outlined at the beginning of this section.[112] It seems clear that the tide of romanisation was weakening by the time it reached the borders and, beyond Exeter, only flowed in the most superficial and ephemeral way. Iron Age settlements continued their existence, with only the development of the characteristic south-western court-yard house, throughout the Roman period and into the Dark Ages beyond. There is little evidence for the growth of villas, and only one, at Magor Farm, Illogan, is known to exist in the extreme south-west. It is often claimed that an obvious lack of right angles in its lay-out proclaims its rusticity.[113] For its date in the mid second century, it displays the typical development of a modest winged-corridor villa. Lack of right angles need not distress us, or mislead us, as there are innumerable buildings in more sophisticated areas of Britain which

334 *Flavian Expansion* [440]

display no better symmetry, and the myth that all Roman buildings were accurately surveyed deserves to be exploded once and for all. Obviously the venture of villa ownership in East Penwith was not entirely a failure, as the original villa was added to, and was not abandoned until the third century. It therefore had a life-span representing at least two and possibly three generations. Presumably it lay at the centre of a farm; or was it possibly the residence of an early Cornish mining captain?

It is often assumed also that the reason for the rejection of *romanitas* by the Dumnonii lay in the essentially highland nature of their geography. This may, and probably did, have an effect, but it will not do alone. The Parisi of East Yorkshire occupied country not so very different from Lincolnshire, Norfolk or even parts of Kent. Yet they seem to have rejected urbanisation just as firmly, if not more so, as the Dumnonii. There was a kinship, dating back to the period of Iron B immigrants, between the people of the south-west and parts of the lower Severn valley. Yet the latter developed a villa economy which was second to none and cannot be entirely attributed to earlier Belgic, or later immigrant influence, whereas the inhabitants of the south-west rejected such a system even though in parts of their country it was quite feasible. Indeed, the two quite different and contrasting situations outlined above enable the position of the south-west to be classified. In the first place, having largely rejected urbanisation and vicanisation, there was no need or incentive to build up a more advanced agricultural system than they already had. Secondly, the situation depended once again on individual inclinations; little compulsion was employed and if the people did not want romanisation it was not necessarily forced upon them. The opportunities were probably there in equal measure as in other parts of the country; they were not taken.

Extensive alterations were made to the forum and basilica at Exeter early in the fourth century. By AD 380, grass and weeds were apparently growing in the palaestra of the baths, which seems to point to a curtailment of civic life before the end of the fourth century. Indeed, Aileen Fox concluded that, since few coins later than Gratian seem to have circulated at Exeter, commercial life was dying also. Nevertheless some caution is required before the state of affairs is accepted at its face value. We need not conclude from this alone that the town was deserted, but fifth-century alterations at the south-east end of the basilica, with walls made of dry stone, might suggest that the old order of civic authority had ceased. Important also in this context is a wall which was constructed across the street south-east of the basilica, so severing the direct route from the East to the West Gate. Remembering that streets in a town were dedicated to the public in perpetuity, the blocking of a main street would strongly support the suggestion that authority had passed to other hands.

The continued trading connexions in the fifth century between the civitas, and especially Exeter, and the Mediterranean have been emphasised by Aileen Fox.[114] Indeed, Exeter, or its port at Topsham, would have been the first major British centre reached by vessels which had rounded the Iberian peninsula. Was this connexion with the east perhaps responsible for the arrival of an epidemic at Exeter, and the premature decay of the town?

There is a good deal of evidence that the civitas Dumnoniorum was being colonised by both Welsh and Irish Celts during the later fourth and fifth centuries, and their memorial stones, using the Ogham script, are widespread over Cornwall and West Devon. There is some evidence also that the centre of gravity of the civitas was shifting westwards away from Exeter, and it has been suggested that Castle Dore, near Fowey, became the new centre.[115] Despite these changes, however, the south-west peninsula, including parts of the Dobunni and Duro-triges, retained its Mediterranean trading links, as is shown by the numbers of imported amphorae which turn up with considerable frequency at Exeter and on other contemporary sites.[116] An oft-quoted reference to a cornship arriving from Alexandria in time to relieve a famine and returning with a cargo of tin, could be taken to apply to Exeter, or equally to its early sixth-century successor.[117] But some form of life, probably far removed from Romano-British customs, may have lingered on in the town until the arrival of the Saxons in the late seventh century. Certainly Britons continued to live peacefully in Exeter with Saxons until the early ninth century,[118] when they were expelled from the town. But this, in itself, is not proof of continuity.

LEICESTER (*Ratae Coritanorum*)

The Coritani, like their south-western neighbours the Dobunni, had come under the control of Belgic people some little time before the Roman conquest. Stretching north-east in a wide belt from the west Midlands to the Lincolnshire coast, they had a very considerable length of common frontier with the Catu-vellauni. Although the tribe issued coins, some of which had pairs of names on them,[119] strata of earlier Iron A and B cultures survived up to the time of the conquest.

Two main pre-Roman tribal centres have so far been identified: Old Sleaford, Lincs., where much Belgic pottery has been found with moulds for casting coin flans, and Leicester. Miss Kenyon's excavations on the Jewry Wall site produced early levels containing imported Gallo-Belgic and locally produced wares.[120] Coritanian coins from the town and a number of Belgic pots, recently rescued from some commercial excavations, would seem to prove its pre-conquest origins. There is though perhaps a small measure of doubt; such pottery and coins continued in use after the Roman conquest, are extremely difficult to date accurately, and could have been brought to Leicester after the Roman army had arrived. It must be admitted that no structures have yet been convincingly proved as belonging to the period before AD 43, but this may be achieved before long. However, the name of the town, Ratae, is derived from a Celtic word meaning ramparts, or banks, and it might be thought therefore that the Iron Age site was a defended oppidum.

It is not known how the Coritani greeted the Romans, but it is possible that their rulers were among those who submitted to Claudius at Camulodunum. Certainly there is no evidence yet that they resisted, and by AD 47 their land had been put into the straightjacket of the new provincial frontier.

The form taken by the military occupation of Coritanian lands is reasonably familiar. Although there is evidence for more than one fort at Leicester, the other tribal centre at Old Sleaford does not seem to have been garrisoned, perhaps indicating its waning importance. At Leicester a length of military ditch has been found near West Bridge, although no clue was provided to the area enclosed.[121] Early timber buildings have been found below the west central area of the later town. The base of another ditch and parts of other timber structures, built after the manner of military buildings and dating to the Neronian period, were uncovered below the later town defences in Elbow Lane.[122] The two lengths of ditch mentioned above are unlikely to belong to the same circuit, as not only are they too far apart, but they are also on unrelated alignments.

Although the evidence for the early military period at Leicester is scanty and not as clear as it might be, we can detect something of the events which probably took place. It would seem that both the strategic and tactical requirements of the Roman army here coincided with a major native settlement. The nucleus for a vicus was therefore already on the site when a fort was established.[123] The native settlement continued and grew as a vicus. An early street belonging to this period, some 30ft (9m) south of the later street north of the Jewry Wall[124] may represent an attempt at creating a regular lay-out. Alternatively, it might be the approach road of the fort to the east, and if so, is of some importance when considering the later lay-out.

It is unlikely that military government of the Coritani continued after AD 80, although what happened then is not so easy to perceive as with the three civitates already considered in this chapter. What appears certain is that the street system of the new town was being laid out immediately after the withdrawal of the army and these typical provisions for a capital would imply that the civitas had been formally constituted. It would seem, however, that no immediate plans were drawn up for a forum building, but an insula at the centre was left vacant. Many of its functions would have been adequately provided by an open space. We cannot say why the Coritani took no immediate action to provide themselves with the outward symbols of public life, as three other tribes then did. It may have been that, at first, they were attributed to the new colonia at Lincoln, which had been founded on their territory, while retaining their own identity. Or it may have been that the foundation of the colonia and the effective removal of a large part of the civitas to its jurisdiction, deprived the tribe of much of its collective wealth. Certainly in the later Iron Age, the country around Leicester was culturally the most backward, and the most impoverished. Certainly also, their neighbours to the west, the Cornovii, although constituted as a civitas slightly later, were just as lackadaisical when it came to the provision of public buildings. Yet for both, their ultimate wealth is not in question, if the size of their

CESTER   (Ratae)

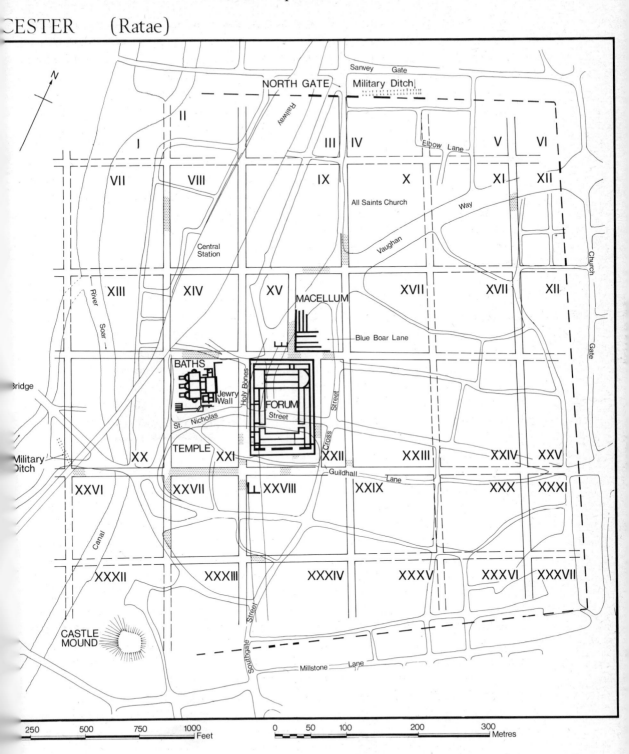

NORTH GATE   Sanvey Gate   Military Ditch

II

I

III   IV   Elbow Lane   V   VI

VII   VIII   IX   X   XI   XII

All Saints Church   Way

Central
Station   Vaughan

River Soar

XIII   XIV   XV   MACELLUM   XVII   XVII   XII

Blue Boar Lane

Bridge   BATHS   Jewry Wall   Holy Bones   FORUM   Street

St. Nicholas   Street

Military
Ditch   TEMPLE   XX   XXI   XXII   XXIII   XXIV   XXV

Guildhall Lane

XXVI   XXVII   XXVIII   XXIX   XXX   XXXI

Canal

XXXII   XXXIII   XXXIV   XXXV   XXXVI   XXXVII

CASTLE
MOUND

Southgate Street

Millstone Lane

250   500   750   1000
Feet

0   50   100   200   300
Metres

75   Plan of Leicester (*after J. E. Mellor*)

capitals and the scale of their public and domestic buildings is taken as a measure. Herein lies the paradox.

There is only slight evidence for the buildings of the Flavian town, although what there is suggests a fairly rapid development in the centre. Some of the buildings which may have been part of the military vicus were razed and replaced by more regular and spacious ones,[125] although timber frames and wattle and daub walls were still used. For instance, a wooden floor had been inserted in the front room of a shop in place of earlier mud floors.[126] The sites of both forts were almost certainly included in the developing area, but an inhumation burial beneath the town rampart in the Elbow Lane section[127] would imply a later expansion of the town boundaries. No plans seem to have been made for a bath-building, and the part of the insula which it was later to occupy was used, unlike the forum insula, for shops and houses.

The beginnings of the town were therefore modest: an open space for a forum and little if anything provided in the way of amenities. It was essentially a commercial centre, and its later wealth might be attributed to the early enterprise and possible frugality of its inhabitants. Nearly two generations were to pass before the fruits of accumulating wealth became outwardly apparent. It showed first as better quality houses and shops were built to replace those which, after 20–30 years, were nearing the end of their useful life (fig. 75). Economies were, however, still effected. The early second-century house in the south-west corner of Insula XVI, which replaced Flavian timber buildings, was built on a spacious plan round a large open courtyard, but the walls were constructed of clay blocks, cut to standard size, laid on low masonry foundations.[128] The most frequently used building stone in Ratae came from the granite outcrops of Charnwood forest, especially from Groby, and from nearby Enderby; it was a stone which at the time was difficult to work and it lent itself only to the construction of rubble masonry. For better-class work and architectural decoration, a millstone grit from near Melbourne, Derbyshire, about 30 miles (48km) north-west of the town, or a sandstone from Danehills, was used. The use of stone which was not always of the best quality and which was obtained almost entirely from quarries north-west of the town and often at some distance away, requires explanation, as better-quality freestone was available at half the distance to the east and south-east, where oolites of the Jurassic zone are found. It is possible that this provides a glimpse into some of the problems of land ownership, which are at present all too indistinct. But considerable use continued to be made of substitutes for masonry in private houses and shops, even if the outward appearance of the buildings was much improved with plastered and painted walls and concrete and mortar floors.

Some time during the late Hadrianic period work was started on the construction of a forum and basilica in the reserved central insula (XXII). It is possible that exhortations made by Hadrian during his visit to Britain were responsible,[129] for the period saw other municipal works put in hand, such as the fora at Wroxeter and Caistor-by-Norwich, and the return to civilian government of other civitates (Chapter 8).

LEICESTER

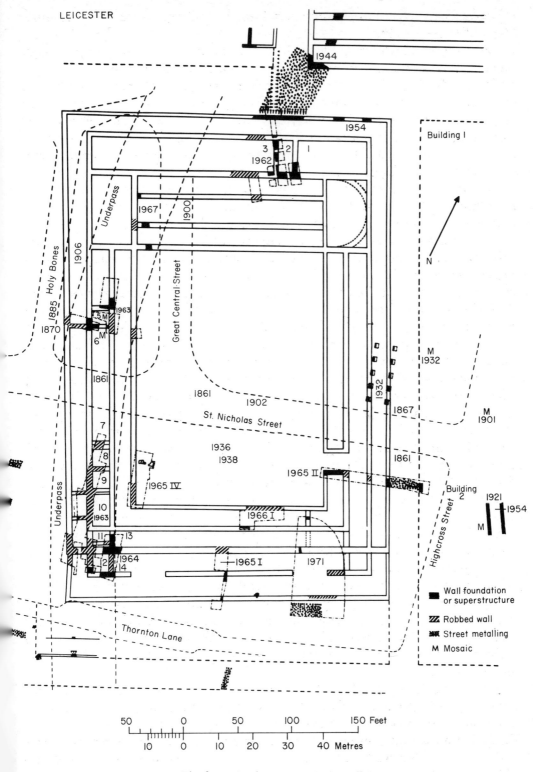

76 The forum insula, Leicester (*J. E. Mellor*)

The reserved insula proved larger than the resources of the civitas. It was reduced on the east by a new street which cut off about a third of the original area, while to the south the street was extended northwards to the forum walls. Even with these economies the original plan seems to have envisaged a forum and basilica only 387ft (118m) by 298ft (81m). This plan provided only for rows of double porticoes in the east, south and west ranges, with the basilica across the north end. The changes of plan (fig. 76) during construction saw rooms added to the inner portico of the west range with a new inner portico provided, and to the outer portico of the south range, with the wholly new element of a row

65   Painted fresco from the west wall of the courtyard of a house in Insula XVI north of the forum, Leicester (*F. M. B. Cooke*)

66   Painted fresco from the north wall of the courtyard of a house in Insula XVI north of the forum, Leicester
(*F. M. B. Cooke*)

of rooms and an outer portico added to the latter, so effectively increasing the overall length of the building to 433ft (132m). Too little work has been done on the east range to be able to say if similar changes took place there, but it was probably made symmetrical with the west. Entrances seem to have been provided in the east wing near its south end, and possibly in the west wing near its north end, with two more arranged symmetrically towards the ends of the south wing. The latter appear to have been supplemented by a single monumental porch added axially to the south wing. A number of columns, bases, parts of stylobate blocks and sections of stone drainage channels have been found from time to time beneath St Nicholas Street, Holy Bones and under nearby buildings. They must have belonged to the forum and were probably part of the colonnades. A restored length of the stylobate with a column in position can be seen outside the Jewry Wall Museum (pl. 68).

The basilica, covering the north end of the forum, appears to have been conventional in plan, although the positions of the tribunals have yet to be accurately established. It was flanked on the north by a row of rooms and an outer portico. Some at least of these rooms opened on to the portico and not towards the hall. An interesting observation was made by Hebditch in this area. A tree had stood in the builders' way on the edge of the street and had been cut down, leaving the stump and roots to rot; they appeared as hollow cavities in the surrounding road metalling.[130]

With work on the forum and basilica completed, or nearing completion, attention seems to have been turned to the provision of a public bath-house in the next insula west (XXI). This site embraces the well-known stretch of standing masonry called the Jewry Wall, and the site itself, west of the Jewry Wall, was the subject of excavation by Dr Kathleen Kenyon between 1936–9.[131] Time has not, however, dealt kindly with her interpretations, and it is therefore expedient briefly to recapitulate some of the theories which have been advanced from time to time to explain the building's function.

Dr Kenyon claimed that the first major building on the site, erected during the early part of Hadrian's principate, was the forum and basilica of the town, although the plan was abnormal for such structures. Furthermore, she concluded that the forum was never completed because instabilities in the subsoil would have caused the collapse of the walls in the south range. Her next stage involved the removal of the forum and basilica elsewhere and the construction of a large bath-house on its site during the early Antonine period, with further additions taking place in the fourth century.

Objections to these conclusions arise on two counts: function and date. We have already seen that the forum and basilica have been found in the neighbouring insula since Dr Kenyon's excavations and that they are dated a little later than her first building, which should itself now be dated somewhat later.[132] More-over, according to her interpretation, there were two main phases of construc-tion, and it is difficult to see how a building, which was provided with such monumental drains as the first, could convincingly be interpreted as a forum, particularly with its irregular and abnormal plan.[133] Moreover, if the subsoil was unsuitable for a forum it would surely have been equally unsuitable for a bath-building, with its even greater weight of masonry.

Most recent opinions, therefore, have accepted that the building was from the first intended as a bath-house and that work was started about AD 145–50, perhaps to be discontinued for a very short space of time either because money temporarily ran out, or because of the unexpected difficulties over the foundations and the need to replan. Ultimately, the building was completed, after some alterations in plan had possibly taken place, about AD 155–60.

East of the main baths, and now partly under St Nicholas' Church, was a palaestra, possibly covered, which extended for some 80ft (24m) to the eastern street. Entrance into the baths was through a pair of doors set asymmetrically in the west wall of the palaestra, which can still be seen in the surviving structure. Blind arches and niches between, and on either side of, the doors probably formed part of the architectural decoration and may have contained statuary. One may have been occupied by a statue of the goddess Fortuna, who was frequently associated with baths. The apparent asymmetry of this part of the structure might suggest that existing work was freely adapted in the finished building, although another explanation envisages companion doors further south along the wall to balance the effect. Although there would then have been a symmetrical appear-ance from the palaestra, it would have been difficult to justify the second pair of doors, as they would have led only to the service area, and would have borne little relationship to the rest of the building.

The main bath-house had a plan (fig. 8) which was somewhat rare in Britain. Access to rooms was obtained from a central concourse entered directly from the palaestra. It will be apparent from earlier discussion that, in the commoner type of bath-house, each room of greater heat is approached through those of lesser, thus imposing as it were an order in which the bath should be taken. It is probable that, at Leicester, the main concourse acted as a frigidarium and would have been equipped with basins and running cold water. As a bather entered this room, there were on either hand small suites of three rooms each. There is no indication that they were heated, although it must be remembered that little more than wall foundations or robbing trenches had survived post-Roman building works; all these rooms were part of the earliest phase of construction. On his immediate left was probably a latrine, which was perhaps inserted in the later phase, although there is room for doubt, as it would otherwise be difficult to explain a massive drain in the first phase, south of the block and apparently having no useful function. One or more of these rooms probably acted as changing-rooms.

Also facing him as he entered were three heated ante-chambers, probably tepidaria, each leading to another heated room of considerable size (approximately 47ft (14·3m) by 35ft (10·7m)) and arranged side-by-side. Presumably caldaria, they would have been raised to higher temperatures. The centre room was equipped with a rectangular plunge-bath in the end wall, while the two flanking rooms had semi-circular plunge-baths situated beyond both the end and side walls. Each room appears to have had its own stokehole in a rectangular room placed beyond the terminal plunge-bath. Part of one of the iron beams (pl. 69) which supported the boiler over the flue entrance was found during the excavations.[134]

The building (fig. 80) seems to have been enclosed on the north and south sides within porticoes, and it is possible that a row of shops was included on the north side.

The drains which served the baths are worth a comment, not only for their size, but also because they reflect on the problems of the aqueduct. In the completed building two major drains were probably operative and ran virtually round three of its sides. That to the north was constructed in the first phase, according to Dr Kenyon, but is apparently cut by the north apse of the caldaria in the second phase. But this point is glossed over in the report, although on Plate XI two superimposed drains show clearly that reconstruction had taken place at some time. Re-excavation enabled this point to be confirmed before the construction of the Jewry Wall Museum.[135] The drain running beneath the frigidarium was said to have flowed from south to north, although its continuation could not be found owing to massive disturbances. The direction of flow is surprising if its southern end is to be interpreted as a latrine, although it must be admitted that this suggestion was not made by Dr Kenyon, who considered the

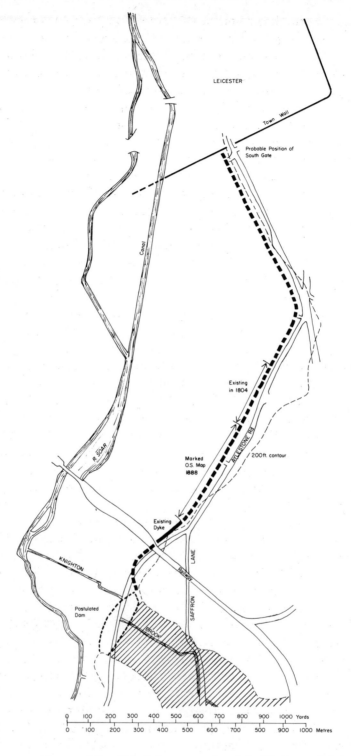

77   Suggested line of the Leicester aqueduct (*after W. Keay and Astley Clarke*)

drain to be a channel bringing water to the baths, and possibly connected with an arch which pierced the palaestra wall near it. This seems to be ruled out by the low level of its bed. The drain branched by the arch, running both directly south and south by west. It is here that it reaches its most massive proportions, the channel being 2ft (609mm) wide and having sufficient headroom for a man to walk down it. It was roofed with foot-thick (305mm) blocks of millstone grit.

Such a channel, no matter whether it was carrying water to the site, or away from it, was intended for a heavy and continuous flow. Yet we find Dr Kenyon making the suggestion that the Raw Dykes, if the town's aqueduct, was a failure because it was cut at too low a level to serve the baths; thereafter she implied that they had no supply of running water until the fourth century when a water tank was constructed in the south-west corner, the tank being filled by hand from the nearby river Soar. This hardly accords with high capacity drains, not only in respect of their building, but also with their maintenance and with the additions made to the system. Clearly we should assume that a free flow of running water was provided for the baths from the beginning. How was this done?

If we turn first to the Raw Dykes, of which a length still survives near the junction of Aylestone Road with Saffron Lane, it can be seen that it appears to consist of two components. The upper was a shallow channel just over 50ft (15m) across and no more than 8ft (2·4m) deep, which was in part formed by the upcast having been tipped on the downhill side. Centrally in the bottom a deeper cut had been made, 13ft (4m) wide at the top, sloping to a flat base only 3ft (0·9m) wide and 5ft (1·5m) deep.[136] Originally the dyke was known to have extended as far as the southern limit of the town, but most of its course is today obliterated. It is interesting, though, that the 198ft (60m) contour, on which the surviving section of the dyke lies also continues as far as the town boundary, which it strikes near the Newarkes. If this contour is traced southwards it meets the Knighton Brook no great distance away. Dr Kenyon indeed suggested that damming the brook would have created a reservoir to supply the aqueduct, which, as we have seen, could carry the water as far as the town. We might elaborate further and suggest that the course of the brook was diverted into the aqueduct, a suggestion which was first made by Mr William Keay and Mr Astley Clarke in 1935. Their proposed scheme is shown in figure 77. It is not a large stream today, and most of its flow could have been contained in the lower part of the dyke which, by concentrating the water in a narrow channel, would have increased the rate of flow. When the water level rose higher, the upper part of the ditch would have ensured that the valley below was not flooded. Once the water had been brought to the town boundary, it was well within the capacity of Roman hydraulic engineers to lift it by means of water-wheels or other devices into a tower, from which it could flow by gravity to sites in the town, including the bath-house. It seems strange that Dr Kenyon herself should have suggested this method for filling from the river the fourth-century water-tank on the bath's site, without apparently thinking of applying it to the related problem of the Raw Dykes.

Small scraps of evidence support these suggestions. In 1966, within the town and a short distance east of Southgate Street, a ditch was found, 4ft (1·2m) wide and 4ft (1·2m) deep, running northwards away from the approximate point where the Raw Dykes probably reached the southern boundary. A square cut channel had been dug at the bottom of the ditch, which appeared to date to the second century; a military origin is therefore unlikely.[137] It might be suggested that this channel was dug for a water distribution pipe, either of lead or wood, which was subsequently removed and not replaced. It is not unlike some channels known to have contained such pipes. Another indication of a running water supply is the stone basin drinking-fountain found in 1862 on the site of 52 High

67 Painted ceiling from the market hall, Leicester (*Crown Copyright—reproduced with permission of the Controller of Her Majesty's Stationery Office*)

68 Part of the forum stylobate re-erected outside the Jewry Wall Museum, Leicester (*J. E. Thawley*)

Cross Street, where it must originally have been situated beside the main north-south street.

Only one other certain public building is well known at Leicester, and this dates to a later period than the forum. Towards the end of the second century, or more probably early in the third, a need must have been felt for extra market space. Consequently, a derelict house (see p. 348 below) in Insula XVI north of the basilica was levelled and on the site so provided a large market hall of basilican plan (fig. 10) was built. Its long axis lay east-west, but it does not seem to have extended for the full width of the insula, which was itself only about half the normal size. Its overall length, suggested by a north-south wall recently seen under High Cross Street, was about 180ft (55m) and its width was 96ft (29m). Fragmentary columns, one 5ft $8\frac{1}{2}$in (1·75m) in diameter, carved impost mouldings and other architectural pieces found below Blue Boar Lane and High Cross Street would appear to have come from the east end of the building. A wing projected northwards from the hall's west end and is likely to have been matched by a companion wing at the east end. They seem to have contained rows of shops or offices set between colonnades, with an open court enclosed in the middle between them. Some of these rooms had plastered and painted ceilings (pl. 67). The plan is therefore markedly similar to a forum and basilica complex and, indeed, was so called when first discovered.[138] But its secondary date and small size, when coupled with the lack of tribunals in the hall, would imply that it was never intended to serve as the principal administrative forum in the town, whose functions were always retained by the earlier and larger building in the next insula south. It must therefore have been built to increase the market area of the town, and so had a purely commercial purpose. Its provision shows how trade had grown and also indicates how, despite the seeming lack of villas, the surrounding countryside had increased its productive capacity.

This prosperity was mirrored in the private houses. The most spectacular dwelling to be found so far is the second-century house in Insula XVI, north of the basilica, already mentioned on p. 338 in connexion with the early development of the town. The house, built originally in the early second century, was extensively renovated towards the middle of the century. It had been constructed some distance back from the street to the south and its rooms had been ranged round the sides of a peristyled courtyard (fig. 78). Parts of the north and west wings were excavated,[139] and at least seven rooms identified. The mid second-century renovation had resulted in tessellated floors being laid in all the rooms examined, while at least two, and probably more, had mosaics. The walls had been replastered and painted with new designs, of which that decorating the interior wall of the peristyle was the most impressive. Here a continuous frieze, incorporating perspective drawings of architectural features such as niches and alcoves, was interspersed with areas of red fresco. The arched niches seemed to have been flanked by columns and displayed coffered soffits, while entwined foliage grew up the centres, with dovelike birds and winged cupids sitting on the branches. Above one niche there seems to have been an elaborate architectural facade surmounted by a panel containing a tragic theatrical mask.[140] The red fresco was decorated with candelabra connected by swags and garlands of flowers, on which pheasant-like birds were perched, and which also incorporated human figures. Top and bottom of the walls were defined by a continuous scroll and a dado respectively (pls. 65–6). The wall plaster recovered from inside the rooms tended to be plainer, with only geometrical and imitation marble patterns, but nevertheless indicated the positions of some structural features such as windows and doors.

The luxuriousness of the house clearly proclaims it to be the residence of a wealthy family, who probably provided decurions or magistrates for the civitas. We can read in the development of the house their rise to power over a matter of little more than a generation. Their fall seems to have been equally rapid, for, by the end of the second century the house was ruinous with its roof removed. An early example of clogs to clogs in three generations! People were scrawling obscene epithets and other remarks on the painted walls of the peristyle[141] while parts of the building were converted to industrial use. In most rooms the

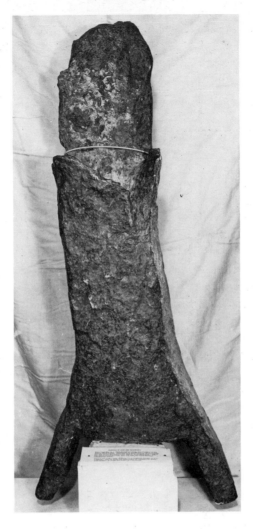

69   Iron beam from a stokehole in the Jewry Wall baths, Leicester (*F. M. B. Cooke*)

mosaics and tessellated floors had been hacked out and the stones salvaged, and on the concrete base so exposed in one room a number of cows' heads had been tipped. A deep pit had been dug in the north-west corner of the courtyard and a gulley running into it was presumably to feed it with water. It would seem that a tannery or, perhaps more likely, a factory for making horn had taken over.[142] Ultimately, as we have seen, the site was requisitioned for a public market, presumably under a regulation that required buildings which had been pulled down, or were ruinous, to be replaced within a given time. Failure to do so may have meant forfeiture of the land to public ownership.

Other private houses representative of equal wealth are indicated by the

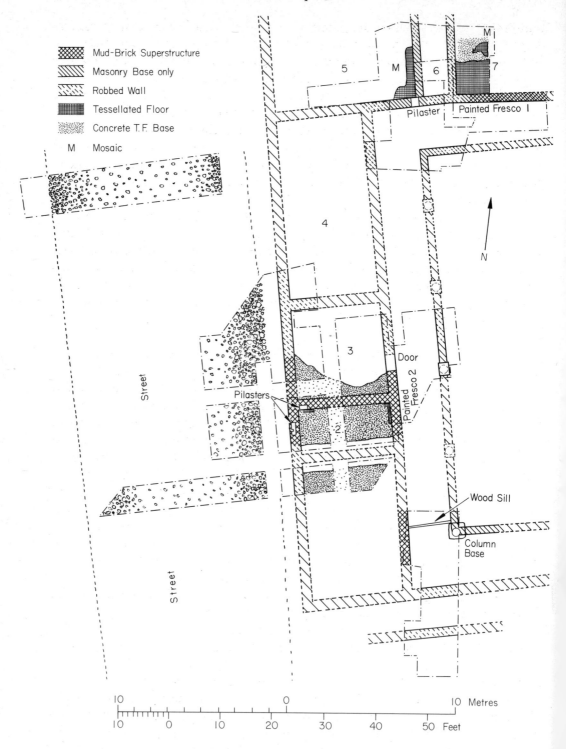

Mud-Brick Superstructure
Masonry Base only
Robbed Wall
Tessellated Floor
Concrete T.F. Base

M   Mosaic

78   Second-century house, Insula xvi, Leicester

number of mosaics which are known from the town.[143] Two in particular deserve mention: the Peacock pavement from a house in the same insula as, and south of, the public baths, and the pavement found beneath the now-defunct Central Station, lying in Insula XIV north of the baths. Both the pavements were large and almost entirely made up of panels of conventional floral and geometric patterns. However, the central panel of one pavement contained a peacock, with tail spread, and with the eyes in the tail picked out with blue glass tesserae: hence the modern name of the mosaic. It was probably mid second-century in date. Very few pavements made use of extensive pictorial scenes, although one small panel depicting Cyparissus and his Stag was found near All Saint's Church at the north end of the town.

Another house, or possibly a shop near Southgate Street, possessed a deep cellar (pl. 70), with walls still surviving to a height of 6ft (1·8m). Two walls had windows with splayed sills, probably designed to admit light from an 'area' outside. Entrance was by a single doorway at the foot probably of some wooden steps, and niches, possibly for lamps, had been provided in each wall. The walls had been plastered and whitewashed and a simple decoration of red and blue lines painted over it.[144]

A suggestion has already been made that the second-century town boundary perhaps enclosed a smaller area on the east than was later walled. Certainly burials and a pottery kiln have been found inside that part of the circuit of the later wall, although this is not decisive. Pottery kilns have been found at Canterbury and Gloucester apparently within the town, while occasional burials, as the result of foul play, could also have taken place inside the boundaries. This conclusion, however, conflicts with foundations of timber buildings found beneath the east rampart in Churchgate, and with the information provided by the Thurmaston milestone.[145] According to its inscription, the town boundary should have lain further out during the Hadrianic period if indeed the distance of two Roman miles had been measured from the boundary and not from the centre. It is possible, however, that the milestone was not in position when found in 1771.

Leicester appears to have been one of the few towns in Britain which was not fortified with earthworks at the end of the second century, although their existence on a hitherto unexpected alignment cannot be entirely ruled out. Perhaps a hint of what might be expected was found below the town wall footings on the south side near Southgate Street, where there was a palisade or fence with post holes 1½ft (456mm) in diameter and 3ft (914mm) apart.[146] The earliest defences therefore seem to have been the stone wall with contemporary bank and ditch system, which was erected round the town in the third century: more accurate dating is not at present possible. It is unfortunate that this wall seems to have been destroyed by river action on the west side, while on the north, east and south sides it everywhere coincided with the medieval walls, which were severely damaged in the early middle ages and subsequently robbed to foundation level and below. So little has survived, and so shallow were the foundations, that it has often been difficult to ascertain its line. Nevertheless, the

70   Cellar of a house, Southgate Street, Leicester (*City of Leicester Museum*)

rampart still stands in most places to some height behind the line of the wall, while the ditches, recut in the middle ages, also help to mark its course. As far as can be seen from the slight remains, the wall had a foundation about 9–10ft (2·7–3m) wide, but the trench was shallow, hardly penetrating the undisturbed subsoil.

Excavations have established the line of the defences on the north, east and south sides.[147] That on the west has long been open to speculation. Early theories dispense with a wall on this side allowing the river Soar to be an adequate defence. But Haverfield and others have cast doubt on such an arrangement.[148] Recent excavations have made it appear likely that the river has encroached on the town since the Roman period, possibly destroying the western fortifications. Certainly the town once extended beyond the present river course, as a north-south street of the grid has been found at West Bridge,[149] but it is not yet known if this part was excluded when fortifications were constructed.

No gate structures have yet been positively identified, although a mass of heavy masonry, recorded from below the Cumberland Inn, may be part of the north gate, which carried a minor road to the Charnwood area. Consequently it was relatively unimportant except that it led to the main stone quarries. Undoubtedly the two most important gates were those carrying the Fosse Way through the east and west sides respectively, but it is not yet at all clear where these gates stood. Some claim that they were on the same sites as the medieval gates and so at either end of the street running past the south end of the forum.[150] But it is not impossible for the next street north to have served as the decumanus maximus, and the existence of an early predecessor, belonging to the period of military occupation, on nearly the same alignment suggests that there is some substance in this claim. Similar doubt arises over the position of the south gate. It may not coincide with the medieval gate at the end of Southgate Street, but instead may be 440yds (402m) east, and so directly opposite the north gate. Through this gate ran the Gartree Road to Medbourne and beyond. It is worth mentioning that another road, leaving by the west gate, acted as a short route to Mancetter.[151]

There is much varied evidence for the commercial and industrial life of the town. Some shops have already been mentioned. Other blocks are known at the south-east corner of Insula xv, and the north-west corner of Insula xxviii. References have also been made to the manufacture of pottery and either horn objects or leather. Metal-working was being carried on as early as the middle of the first century, and crucibles and a fine stone mould for thin ornamental bronze plates have been found in Friar's Causeway.[152]

Other metal-working, albeit of a more unusual nature, was carried on in the late fourth century in the outer west colonnade of the market. A small circular hearth had been used for a preliminary process in the recovery of silver from late base coinage. Nearby was found a cake of metal, weighing 5lb (2·3kg) which was composed of 15 per cent copper, 55 per cent lead and a trace of silver, and which had probably come from a cupellation furnace. Such activities were illegal if carried out by private individuals and punishable by the death penalty,[153] so it is an interesting commentary on the state of law enforcement that such operations were allowed to be carried out openly in a public building. Considerable amounts of once molten glass, mainly in the form of droplets and threads, probably imply that glass vessels were made in the same furnace. Leicester had the usual trading contacts with other parts of the province, as is witnessed by the fragment of carved shale table leg, probably from Dorset, found in the nearby villa at Rothley.

Less is known about the religious life of the inhabitants. A temple is perhaps

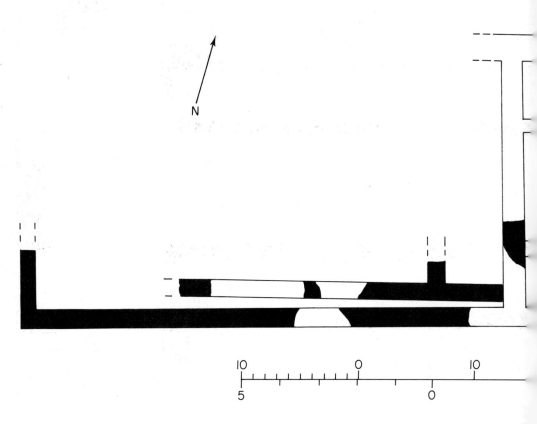

79   Plan of a temple, possibly a Mithraeum, in Insula XXI, Leicester (*after J. E. Mellor*)

indicated in the narrow insula east of the forum, where columns standing on a stylobate and part of a triptych, carved in stone and depicting the upper half of a male figure, have been found.[154] Another, more certainly a temple (fig. 79), has recently been excavated in St Nicholas' Circle, beneath the modern Holiday Inn,[155] and therefore lying in the same insula as, but south of, the public baths. It was an aisled building 20ft (6·1m) wide with a nave 50ft (15·2m) long, and it was aligned east–west with the entrance to the west. The floor level of the aisles was higher than that of the nave and at the east end were two transepts which cut short the aisles and terminated in apses. At the west end there was an ante-room, or possibly a courtyard at least 40ft (12·2m) long and the same width as the building. A carved stone male torso and two small column bases were found in the building, as well as incense burners and beakers. It appears to have been built in the late second or third century, and a scatter of coins on the latest floor suggest a declining use after *c.* AD 360. Immediately south of the building was a well, which had been filled during the third century. The temple, for so it would

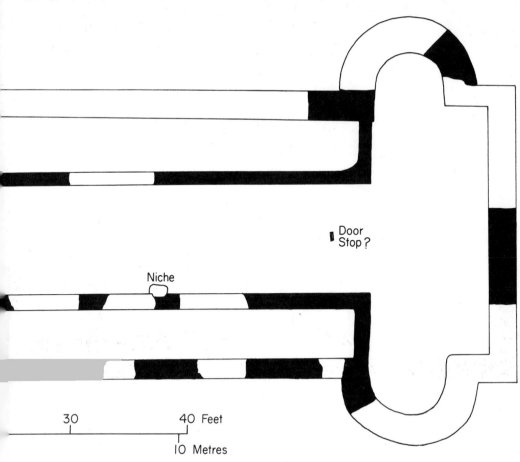

Door
Stop?

Niche

30   40 Feet

10 Metres

seem to be, has been provisionally identified as a Mithraeum, but it should be
remembered that basilican-plan buildings were by no means confined to temples
of this cult. It also lacks some of the features that might be expected of a
Mithraeum. Just east of the market hall, and probably in the same insula, an altar
depicting a bearded river or sea god may be associated with an earlier discovery
of a frieze or pediment ornamented with sea-serpents.

Cemeteries, which have never been properly investigated, are known outside
the four principal gates and also beyond the north-east corner. Three lead coffins
came from those to the south, but so far only a fragmentary tombstone has been
found from the western cemetery and the name of the person commemorated is
not decipherable,[156] so, little is yet known of the people of the town. One,
however, was Adcobrovatus, whose son M. Ulpius Novanticus was serving in
the Roman army in AD 106. Novanticus presumably enlisted either very soon
after the town had been founded as the civitas capital or even while it was still a
military vicus.[157] He gained his Roman citizenship during his service with

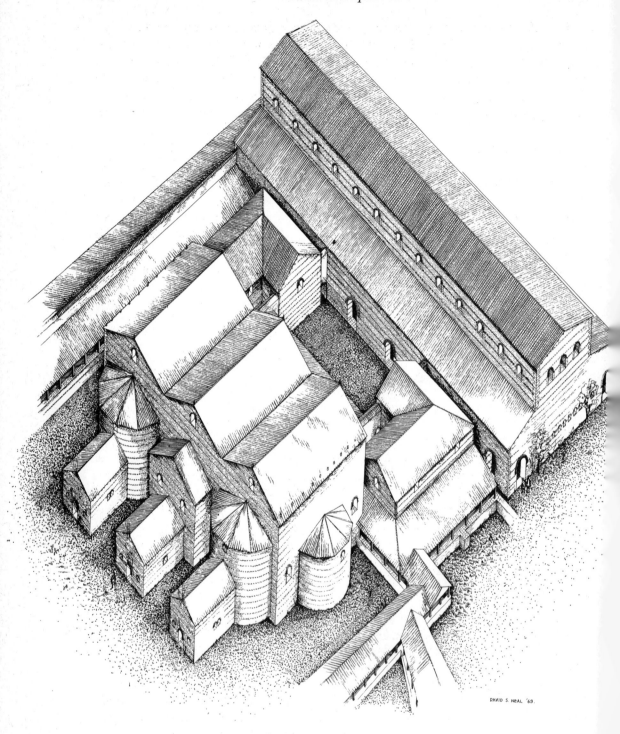

DAVID S. NEAL '69.

80   Restoration of the Jewry Wall bath-house (*D. S. Neal*)

Coh. I. Brittonum and was serving at *Porolissum* (Dacia), where his discharge
certificate was found. Because his origo is quoted as Ratae and not civis Coritanus,
the rank of municipium has been claimed for Leicester.[158] But from the unusual
nature of this particular diploma and from what we now know of the early
development of the town, it would seem extremely unlikely.[159] Two other
people possibly associated with the town are known from their names scratched
on a piece of Italian red-ware pottery: Verecunda, who may have been an
actress, and Lucius, a gladiator.[160] The rarity of such pottery in Britain might
make this piece suspect, but, if genuine, it probably implies that they were only
visitors to the town in their capacities as entertainers. Their presence would imply
that Leicester either had an amphitheatre and possibly a theatre as well, or
compromised with a Romano-Gallic theatre as at Verulamium (p. 210). No
evidence for any such building has yet come to light. But at least someone in the
town was probably wealthy enough to be able to stage gladiatorial shows, and a
fragment of a fairly common type of moulded glass beaker, displaying gladiatorial combats and the names of the performers, is additional evidence of an
interest in such contests.[161]

Another citizen, probably an oculist, C. Pal. Gracilis is known from a stamp
with which cakes of ointment were marked,[162] while Primus, a labourer in a tile
factory somewhere in the civitas, recorded in a fit of pride or boredom that he
had made ten tiles.[163]

What was the later history of Ratae? Private shops were being rebuilt in stone
in the early fourth century, so we can assume that the town was as busy as before,
despite the fact that it may no longer have been at the centre of so large a civitas
(see p. 22 above). In the late fourth century, a detachment of the Roman army
were probably stationed in the town, although there is only very slight evidence
to show that the defences had been strengthened with external towers. Some time
during the last quarter of the century a serious fire swept through the centre of the
town, burning the forum, basilica and the market hall.[164] We do not know if it
was started intentionally or by accident, but no attempt was made to rebuild
afterwards. What happened then is shown best by conditions observed in a
corner of the west wing of the market.[165] Here the burnt and collapsed roof
timbers and tiles were found as they had fallen. On top was a layer of small,
rubbly building stone and mortar, derived perhaps from weathering of the
exposed wall tops. A stage of equilibrium was then reached, when only fine
gritty soil had built up over the fallen masonry, the product of weed growth,
wind and rain: similar layers formed in the open cellars of houses bombed during
the last war. But at one point in time the process had been halted by a rough
pebble floor, on which were a few scattered nails, but no pottery, coins or other
finds. Someone had made a rough shelter in a corner of the ruins, so the site cannot
have been entirely deserted, even though past glories had long since fled. Early
Saxon burials are known from some of the cemeteries,[166] and it would seem that
perhaps Leicester, like Caistor-by-Norwich and some other eastern towns, slid
rapidly from Roman Britain to Saxon England.

WROXETER (*Virconium Cornoviorum*)

The tribal territory of the Cornovii lay in an area which was not immediately occupied by the Roman army, when the first frontier was laid out. It is possible, however, that they made their peace with Claudius, and would therefore have early allowed troop movements within their boundaries; yet there is some evidence of hostility from hill-forts in the Marches. This situation did not last long, and by the time of the governorship of Ostorius Scapula the frontier zone had been extended to the Welsh border to cope with the continued hostility of the Ordovices and Silures. The need to control the valleys of the rivers Severn and Dee, which form natural routes into the heart of Wales, was justification enough for this occupation.

At the moment when they submitted to occupation by Roman forces, the Cornovii seem to have been at about the same stage of cultural advancement as the Dumnonii. No breath of Belgic culture had touched them and their society was based on a multiplicity of hill-forts, which occur wherever there is suitable terrain. However, we can probably no longer claim with the confidence of Richmond[167] that, in the west midland plain of Staffordshire and Cheshire, settlement was thin. Recent surveys have tended to show that river valleys, especially on the gravels, were just as thickly settled in prehistoric times, as they were in later periods.

The first military occupation at Wroxeter was probably by a cohort of Thracians,[168] placed in a fort about a quarter of a mile south of the later town.[169] But knowledge of a number of marching-camps in the vicinity would suggest a high level of military activity from time to time, as campaigns were mounted against Welsh tribes. Later, a fortress for Legio XIV was established to replace the auxiliary fort on a new site just east of a southward turn in the course of the river Severn. So far three phases of timber buildings have been discovered[170] within an area possibly bounded by a double-ditched fortification.[171] The earliest of the phases dates to *c.* AD 60, possibly slightly earlier, while the third probably extended beyond the 80s, but the fortress was probably empty between the withdrawal of Legio XIV from Britain and the return of Legio XX from Inchtuthil to Wroxeter.[172] In the circumstances the third phase of construction was probably put in hand by Legio XX, and Frere has suggested that the un-finished bath-house on the site of the later forum, and another structure nearby, were part of this building programme, which was interrupted by the removal of the legion to Chester. Webster has, however, suggested that the baths were intended as a parting gift by the legion to the newly-founded town, left incomplete because warfare in the north *c.* AD 100 required the departure of its builders. But it is difficult to envisage the mechanics of such a gift or to find a parallel for it.

The abandonment of the legionary fortress in the 90s led to the constitution of the civitas Cornoviorum, and the foundation of its capital at Wroxeter, to fill the void. Thus, although a somewhat late arrival on the Flavian constitutional scene, it nevertheless belongs to that time rather than to the next bout of civic activity during the Hadrianic period, which is the subject of the next chapter.

Yet Frere's solution for the unfinished bath-house presents difficulties, if the conclusions of earlier excavators are to be taken at their face value. Atkinson considered that the bath-house was constructed after the street grid was laid out,[173] although he reached this conclusion by a consideration of general levels rather than by a meticulous study of stratification, and it might be unwise to place too much reliance on it. But if we accept that the streets belonged to the early town, so too must the bath-house. A way out of this difficulty can, however, be found if the principal town streets perpetuated those of the fortress, as seems to be the case. Then there are the open-fronted timber buildings which Bushe-Fox found lining the west side of the street, running south from between the two unfinished masonry buildings, and which he dated to the period AD 75–85.[174] He inferred that the occupation was considerable, from the amount of pottery and other articles found, and considered that a certain amount of rebuilding had taken place. In a civilian context these buildings would probably have been shops, but in a military context such as Frere envisaged they could have been stores buildings lining the main roads of a fortress, as at Inchtuthil.[175] However, the intensity of occupation postulated by Bushe-Fox is hardly in accord with an unfinished fortress. Neither could the buildings be interpreted as shops in a canabae outside, for their position would seem too central to the site as a whole. Bushe-Fox, however, also records that, early in the second century, reconstruction took place in a more readily recognisable way. Long houses with open fronts and porticoes were constructed on the site, and he is clearly describing shops which belonged to the initial lay-out of the town. It is probably best therefore to assign his earlier structures to the military period in spite of the intensity of occupation, and to associate the shops with the first town plan. Certainly the main street grid in the central area was being laid out in the last decade of the first century, which would seem to fit with this suggestion.

Nevertheless it is as well to interpret these early developments cautiously until more precise information is available. Frere's view that it is difficult to explain the failure to complete the baths if they were civilian in character because the impetus to urbanisation in civitas capitals was provided by government policy, needs modification.[176] We have already seen that some civitates were exceptionally slow to provide outward displays of civic authority. If it was government policy, it seems not always to have been pressed and much must have depended on the energy and inclinations of individual governors. It is probably true to say that baths were seldom built before a forum, but both could have been started together in a wave of zeal. So the possibility that the baths, and the basilica opposite, represent failed civic building programmes, must linger for the present.

Although Wroxeter was close to one of the most imposing Cornovian hill-forts on the Wrekin, there is nothing to indicate that the latter exercised any paramountcy over the tribe. The situation is closely akin to that of the Dumnonii, where a legionary fortress also provided an additional attraction to the tribesmen and gave them the incentive to settle within its neighbourhood. The legionary fortress would undoubtedly have attracted more and richer traders than an auxiliary fort would have done, not only from within the tribe, but also from other parts of the province, if not from other provinces as well. The legionary canabae, as at Exeter, gave the town a fair start.

It is at this point that we come up against the main paradox of Wroxeter. Many writers have taken pains to point out that, with at least 180 acres (63ha) enclosed within its defences, it is one of the largest towns in the province; not as large as Cirencester or Verulamium, but certainly larger than Canterbury and other civitas capitals. It was on the very fringe of the civilised areas of the province, although neither Caerwent nor Aldborough can be compared with it. An important point here is whether it is wise always to equate prosperity with size, as measured by the area enclosed by fortifications. If we work on the assumption that defences were seldom built to encircle areas not occupied by buildings, then it is probably safe to make the equation. But at Wroxeter, much of the northern end seems to have been devoid of major buildings and its enclosure within the defences must have been for other reasons. A safer guide to prosperity is perhaps to be found in the size of the forum; it is worth noting that the piazza, measuring 242ft (74m) by 225ft (69m) is very nearly twice the size of that at Silchester, though considerably smaller than the one at Cirencester. There is probably therefore some justification in claiming that Wroxeter was a rich town. Richmond suggested that the reason for this concentration lay in the unsettled conditions obtaining in the civitas, much of which was subject to continuous military occupation.[177] Certainly villas are few and far between, so that tribal landowners may have left their estates in the care of bailiffs to seek not only power and entertainment but also the protection of the town. But we might also argue that continued military occupation of much of the territory, which included a legionary fortress at Chester, would have reduced the area of the civitas under civilian control and hence its revenue.

How and when did the town become rich? It was not an immediate process, for there was a delay of some twenty-five years before funds and inclinations were sufficient for a forum, and, as at Leicester, its construction may have followed Hadrian's visit to Britain. The prosperity may have grown from the fact that the town lay astride one of the main natural routes into Wales. In this sense it early became a major frontier town, probably enjoying benefits from trade not only with civilians, but also with army personnel stationed in the region. In later years in Britain both Corbridge and Carlisle possessed similar advantages, and analogies are common on other frontiers.

We have arrived, therefore, at a point where we can see that the town developed from the nucleus of the legionary canabae in the closing years of the first century. The central part of the street grid had been laid out around the unfinished baths, while private enterprise was responsible for the erection of shops and houses in insulae further south.

Some time during the 120s work must have started on the forum. It is difficult to explain why the insula containing the unfinished bath-house should have been

WROXETER   (Viroconivm)

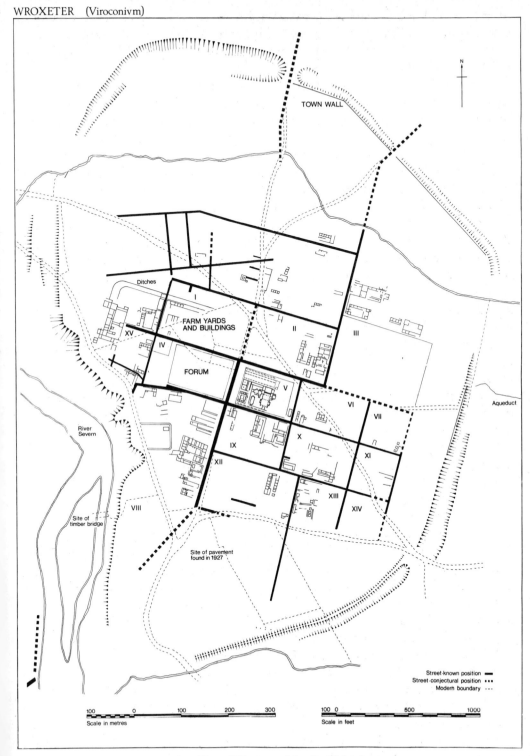

81   Plan of Wroxeter (*after G. Webster*)

chosen for it. Any attempt at forward planning by the local authority should have envisaged a public bath-house for the town, and the most sensible arrangement would have been to utilise the unfinished foundations, with their part-completed services, which would have had little meaning in the context of a forum. The insula which was ultimately used for the bath-house may have been vacant at the time, although not all of it has been investigated, and certainly it was not inferior in size. It seems most likely, therefore, that the insula containing the unfinished bath-house was the only one in the centre which was immediately vacant and contained no private buildings.[178]

The forum and the unfinished bath-house beneath it were excavated by Professor Donald Atkinson from 1923 to 1927.[179] The original lay-out (fig. 5) closely resembled the contemporary forum and basilica at Leicester. The basilica occupied the west end of the forum: the nave was 38ft (11·6m) wide and the aisles 15ft (4·6m) each. The floor level of the nave was slightly below that of the aisles. A raised tribunal with an open platform in front was identified at the south end of the nave and another should be inferred at the north end, making the length of the nave about 170ft (52m). Atkinson considered that various changes in the plan had been incorporated in this end of the structure before it was completed. The west wall of the nave was reduced in width south of the tribunal platform, and the west aisle was also terminated on the same line, suggesting that an inner office led off from the tribunal. The back range, 30ft (9·1m) wide, contained six identified rooms; Atkinson restored seven on his plan so as to make it symmetrical about the central room, which had a wide opening on to the west aisle, and it is to be supposed that it formed a shrine. The most interesting room in the range was that at the north end, which could only be entered from the adjacent room to the south. When the basilica was burnt in the middle of the second century, the contents of the room perished with it and were never recovered. They included iron locks and fittings from cupboards or chests, styli, a samian inkwell, six bone counters, some glass jars or bottles, three Trajanic coins, and part of the discharge certificate, dated 14 April AD 135, of an auxiliary infantryman, whose name was probably Mansuetus. Whether or not he was the last occupant of the room before the fire, as Atkinson suggests, it was clearly the office of a clerk and possibly where records of the civitas were kept.

Entrance to the basilica was gained at either end of its east aisle, through doorways opening from the inner portico of the forum and Atkinson considered that there had also been a central entrance from the piazza. The piazza was surrounded on the north, east and south sides by a colonnaded portico about 18ft (5·5m) wide; no rooms lay behind the portico on the north and south sides, but, on the latter, an external portico was provided which extended across both the forum and the basilica beyond. Two subsidiary entrances into the forum were situated at either end of this portico. On the east side a range of eight rooms, 35ft (10·7m) wide and penetrated by a central entrance passage, lay between the inner and an outer portico. The main entrance was 18ft (5·5m) wide, and coincided with a similar space in the colonnade of the outer portico. It was from outside the latter that 169 fragments of an inscription were found where they had fallen (see below). The inscription, measuring 11ft 9in (3·5m) by 3ft 9in (1·1m), had originally been set over the main entrance to the east portico and recorded the dedication, and therefore presumably the completion, of the forum between 10 December AD 129 and 9 December AD 130, during Hadrian's principate.[180] As it is unlikely that major building works could have been carried on in the depths of winter, when frosting of mortar would have been a very real hazard, the date of completion is more likely to have taken place in the summer of AD 130 than in the previous year. The inscription also tells us that the civitas Cornoviorum were the dedicating authority.

Two parallel walls, 18ft (5·5m) apart and running north-south, apparently divided the piazza into two approximately equal halves, and Atkinson supposed that they formed a cross colonnade which helped to remedy lack of covered accommodation in the north and south ranges. The west wall of this colonnade certainly belonged to the earlier bath period, and, on reading the excavation report, one is left with the strong impression that its fellow did too. It is difficult to believe in the existence of this colonnade when (a) the piazza gutter runs through it and not along it; removal of water run-off would seem just as essential for the cross portico as for those surrounding the piazza: (b) two column bases, which Atkinson discovered as continuing the line of the south colonnade through the cross portico, would not only have been superfluous in the circumstances which he envisaged, but were also placed asymmetrically with respect to the latter. Nevertheless a single cross wall on the line of that to the east may have existed as a screen wall, in the same way as that in the piazza at Cirencester (p. 305). Re-excavation is required to settle the point, but the modifications of the second period certainly made use of a wall on this line. It seems probable that the ragged end of wall which was discovered projecting westwards from the north-west corner of the basilica was likewise a survival from the baths, as were also the large drains north-west and south-west of the block. Their projected capacity was clearly unrelated to the removal of surface water from the forum buildings and piazza, for they were obviously designed with greater flows in mind. Moreover, the unfinished south-west drain, although in keeping with the general incomplete state of the baths, would have been quite adequate, even as it was left, as a soakaway for the forum gutter.

Two masonry foundations were situated in the piazza, some 20ft (6·1m) out from the east wall of the basilica and seemingly arranged symmetrically about its entrance. Presumably they carried statues, and fragments of cast bronze decoration were scattered over the surface in the area.

Some time during the decades AD 165–85 the forum was destroyed by a fire, which also spread to shops and houses in the next insula south,[181] but not apparently to the baths opposite. It is not clear what caused the fire, but the limited area affected would suggest an accident followed by inadequate control. However, it must have occurred in the day time when stalls were set up and in use. In the panic following the outbreak, some in the outer east portico were overturned and their wares fell into the external gutter. The south end of the portico seems to have been occupied by hardware merchants. At the very end, a stall holder had been selling mortaria made by Sennius, a manufacturer working at Mancetter.[182] Farther up the portico and nearer the entrance were stalls of samian merchants, who were offering for sale a variety of different vessels made both at the Central Gaulish potteries of Lezoux and the East Gaulish centre at Rheinzarbern. The preponderance of no one potter among 210 vessels recovered suggests the presence of a middleman who had for convenience sake put together similar bowls from different factories. Atkinson reckoned[183] that the bowls, stacked neatly in piles one inside the other on shelves or benches, had slid gently into the sand filling the gutter. This is hardly in accord with fire and panic; the sudden upheaval of a bench or table on which such piles of bowls were set, and their fall several feet to the ground below, would have led to a much wider scattering than actually happened. We might infer therefore that the nests had been either contained in rough boxes or tied together in some manner. As a side line one merchant also had a crate of whetstones for sale. The number present (about 100), and the way in which they fell, make it appear as though the box had been nearly full, so that few can have been sold, from which we might infer that the fire started early in the day. The stone from which the whetstones had been fashioned came either from near Stony Stratford, Bucks., or, less likely, from the Craven Arms district south of Wroxeter.

When the forum was rebuilt after the fire, certain modifications seem to have been put in hand. Two foundations, which sprang from the eastern wall crossing the piazza, curved inwards towards the main entrance, but were not traced further than the line of columns forming the east internal portico. Atkinson considered that these were constructed to increase the proportion of covered space, a suggestion which has little to commend it when it is seen that as much, if not more, was lost from the north and south porticoes as was gained in the north-east and south-east corners of the piazza enclosed by the new foundations. Indeed, it is difficult to see the purpose behind the alterations, as they seem to change nothing but the appearance of the building.

The public baths (fig. 9) in the insula east of the forum present a much more complicated structural history than the forum and basilica. It is possible that the building was started at about the same time as the forum, but that, with delays of one kind or another, it was not fully operative until some thirty years later.[184] It seems most likely that the final delay was caused by the need to rebuild the forum, which would have been a prime necessity. An earlier stone building has been identified on the site of the baths, but is only imperfectly known.

The main building was made up of a long aisled hall measuring 240ft (73m) × 65ft (19·8m) on the north side, which served as a covered palaestra, not unlike that already discussed for Leicester (p. 342). It may, however, have had a secondary use as a market hall, as Wright found a number of weights of different sizes; moreover Webster commented on the large dump of animal bones found outside the south-east corner. The main entrances seem to have been at the west end, and

Aerial photograph of the north-west part of Wroxeter, showing the outlines of a large house (p. oo)
(*Arnold Baker*)

a changing room was situated at the opposite end. An external portico ran down
the north side between the hall and the street. Two wings projected southwards
from each end of the hall. That to the west contained two large, approximately
square rooms, with central square pedestals; pairs of wide openings in each room
gave on to the street to the west, and a corridor passed to their rear. The rooms
do not seem to be part of the main baths, although they are attached, and their
appearance would suggest large shops rented to manufacturers or merchants by
the ordo of the civitas. Indeed Wright's excavations in 1836 clearly showed that
the south room had been used by a metal worker or enameller (p. 369 below).
Behind the corridor was a large public lavatory almost certainly not connected

with the rooms just considered, but entered at its north end from the palaestra. The eastern wing contained the main bathing establishment, consisting of three very large rooms which acted as frigidarium, tepidarium and caldarium respectively. The cold and hottest rooms were provided with their own plunge baths of equivalent heat and separate laconica were originally provided each side of the tepidarium. The main entrance from the palaestra to the frigidarium still survives as a piece of standing masonry, normally referred to as the Old Work. Attempts at a restoration on paper have been carried out by Webster and Wood-field,[185] basing their account on the excavations of Wright,[186] Fox,[187] and Kenyon[188] and on Webster's own more recent work. They postulated a double central entrance through the wall leading from the palaestra, flanked by blind arches, which were embellished with architectural detail. The springing for the frigidarium vault, whose long axis ran parallel with the main wall, probably started from a level at the heads of the decorative arches. The whole scheme was not dissimilar to that at the nearby contemporary public baths at Leicester (p. 342). The frigidarium is one of the few buildings in Britain which had part of its wall covered with mosaic.[189] A secondary set of hot rooms, incorporating the west laconicum, was later built to open off the tepidarium, extending almost as far as the latrine, while to their south lay a large piscina or open air swimming pool, which is a most unusual feature in a Romano-British bath-house.

The excavation of the bath-house is not yet complete; it is clear that even now not all has been uncovered and by no means all is known of its history. Large though it was it did not occupy the whole insula, and one other building excavated by Wright near the south-west corner may have been a small market or a collection of guild offices (fig. 11). It is made up of small squarish rooms arranged round three sides of a courtyard, to which access was gained from the main street to the west. It resembles to some degree both the markets at Verulamium (p. 207) and Cirencester (p. 299).

In the centre of the town the streets were laid out in a reasonably regular manner, although there is some variation in the size of insulae, and this part of the town plan is undoubtedly the earliest (fig. 81). But there are some inconsistencies. For instance, the main north-south street, which separates the baths from the forum, does not appear to extend northwards between Insulae I and II,[190] while Watling Street, entering the town from the north-east seems to turn towards the south to link with the street which formed the eastern boundary of Insulae XVI and II. This line was not, however, continued beyond the southern boundary of Insula II. The behaviour of these streets may have been conditioned by the siting of early military roads in the area and possibly also by an existing religious site, represented by a small Romano-Celtic temple, which shows on aerial photographs (pl. 72). The temple enclosure may have caused the re-routing of Watling Street into the heart of the town, in the same way that a similar enclosure caused a change in alignment of the main road system at Silchester's east gate (p. 261). The initial street lay-out seems to have extended north as far as the Bell Brook, which bisects the north part of the town from east to west; but the system was not fully completed. It is linked on the west to another system of streets on a different alignment, which are almost certainly later in date, and which were possibly influenced by the boundaries of the temple compound in the centre. There seems no reason why this change in alignment should be associated with an earlier, but unidentified, line of fortifications. Nevertheless there is a possibility that the first boundary did not cross the Bell Brook; a large bank and ditch south of the stream may be no more than an earlier water course, or perhaps attempts

72   Aerial photograph of the central area of Wroxeter, north of the forum, showing a Romano-Celtic temple and a large foundation beside it (*Arnold Baker*)

to canalise the flow.[191] Neither does a defensive alignment here help in explaining the change in the street plan in the north-west quarter. Outside the central area both to south and west, the street system is equally confusing and seems to represent piecemeal development. It would seem right therefore to modify our proposition in Chapter I (p. 21), that towns were from the first planned, by making an exception of what would seem to be later suburbs and additions to the main plan. The road line out of the town to the south-west is marked by the site of the bridge, of timber on stone piers which crossed the river Severn.[192]

The Wroxeter aqueduct has fortunately been identified over much of its course, and it was similar to that at Dorchester (p. 319). Water, drawn from the Bell Brook about three-quarters of a mile east of the town, was conveyed in an open channel which followed the contour of the ground as a series of short, straight lengths, to a point on the highest ground inside the town north of the baths. The channel was 3ft (0·9m) deep and originally appears to have been about 8ft (2·4m) wide across the top, narrowing to 2ft (0·6m) at the base. The excavated material had been heaped as a bank on the downhill side and there was slight evidence to show that the sides had been lined with clay. With a foot of water in the channel, it has been calculated that nearly 2,000,000 gallons (9×10^6 litres) of water could have been delivered daily to the town.[193] Presumably the channel was constructed long before the defences were erected, and it is not yet known how they were adapted to accommodate it. However, we might postulate a distribution tank in the area north of the baths, which we have already seen was partly occupied by a temple and its enclosure. The temple itself seems, in aerial photographs,[194] to have a massive square foundation situated close to its south-east corner with a fainter line approaching it from the east (pl. 72). We might suggest that this arrangement represents a temple inside a sacred enclosure associated with the aqueduct head. The sanctifying of an aqueduct source or head is not unknown elsewhere.[195]

From the distribution-point pipes must have led to the baths, to public fountains and to private users. Atkinson discovered a considerable length of a timber pipe-line running along the edge of the street south of the forum and a shorter length of lead pipe near the north-west corner. He considered that both belonged to the later forum period, dating to the late second or third century. The lead pipe had burst at no less than six places in the length uncovered, and it had clearly not been buried deep enough to escape frost damage.[196] Both pipes were presumably fed from a water main running south along the east side of the main street between forum and baths. This main must also have fed the channel which Bushe-Fox found on the west side of the same street beside Insula VIII.[197] Side channels from it carried water into the buildings flanking the street and control of water entering them was managed in two ways. First the floor level of the side channels was higher than that of the main channel, so that if the water level in the latter fell below 7 inches the supply to the houses was cut off. But by inserting a sluice gate across the main, just below the outfall to a house, the whole flow could for a time be diverted to it (pl. 73). Such a system closely follows the equitable arrangements suggested by Vitruvius and other engineers,[198] so that we can see in use at Wroxeter a developed system of water distribution, such as we can only suspect in most other towns, where control was exercised over private users who would have had to pay a tax to the local authority for water consumed.

The fortifications of the town seem to have followed the normal pattern. An earth rampart with two ditches was first created towards the end of the second century, to be followed by a stone wall at a later date, probably during the third century. As at Dorchester, the stone wall seems to have been built more on top of the existing rampart than at its front. The ditch system was at some stage reduced to a single wide ditch, and it is possible that this was associated with the construction of external towers.[199] No gate structures have been identified, although the positions of at least four can be suggested with reasonable confidence. Investigations are also required at the points where the Bell Brook entered and left the town, to see if water gates were provided, perhaps on the lines of those constructed at Silchester.

Apart from the row of buildings explored by Bushe-Fox, and some remarkably clear and detailed aerial photographs, only little is known of the town's private houses and shops. Those excavated by Bushe-Fox in 1912–14 were on the west side of the main north-south street and south of the forum. For the main part they consisted of strip-like buildings set behind a continuous portico with their long axes at right angles to the street; they were open at the front and had one or more rooms at the rear of the premises. They therefore conform closely to the general pattern of Romano-British shops and workshops. As already recorded, they first appeared on the site early in the second century, only to be burnt in the same fire which destroyed the forum. There were indications that rebuilding after the fire did not always follow the same plan. On one site a temple had been built, and immediately north of it, several shops had been amalgamated into a single block. The latter is presumably an instance, similar to that already cited for Cirencester (p. 310), where a shopkeeper enlarged his premises by buying out his neighbours. As a result he was able to extend his domestic premises across the rear of all three shops to make a comfortable-sized house, which, for a time, even had its own small bath suite and latrine, flushed by water from the aqueduct. An interesting common feature in almost all these shops was the number of ovens and furnaces which they contained and the liberal traces of metal-working. Evidence was obtained for casting: bronze brooches, and small bronze busts were made by the lost-wax process and silver objects were also manufactured. A fragment from a piece of cast bronze showed that, exceptionally, two runners had been used in some moulds to allow air to escape when the metal was poured. There was also evidence for cupellation furnaces by which silver was extracted from lead alloys.[200]

The shop west of the baths, which was used by another metal-worker, also contained some interesting features when found by Wright.[201] Nearly half the floor at the back of the shop was covered to some depth with very find sand,

73   Water distribution at Wroxeter. A junction of the main and branch channels on Site VI (*Society of Antiquaries of London*)

which may have been used for making moulds for casting objects. Near the north door was a small furnace situated on top of a beehive-shaped block of clay, which had been heavily vitrified, while beside it was a column base which may have supported a small anvil. A quantity of powdered granite and fragments of glass might suggest enamelling processes, while pieces of dross and slag clearly indicate metal-working on some scale. In the disturbed soil outside the east forum entrance was found a massive block of iron, $11\frac{1}{4}$in (285mm) long, $3\frac{1}{4}$in (82mm) wide and $\frac{9}{16}$in (14mm) thick. On both flat faces designs were embossed which had been used as matrices for producing patterns on thin bronze plates.[202] It is possible that this dye came originally from the workshop on the opposite side of the street.

The metal-working processes which were extensively carried on in the town probably made use of local deposits of copper and silver. Although lead and silver mines were at first usually controlled by the army, later control was often vested in the local curiales. Can one glimpse here perhaps the basis of Viroconian prosperity?

Another minor industry is indicated by three soapstone palettes, also found near the baths by Wright, which were probably used for grinding pigments in preparation for fresco painting. In the fourth century there was also a pottery manufacturer whose kilns were situated about $\frac{3}{4}$ mile (1·2km) north-west of the town,[203] and no doubt other kilns have yet to be found. We cannot yet say if the three roof tiles stamped LCH, and found in the debris of the destroyed forum, indicate a local tileworks,[204] but it is more than likely.

Two temple sites have been identified in the town. One, known only from aerial photographs, has already been discussed in connexion with the aqueduct. The other was excavated by Bushe-Fox in Insula VIII. It had been built over the burnt remains of earlier shops and therefore probably dates to the later second century.[205] The temple consisted of a rectangular podium 30ft (9·1m) wide and 24ft (7·3m) deep contained in a temenos 98ft (29·9m) by 56ft (17·1m). The cella appears to have been somewhat shallow and lay behind a portico. Another portico of six columns, which was probably part of a continuous colonnade down the side of the street, provided access to the temenos. Pedestals were situated slightly forward, and to one side, of the two front corners of the temple portico, while a pair of gutters drained surface water from the temenos into the 'aqueduct' beside the street.[206] Two uninscribed altars and many fragments of sculptured stone were found, including parts of human figures. The temple is definitely of Italian type; the columns in front of the cella were about 20ft (6·1m) high and were surmounted by an elaborately decorated facade. Despite the sculptures, which included a relief of naked figures and part of a life-size horse's head, it is not possible to say to which divinity the temple was dedicated. It was clear, however, that the building was derelict by the early fourth century.

Lewis has suggested that another building, visible in aerial photographs, in an insula south-east of the baths is a temple of classical pattern,[207] but there would seem to be some doubt over this interpretation. Two other areas inside the town walls are worth considering as temple enclosures. The south-west corner of Insula III, although apparently devoid of buildings, is surrounded by a stone wall, enclosing an area approximately 550ft (168m) by 500ft (152m). It also covers the highest part of the town, which might be thought a suitable site for a shrine. North of the Bell Brook is a considerable tract of land within the northern defences which shows no sign of major houses. Richmond, seeking a reason for the inclusion of this area, suggested that it may have been the site of a sacred grove or precinct.[208] However, a more prosaic suggestion for its use is considered below.

An insight into domestic religious practices was provided by a late first-century deposit below the house north of the temple in Insula VIII. Two fragments from an aedicula, or household shrine, with an arched niche to contain a statue, were found there, and it may have been set up in one of the early shops. Similar provisions were made in a shop in Insula XIV at Verulamium (p. 223). Several fragments of pipeclay figurines, including a Dea Nutrix, have also been found in the town and these would most likely have come from aediculae.

It is often claimed that there are more large private houses at Wroxeter, representing residences of decurions, than there are in many other towns. Yet a careful examination of aerial photographs seems to reveal no more than a dozen or so of such quality, which is not all that different from the situation elsewhere. Certainly it seems an insecure base for the conclusions normally drawn, that insecurity in the civitas forced the landowners to take up residence in the town.[209] Certainly also few top-quality mosaics have been found in private houses at Wroxeter, although public buildings were not thus deficient. One house is very large, measuring nearly 300ft (91m) from end to end. It lies near the west defences in Insula XVI, and shows clearly in aerial photographs (pl. 71). It is interesting, because, apart from its size, it seems to stand astride two insulae and its front portico lies at the end of the street which runs past the north side of the baths and forum. In this sort of situation it resembles the so-called mansio at Silchester (p. 263), and the Wroxeter building may have been similarly used. An alternative suggestion may, however, be made. If it was a private house, it was certainly one of the largest and most imposing in the town. The plan, moreover, resembles that of a winged corridor villa, and we may repeat the suggestion already made for Silchester and Cirencester, that it is possible to have a farm inside a town. This in turn might explain the apparently vacant area at the north end which appears to be covered by a rectilinear pattern of narrow ditches, looking not unlike modern allotment gardens and perhaps used for horticulture.[210] Some towns seem to have had a farm closely attached to them, as at Cirencester, Dorchester, Leicester and Verulamium. In those parts of the country the major part of the farm could be left outside the defences, but cattle rustling, or its equivalent, from the hills and border country of Wales may well have made it more politic for a considerable part of the farm to be enclosed at Wroxeter. In turn this could explain the inflated size of the area within the defences.

No extensive provision seems to have been made for amusements in the town.

A 'gladiators' cup, engraved with names, of a type already described under Colchester and Leicester, bespeaks an interest in such shows, but there does not seem to have been an amphitheatre for their performance.[211] There was, however, an unusual enclosure behind the temple in Insula VIII. It consisted of a pair of concentric walls, 12ft (3·7m) apart, and was rectangular in shape with rounded corners. A double entrance was situated in the outer wall at the north-east corner, and there was an alcove in the same wall, placed centrally in the shorter side. Another expansion in this wall occurred a short distance west of the entrance. Bushe-Fox put forward[212] the explanation that the structure carried tiers of seats between the walls for spectators attending amphitheatrical shows; he also decided that the building had been largely destroyed by the mid second century, as a drain from the house to the east cut through the walls. Webster rejected the latter argument and proposed that the building was associated with the nearby temple and was used for the enactment of religious ceremonies and dramas.[213] Neither explanation is entirely convincing.

In the almost complete absence of civilian tombstones and the scientific investigation of cemeteries, there is little that can be said about the inhabitants. One tombstone records the burial of Placida, aged 55, and probably her son Deuccus, aged 15. Neither would seem to have held Roman citizenship.[214] A circular oculist's stamp, not unlike the Leicester example, carried the name of Tiberius Claudius M(essor). According to Haverfield, he may have been the same man who lost a stamp near Valenciennes, in northern France.[215] Wright records a burial, possibly of a surgeon, north of the town; it was apparently associated with a case of surgical instruments which included a lancet.[216]

The picture described by Wright of fire and slaughter as Wroxeter disappeared before the Saxon onslaught has had to be much modified in recent years. As Richmond pointed out, the Cornovii had probably for long been used to raising their own militia, some parts of which had, by the fourth century, been absorbed into the regular army as *Coh. I Cornoviorum*.[217] This ability to protect themselves and their town must have been a great asset in the closing years of the fourth century and beyond, as units of the regular army were withdrawn from Wales and the borders. Recent finds of *martio-barbuli*, or lead-weighted javelins, suggest that detachments of the regular army were passing through Wroxeter in the very late fourth or early fifth century. But by then the town had for some time been deprived of its forum, basilica and bath-house. Atkinson reckoned that they had been destroyed in the barbarian invasion of AD 296, and certainly the datable evidence does not take it much later. However, it is probably best, in view of the limited nature of the destruction, no longer to associate it with enemy action. Although the forum was not rebuilt, the site continued to be used and we might ask how the commercial life and administration of the town was continued. The only real loss sustained was the basilica; the forum had never provided a great deal of permanent covered accommodation, so that its loss would have been less seriously felt. As in the town's beginning, so at the end, an open space would have served adequately as a market. There is a strong contrast here with many other towns; at Wroxeter shopkeepers seem to have preferred to build their own private premises, rather than to use rented accommodation in public buildings. Moreover the town already possessed an alternative basilica attached to the baths, which had been unaffected by the destruction and was certainly used until the end. Indeed, in the final stages, part of the bath-house seems to have been converted to a granary. Might we suspect that the administrative business of the civitas was henceforward carried on in this basilica? It might be objected that the palaestra of a bath-house was no place for the law courts to sit.[218] But magistrates' courts were not always the quietly-ordered scenes that we expect today. Even as recently as the Victorian period, Dickens vividly described a remarkable magistrates' court scene in *Great Expectations*.

Recent excavations by Barker on the site of the same building have shown that, even after it was ruined, an extensive series of large timber buildings were erected on the rubble.[219] A comparable situation, of rough timber shacks being built in the ruins of the market-hall at Leicester, has already been described (p. 357). It is not yet possible to say what the Wroxeter buildings were, as Barker has by no means finished his excavations, but they show a continuation of life in the town, if not of town life, long after the stage had been reached when the last Roman buildings were falling down. Sometime during this period an Irish chieftain, Cunorix, son of Maqqos-Colini, visited Wroxeter and met his death. He was apparently buried inside the town walls, which shows that the old order had broken down.[220] Other bodies have been found from time to time in excavations, and one at least was found lying unburied on the edge of the main street by the forum, while another was found, apparently clutching his life-savings, in one of the hypocausts of the bath-house, into which he had crept to die. The overall picture obtained is not dissimilar to that at Cirencester during the closing years, when unburied bodies were lying in the streets. It has been postulated that there a small band of survivors from a serious epidemic had withdrawn to the safety of the amphitheatre. In the Gloucestershire region we find Celtic overlords assuming control. The analogy can be taken further. In Shropshire, as in parts of Wales and the south-west, there was a return to abandoned hill-forts in the late fourth or early fifth centuries. Near Wroxeter the Breidin was refortified and it is possible that the hilltop on which Shrewsbury stands was treated as a similar refuge. A picture, therefore, is beginning to emerge in the west, of small bands of refugees, usually only a fraction of a town's population, seeking safety in the nearest easily-fortified place. There were no doubt Romano-Britons among them, but there were probably also Irish and Saxon foederati or immigrants. Although many questions remain to be answered, it is just possible to detect the glimmerings of a common pattern, which will explain the abandonment, albeit sometimes temporary, of the Romano-British towns, and which is developed more fully in the final chapter.

8

Hadrianic Stimulation

CAERWENT, CARMARTHEN, BROUGH, ALDBOROUGH

The four towns considered in this chapter represent the last major extension of the truly civilian areas of the British province. Thereafter, further limited expansion of civilian government took place only in areas which continued to be occupied by the army. Moreover, some subsequent contraction probably occurred in certain districts of the Brigantes.

Hadrian's visit to Britain in AD 121 or 122 came early in his protracted tour of the Provinces. His appearance in Britain seems to have restored confidence and stimulated renewed building activity in towns; the impetus from the Agricolan encouragement had by then been largely exhausted, and confidence undermined by a series of military reverses in the north. We might suspect that Hadrian, in view of his interest in construction, contributed financially. He was also responsible for a complete reassessment of the military occupation, which resulted in the creation of a permanent linear frontier in the north. The greatly increased troop concentration required by the new frontier work was only achieved by withdrawing units from forts in Wales and Brigantia. As earlier, under the governor Agricola, it could only be done if suitable civilian administrations could be established to replace military government. In taking this action, Hadrian to some extent gambled on the continued peacefulness, after military control had been removed, of potentially troublesome areas. It proved a gamble which did not entirely succeed.

The areas in question, which were now thought ripe for local self-government, were in south Wales, the *civitas Silurum* and the *civitas Demetarum*, and in north England, east of the Pennines, the *civitas Parisorum* and the *civitas Brigantum*.

CAERWENT (*Venta Silurum*)

For many years the Silures had showed an implacable hostility to Rome, which sometimes vented itself in aggressive attacks on the Roman army.[1] At first allied with Caratacus, later on their own, they resisted fiercely all attempts to subdue them,[2] and it was not until the mid 70s, when the governor Julius Frontinus had defeated them, that a permanent occupation could be imposed.[3] In a classic passage, Richmond has summed up the way in which they were broken, first by attrition and encroachment, finally by pitched battle.[4]

Military occupation ensued, which pivoted round the new fortress of Legio II Augusta at Caerleon. A network of roads linking a number of auxiliary forts put the tribal territory into an effective straitjacket. It is unlikely, therefore, that the years of Frontinus' and Agricola's governorships will have seen the emergence of a properly constituted civitas with its capital, controlling its own affairs. In consequence, Nash-William's claim, that the fortified town of Caerwent was founded in the Flavian period, must be reconsidered.[5] Yet there is Flavian pottery from the area of the town as Hartley has pointed out,[6] and it is best explained as coming either from a fort, or from a vicus attached to a fort. This revision would also conveniently explain why the late first-century bath-house, probably belonging to the fort, and considered by Nash-Williams as the first town baths, was almost completely demolished and rebuilt during the early second century. However, it must be admitted that the published dating evidence of both early periods is distinctly thin, while it is not at all certain that the first building was even a bath-house.[7] Further work is needed to identify the exact site of the fort.

Having established, however, the probable existence of a fort at Caerwent, we can see that the formation of the town followed the classic pattern, already repeatedly described. What is not known is whether the not far-distant site at Sudbrook acted as the tribe's main centre before their conquest. On the whole the situation seems most closely matched among the Dumnonii and Cornovii, where apparently no centralised control was exercised. But the name of the town, which emerges as the Latinised *Venta*, does suggest that, like the two others with the same name in Britain, a tribal gathering-place existed on the site either before, or very soon after, the conquest. Excavations ascribed an abrupt ending to the occupation of Sudbrook in the late first century, but no sign of destruction was observed. If the ending was as abrupt as the excavator concluded, we might suggest that this was one of the few instances where the inhabitants of a defended native settlement were compelled by the Roman army to vacate them, perhaps because of their long resistance.

The probable circumstances under which part of the tribal territory was returned to civilian administration have already been discussed in the opening paragraphs to this chapter. How much of it was left under military control we do not know, but certainly the legionary *prata* of Caerleon must have covered a considerable area. A boundary stone washed out from below the modern seawall near Goldcliff Priory, Mon., about 3 miles (4·8km) south of the fortress, may partly indicate its delimitation.[8]

Although much of the town has been excavated (fig. 82), so that, as at Silchester, a reasonably complete plan is known, it is unfortunate that most of the discoveries were made before strict archaeological records were kept. Consequently the

CAERWENT (Venta Silvrvm)

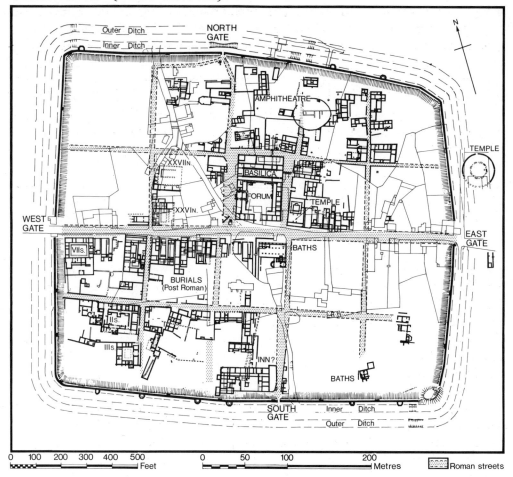

82   Plan of Caerwent (*Dept. of the Environment, Crown Copyright—reproduced with permission of the Controller of Her Majesty's Stationery Office*)

history of many of the buildings, including the forum and basilica, is imperfectly known. Nash-Williams, on the evidence of the coin sequence from the forum, and presumably influenced by his own views on the date of foundation of the town, ascribed a late first-century date to its construction, which must be revised. There is a contrast between the forum evidence, which starts with a coin of Nerva, and the baths where the earliest coin was Vespasianic.

   In the absence of specific evidence to the contrary it is likely that the forum and basilica belonged, with the baths and street grid, to the early days of the town's lay-out. The forum occupied the whole central insula, north of the main east-west street. This insula was somewhat smaller than the rest although the streets to east and west of it were broader. The baths lay at the north-east corner of the insula opposite.

As befitted a tribe which must have been impoverished by long years of fighting against Rome, the forum and basilica were built on a modest scale, the piazza measuring only 107ft (33m) by 101ft (31m). In this respect the tribe resembled the Iceni, who had become emasculated through the Boudiccan rebellion, and there is a remarkable similarity in the development of their capitals.

The forum piazza at Caerwent (fig. 7) was enclosed on three sides by colonnaded porticoes, floored with concrete, behind which were the normal ranges of rooms. In the east range there were probably six shops with wide doorways giving on to the portico while another room, subdivided by a cross wall to provide two small ante-rooms at the front, may have been an office. The south wing was divided by a central entrance, nearly 16ft (4·9m) wide, which coincided with a gap in the inner colonnade. There appear to have been four shops each side of the entrance, all of which opened to the south on to an outer portico. The west wing, although confused by later alterations, seems to have contained a single long hall at the south end, with one other room between it and the basilica. The original floor of the piazza was not discovered, but it had been resurfaced with sandstone paving stones in the late third or early fourth century, and a gutter, cut in the surface of stone blocks, ran round all four sides. The gutter discharged into a large drain that carried the flow underneath the basilica and the north street beyond.

The basilica at the north end could be approached either by a flight of three steps from the piazza, or by doors set at each end of the south aisle which gave on to the adjacent streets. The basilica measured 126ft (38·3m) by 62ft (18·9m) internally and was raised above the forum level. Enough architectural fragments were recovered to show that the nave was ornamented in the Corinthian style and the columns had probably risen to a height of about 30ft (9·1m). Both ends of the nave were separated from the main body of the hall by wooden screens, which were also extended across the north aisle. Although Nash-Williams implied that only the room to the east was used as a tribunal, there seems no reason why both should not have served. But the eastern tribunal had a raised floor, heated from a small hypocaust flue in the south aisle, reminiscent of the small heated block in the first basilica at Caistor-by-Norwich. The floor may have been tessellated and the walls were decorated with formal patterns of painted plaster. The back range behind the hall was made up of a central shrine flanked by three offices on the east and a large room on the west which was probably the curia. The latter could only be entered from the room at the west end of the north aisle and from a small ante-room beyond. In the extreme north-west corner of the block was another room, entered from the same ante-room, which may have served as a records' office. The curia was the best-furnished room, with a mosaic panel set in a concrete floor, an unusual arrangement suggestive of economies, and painted walls embodying architectural perspectives.[9]

It can be seen by comparing the above description with other fora that the whole building had been reduced to its simplest essentials, not only in size, but also in its appointments.

The bath-house, the second of the four main public buildings known in the town, was equally modest in scale (fig. 9). Unfortunately only the northern part, consisting of a covered hall, or palaestra, a frigidarium and cold plunge, a large cistern and a small block of later hot rooms have been excavated,[10] and the remainder is covered by farm buildings. Both north and west sides had external covered porticoes. It is interesting to compare the palaestra with the roughly contemporary buildings at Wroxeter and Leicester. The replacement of an open, peristyled courtyard, of the type that can be seen in the first-century baths at Silchester, by a covered hall of basilican plan was a sensible acknowledgment of the British climate. The hall was nearly 110ft (34m) long and just under 40ft (12·2m) wide. Two lines of heavy stone pedestals marked the positions of the internal columns, while the outside frontage was decorated with engaged columns on masonry plinths. The latter can hardly have played any structural part in the building as their positions did not coincide with those of the internal columns. The main entrance seems to have lain between the second and third external columns from the east. Two probable changing-rooms and a small latrine were situated in the north-west corner of the hall.

The floor of the cistern was 7ft (2·1m) below the general level and it presumably held the water for filling the boilers. Although no aqueduct is known, one may be assumed, for a wooden pipe-line was discovered running southwards through the north gate and was again picked up outside the north wall of the basilica, with a branch down the street to its east. The latter may have served the baths, and a cement-lined conduit crossed the palaestra from the north towards the bath wing. A narrow street, about 10ft (3·1m) wide, separated the baths from the neighbouring buildings to the west, and the main drain lay between the portico and the street. At one point, approximately level with the frigidarium, a lead pipe discharged into the drain. The extension of this drain can probably be seen in the next insula south, which it crosses to lead towards the mansio. Thereafter it most likely discharged through the culvert beneath the south gate.

Various structural alterations took place in the bath-house during the third and fourth centuries. Coins recovered from the site imply a continued use into the fifth century, followed by a rapid dissolution.

The house interpreted as a mansio lay immediately on the left of anyone entering the south gate, but it should be noted that some other buildings might be thought to have equal claims. It was excavated in 1904 and little is known of its history, although some can be inferred from its close proximity to the defences.[11] Nash-Williams' published section through the latter,[12] despite the fact that its position is not precisely known, shows the wall of a house level with the tail of the rampart and obviously later than both phases of fortification. That being so we should assume that part of the building at least belongs to the fourth century. But that need not apply to all of it, as the line taken by the fortifications seems to make a southward detour before reaching the building so that the latter occupies

74   Inscribed pedestal erected in honour of Ti. Claudius Paulinus, at Caerwent (*Crown Copyright— reproduced with permission of the Controller of Her Majesty's Stationery Office*)

a slight bulge, suggesting that they had to be aligned to take an existing building into account. The building was arranged round three sides of a courtyard; the fourth side, although enclosed by a wall, was against the town rampart. A large forecourt stretched across the front of the building, and a number of rooms were equipped with hypocausts. A fine mosaic was discovered in the large room at the north-west corner. Apart from its size, and it is almost the largest house in Caerwent, there is nothing to confirm its identification.

The administration of the tribe and its capital by the ordo of the civitas Silurum are specifically attested in an inscription, carved on a pedestal for a statue (pl. 74), which was erected in the town in honour of Ti. Claudius Paulinus, sometime legate of Legio II Augusta, proconsul of Gallia Narbonensis, propraetorian legate of Gallia Lugdunensis, and later of Britannia Inferior. The latter post, not mentioned on the pedestal, was held by Paulinus in AD 220, so that the inscription dates to a year or so before.[13] The stone was found incorporated in a heavy plinth below the village green, not far from the forum, and was said not to have been in its original position.[14] It had, no doubt, been erected originally in honour of a man who had probably been made a patron of the civitas, or who had in some way aided them when he commanded Legio II Augusta. In this respect it demonstrates a continuing relationship between the army and a neighbouring civilian authority. Most important, however, it shows both the administrative organisation of a civitas at work issuing decrees, and the ascendency of civitas over town in local government affairs.[15]

However Bogaers has argued that this particular inscription is of no help in determining the relative importance of civitas and town, because it is dated to the period after Roman citizenship had been granted by Caracalla to all free men and women of the Empire (AD 212). He goes on to claim that, following this move, the distinction between genuine chartered towns and tribal civitates disappeared and that the name civitas was preferred for urban centres.[16] This will not do in this case, for it overlooks the evidence of name survival, and it would also have been a gradual change, brought about by usage and not by litigation. Rivet has drawn attention[17] to the essential difference in this respect between Britain and Gaul: in the former it is the town name which most often survives in modern language, while in the latter it is the tribal name. Hence, working back from the modern name Caerwent, we can deduce that the town was commonly known in the late Roman period as Venta, and that it was the Silurian part of the title which became lost. This is in direct contrast to Venta Icenorum which appears in the Antonine Itinerary as *Icini*, so that the distinction is very real. For Bogaers to be right, therefore, the inscription should have read *civitas Ventensis*. Although we can agree with him that ultimately the civitas became synonymous with the town at its centre, it was obviously still far from being so when Paulinus' statue was erected.

The town's fortifications as far as is known followed the normal pattern. An earth rampart, with a ditch in front, was erected not earlier than AD 130, and probably belonged to the late second century. The stone wall was added to the front of this rampart sometime in the second half of the third century, but on the north and east sides there is evidence to show that the wall was built more over the ditch.[18] Lengths of the wall have survived to a considerable height, especially on the south side (pl. 75), where they form one of the most impressive sights in Roman Britain. The southern defences were investigated by Nash-Williams in 1925, while earlier excavations took place on other sectors between 1899–1913, which were later summarised by Ward.[19] The area enclosed within the fortifications was about 44 acres (18ha), which is not so different from that of Caistor-by-Norwich within its second defences.

The width of the early bank is not known, but it exceeded 34ft (10·4m) in places, and had survived to a height of 6ft (1·8m). The stone wall averaged 10ft (3·1m) thick at the base but was reduced by internal scarcements to 6ft (1·8m). In places it still rises to a height of 17ft (5·2m). On the south side, it is clear that the wall was built in sections with straight joints between each although the joints were masked by the front skin of facing stones. Behind the wall, at various intervals, were so-called counterforts, in which the superstructure had been carried up at its full basal width. They may have provided supports for stairs leading to the wall walk (cf. Silchester, p. 265 above). There were two ditches in front of the wall of varying size and spacing.

75   South wall of Caerwent, looking west from the south gate (*J. S. Wacher*)

Four gates are known. The largest were the east and west gates, placed nearly centrally in the respective walls, on the line of the most important road through the town. The only parts that survive of these structures are fragments of the square, south gate-towers of both gates, which projected forward from the front face of the town wall. The width and number of the carriageways is not known, but it is interesting to observe that the town wall abuts the masonry of both gates with straight joints, and in the west gate at least the tower seems to be an addition to the original plan, with its fortifications oversailing those of the wall.[20]

The south and north gates (fig. 20) were both single-arched openings in the town wall. The south gate lies at the end of the street to the east of the public baths. The gap in the wall measured $15\frac{1}{2}$ft (4·7m) wide and it contained a passage way 9ft (2·7m) wide, and 16ft long (4·9m), which was formed by walls projecting 4ft (1·2m) in front of the town wall and 2ft (0·6m) behind it. The gate structure was therefore about 16ft (4·9m) square and may have supported a single tower over the entrance. Nash-Williams noted that, at this gate, the town wall had been built later, and it is possible that the gate was originally built at the same time as the earthworks. The front of the gate was partly dismantled when the gate was blocked, but the inner arch still stands for seven stones above the springers, where it was kept in place by the later blocking. A drain emerges through the gate below the level of the sill.[21]

The north gate, excavated in 1901–3 and more recently restored by the Directorate of Ancient Monuments, was placed somewhat west of its street, which lay on the west side of the forum, so that the street had to be bent towards it. It was joined at the gate by another street running westwards away from the gate along the back of the rampart. It is difficult to see why this arrangement was necessary, or for that matter why both north and south gates were not placed in opposing positions. However their staggered placing was probably due to buildings having earlier been constructed across the north end of the street to the east of the forum and the south end of that to the west. Presumably these rights of way had been extinguished before the fortifications were constructed. The plan of the north gate is similar to that of the south, except that there is no forward projection, but only one of 5ft (1·5m) to the rear. The pivot stones for the double doors are still in position, level with the outer arch, which is better preserved than at the south gate.[22]

Caerwent is richly endowed with evidence of the religious practices of the inhabitants. On the south-west corner of the insula east of the forum was a Romano-Celtic temple within a trapezoidal enclosure (fig. 84). The south door-way led into a long, narrow entrance-hall or ante-chamber, with an apsidal east end and tessellated floor. The suggestion of Nash-Williams that the building east of the temenos acted as an entrance hall lacks conviction; with its furnaces, it sounds far more like a workshop. Moreover the alleyway for the eavesdrip gutter, between it and the temenos, would suggest separate ownership. Beyond the south hall lay the precinct proper, with the temple placed symmetrically within it. The temple was of normal form, with an apse projecting from its north side across the rear portico. Behind the temple was a house set in its own courtyard, with an entrance portico opening from the street to the west. A series of buildings, east of the temple and fronting the north side of the main east-west street, are best interpreted as shops. The whole complex may have been enclosed with a boundary wall, and it has been suggested that it resembles the *tempelbezirk* of the continent,[23] with temple, priest's house and attendant shops. However, the shops seem in part to have been vested in different owners and there may have been no connexion. Finds within the temple included the broken head end of a bronze serpent and a fragmentary bird's head carving of bone, both of which are normally considered attributes of Celtic deities.

A statue base and an altar found within the town may provide a clue to the dedication of the temple. The statue base found in house XI s, where it had been incorporated in later building work, was dedicated to the Rhenish god Mars Lenus, 'otherwise Ocelus Vellaunus' by M. Nonius Romanus on 23 August AD 152.[24] The altar had been set up in house XXVI s; it was dedicated to Mars Ocelus by an *optio*, Aelius Augustinus.[25] Mars Ocelus is probably a variant of Mars Lenus, and was a particularly British, or even Silurian deity. The only other dedication comes from Carlisle.[26] These inscriptions have led to suggestions that the principal religious site at Caerwent, next to the forum, was dedicated to Mars Ocelus/Lenus, although one of the other temples might equally claim the title. One of the most interesting points about the first inscription is the condition under which the dedication was made, on the occasion of an immunity being granted to the guild. We do not know what guild was intended, but it shows that, within 20–30 years of the town's foundation Roman institutions of this kind had been introduced, and that Roman citizens, possibly from other provinces, had settled there. The dedication of the *optio*, a junior non-commissioned officer in the army, shows again the connexion between military and civilian.

Two other religious sites are known, one of which involved alterations to the west wing of the forum. In the centre of the wing, and across the long hall-like room, a massive podium was constructed. Its front lay slightly in advance of the stylobate of the portico, while the rear projected some 6ft (1·8m) into the street behind; the width was 35ft (10·7m). Fragments of fallen tufa voussoirs were scattered over the podium, indicating a vaulted structure. Although no proof was obtained of its religious nature, a temple is certainly the most plausible explanation.

The other temple had either been excluded from the town when the defences were built, or else constructed later. It lay to the east, and was so close to the wall that there was no space for the outer ditch. A recent geophysical survey by the Ancient Monuments Directorate has shown that the outer ditch was seemingly never dug on the east side of the town. The plan was unusual: the temple was a regular octagon surrounded by a circular wall.[27] The overall diameter was 130ft (69·6m) and the north side of the circle contained an entrance $8\frac{1}{2}$ft (2·6m) wide. Subsidiary doors lay to the east and west. The most likely arrangement is the conclusion of Lewis,[28] that the portico and cella were both octagonal, with a

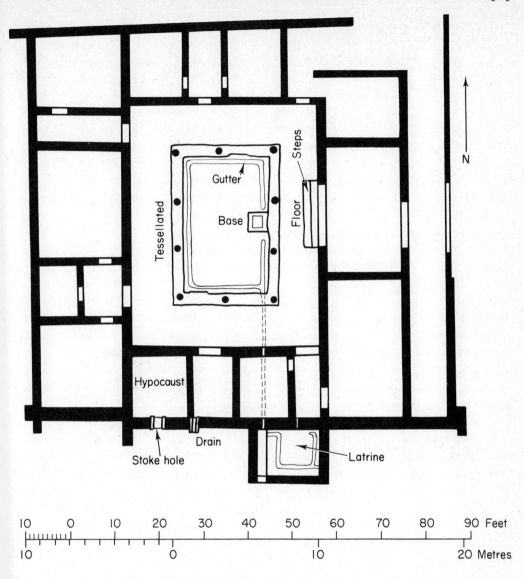

83   House III S, Caerwent

circular temenos surrounding it. It would then resemble the temples at Pagan's Hill and Chelmsford.

Two other finds of religious significance are the stone carvings depicting a man's(?) head and a seated Mother Goddess. The treatment of both faces is so crude, yet so alike, that we must conclude that both were the product of the same untutored craftsman, working in local sandstone. There might almost be a connexion here with the series of rough plaques and statuettes of the neighbouring Dobunni.

Evidence for fourth-century Christianity is provided by a Chi-R scratched on the underside of a pewter bowl from house VII N.[29]

Attempts have sometimes been made to link the so-called amphitheatre with the temple precinct east of the forum. This building (fig. 15), roughly elliptical in shape, with the long axis orientated east-west and with diameters of approximately 145ft (44m) by 121ft (37m), is something of an enigma. It was constructed at a late stage in the town's development, for it overlay foundations of earlier buildings and also interrupted the line of a street. But it is not possible to say on present evidence how many of the surrounding houses still stood when it was built. If it was intended for use as an amphitheatre, it is difficult to see where spectators would have sat; however, a short length of outer wall, 25ft (7·6m) away from the inner, is recorded on the south-west part of the circuit, with a short spur wall projecting inwards from its end. Only one entrance has so far been discovered on the east side; it was 8ft 6in (2·6m) wide with a door socket still in place.[30] It is worth noting that the main dimensions almost exactly coincide with the arena measurements at Cirencester. If an amphitheatre, it was of slightly unusual form, or perhaps it was even left unfinished; moreover it would have been one of only two amphitheatres in Britain to have been included within a town's fortifications, probably because, in each case, they were erected first (SILCHESTER, p. 264). Alternatively it may have acted as a livestock market.

Although 7 of the 20 insulae in the town have hardly been touched by excavation, the general impression gained from the town plan is that not only are the insulae smaller than in many other towns, but they are also more closely packed with buildings. There are open spaces and it is possible to detect walled gardens, or perhaps orchards, attached to many of the larger houses; these are usually situated in the central parts of insulae. But street frontages are altogether more densely used. Almost the full extent of both frontages of the main east-west street, except where they are taken up by public buildings and one or two private houses, seem to have been owned by shopkeepers, for their narrow-fronted buildings jostle one another for space. Some, judging by the way in which the shops had been extended to the rear, were more prosperous than their neighbours, but in general there seem to have been fewer instances of corporate enterprises being built by the merging of premises. Greater individuality seems to have survived, as is indicated by the number of narrow alleys separating shops. As already explained in the section on Verulamium (p. 63), these alleys were used for gutters catching the eavesdrip from roofs, which must have extended along each building at right angles to the main street.

Apart from a possible sea-food shop in the east wing of the forum, there is little indication of trades carried on in individual shops, but we might expect the normal ones. A selection of carpenters' and masons' tools are not unexpected, while a shoe-last can only have come from a cobbler's shop. A fragment of a bone carding-comb is a reminder that this Venta has been considered as a candidate for the site of the imperial weaving mill mentioned in the Notitia (see p. 237). The large number of agricultural implements which have been found scattered

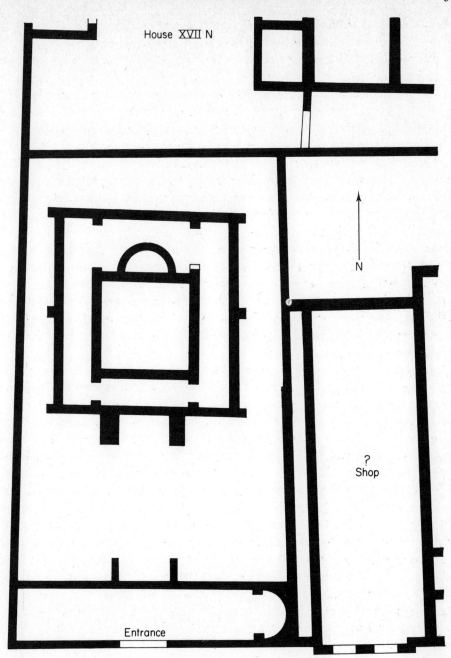

House XVII N

N

?
Shop

Entrance

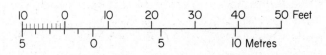

84 Temple and enclosure west of the forum, Caerwent

about the town emphasises the point already made under Silchester, that not only did outlying farms often depend on towns and villages for essential services, but also that farms might exist within the town's boundary. In this connexion a blacksmith's shop has been identified on the south-west corner of the next insula west of the forum, and Forest of Dean iron was probably readily available.

About 16 houses in the town can be identified as being probable residences of the curial class, so that Caerwent, despite its small size, does not lag far behind in the number to be found in other, larger towns. Some of the houses are perhaps slightly smaller, but the general standard does not fall far short of the norm. One or two are of the compact, peristyled form, a type already noted at Colchester and Gloucester, but somewhat rarer in civitas capitals. It is possible to detect here a Mediterranean influence, perhaps derived from the nearby legionary fortress, or perhaps introduced by traders, who, with army supply-contracts in their pockets, had chosen to settle here rather than in the civil settlement outside the fortress. M. Nonius Romanus, although probably from around Trier and not from the Mediterranean, may have been influenced by such considerations. Certainly the houses here have so far produced more mosaics than are known from Wroxeter. Indeed, there is an impression about Caerwent, despite its size and the obvious presence of native Silurians, that is more Roman than British; but it must be admitted that the impression may only be created by uneven survival of the evidence.

Most typical of these houses is III s (fig. 83). It formed a compact block around a courtyard, with the peristyle supported on columns. The courtyard probably served as a garden and contained a statue-base opposite the main entrance in the east wing, and a drain round all four sides to catch water from the roof. The water collected was used to flush a latrine outside the south wall. A wooden water-pipe had brought a supply of water through the main entrance and sections of lead pipe indicated its distribution. It is possible that the overflow from the pipe ran into the courtyard drain. The floor of the colonnade was tessellated, but the rooms seem only to have had concrete floors.[31]

Two other houses in the same insula, although slightly more spreading, produce the same impression. House II s had a bath suite attached on the west and a number of mosaics in rooms in the north range. As in the case of III s a water-supply was indicated by a section of lead pipe.[32] House VII s was similar and had two fine mosaics in the principal rooms of the south-west corner.[33]

The middle of the fourth century saw the strengthening of the defences by the construction of six external towers on the south,[34] and at least five on the north, walls; it is possible that the east and west gates were rebuilt at the same time with their projecting towers. The towers on the walls were heptagonal in shape, probably similar to those constructed at about the same time at Cirencester. Their spacing, however, was by no means regular, and neither east nor west walls were so equipped. As their foundations in part overlay the inner lip of the inner ditch, steps must have been taken to strengthen them, as at Cirencester, although the published account of their excavation does not make it clear how this was done. The bastion at the west end of the south wall had a sally-port in its base. However, the practice in many other towns, of recutting the ditch system, does not seem to have been followed. Caerwent was in some ways fortunate in lying in the shadow of the late fort at Cardiff, which, with its sea patrols, would have helped to fend off raiders from Ireland approaching up the Bristol Channel.

As in other towns in the west, life of a sort lingered on in Caerwent during the fifth century. Rough graffiti scratched on the walls of the curia in the basilica would seem to belong to the period,[35] at any rate they must have been cut before the building perished in flames.[36] However, the forum remained in use for some time longer than the basilica. Both the north and south gates were blocked with rough masonry. However, the need was still felt for adequate drainage, as the drains running through the gates were rebuilt through the new masonry at higher levels, which could imply the continued functioning of the bath-house. A sally-port was provided at the north gate. Later still, long after use of the bath-house had ceased, and the shell of the building had fallen down, another structure was erected partly over the west-end of the palaestra, and partly across the passage to the west and the main street to the north.

Nash-Williams, who excavated the building, considered that it was part of a Christian church, with flattened apse at the end of a presbytery. He also considered that the plan indicated a lingering survival of Romano-British building methods, but he was inclined to associate the 'church' with the sixth-century settlement founded at Caerwent by the Irish Saint Tathan.[37] Doubt has, however, been cast on this interpretation, and it has been suggested that foundations of the 'church' are, in fact, those of a post-medieval cottage.

Nash-Williams found two bodies lying beside the main street in front of house XXIV s,[38] on a level with the top of a dismantled boundary wall. He assumed that they had been properly buried, with an orientation to the east, and that they were therefore related to the nearby Christian church. Their position, however, is strikingly similar to the bodies found beside streets at Cirencester (p. 313) and Wroxeter (p. 374) and we might therefore be excused for suggesting a common association.

CARMARTHEN (*Moridunum Demetarum*)

The nature of the Roman site at Carmarthen has been under discussion for a long time. It has been identified with the Muridunum of the Antonine Itinerary,[39] and with Ptolemy's Moridounon,[40] and Professor Jackson has shown that the correct name, as derived from the Celtic, should be Moridunum.[41] Although earlier this century the site was more often than not considered to be a fort, Haverfield, acting largely on guesswork, suggested that it might be a town.[42] St Joseph more recently referred to the 'platform' as the likely site of a fort, measuring 600ft (182m) by 400ft (122m) approximately, with a probable vicus to the south-west.[43]

However, a series of investigations begun in 1968 by Barri Jones, and more recently continued by J. H. Little, have shown that the 'platform' site referred to by St Joseph appears mostly to be occupied by a town of some 14 to 15 acres (5·7 to 6·1ha). That being so, it is probably correct to identify it as the civitas capital of the Demetae, who covered Pembrokeshire and most of Carmarthenshire. This tribe seem never to have been intensively garrisoned by the Roman army,[44] so that we can infer a peaceful occupation, once their neighbours to the east, the Silures, had been defeated. The only fort so far known in their territory was established, either under Frontinus or Agricola, at Carmarthen on the right bank of the river Towy. The exact position of the fort is not known, but Flavian samian from the area south-west of the town might be thought to indicate it, and this evidence is partly confirmed by a ditch section obtained in 1968 in the grounds of the Royal Ivy Bush Hotel.[45] However, some caution still needs to be exercised. Other 'forts' have been changed to 'towns', only to revert to 'forts' again as more information was obtained about their history and interior arrangements.[46] The position of Carmarthen would have made it ideal for a naval station, especially in the fourth century, when coastal defence work was being carried out in Wales. The situation at Brough-on-Humber, where a 'town' of equivalent size to the fortified area at Carmarthen is now generally accepted to have been primarily a naval base from Hadrianic times onwards, might be considered as closely analogous.

It has been claimed by recent excavators, following the find of a coin of Aurelius Caesar in the primary level of a south-west to north-east street, that the lay-out of the town and consequently the constitution of the civitas took place late in the second century.[47] But the links in this argument are most tenuous. To begin with there appears to be an earlier alignment of streets, which may belong to the first foundation of the town and civitas. Secondly, even if it was part of a grid, it is well known that peripheral streets in towns were not always laid out as early as those at the centre,[48] and it is by no means yet known where the centre lay. Even if it can be shown that the whole town plan does belong to the end of the second century, it does not necessarily follow that constitution of the civitas was as late, for, on general historical grounds, it should have taken place almost fifty years before.

It was anticipated in the opening of this chapter that the emergence of a self-governing civitas, in an area under military government, would take place when that government was withdrawn. The apparent peacefulness of the Demetae, under the army, provides sufficient justification to propose the joint withdrawal of military control both from their territory and from that of their more hostile neighbours, the Silures. It might be claimed that a general remoteness, or backwardness, of the Demetae caused a delay in the grant of self-government. But neither the Silures nor the Dumnonii seem better placed in either respect. Both civitates, therefore, probably returned to civilian government at the same time, when the Roman army's commitments in Wales were drastically reduced early in Hadrian's principate. It is difficult to envisage a fort at Carmarthen after this date, and, with the only fort in Demetian territory abandoned, military government could no longer have continued.

The fort at Carmarthen probably attracted a settlement on its north-east side, and in due course this vicus assumed the responsibilities of a civitas capital, or so it would seem at present (pl. 76). Here we can see the process whereby a military vicus became a civitas capital working most clearly. If Carmarthen was the only fort in their territory, as it seems to have been, only one vicus was available to be chosen as capital; there was no alternative.

At the present incomplete stage in the investigations, it is not possible to say a great deal about the town. No public buildings within the fortified area have yet come to light, but an amphitheatre is known on the north-east side beyond the defences. Although doubt has been cast earlier on the existence of a regular street grid, one may yet emerge. There is also a possible bath-house, parts of which were discovered many years ago in the gardens behind East Parade, and which was re-investigated in 1961. But it would seem to lie outside the walls, and may possibly have belonged to the earlier fort.

76 Aerial photograph of Carmarthen, looking north-west (*G. D. B. Jones*)

The amphitheatre (fig. 16) was first recognised for what it was in 1936, and a trial excavation in 1968 showed that the arena measured 150ft (45m) by 90ft (27m). It had been constructed by cutting back into the hillside, and using the excavated soil and rock to form the outer seating bank, probably in much the same way as had been done in the first stage of the amphitheatre at Cirencester (p. 299). The overall dimensions were 300ft (91m) by 220ft (67m), a size which, when associated with a town of this size poses some problems, as it could have provided accommodation for the population of a town as large as, if not larger, than Cirencester. It must, therefore, have been intended as a gathering ground for a large part of the tribe. This fact, rather than the uncertain information provided by the town, seems the most cogent reason for considering the site of Carmarthen as the civitas capital of the Demetae.

The arena wall and entrance passages of the amphitheatre were constructed of masonry, but the revetments for the terraces on the seating banks had been made of wood. It is not yet known if an all-timber phase preceded the masonry. On the north-west seating bank, the terraces, each about 2½ft (762mm) wide, were retained with planks, which were themselves secured laterally by beams beneath them running down the slope of the bank. The system used is not so very different from the dry-stone terrace walls at Cirencester. The north-east entrance, on the side away from the town, is, so far, the only one to be identified, and it was about 20ft (6·1m) wide. A complicated drainage system of stone-filled soak-aways had been constructed on the north-west bank to carry water from the hillside above into a drain running round the inside of the arena wall. Similar methods are used today on railway and road embankments to prevent soil slip. The slight evidence recovered indicated a construction date in the first half of the second century. If correct, this date might be in closer agreement with the emergence of the civitas than that provided by the street lay-out in the town.[49]

The defences have been sampled on the north-east side, while their line is indicated on the south-west and north-east parts by a marked change in the modern ground level and subsidence cracks in buildings. The south-east side is to a large extent masked by the present town.

As with most towns, the earliest fortifications were a turf and clay bank, about 19ft (5·8m) wide and surviving in the core of the later rampart to a height of nearly 5ft (1·5m), fronted by a single ditch, 18ft (5·5m) wide and 9ft (2·7m) deep. Antonine samian in the rampart provides a mid to late second-century date for its construction, and it is probable that Carmarthen fits the pattern of other urban earthwork fortifications. The excavators considered that its erection represented a development contemporary with the laying-out of the street grid. If the defences were, however, an emergency measure, as seems most probable, it is hardly likely that streets would have been incorporated in the scheme.

At a later date, which has not yet been established precisely, the ditch was filled, after a thick layer of silt had accumulated in it, and a stone wall built partly over the old berm and partly over the filled ditch. The wall was only about 5½ft (1·7m) wide, which, for a town wall, is less than the normal width and more in keeping with the narrow-gauge wall at Cirencester (p. 302). The rampart behind the wall was augmented with a clay tip, bringing the total width to nearly 60ft (18·3m), which may have been a way of strengthening a sub-standard wall. The ditch beyond the wall is indicated by the earlier name of Sunken Lane applied to Richmond Terrace.[50]

No gates are known, and it is not yet certain if external towers were ever added to the wall.

Some buildings have been sampled near the west corner and they show an extended sequence of development. The earliest main structures seem to have been narrow shops fronting the north-west side of the street referred to above (p. 390), with larger domestic buildings on the south-east frontage. The latter may, however, have still been connected with trade.[51] In the earliest stage most of the buildings were constructed with timber frames. Furnaces, and a copper-smith's crucible, suggest metal-working in the shops.

On the south-east side of the street, the houses seem to have been rebuilt in masonry in the third or early fourth century. In one, wooden floors had been laid. Later still, in the second half of the fourth century, the whole site was levelled for a much larger house which lay partly behind a colonnade beside the street. One large room contained a hypocaust and it appeared that most of the rooms had tessellated floors, but not apparently any mosaics.[52]

Later occupation is attested by the general coin sequence and by the association of Carmarthen with the usurper emperor, Magnus Maximus (AD 383–8). No signs of violent destruction have yet been found, but the final chapter in the town's history must await further work.

BROUGH-ON-HUMBER (*Petuaria Parisorum?*)

Petuaria is the only πόλις attributed by Ptolemy to the civitas of the Parisi,[53] so it is reasonable to suppose that it was the tribal capital, although it does not carry the tribal suffix in his account, in the Ravenna list,[54] or in the Antonine Itinerary.[55] The identification of Petuaria with Brough-on-Humber has depended so far almost entirely on the inscription (pl. 77) found in 1937,[56] which refers to an official of the *vicus Petu[ariensis]*. Since the inscription was found within the irregularly-shaped, walled enclosure at Brough, it was natural that this particular site should be called a walled town and the tribal capital of the Parisi.[57] However, the site had many features which were uncharacteristic of a civitas capital, and more recent excavations have shown an almost exclusively military chronology for the sequence of defensive circuits. Consequently grave doubts have been cast on the earlier identification and it has become necessary to acknowledge the military or naval nature of the fortified site, hitherto called the town, and to look for the latter elsewhere.[58] So we now seem to be in a position where we have one of the few inscriptions relating to the status of a British civitas capital completely unrelated to any structural remains.

77   Dedication of the new proscaenium of a theatre at Brough by M. Ulpius Ianuarius (*Hull Museums*)

So much for the changing views of archaeologists. The site at Brough must now be considered from its beginnings (fig. 85).

An extensive Iron Age settlement is known in the area at North Ferriby,[59] which may have extended westwards as far as Brough.[60] It is probable that the Brough-Old Winteringham ferry route was used in prehistoric times, as both sites lay on convenient havens off the Humber. Consequently it was the natural approach line from Lincoln of the Roman army when Petillius Cerialis mounted his Brigantian campaign in AD 71–2. It is not known if the Parisi greeted this advance in a friendly manner. It might have been so, if they had been under pressure from their western neighbours; certainly with only two known forts in their territory, if we exclude York, hostility cannot have been either great or prolonged. The two forts were situated at Malton and Brough and, as it were, bracketed Parisian territory. The latter was built conjointly with a large stores depot, which must have made use of the excellent access by river. Yet the fort also faced south-east, or towards the main native settlement, as though some degree of control was still needed, and that a threat, if threat there was, lay more in that direction than from the west.

The fort at Brough was evacuated in the late seventies, probably in connexion with Agricola's reorganisation, but the stores depot was retained. The fort site then lay vacant for over forty years, but it was still demarcated by its rampart and ditches. There seems to have been no question during this time of the civitas being constituted with a civil government, as, not only was the stores depot at Brough maintained, but also the large fort at Malton. It is also possible that the legionary fortress at York included some Parisian land in its prata.

Early in the Hadrianic period, the long-vacant fort was reoccupied for a brief spell, possibly in connexion with troop movements between the Humber and the Tyne and possibly also in anticipation of the next stage of development, which saw both fort and stores depot removed and a defensive circuit erected on a new and much extended line.[61] These new fortifications were most likely intended to protect a base for the *classis Britannica*. It is probable that, at the same time, much of the civitas was reconstituted under civilian government with a new capital not far from the base. It would be extremely unlikely, at this time, for both to have occupied the same enclave.

During the earlier military occupation, a slight movement of people seems to have taken place from the civil settlement at North Ferriby westwards towards the fort. Admittedly the migration may have been very slight and, indeed, the fort was so close as to render it almost unnecessary. The vicus so formed may have included North Ferriby and may have survived the first military evacuation. What happened afterwards is, for the time being, largely a matter of guesswork.

The inscription mentioned above clearly states that, by AD 144, the *vicus Petuariensis* possessed junior magistrates of a class that are normally only found in towns of the rank of civitas capital or above. It also implies the existence of a theatre, which was a public building normally, if at all, only provided after more functional structures such as a forum and bath-house had been erected. We may therefore infer their presence.

Where was the town? The inscription was found incorporated in the masonry of an early fourth-century building inside the naval base, so that the theatre cannot have been more than a mile or two away at the most.[62] But, apart from North Ferriby, there is no indication of a major settlement either east, west or north of the naval base. North Ferriby itself, while apparently still occupied in the fourth century, has never produced evidence for massive public buildings, although they must have existed somewhere, if not there. Moreover, the area

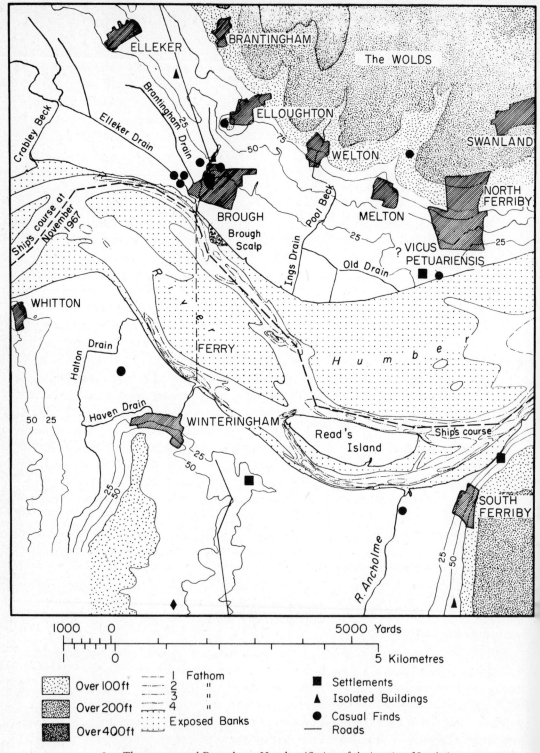

85   The area around Brough-on-Humber (*Society of Antiquaries of London*)

has produced no trace of fortifications, which would be expected at a civitas capital.

A possible solution may perhaps be sought along the following lines. If a civitas capital was founded soon after military government had ceased, it presumably developed at first along normal lines. Traces of its structures are most likely to be found somewhere between the naval base and North Ferriby, probably nearer the latter, where the local topography is more suitable. Its theatre, however, was apparently in ruins by the late third century, if not before. The town never seems to have been fortified, and we might suggest that, by the time that urban defences were generally being constructed, the site no longer warranted them. That being so, it is difficult to escape the conclusion that we are dealing with another failed town like Chelmsford (p. 198). Had this happened, it is more than probable that disused buildings would have been robbed of their stone when the defences were built at Brough.[63]

Was the finding of the theatre inscription at Brough, therefore, a red-herring which has misled archaeologists for nearly four decades? Is North Ferriby the *vicus Petuariensis* of the inscription and hence also *Petuaria Parisorum*, and Brough the *Praetorium* (*Petuaria*) of the Antonine Itinerary? The answer lies in excavations at the former site, and until they have been undertaken, speculation is useless.

Apart from the theatre attested by the inscription and the implication which this has for the sometime existence of other public buildings, there is little more to be said about this unknown town. The dedicator of the inscription was a Roman citizen, M. Ulpius Ianuarius, whose father or grandfather had been enfranchised under Trajan. He was perhaps not a native Parisian but a retired soldier, and he and his like may have given the town its initial impetus, which later faltered because of the lack of local support.

Smith has suggested that Petuaria was the centre for a mosaic artists' workshop,[64] who were responsible for a number of fine, characteristic pavements both north and south of the Humber in the mid fourth century. The patterns used suggest an off-shoot from the Corinian workshop (p. 306).

We cannot say what would have happened to the civitas, if its capital town and system of local government collapsed, but there are two possibilities. It might have been attributed to the nearby colonia at York (p. 176 above), or a prefect or *princeps* appointed to manage its affairs.

A residue of the inhabitants of the town probably remained, and it was possibly they who, after the abandonment of Brough as a naval base soon after AD 360, moved inside the fortifications and occupied the south-west corner.[65] Certainly a slight occupation there continued to the end of the fourth century, but probably not much later. The defences had already been breached by the rising level of the sea and river Humber, and can have afforded little security. This part of the country was also one of the first to be subjected to increasing waves of Anglo-Saxon settlers, and it is not surprising that fragments of at least one urn have come from Brough itself, suggesting a cemetery no great distance away.[66]

ALDBOROUGH (*Isurium Brigantum*)

The tribe of the Brigantes occupied the largest area in Britain, but before the Roman conquest they were probably only a loosely-knit confederation. This may have been the reason why the attitude of different parts towards the Romans varied. To begin with, their paramount ruler, Queen Cartimandua, who was primarily concerned with the southern area, was well-disposed towards them but more hostile feelings pervaded other parts. Indeed, Cartimandua may have established treaty relations with Rome, even though her kingdom then lay beyond the provincial frontier. Treaty or not, the Romans obviously considered her a useful and valuable ally, who was able at first to preserve moderately peaceful conditions beyond the northern frontier, while the troublesome tribes in Wales were being dealt with. She attached herself more strongly to the Roman cause when she handed over the much-wanted fugitive, Caratacus.[67] To what extent this action aroused hostility in other sections of the tribe we do not know, but it may have exacerbated an increasingly delicate situation. Trouble grew from then on, and was made worse by Cartimandua's separation from her consort, Venutius. On two occasions at least, Roman armed intervention was required, and on the last, in AD 69, she was only rescued with difficulty from her kingdom.[68] At the time the Empire was riven by civil war, the garrison in Britain was dissatisfied and mutinous, and the governor had lost control to such an extent that he had had to flee the province. Thereafter Venutius held undisputed control for the next two or three years in Brigantia, and the kingdom, instead of being a friendly buffer state, became a threatening menace on the northern frontier. As with Wales, the only ultimate solution lay in conquest and control.

The arrival of a new governor, Petillius Cerialis in AD 71 drastically changed the situation. His vigorous campaigning in Brigantia, east of the Pennines, led to the defeat of Venutius at Stanwick.[69] This oppidum, enclosing in its final stages an area of over 700 acres (284ha), had been constructed in the manner of the great Belgic oppida further south, and might be taken as a pointer either to Venutius' antecedents or to his military advisors. With Venutius defeated, Cerealis continued by way of the Stainmore Pass at least as far as Carlisle, subduing resistance as he met it. Despite victory, occupation did not follow immediately, probably because of a shortage of auxiliary regiments, many of which were still in forts along the original frontier zone of the Fosse Way.

The consolidation, which was the natural sequel to the conquest, only came nearly a decade later under the governor Agricola, when, with considerable flair for strategy and tactics, a rigid network of roads and forts were constructed to control the tribal territory in the same way as Wales had previously been dealt with. On each side of the southern Pennines lay a legionary fortress: York and Chester. The latter was also intended to prevent collaboration between the Brigantes and the tribes of north Wales.

From what happened later, we can deduce that those parts of the tribe which occupied the western Pennines, the Lake District and parts of Durham, remained hostile to Rome, while that east of the Pennines, especially in the Vale of York, settled down to a more peaceful existence.[70] Consequently, the reorganisations of Hadrian saw the relaxing of military control and the evacuation of forts in the eastern part, and the constitution of the civitas Brigantum, while a firm grip was maintained on the west. The area which came under civil government was, therefore, somewhat less than half the total tribal territory. However, the situation was drastically changed after the Brigantian rebellion of AD 154–5, for then many of the Pennine forts were reoccupied at full strength and much of the civil area of the civitas probably returned to military government (see also p. 406 below). Further trouble was experienced again in the later second century, and it is interesting how the time span between each Brigantian rebellion from *c.* AD 100, and indeed from AD 69 onwards, represents the rise of a new generation to take the field.

It must be apparent that there had been a fort at Aldborough, although convincing evidence for its existence has yet to appear. But as a link in the chain of forts on the road north from York, one would have been desirable. Moreover, there is evidence for Flavian occupation, which, if not belonging to the fort itself, may have been part of its attached vicus.[71] An iron entrenching tool illustrated by Ecroyd Smith would be best suited to a military context. There seems to have been no native settlement in the vicinity before the fort was established, so that the selection of its vicus as the civitas capital must have been mainly for arbitrary reasons, although a concentration there of the most influential natives may have been a deciding factor, as with Dorchester or Cirencester. Other possible factors were the need to keep a distance from York, and the existence nearby of a site of possible religious significance to the tribe.[72] It is interesting, moreover, to observe the complete eclipse of Stanwick and Almondbury, both centres which had had earlier associations with the Brigantian ruling classes.

The vicus at Aldborough contained substantial buildings before it became the civitas capital, as excavations near the site of the supposed east gate have exposed late first-century masonry structures.[73] But although sporadic excavations have taken place in the town in more recent years, our knowledge of the internal buildings, such as it is, has been mainly derived from much earlier sources.[74] Most energy in recent years has been expended on the fortifications, which are now tolerably well understood (fig. 86).

So far the only indication of a major public building has been found north of the church, where walls representing a range of rooms over 270ft (82m) long were found in 1770. It could represent a wing of the forum, or perhaps more probably the offices and other rooms behind the basilica, so placing the latter on the more favoured north side. This would put the forum insula south of the street joining the east and west gates, although it would in this position interrupt the line of the main north-south street. Since the cardo and decumanus maximi were seldom interrupted by any building, the position of the forum at Aldborough is surprising and more reminiscent of the placing of the principia in a fort.

Although part of a bath-house was found close to the back of the rampart just

ALDBOROUGH, YORKSHIRE.   (Isvrivm Brigantvm)

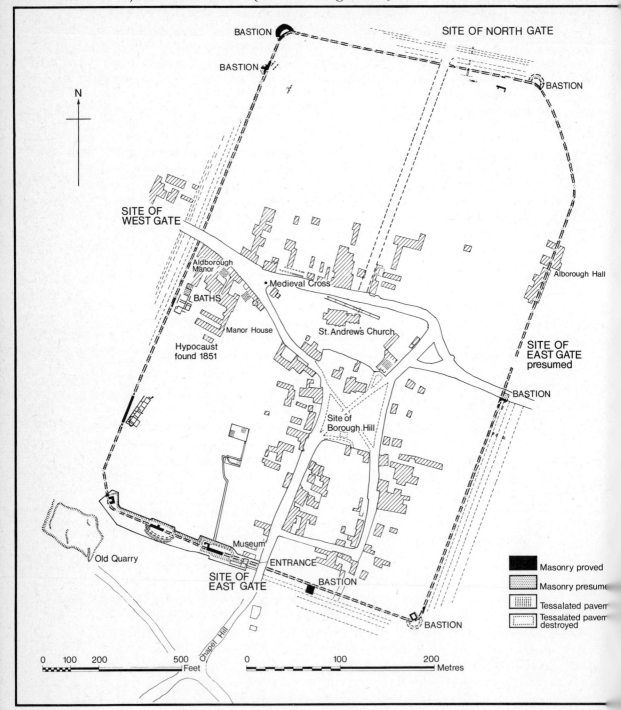

BASTION

SITE OF NORTH GATE

BASTION

N

BASTION

SITE OF
WEST GATE

Aldborough
Manor

Alborough Hall

• Medieval Cross

BATHS

Manor House

St. Andrew's Church

Hypocaust
found 1851

SITE OF
EAST GATE
presumed

BASTION

Site of
Borough Hill

Old Quarry

Museum

ENTRANCE

SITE OF
EAST GATE

BASTION

BASTION

Chapel Hill

	Masonry proved
	Masonry presume
	Tessalated pavem
	Tessalated pavem destroyed

0   100   200   500
Feet

0   100   200
Metres

86   Plan of Aldborough (*after D. Charlesworth*)

south of the west gate, there is nothing to show that it was a public baths, even though it was greater in size than the normal suite attached to a private house. It could, however, have belonged to a mansio, and the situation not far from a gate would favour this interpretation.

Like most other Romano-British towns, Aldborough received its first defences, of earthworks, late in the second century. The bank was built of dirty sand, some crushed sandstone and a good deal of domestic refuse, and seems to have exceeded 15ft (4·6m), in width. It was fronted by a single, flat-bottomed ditch of roughly the same width and about 5 to 6ft (1·5 to 1·8m) deep. Nothing is known of the gates of this period, and, although masonry internal towers occur at close intervals on the town wall, there is, as yet, no indication that they, and possibly masonry gates also, were part of the earlier circuit of fortifications as at Cirencester. However, it is noteworthy that the gates were built of millstone grit quite different from the soft red sandstone used for the wall; yet this fact can also be used to equate the known gate structures with the late fourth-century bastions.

At some date, not earlier than the middle of the third century, the existing defences were strengthened by the addition of a masonry wall, 10ft (3·1m) thick at the base; some variations of width from 8 to 9ft (2·4 to 2·7m) have also been recorded. A stretch of this wall between the south-west corner and the south gate is exposed to view. The rear face was strengthened by a heightened rampart and another, smaller ditch seems to have been dug beyond the existing ditch on parts of the circuit. Internal, hollow towers were probably an integral part of this work and two are known on the stretch of wall between the south gate and the south-west corner, with an additional tower there and another at the south-east corner. Surprisingly they were not found at either the north-west or north-east angles.[75] Three milestones,[76] one from inside the town, the other two outside, can be dated to the principate of Decius Trajan, AD 249–51. Extensive roadworks around the town might have been the counterpart of masonry defences (CIRENCESTER, p. 301).

Four gates may be presumed, approximately in the centres of each side of the circuit. The north gate has been partly excavated on two occasions with confusing results.[77] The gap in the wall seems to have been about 30ft (9·1m) wide, implying at least two carriageways, but it is not at present possible to say if there were internal or external projecting towers. But the use of millstone grit in the gate, as already suggested, might indicate an earlier structure or more likely a later rebuild, for it is of this material that the fourth-century external towers were built and not of the more normal red sandstone. The east corner of the south gate was encountered in more recent excavations.[78] The west gate lies beneath the modern road to Boroughbridge, and the east gate under the grounds of Aldborough Hall. A sill-stone from the latter, with socket for the gate pivot, was recorded by Ecroyd Smith.

An interesting structure, found just inside the north gate, was the base of a large stone-lined water tank, measuring internally 8ft 9in (2·7m) by 6ft (1·8m). The sides of the tank, to judge from the width of rebates near the edges of the base, were made of vertical slabs 10in (254mm) thick. An oddity is the apparent lack of provision for an overflow. It seems that other tanks may have been provided at both the east and west gates, where similar rebated base stones have been found. All were probably intended to act as cisterns for fresh water, but whether they were fed from an aqueduct or whether they collected water perhaps running off the gate structures, is not known.[79]

Evidence for the houses inside the town has mainly been obtained by chance discovery or by excavations carried out before sufficient attention was paid to structural history. Consequently, it is only possible to make some general comments. Remains of two substantial houses have been uncovered in the south-west quarter, one close to the west defences, the other more centrally placed within the area. The former, according to Ecroyd Smith's plan, obviously represents a house of more than one structural phase. It seems to have consisted in part of a long wing, with what may have been a corridor running down the west side and with the southernmost room terminating in an apse. Another apse was later added to the adjacent room so that it extended across the corridor, which was itself then subdivided. The walls were decorated with painted designs to imitate marble veneers and with simple foliage patterns, and seem to have incorporated some perspectives.

The second building had at least two wings with an internal colonnaded courtyard. It was equipped with hypocausts and the main corridor and principal rooms had fine mosaic floors. It is not possible to say whether another large apsidal room found further south was part of the same building. Most of the mosaics were of geometric and conventional floral patterns, but that in the large apsidal room, although badly damaged when found, appears to have been a figured mosaic of better quality. The surprising feature of this pavement is the inclusion of an inscription in Greek beside the figure of a man who, having risen from a chair, reads from a scroll.[80] The style is very similar to some pavements from the Mediterranean, where a few lines of text describe either the activities taking place or persons and animals shown in the mosaic. The most likely explanation for such a pavement at Aldborough would seem to lie in slavish copying from a pattern book, or in the inclinations of a retired soldier or merchant. It is all the more interesting, therefore, that the Venus pavement at Rudston should incorporate Latin descriptions. Yet another mosaic in the same building at Aldborough contained a central panel, unfortunately damaged, but showed an animal, probably a lion, sitting beneath a tree. Although in a very different category of workmanship, there is a striking similarity in general design between this pavement and another found near Aldborough Hall, which depicts the mythological suckling of Romulus and Remus by a wolf.[81] The execution of the latter, by an obviously unskilled artist, shows a wolf which looks more like a friendly domestic cat. The lack of proportions exhibited is reminiscent of the Venus pavement in the not far distant villa at Rudston.[82]

The standard of the few houses known at Aldborough provides the impression of a well-appointed town with a fair number of comfortable houses. Perhaps as at Wroxeter, similarly situated on the fringe of an unsettled area, the safety of town walls was sought in preference to existence in isolated country villas, of which few are known in Brigantian territory. Certainly the general impression gained is of a civitas capital not so very different from others further south, some of which had an earlier start. Although little is known of the internal street plan, the regular alignments of the main buildings would suggest a grid based on the two main cross streets.

There is little evidence of the commercial and industrial life of the town. A reputed butcher's shop on the main north-south street, found behind the Ship Inn, may represent no more than the normal collection of domestic refuse.[83] A collection of iron tools, not unlike those used by a farrier, was illustrated by Ecroyd Smith. A fragment of a horn shuttle, illustrated by the same author, shows that weaving was carried on, probably on a domestic scale. Neither must it be forgotten that much of the legendary wealth of the Brigantes lay in cattle and we might expect tanning and bone or horn industries. The fine pieces of enamelled bronze found from time to time in the town might also suggest the manufacture of such goods. Local pottery industries were hardly necessary, as most requirements were supplied by the east Yorkshire potteries; but one of the so-called 'Red Graves' described by Ecroyd Smith, which were found outside the southeast wall, appears remarkably like a pottery kiln, while the other, although more in the character of a sarcophagus, could have been re-used for some industrial process, as it was found half full of ash.

No temples have yet come to light, but two stone reliefs of Mercury imply a shrine to this deity somewhere in the town. A number of altars, both inscribed and uninscribed, and including one dedicated to Jupiter Optimus Maximus and the Deae Matres, have also been found.

Fragments of two tombstones tell of Felicula Gaius and of another unnamed person.[84] A number of burials are known from outside the walls, and reference has already been made above to a possible stone sarcophagus.

At some stage in the town's history a by-pass road seems to have been provided round the north-east corner so that through traffic from York to Catterick could avoid the centre. An extra-mural settlement grew in the vicinity, presumably formed for the most part of the shops of traders anxious not to miss even this opportunity for gaining customers.[85]

Aldborough is among those towns in Britain which had its fortifications reorganised in the second half of the fourth century. Massive, hollow segmental towers were added to the outer face of the wall at the main corners, with rectangular towers at intervals along it. The inner ditch was filled where they were constructed and the outer ditch seems to have been filled entirely, while a new ditch, 40ft (12·2m) wide, was excavated 25ft (7·6m) out from the fronts of the towers.[86] Repairs also seem to have been carried out on the curtain wall in places.

Despite the strength of its new defences and the obvious wealth in the town represented by the large comfortable houses, a decline in its affairs seems to have set in before the end of the fourth century. There is no indication so far of violent destruction to equate with any of the rebellions or invasions known to history which troubled this part of the country. In this respect it seems to resemble Catterick and not the legionary fortress at York, where parts perished in flames during the later second century. No doubt Aldborough was affected, during these times, but not so intimately. As a town it certainly seems to have weathered the barbarian conspiracy of AD 367, and the remarkably high proportion of coins dated to the House of Valentinian, when coinage was generally scarce, might indicate that a unit of the field army was quartered here temporarily, simultaneously with another detachment at Catterick. At Aldborough, however, with 55 acres (22·3ha) enclosed within the walls, there was probably sufficient room for billeting troops without large-scale expulsion of the civilians. The sharp decline in the number of coins thereafter is equally noteworthy, with the House of Theodosius poorly represented in the list, suggesting perhaps the removal of the unit under Magnus Maximus.

9

Some Exceptions

The towns considered in the foregoing chapters were all established during the first eighty or so years of the Roman occupation. This time-span saw, therefore, virtually the full extension of the areas of the province which came under civilian government. In fact, however, the main period of urban development was more concentrated, and no less than seventeen of the twenty-one towns so far considered showed their major development between *c*. AD 80 and 130. It is hardly surprising therefore that despite such variable factors as size, wealth and status, they had much in common. It was this similarity between them which, at the beginning of this book, enabled us to define the term 'town', as a settlement which had specific functions: administrative, social, economic, educational, protective; which provided facilities for amenities and amusements, and which was planned. They were therefore more sophisticated than other settlements of the same date. But this definition, adequate though it is for the towns which have been considered, is restrictive since it largely fails to take into account later developments.

Since the situation was not static, a number of sites developed, which, while not strictly towns according to the above definition, were nevertheless close approximations to them. Some lacked one or more of the prescribed functions or facilities, but might show an element of planning in their lay-out; others might have functioned as towns, yet lacked the planning. In the former class we might include Bath, Corbridge and Catterick, while in the latter were those which, as the result of the promotion of a pagus to a civitas, became civitas capitals. Although there is no definite information for such promotions in Britain, it might be suggested that Ilchester, Carlisle and Water Newton were so treated.

The appearance of the duly constituted *civitas Carvetiorum*, of which Carlisle was most likely the capital,[1] in an area on the frontier containing large troop concentrations, raises several problems. We need not doubt that, for a long time, this and similar areas had been subjected to military government, and that in them the writ of the civitas Brigantum, to which tribe the land had once belonged, did not run, even though purely local and strictly controlled autonomy may have been granted to the many vici. Salway has considered the constitutional position of these tribal areas and doubts whether the army could have carried out all the duties required of a civilian authority.[2] Yet there are instances of fort commanders acting in various capacities as civil administrators, especially in the later Empire: adjudicator, tax-gatherer, census-taker, police officer.[3] There is also evidence of army officers being seconded to supervise areas of civilian settlement, the best example in Britain being the *regionarius* from Ribchester, who was a centurion of Legio VI detached from legionary duties to command an auxiliary regiment and to manage a settlement of veteran auxiliaries.[4] In an area where military occupation was a necessity caused by potential sedition or invasion, it is obvious that the last word must always have remained with individual commanders or their superiors.

The much-disputed passage of Pausanias[5] if interpreted in its simplest way, helps to confirm this reasoning. He states that Antoninus Pius deprived the Brigantes of much of their territory because they had invaded the Genunian district. Despite much argument to the contrary, it is best taken as a reference to the Brigantian rebellion of AD 154–5. Nor need the whereabouts of the Genunian district bother us; it need not even have been part of Brigantian territory, but could have lain anywhere beyond its borders, either north, east or south. The essence of the passage is quite clear: a large segment of the Brigantes, presumably governed at the time by the civitas, misbehaved themselves and had to be placed once more under military government. Judging from the forts reoccupied between AD 155 and 161, the hill-folk of the Pennines had been the cause of the trouble (p. 399 above); little more than the Vale of York was therefore left within the ambit of the civilian authority. Government either by the army or by the civitas could not be better distinguished; the area retaken by the army was no longer part of the civitas Brigantum. That being so, there was no reason why, at a later date when some areas had become more peaceful, parts should not have been resurrected as civitates. If they were physically separated from the civitas Brigantum it would have been a wise decision to give them a separate identity, no doubt derived from one or more of the pagi of the tribe: hence the civitas Carvetiorum, which lay in the north-western part, and which probably embraced much of the Cumberland plain.

It is unfortunate that so little is known of Carlisle, possible *Luguvalium* (*Carvetiorum?*), although it seems to have grown to a considerable size and may have exceeded 70 acres (28ha). Saint Cuthbert perambulated its walls in the seventh century, and also saw a 'fountain'[6] which, together with another elaborate water tank found in the grounds of the Tullie House Museum,[7] implies a working aqueduct. The defences present problems, but it now seems unlikely that the triple row of stakes, recorded by earlier excavators as a stockade or palisade, is the underpinning of a defensive masonry wall, made necessary by marshy ground. Moreover, in 1973, Dorothy Charlesworth failed to find any trace of the urban defences where they were expected on the north side of the town. William of Malmesbury mentions an arched building with an inscription to Mars and Victory, presumably a temple or shrine.[8] Stone columns and bases suggest buildings of substance, and there are slight indications of a regular street grid.[9] Somewhere there must be the requisite public buildings for a civitas capital and, in the late fourth century, the praetorium of the provincial governor.

Fortunately a number of inscribed stones help to fill the gap caused by the lack of structural remains. A joint dedication to the Fates and Mother Goddesses is a good example of the conjunction of classical and native deities, while a mention of Cautes implies the presence of a Mithraeum.[10] Mars Ocelus, a temple of whom has already been noted at Caerwent (p. 384), and Hercules, probably as a cloak for the emperor Commodus, also had their followers.[11] A number of tombstones show a strong element of Roman citizenship among the inhabitants and one, of a Greek, shows a little of the cosmopolitan nature of the town.[12] Nor should it be forgotten that Carlisle was probably the starting point for many merchants venturing beyond the frontiers. Antonianus set up an altar at nearby Bowness in anticipation of the success of his trip.[13]

It is difficult to decide on the date of emergence of the civitas Carvetiorum and its capital. The tombstone and the milestone from which its existence can be deduced cannot be dated earlier than AD 258.[14] As a reasonable proposition, but one with no firm evidence to back it, we might suggest that its constitution was part of the settlement of the northern frontier by Caracalla in the early third century which resulted in a long period of peace and considerable prosperity. It must have meant a new departure for Britain with a civilian authority acting on the same level, and in the same general area, as a military authority. Presumably military territoria were now more restricted and ran side by side with the civitas.[15] Can we detect here, as in some other provinces, the trend which came to fruition in the early fourth century, when civil and military affairs tended to be separated, from the highest officers downwards, by the reforms of Diocletian? These reforms must have likewise affected those other civitates which, in whole or in part, had hitherto been under military government. The system, whereby regionarii or beneficiarii were made responsible for regions still unable to cope with problems of self-government, was probably extended. But the duties of existing curiales, already in some cases expanded at an earlier date to take over official mining ventures, could have been enlarged to assume control of parts of their territories previously under the army. If so, the reforms of Diocletian were the logical rationalisation of trends which had started nearly a hundred years earlier.

The probable promotion of pagi to the status of civitas must have led to the fragmentation of some of the larger tribal areas, and to the creation of a new generation of civitas capitals.

Unfortunately in Britain there is no firm evidence for such promotions, but there are some slight indications, and we can consider first the case for the division of the Durotriges. The two well-known inscriptions from Hadrian's Wall which refer to a civitas Durotrigum Lindinensis,[16] have normally been accepted as evidence for the splitting of the Durotriges in two, with Ilchester as the capital of the north-west part.[17] More recently, Bogaers has cast doubt on this view.[18]

He argues that the date of the inscriptions, as yet undecided between the Severan period and the late fourth century, places them in a time when constitutional changes in the Empire had altered the meaning of civitas in Britain from a tribal area to a town. There is substance in this argument, especially when applied to the present example, and the inscription could refer, according to Bogaers, to the people of Lindinis, a town of the Durotriges; the name of the town itself is quoted. But for reasons already given under *Venta Silurum* (p. 381 above) his arguments, when applied to the other, similar inscriptions from the Wall,[19] carry less conviction, because of the question of name survival. The civitas Dumnoniorum, which is recorded by another inscription, is referring, again according to Bogaers, to the people of Exeter (*Isca*). But since it is the Isca part of the town's name which has survived today and not the Dumnoniorum, the inscription should properly have read civitas Iscensis for Bogaers to be right. Either an archaic form of words was being used, or the inscription was quite correctly referring to a group of people who had their origins in the whole territory of the Dumnonii.

Two further reasons for believing that the latter explanation is correct may be considered. A common formula seems to have been used in all the inscriptions; if therefore it had a particular meaning for one, it probably had the same meaning for all. Moreover, Ilchester was a small settlement, with no more than about 35 acres (14ha) enclosed within its walls. It is unlikely that its population could have provided a working-party large enough to be of much significance in the rebuilding programmes which took place on Hadrian's Wall, during either of the two surmised periods. Yet the party is known to have carried out work on two sections of the curtain wall, and it is best seen as a group raised from the estates of the many rich landowners, with large numbers of slaves and retainers, who inhabited the area round Ilchester; in truth from the civitas Durotrigum Lindiniensis.

Having thus established a case for the independent existence of this civitas, we may now consider its capital at Ilchester (*Lindinis*). Unfortunately, as at Carlisle, there is little information available. Some work was carried out on the defences in 1948–9 and again more recently. It has revealed a three-stage work, which started as a simple clay bank dated to the late second or early third century. At a later date a timber revetment connected by tie-beams to a series of posts at the rear was added. In the fourth century, the timber was replaced by a stone wall at the front of the bank. Part of a gate-tower belonging to the south gate has also been uncovered.[20]

The little excavation which has been carried out in the interior has shown that the main development took place in the third and fourth centuries. Nothing is yet known of streets or public buildings, if indeed Ilchester was so equipped. It carried out the main functions of a town, therefore, apparently without the amenities, or the evidence for planning, which would enable it to be classified as a town.

Another site probably in much the same category as Ilchester is Water Newton (*Durobrivae*). Slight evidence, in the form of a milestone[21] showing that distances

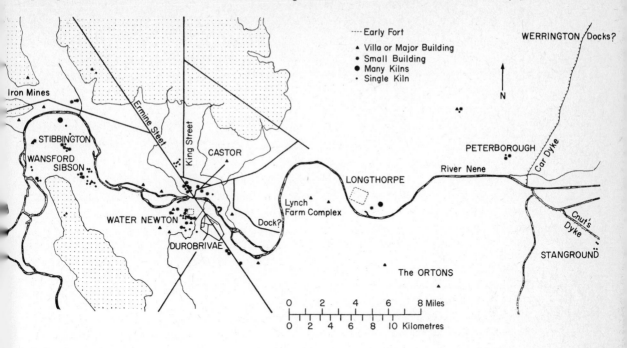

87   The area around Water Newton (*after J. P. Wild*)

were being measured from it, might suggest that it too had become a civitas capital. The unplaced *civitas Corielsoliliorum*, attested by a stamped tile from Cave's Inn,[22] might have been created from the northern section of the Catuvellauni, in which area Water Newton, at about 44 acres (17ha), is by far the largest fortified site, and therefore the most likely candidate for capital. But, as at Ilchester, little is known of its history. The defences have been sampled, and a good deal of excavation has taken place in the extensive extramural settlements, but the interior is mainly known from the aerial photographs of Dr St Joseph.[23] Apart from Ermine Street, the main road north, which cleaves the site in two, all the other internal streets are laid out in a completely random fashion, showing not the slightest attempt at planning. The fortifications, not yet accurately dated, appear to have been a one-phase work incorporating a wall, contemporary bank and ditches.[24] The absence of independent earthworks is perhaps a pointer to the late development of the site. But Durobrivae also became the centre for a great industrial complex, which extended on all sides (fig. 87). It was certainly one of the principal potteries in Britain during the third and fourth centuries, and the peaceful conditions are emphasised by the private houses of master potters which were built outside the defences.[25]

Again, however, despite the total size of the settlement and the obvious wealth which it must have represented, the general impression gained is similar to that given by Ilchester: a settlement probably carrying out many of the functions of a town but lacking some amenities and coordinated planning. It is probable that other settlements in this same category will be identified in the near future, and certainly more are needed if we are to make up the 28 civitates of Gildas and Nennius. The number which they quote, less the coloniae, might possibly be taken as representing the final count of civitas capitals in Britain.

It can be seen therefore that, apart from Carlisle, this class of civitas capital does not fall strictly within our definition of a town. The changes which occurred in the later Roman Empire often defy easy analysis, owing to the increasing complexity of administrative, military and economic affairs. The Empire was a growing organism. So our definition of a town, although adequate for the first two centuries AD has to be adapted too, in order to take in the later modifications. We can extend it therefore by qualifying the administrative functions which are part of our definition of a town, to include those organisations which, during the third and more especially the fourth century, held the rank of civitas or above. Despite the reservations made above about Bogaer's deductions, there came a time when there was an identity between the tribal civitas and the town at its centre, so that the term civitas became more and more used to denote the capital.[26] Consequently we can take all those sites, which in later contexts were called civitates, and justifiably call them towns. The number which this will add to our original list of civitas capitals is not yet fully known; neither are all their identities certain. What is sure, however, is that when they are better known they will deserve separate treatment.

Town Life
or Life in Towns?

What became of Romano-British towns once the link between them and the central government was severed? Documentary sources for this period are scarce and confusing and it is only in the last twenty years or so that archaeological evidence has begun to provide part of the answer. But the interpretation of this evidence is not easy, and so far it has taken place mainly on a piecemeal basis, with only a few attempts at synthesis.[1] It is probably best, therefore, if we start by analysing the problems involved.

To begin with, there is the important question of continuity between Romano-British and English towns. Recent trends among archaeologists have tended to emphasise this aspect without it seemingly being always appreciated what was continuing. It is comparatively easy to demonstrate a continuity of occupation of a town by simply showing that people still lived there. It is much more difficult to produce evidence for social, economic or administrative continuity, or even to be able to show that the population still contained descendants of the earlier inhabitants, when so much of the tangible, cultural material ceased to be used early in the fifth century. It is probably safe to predict that a degree of continuity of occupation existed in almost every former Romano-British town. There may have been relatively short periods when some were completely deserted, but even the so-called 'migrated' towns such as Wroxeter, Caistor-by-Norwich and Silchester have retained a village nucleus today, which was probably all that any could boast in the early Anglo-Saxon period. Many of the towns of the Roman period were so sited, that they automatically remained principal centres throughout the middle ages and down to modern times. There is probably little to be gained therefore in formally demonstrating that each and every town was occupied continuously from Roman times until the middle ages, unless we can specify its nature, for such continuity is in accordance with probability, even if the evidence has no longer survived, or is inaccessible to modern investigators. For this line of enquiry to be of real use, other aspects of Romano-British cultural survival must be taken into consideration, which is a difficult if not almost insuperable task. The evidence is tantalisingly slight. It may be likened to the viewing at random of individual frames in a cinematograph film.

The second main problem is the degree to which general deductions can be made about the chaotic conditions in the fifth and sixth centuries. The historian can most readily define a period when order and discipline reign: chaos presents a much greater challenge. Given our present knowledge it is probably best to treat each town primarily on its own merits while drawing comparisons and contrasts wherever possible.

Having defined the main problem we can next consider the questions of continuity of a Romano-British culture. It is now possible to trace the existence of civilised life down to at least the middle of the fifth century at Verulamium, Cirencester and Silchester, and each has been described in earlier chapters. There is evidence that the Church was far from idle, as it was threatened by a major heresy in Britain; hence the visits of St Germanus of Auxerre in AD 429 and again in AD 440. It has indeed been suggested that this heresy—Pelagianism—had its greatest strength in towns and helped their survival, after Britain had thrown out the official government.[2] However, this view has been seriously questioned by Liebeschuetz.[3]

At about the time of Germanus' first visit, the father of St Patrick was trying to make him accept public office. So we can deduce that the curial classes had survived not only to receive the rescript of Honorius of AD 410, but later also to send a request for help to Aetius in AD 446. There were people living, who, a generation after Britain had been officially abandoned, could still with confidence send to Rome for aid. Although the tide of chaos was lapping at their feet, something of the old standards of civilized life still survived. A civitas was still centred on a town, even if it no longer entirely controlled its surrounding area and was ruled by a 'tyrant' instead of by elected magistrates and a council. We might suspect that, for many people, little difference was detectable in the running of affairs from the days when they had been controlled by a virtually self-perpetuating minority.

Evidence has yet to be produced that the towns were still properly functioning in the period of peace and British prosperity which came after the Anglo-Saxons had suffered a major defeat at Mount Badon, towards the end of the fifth century. If some were still occupied by decurions and their like, maintaining the same sort of standards, then modern excavators are foreshortening by a considerable time-span the dates of dissolution of their houses. The evidence may be there, but, if it is, we cannot yet see it. But there is some reason to believe that by then many towns had already been deserted by the classes which had been foremost in their maintenance.

Indeed, one of the most surprising aspects of this whole period is the almost complete disappearance of what may be called the Romano-British culture, in contrast to other provinces in the western Empire, which, in many ways, preserved far more in the face of similar odds. Its apparent inability to survive in Britain has, in the past, often been used to illustrate the supposed weakness of the

culture, even in its prime. It has also been pleaded that it was only a veneer confined to the upper classes, and that this veneer extended to the British peoples'
restricted use of Latin. It was claimed in consequence that once the upper classes
had been removed from the scene nothing remained of the old culture to be
absorbed by that being newly established. Yet the solid weight of evidence is
against such an assumption.

It is highly probable that in the lowland area at least, a common culture had
permeated almost all classes in Britain in the fourth century, except perhaps the
very lowest class of country peasants. There certainly seems to be no reason why
brickmakers should have had a monopoly of literacy among the working class
and decurions would hardly have amused themselves by scratching their names
or messages on pots. Attention has already been drawn to the implications arising
from writers of graffiti swearing in Latin (p. 47). Recently also Mann has suggested that the Latin of Roman Britain, archaic though it may seem, was by no
means a second language learnt at school.[4] Why therefore was the language and
culture eclipsed from the lowland area, even though Latin loan words were taken
into Welsh?

If it failed to survive, for so it would seem, it is probable that the people who
maintained the culture had either fled from lowland Britain, or had perished with
it. Many scholars have already discussed when this came about, but fewer
satisfactory attempts have been made to explain how and why it happened, and
attention must now be turned to a consideration of the causes.

Throughout history the classic causes of depopulation have been war, famine
and pestilence. All seem to have played their part in the collapse of Roman Britain
and the rise of Anglo-Saxon England during the fifth and sixth centuries.

The literary sources of the period make numerous references to fighting, but
in the confusion it was probably not always Britons on one side and Saxons, Jutes,
Franks or Picts on the other. The wealthy British ruling classes still depended a
great deal on German foederati to beat off raiding parties, and even attacks by
rivals. One of the prime causes of the weakening of the ruling classes may have
been internecine strife. An account,[5] dating shortly after the severance of Britain
from the Empire, tells in glowing terms the possible effects of this warfare. With
the restraining influence of the central government removed, it was left to the
ruling classes to fight out among themselves the question who should wield
power. As for its effects on population, such conflicts could have removed permanently from the scene a large proportion of the people relied upon to provide
leadership and to maintain standards. When we add raids by Saxons and others
and, slightly later, a serious rebellion of foederati, a considerable drain on the
indigenous population might be envisaged. To this might also be added the
major schism in the Church, which may have been linked with politics,[6] so
further weakening British resistance to external forces.

Despite this knowledge of intermittent warfare throughout the fifth and sixth
centuries it is surprising that so little tangible evidence has been found to confirm
it. Contrary to some still current views, it is now known that few towns suffered

violent destruction; some villas went up in flames with their inhabitants massacred, but the majority slid into slow decay. The opinions canvassed by Collingwood forty years ago can still hold good.[7] There is virtually no evidence of battle cemeteries such as were connected with native British sites during the Roman invasion period of AD 43, although some of the early Saxon cemeteries, containing the graves of warriors and apparently dissociated from settlements, may perhaps represent their sites. The total inability of Saxon raiding parties to capture fortified towns,[8] unless aided by ruse or treachery, may also have extended to rival British factions. Towns therefore, if occupied, were safe, and warfare must have largely passed them by unless they were affected by a rebellion from within. Such battles as there were would have taken place in open country, and mainly between small parties of contestants, perhaps no more than a few hundred strong.

If warfare did not greatly affect the towns, other causes following in its train touched them more closely. Serious famines had been known in the Empire before law and order had broken down.[9] The situation would have been doubly exacerbated in fifth-century Britain. Not only would cultivation of the land have been made more difficult, but the destruction of standing crops was probably more frequent. Moreover the towns had been mainly dependent on the villas to supply their agricultural needs. Once the villas themselves were in decay and communications severed, the plight of the towns would have been greatly increased. Hence the understandable desire of townspeople to get what crops they could within the walls as quickly as possible, as is shown by the existence of corn-drying ovens in late contexts inside towns. In such circumstances also, towns which possessed large vacant areas had a distinct advantage over those which were more cramped inside their fortifications. Perhaps this factor helps to account for the apparently longer survival of Verulamium and Silchester. The local Dumnonian famine of the sixth century, relieved by the arrival of an Alexandrian grain ship (p. 335) was probably but one of many in the period in question. The results can be foreseen. Apart from outright deaths, a progressive weakening will have occurred in the surviving population, making them more susceptible to ever-prevalent diseases. Those who could, possibly migrated to other areas. It should be remembered also that famine would have affected Briton and Saxon alike, but that Saxon stock could be renewed by fresh migrations.

Most of what we might call the 'killer' diseases were probably endemic in the ancient world, and no doubt from time to time reached epidemic proportions. Major epidemics are recorded by contemporary writers, but it is rarely possible to decide on the nature of the diseases from the symptoms which they describe. Smallpox, typhus, acute bacillary dysentery, cholera, anthrax, bubonic plague and many others were probably all present, giving rise to serious epidemics from time to time. Outbreaks of bubonic plague, which was undoubtedly the most deadly, are recorded in Libya by both Dioscorides and Posidonius *c.* 50 BC; the symptoms in this instance are accurately described. Less certainty can be attached to the succession of pestilences which were spread over the last thirty years of the second century; more than one disease, probably including smallpox, may have been involved, but no certain diagnoses can be made.[10] However, the effects were serious; it reached Gaul and Germany, so we might assume also its presence in Britain.

Other major epidemics are recorded between the third and sixth centuries AD, terminating with the well-attested pandemic of bubonic plague which started *c.* 540 during Justinian's principate.[11] Most other outbreaks, however, appear to have been severe, but relatively localised, epidemic diseases. The pandemic of Justinian almost certainly reached Britain. It is mentioned by Gregory of Tours and the Irish and British Annals which refer to a *mortalitas magna*.

It is likely that an earlier epidemic also reached Britain. Hydatius, writing in the west, mentions a *pestilentia quae fere in toto orbe diffusa est, c.* 443.[12] Some confirmation is contained in independent references to its presence in Constantinople *c.* 445–6, while yet another author records it in Italy.[13] Gildas mentions a *pestifera lues* in Britain,[14] but we cannot be certain to which epidemic he is referring. If he was writing not later than *c.* 540, as proposed by Morris,[15] then the reference is probably to the fifth-century epidemic, a conclusion reached by both Stevens and Myres.[16] Alternatively he may have been alluding to a completely different outbreak. Slightly later, *c.* 455, there is a mention of an epidemic spreading throughout the Roman provinces, and especially in the provinces of Asia Minor. The symptoms are described as beginning with inflamed eyes, swelling and redness of the skin over the entire body, and ending, usually fatally on the third or fourth day, with severe pulmonary symptoms.[17] It has been suggested that it was a severe form of scarlet fever with secondary streptococcic pneumonia.[18] We do not know whether this was the disease, which a decade earlier had probably reached Britain. When such major epidemics occurred, there was most likely a synchronous prevalence of several diseases, which together gave rise to an enhanced mortality. Moreover, the nature of the disease is largely immaterial to our arguments; it is the consequences which are important.

There is no doubt that a malignant infection in its severest form can have far-reaching effects on the course of history, all too often glossed over by many historians. We have only to remember the appalling effects over the whole of Europe of the Black Death in the fourteenth century, and of the Great Plague two centuries later. Pepys' description of the Great Plague in London leaves little to the imagination. We have bodies lying in grass-grown streets; the deserted houses and closed shops; the empty churches; the flight of organised government and many of the inhabitants to places of safety; the breakdown of civil order; demoralisation of survivors; the refusal of country-folk to harbour refugees, and their sometimes violent reception.[19] But bubonic plague has not only been the cause of high mortality. It was typhus as much as the Russians which defeated Napoleon's army in 1812. In the Crimean war, 63,251 men were killed in battle, but 104,494 died of diseases, principally cholera, but also typhus and dysentery.[20]

It may seem out-of-place to quote such sources in an account of the decline of Roman Britain. It is, however, the only way to appreciate the severe effects of major epidemics of even quite common diseases. Neither is there reason to suppose that the poorly-documented epidemics of antiquity were any less deadly than their more modern counterparts. In discussing the end of Roman Britain, most authorities cite one or more of the pestilences, to which reference has already been made above (p. 415), but usually with little more appreciation of their serious consequences than if they had been mild outbreaks of the common cold. Such an epidemic could spell the end of a society which was already disintegrating. Moreover, we must remember that, in the disease-ridden world of antiquity, a pestilence which attracted the attention of a contemporary writer would indeed have been serious. We should not therefore dismiss too readily the sources which we have, and accuse the writers of distortion. In a world where death from disease was common-place, a reference to a *mortalitas magna* probably meant just that.

Human epidemics are essentially affairs of urban communities. Without gross aggregations of population there can be no major epidemics, and without lively commercial intercourse between towns they cannot spread. Towns, therefore, will be the first sufferers, and will be the most severely affected. When we remember the direct trading contacts between Roman Britain and the Mediterranean, it is easy to see that any epidemics there could have arrived on these shores and spread, by the activities of traders, throughout much of the country. These contacts continued during the fifth and sixth centuries. It is highly probable, therefore, that the pestilence of Hydatius would have reached Britain just at a time when the country could not cope. Once established in the conditions then obtaining it would have been impossible to control. We shall see from the following discussion that, of all causes, a severe epidemic of a virulent disease can most easily explain certain events which occurred towards the end of Roman Britain.

Among the things that we have to explain are: instances of unburied bodies lying beside streets in some of the towns; the apparent decay and desertion of many towns for reasons not connected with warfare, sometimes in favour of other nearby, fortifiable sites such as Iron Age hill-forts,[21] or even amphitheatres, and this despite the fact that walled towns must have been amongst the safest refuges, so long as the walls could be manned; the general manpower shortage in the Empire from the fourth century onwards; the rebellion of the foederati; the reluctance of Germanic peoples to settle in 'captured' towns of the Rhineland even as early as the late fourth century; the description of towns as 'tombs surrounded by nets';[22] and, if we exclude the early foederati, the same reluctance on the part of the first genuine Anglo-Saxon immigrants in Britain. Nearly forty years ago, Myres drew attention to the striking non-urban pattern of the settlement.[23] As he then observed, urban traditions in some other western provinces were often preserved by the Church, whereas in lowland Britain even the Church collapsed, requiring later missionaries from the west and from Rome to re-establish it. The saints and bishops who so often came to the aid of ailing communities during the break-up of Empire, such as St Germanus in Britain in the first half of the fifth century, and St Severinus in Pannonia shortly afterwards, seem to have been inactive in Britain. We have also to explain the flight of lowland Britons to Wales and possibly even to Brittany, and the migration of tribal peoples within the country. We must also account for the fact that the main periods of Anglo-Saxon aggression almost immediately followed our suggested two most serious epidemics in Britain, when confusion would have been at its worst. A Gallic Chronicle[24] records that in AD 441/2, a date which has to be only slightly revised to fit, Britain passed under control of the Saxons. The second Saxon advance began slowly, *c.* AD 550, and continued to *c.* AD 600, by which time most of the remaining areas of what is now England had been permanently taken. One association of disease and aggression might have been coincidence, but two seem to be stretching coincidence too far.

As we have already seen, warfare could to some extent explain all these events, but for the marked absence of evidence. Briton and Saxon were not unequally matched and in some ways the Briton had advantages in a straight fight. They had fortified sites unassailable by their enemy; they had cavalry. When organised and properly led they were more than a match for the Saxons, as happened at Mons Badonicus. For the British to be defeated they had to be more of a rabble than the Saxons. The only advantage which seems to lie on the Saxon side was

78   Worn floor in the forum piazza at Cirencester (*Cirencester Excavation Committee*)

continuous reinforcements of new migrants. Warfare and famine combined could take us further, but the famine would have had to have been both severe and protracted. Only a major epidemic, feared equally by friend and foe, would have had the all-embracing effects needed to account for the conditions described above. In such circumstances the one advantage allowed to the Saxons would have been crucial, for there were no reinforcements for the Britons.

If disease was indeed an important element in the rundown of Roman Britain, and if this disease originally reached the shores by ships trading from the Mediterranean, then it is likely to have broken out first in the towns, the centres to, and from, which traders travelled. Not all towns need have been affected simultaneously. Outbreaks may have been erratic in both time and place. But what better reason could we have for Saxons shunning towns if infected corpses were lying unburied in them, and what better description of them could there be than tombs surrounded by nets? Flight from war and famine are both possible, but the former would not be considered too serious a threat by townspeople behind the protection of their walls, while flight from the latter may have been useless if the famine was at all widespread. Flight from pestilence is altogether more likely and is surely the one readily acceptable reason why people should have left the safety of fortified towns and villages. The flight itself will have spread the disease. Its main effects were probably first felt in the west, in just those areas already burdened with refugees from the fighting in the east, where the greater weight of Anglo-Saxon immigrants had made themselves more immediately felt. It is possible, therefore, that the main Saxon advances came after epidemics had weakened British resistance and had opened voids in the settlement pattern, into which the Saxons pressed after mopping up small pockets of resistance. The victories recorded in the Anglo-Saxon Chronicle might best be seen in this light, if their propaganda value is discounted. They therefore succeeded to the province almost by default.

What of the towns themselves in this degenerative process? Their desertion, and the failure of the way of life which they supported may have been caused partly by famine and partly by disease, of which the latter was probably the most deadly, and by the disintegration of an economic system of which they had been a major prop. The more thickly an area was populated the more quickly an infection would spread, so that towns, if affected, would have suffered most in the earlier epidemics. On present evidence there is little to show the survival of their institutions or of a civilised way of life much beyond the middle of the fifth century; this strongly suggests that the pestilence of Hydatius was the root cause. If civilised life somehow survived in towns after this date, modern archaeologists have entirely failed to produce the evidence for it, presumably because, if it is there, it cannot yet be recognised for what it was.

We can briefly review the evidence. Verulamium provides the most vivid picture with its fifth-century masonry buildings and its working aqueduct, which might extend its period of survival to beyond AD 450; as yet, it is one of the few towns in lowland Britain where so late a date can be demonstrated. At

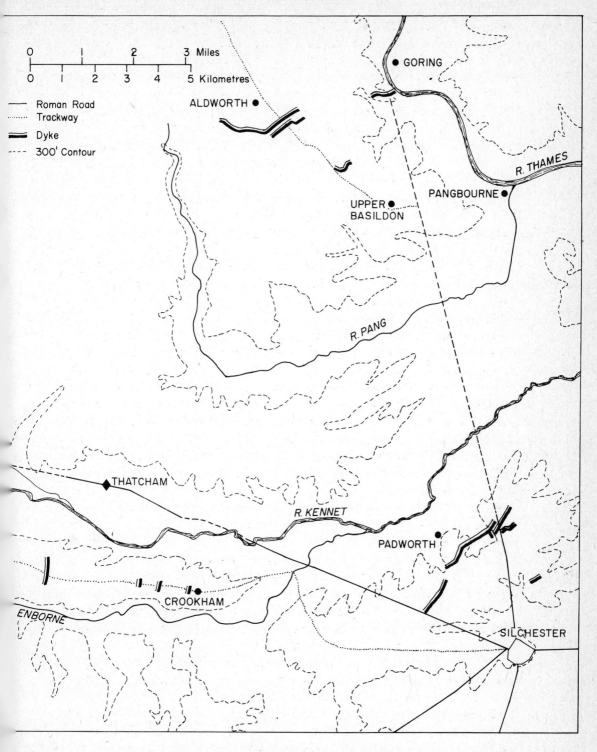

88. The Silchester dykes (*after B. H. St. J. O'Neil*)

Cirencester there is evidence that large crowds were using the forum until after AD 430 (pl. 78), and that enough traffic travelled the streets to turn the surfaces periodically into mud. Continued use was also anticipated as a new ditch was dug beside a main street to contain the mud, but was not needed (fig. 89). The end, when it came, must have been remarkably abrupt and unexpected. Moreover, it was in this ditch that unburied corpses had lain. It would be difficult here to extend the terminal date much beyond AD 450, if as far.

The bodies found near the baths at Wroxeter were originally taken as evidence for sack and slaughter, but this seems unlikely in the view of the absence of supporting material. Frere considered that the old man who crawled into a hypocaust with his life-savings, and with some companions, could not have been suffering from infection, and that all were suffocated. Yet there is no reason why they should have stifled; it is a slow death, and providing poisonous gases are not present, one which could easily have been avoided by crawling outside again, or at least to a point where fresh air would have been obtained. People are known to have lived for days buried in the ruins of bombed houses. A mass suicide by suffocation in a disused hypocaust is not entirely convincing, particularly since a hypocaust, by its construction, would have provided ample ventilation. But to people already victims of a disease, a hypocaust would provide an ideal refuge, safe from interference by bands of vigilantes or Welsh raiders. There was also a body found lying unburied beside a main street, as at Cirencester.

Caerwent also has its quota of possibly unburied bodies, plus a fire which burnt the basilica and some houses and shops. At Exeter, the baths was apparently disused at a comparatively early date, although there were still people around to dig pits through the floor of the palaestra. A breakdown of institutions is indicated if nothing more. It has been claimed that subsequent erosion of the hillside on which the town stood has removed the later levels. But standing walls, even of ruined buildings would have inhibited such erosion until the walls themselves were flattened. With the present work still continuing, however, it would be wise to suspend judgment until more areas have been sampled.

Silchester seems an obvious candidate for survival, and may, like Verulamium, have escaped the first epidemic as well as Saxon onslaught. The Ogham stone implies not only a later date for collapse but also the presence of Celtic foreigners. If, like Verulamium, Silchester retained its functions, perhaps until the sixth century (fig. 88), it was nevertheless a deserted town by the time the Saxon advance was resumed. No sign of violent destruction has been found at either place.

Winchester, Dorchester and Chichester are difficult cases, as information is still lacking, although there are indications of desertion at Winchester after *c.* 450. Apart from Gloucester and York, which may have been partly flooded, Lincoln, Colchester and London were near enough the east coast to have disappeared beneath the first wave of Anglo-Saxons, as also happened at Canterbury. Certainly by the time the second main advance was getting under way, Canterbury was already the centre of a firmly-established English kingdom. At Leicester,

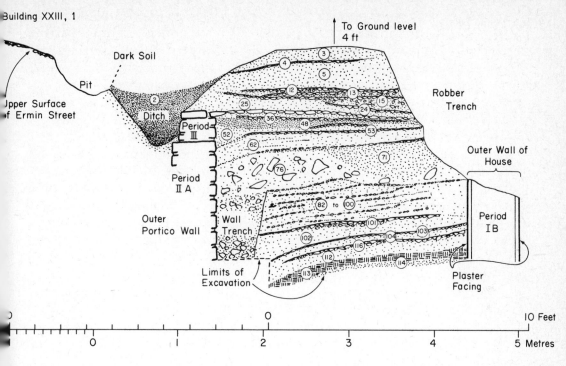

Building XXIII, 1

Dark Soil

Pit

Upper Surface of Ermin Street

Ditch

To Ground level 4 ft

Robber Trench

Period III

Period II A

Outer Portico Wall

Wall Trench

Limits of Excavation

Outer Wall of House

Period IB

Plaster Facing

89 A section through the fifth-century ditch beside Ermin Street, Cirencester

fire destroyed the centre of the town, but people continued, for a time, to live in the ruins of public buildings; one house, however, seems to have had a late mosaic inserted.

Only at Carlisle is there an indication of civilised life continuing into the later seventh century, if the still-operating fountain was the result of deliberate attempts at upkeep and not a naturally-continuing flow. Presumably by then the population had become partly anglicised. Charles Thomas has suggested that it remained the seat of one of the surviving north British dioceses.[25] If he is right, then Carlisle would be one of the few, if not the only, town in Britain where, as in Gaul, urban traditions were kept alive by the Church.

From the above discussion, it can be seen that the majority of towns had ceased to function by the middle of the fifth century, if not before. Isolated pockets of inhabitants seem to have survived in a few, but they cannot be taken as providing evidence for the continuity of urban life and institutions. Such towns as remained alive, perhaps with the exception of Carlisle, can hardly have survived beyond the middle of the sixth century, but whether we can then ascribe to them the functions of towns is doubtful.

Despite therefore the obvious continuity of settlement which took place in most, we must be forced to the conclusion that the towns themselves did not survive as institutions, and with them perished the culture that they had been foremost in sustaining. Town life had been reduced to life in towns and it cannot be emphasised enough that towns did not continue, and by no stretch of the imagination can they be thought to have done so. Any powers of recovery which they might have had, had also been effectively destroyed. Yet an oral tradition kept alive the names of many, so that they became transmuted into the new language. If many were also resurrected in the late Saxon and medieval periods, it was because their sites, by accident of geography, were as suitable for the economics of these periods as they had once been for Roman Britain.

This chapter has been to a great extent an exercise in probabilities. It is extremely doubtful if conclusive evidence of disease could ever be identified on an archaeological site, but attention might profitably be paid to waterlogged areas. Yet it seems wrong to ignore probabilities, just because the archaeological record is lacking, when we know that there were great epidemics in the ancient world, and, from more modern sources, what damage they could do.

Abbreviations
used in Notes

Abinnaeus Archive—H. I. Bell, V. Martin, E. G. Turner, D. van Berchem, *The Abinnaeus Archive.* (Oxford, 1962)
A.E.—*L'Année Épigraphique*
A.J.A.—*American Journal of Archaeology*
A.N.L.—*Archaeological News Letter*
Antiqs. J.—*Antiquaries Journal*
Arch.—*Archaeologia*
Arch. Camb.—*Archaeological Cambrensis*
Arch. Cant.—*Archaeologia Cantiana*
Arch. J.—*Archaeological Journal*
Atkinson (1942)—D. Atkinson, *Report on the Excavations at Wroxeter in the County of Salop, 1923-7.* (Oxford, 1942, reprinted 1970)

B.B.C.S.—*Bulletin of the Board of Celtic Studies*
B.M.—The British Museum
Bonner Jahrb.—*Bonner Jahrbücher*
Boon (1957)—G. C. Boon, *Roman Silchester.* (London, 1957). Extensively revised 1974
Bull. Inst. Arch.—*Bulletin of the Institute of Archaeology,* London
Bushe-Fox (1913)—J. P. Bushe-Fox, *Excavations on the site of the Roman Town at Wroxeter, Shropshire, in 1912.* (Oxford, 1913)
Bushe-Fox (1914)—J. P. Bushe-Fox, *Second Report on the Excavations on the Site of the Roman Town at Wroxeter, Shropshire, 1913.* (Oxford, 1914)
Bushe-Fox (1916)—J. P. Bushe-Fox, *Third Report on the Excavations on the Site of the Roman Town at Wroxeter, Shropshire, 1914.* (Oxford, 1916)
Butler (1971)—(ed.) R. M. Butler, *Soldier and Civilian in Roman Yorkshire.* (Leicester, 1971)

Carm. Ant.—*Carmarthenshire Antiquary*
Carnuntina (1956)—(ed.) E. Swoboda, *Carnuntina*
Chron. Min.—Th. Mommsen, *Chronica Minora saec.* (MGH. Auctores Antiquissimi, Berlin 1892-8)
C.I.L.—*Corpus Inscriptionum Latinarum*

Civitas Capitals of Roman Britain—(ed.) J. S. Wacher, *Civitas Capitals of Roman Britain.* (Leicester, 1966)
Clifford (1961)—E. M. Clifford, *Bagendon, a Belgic Oppidum.* (Cambridge, 1961)
Cod. Theod.—*Codex Theodosianus*
Collingwood & Myres (1937)—R. G. Collingwood and J. N. L. Myres, *Roman Britain and the English Settlements.* (Oxford, 1937)
Corder (1934)—P. Corder, *Excavations at the Roman Fort at Brough-on-Humber.* (Hull, 1934)
Corder (1935)—P. Corder, *Excavations at the Roman Fort at Brough, E. Yorkshire, 1934.* (Hull, 1935)
Corder and Romans (1936)—P. Corder and T. Romans, *Excavations at the Roman Town at Brough, E. Yorkshire, 1935.* (Hull, 1936)
Corder and Romans (1937)—P. Corder and T. Romans, *Excavations at the Roman Town at Brough, E. Yorkshire, 1936.* (Hull, 1937)
Corder and Romans (1938)—P. Corder and T. Romans, *Excavations at the Roman Town at Brough-Petuaria, 1937.* (Hull, 1938)
Cunliffe (1964)—B. Cunliffe, *Winchester Excavations, 1949-60.* (Winchester, 1964)
Cunliffe (1968)—(ed.) B. Cunliffe, *Fifth Report on the Excavations of the Roman Fort at Richborough, Kent.* (Oxford, 1968)
Cunliffe (1971)—B. Cunliffe, *Excavations at Fishbourne, 1961-9.* (Leeds, 1971)
C.W.—*Transactions of the Cumberland and Westmorland Archaeological Society*

Down and Rule (1971)—A. Down and M. Rule, *Chichester Excavations I.* (Chichester Civic Society, 1971)
Dudley and Webster (1962)—D. R. Dudley and G. Webster, *The Rebellion of Boudicca.* (London, 1962)
Dudley and Webster (1965)—D. R. Dudley and G. Webster, *The Roman Conquest of Britain, A.D. 43-57.* (London, 1965)

Ecroyd Smith (1852)—H. Ecroyd Smith, *Reliquiae Isurianae.* (1852)
E.E.—*Ephemeris Epigraphica*
E.H.R.—*English Historical Review*

Foster and Daniel (1963)—(ed.) I. Ll. Foster and G. Daniel, *Prehistoric and Early Wales.* (London, 1963)
Fox (1952)—Aileen Fox, *Roman Exeter.* (Manchester, 1952)
Fox (1964)—Aileen Fox, *South-West England.* (London, 1964)
Fox (1973)—Aileen Fox, *Exeter in Roman Times.* (Exeter, 2nd ed. 1973)
Frere (1962)—S. S. Frere, *Roman Canterbury.* (Canterbury, 1962)
Frere (1967)—S. S. Frere, *Britannia.* (London, 1967)
Frere (1971)—S. S. Frere, *Verulamium Excavations I.* (Oxford, 1971)

Germ. Romana—*Germania Romana*
Grimes (1968)—W. F. Grimes, *The Excavation of Roman and Medieval London.* (London, 1968)

Hawkes and Hull (1947)—C. F. C. Hawkes and M. R. Hull, *Camulodunum.* (Oxford, 1947)
Herts. Arch.—*Hertfordshire Archaeology*
Hill and Jesson (1971)—(ed.) D. Hill and M. Jesson, *The Iron Age and its Hill Forts.* (Southampton, 1971)
Hull (1958)—M. R. Hull, *Roman Colchester.* (Oxford, 1958)

I.L.S.—H. Dessau, *Inscriptiones Latinae Selectae*
It. Ant.—*Itineraria Antonini Augusti*

Jarrett and Dobson (1966)—(ed.) M. G. Jarrett and B. Dobson, *Britain and Rome.* (Kendal, 1966)
J.B.A.A.—*Journal of the British Archaeological Association*
J.R.I.C.—*Journal of the Royal Institution of Cornwall*
J.R.S.—*Journal of Roman Studies*

Kenyon (1948)—K. M. Kenyon, *Excavations at the Jewry Wall Site, Leicester.* (Oxford, 1948)

Lewis (1965)—M. J. T. Lewis, *Temples in Roman Britain.* (Cambridge, 1965)
Lincs. Hist. & Arch.—*Lincolnshire History and Archaeology*
L.M.C.—*London Museum Catalogue*

Med. Arch.—*Medieval Archaeology*
Merrifield (1965)—R. Merrifield, *The Roman City of London.* (London, 1965)
Merrifield (1969)—R. Merrifield, *Roman London.* (London, 1969)

Mon. Antiq.—*Monmouthshire Antiquary*
Myres (1969)—J. N. L. Myres, *Anglo-Saxon Pottery and the Settlement of England.* (Oxford, 1969)

Nash-Williams (Jarrett, 1969)—V. E. Nash-Williams, *The Roman Frontier in Wales.* (2nd edition: M. G. Jarrett, Cardiff, 1969)
Norfolk Arch.—*Norfolk Archaeology*
Northern Hist.—*Northern History*
Not. Dig.—*Notitia Dignitatum* (ed. O. Seeck)
Num. Chron.—*Numismatic Chronicle*

Oxon.—*Oxoniensia*

P.B.S.R.—*Papers of the British School of Rome*
P.D.A.S.—*Proceedings of the Devon Archaeological Society*
P.D.A.E.S.—*Proceedings of the Devon Archaeological Exploration Society*
P.D.N.H.S.—*Proceedings of the Dorset Natural History and Archaeological Society*
P. Hants. Field Club—*Proceedings of the Hampshire Field Club*
Prosopog. Imp. Rom.—*Prosopographia Imperii Romani*
P.S.A.—*Proceedings of the Society of Antiquaries of London*
P.S.A.N.H.S.—*Proceedings of the Somerset Archaeological and Natural History Society*

R.A.C.—*Rivista di archeologia cristiana*
R.C.A.H.M.—Royal Commission on Ancient and Historical Monuments (Wales)
R.C.H.M.—Royal Commission on Historical Monuments (England)
R.C.H.M. (1962)—Royal Commission on Historical Monuments, *Eburacum.* (London, 1962)
R.C.H.M. (1970)—Royal Commission on Historical Monuments, *Dorset* II. *South-east.* Part 3. (London, 1970)
Rev. Arch.—*Revue Archéologique*
R.G.K.—*Bericht der Römisch-Germanischen Kommission*
R.I.B.—R. G. Collingwood and R. P. Wright, *The Roman Inscriptions of Britain,* I. (Oxford, 1965)
Richmond (1963)—I. A. Richmond, *Roman Britain.* (London, 1963)
Richmond (1968)—I. A. Richmond, *Hod Hill,* II. (London, 1968)
Rivet (1964)—A. L. F. Rivet, *Town and Country in Roman Britain.* (London, 1964)
Rivet (1969)—(ed.) A.L.F. Rivet, *The Roman Villa in Britain.* (London, 1969)

Salway (1965)—P. Salway, *The Frontier People of Roman Britain.* (Cambridge, 1965)
S.H.A.—*Scriptores Historiae Augustae*

Stern (1965)—H. Stern (ed.), *La Mosaique Gréco-Romaine*. (Paris, 1965)

Sussex A.C.—*Sussex Archaeological Collections*

Toynbee (1962)—J. M. C. Toynbee, *Art in Roman Britain*. (London, 1962)

T.B.A.S.—*Transactions of the Birmingham Archaeological Society*

T.B.G.A.S.—*Transactions of the Bristol and Gloucestershire Archaeological Society*

T.E.A.S.—*Transactions of the Essex Archaeological Society*

T.L.A.S.—*Transactions of the Leicestershire Archaeological and Historical Society*

T.L.M.A.S.—*Transactions of the London and Middlesex Archaeological Society*

T.Shrop.A.S.—*Transactions of the Shropshire Archaeological Society*

T. St Albans Architect. & Arch. Soc.—*Transactions of the St Albans Architectural and Archaeological Society*

V.C.H.—Victoria County History

Wacher (1969)—J. S. Wacher, *Excavations at Brough-on-Humber, 1958–61*. (Leeds, 1969)

Wacher (1971)—J. S. Wacher, *Corinium*. (London, 1971)

Wheeler (1936)—R. E. M. Wheeler and T. V. Wheeler, *Verulamium, A Belgic and two Roman Cities*. (Oxford, 1936)

Wheeler (1943)—R. E. M. Wheeler, *Maiden Castle, Dorset*. (Oxford, 1943)

Wheeler (1954)—R. E. M. Wheeler, *The Stanwick Fortifications*. (Oxford, 1954)

Whitwell (1970)—J. B. Whitwell, *Roman Lincolnshire*. (Lincoln, 1970)

Y.A.J.—*Yorkshire Archaeological Journal*

Notes

Introduction (pages 13–15)

1. *Man* viNS, no. 3, 391; *Area* iv, no. 4, 223; D.L. Clarke (ed.) *Models in Archaeology* (1972), 887
2. For citizenship, see A. N. Sherwin-White, *The Roman Citizenship* (1972)

Chapter 1 (pages 17–35)

1. e.g. at Carnuntum, Aquincum, Vetera and Moguntiacum
2. *de Caes.* 20, 27. J. C. Mann and M. G. Jarrett accept the description: *J.R.S.* lvii, 63
3. Tacitus, *Annales* xiv, 3: *eadem clades municipio Verulamio fuit*
4. *Bull. Inst. Arch.* 4, 80
5. Frere (1967), 204
6. *ibid.* p. 202. But a Claudian forum might imply no more than the existence of a civitas capital (see p. 26). Early masonry structures were found below the Vespasianic forum both by Wheeler and Page
7. Rivet (1964), 65
8. But see J. E. Bogaers in *J.R.S.* lvii, 233, where he doubts the municipal status of Verulamium
9. (ed.) J. S. Wacher, *Civitas Capitals of Roman Britain* (1966), 105
10. Frere (1967), 258
11. *Arch.* lxix, pl. xi, no. 43
12. *T. St Albans Architect. & Arch. Soc.* (1961). 21
13. *Arch J.* lxxv, 44, no. 29
14. *P.D.N.H.S.* xxi, 162; xxii, p. xxviii
15. It has been suggested that the *canabae* at Chester (E. Birley, *Roman Britain and the Roman Army*, 64) and the civitas capital at Silchester (G. C. Boon, *Roman Silchester*, 76) were promoted to *municipia*
16. J. S. Wacher in Butler (1971), 165; M. Todd in *Britannia* i, 115

17. I. A. Richmond (ed.) P. Salway, *Roman Archaeology and Art* (1969), 150–65. See also S. J. Hallam in *Antiqs. J.* xliv, 19
18. Tacitus, *Agricola* xxi.1; *Namque ut homines dispersi ac rudes eoque in bella faciles quieti et otio per voluptates adsuescerent, hortari privatim, adiuvare publice, ut templa fora domos extruerent, laudando promptos, castigando segnes: ita honoris aemulatio pro necessitate erat*
    Digest I.18.7. (Ulpian): *Praeses provinciae inspectis aedificiis dominos eorum causa cognita reficere ea compellat et adversus detractantem competenti remedio deformitati auxilium ferat*
19. There are apparently some exceptions, e.g. Catterick
20. See C. E. Stevens in *E.H.R.* lii, 198; and also p. 196 below
21. *J.R.S.* lv, 224 (with references)
22. *J.R.S.* lvi, 223. A *civitas Coriosolitum* is known in *Gallia Lugdunensis*
23. *P.S.A.N.H.S.* xcvi, 188
24. As attested by the Caerwent inscription: *R.I.B.* 311
25. Mommsen, *Staatsretht,*[3] III, 138 and 716. A. H. M. Jones, *Studies in Roman Government and Law* (1960), 130; Frere (1967), 204; *J.R.S.* lix, 249
26. Frere, *loc. cit.*
27. Tacitus, *Annales* xiv, 31. *Quippe in coloniam Camulodunum pellebant domibus, exturbabant agris, 'captivos, servos' appellando*
28. No certain date can be ascribed to the Dover and Lympne roads, but they would most likely belong to an early period
29. Of the occasions in Britain when the presence of a *praefectus civitatis* might be implied, the most likely instance would surely have been among the Iceni in the aftermath of the Boudiccan rebellion; few of the tribal aristocracy can have survived it, so creating,

presumably, an acute shortage of candidates for local government posts

30. E. Birley in *Prosopogr. Imp. Rom.* iv (1966), 3, and G. C. Boon in *Arch.* cii, 38
31. *Arch.* cii, 46
32. *Antiqs. J.* xlviii, 255; l, 279. Some doubt has now been cast on this assumption (p. 277)
33. *P.D.A.S.* xxxvi, 3; Fox (1973), 6
34. *Arch. J.* cxxxii, 203; *Antiqs. J.* xlv, 100
35. E. Blank, *Ratae Coritanorum* (1971), 9
36. *T.Shrop.A.S.* lvii, 112
37. *Arch. J.* cxv, 79
38. E. M. Clifford, *Bagendon: A Belgic Oppidum* (1961), *passim*
39. The name, taken from his coins, is not known in full. This account is only one interpretation; another is considered below (p. 289)
40. *Antiqs. J.* xlii, 11; xliv, 11
41. *op. cit.* 20. Mrs Clifford gave AD 50–60 as the terminal date for Bagendon, but analogies between the Bagendon pottery and the more recently discovered, more closely dated, groups from Cirencester would suggest that an advance of about a decade in the date is desirable
42. At a later date Ilchester, the Romano-British derivative of Ham Hill, may have become a centre for one of the parts of the Durotriges, after their division into two. *Vindocladia* (Shapwick) near Badbury never developed to any great extent. See also Richmond (1968), 2
43. E. Blank, *Ratae Coritanorum* (1971), 12
44. *Britannia* iv, 36
45. *C.I.L.* xvi, 160
46. Frere (1967), 117, n. 2
47. *R.I.B.* 288
48. V. E. Nash-Williams in *Carnuntina* (ed. E. Swoboda), 108; *Arch.* lxxx, 274
49. B. R. Hartley in (ed.) J. S. Wacher, *Civitas Capitals of Roman Britain* (1966), 56. Neither is the town mentioned by Ptolemy who was using sources which were mainly Flavian in date
50. *R.I.B.* 397, dated AD 103–11
51. Wacher (1969), 23; J. S. Wacher in Butler (1971), 166
52. *R.I.B.* 707, suggesting *c(ivitas)* [*P(arisorum)*]. Some doubt has however been cast on this reading, and it has been suggested that the letter C is no more than part of the *pelta* decoration. An earlier date of 139 has also been suggested by E. Birley
53. *Northern Hist.* i, 15
54. *J.R.S.* li, 127; *B.B.C.S.* xx, 208; *Carm. Ant.* v, 2; vi, 4

Chapter 2 (pages 36–78)

1. Suetonius, *Vespasian* 4
2. Tacitus, *Annales* xiv, 32, refers to a theatre, a town-hall, and a statue of Victory, in addition to the temple of Claudius, in the first colonia. That he also refers to the lack of defences is often taken to mean that the provincial administration was careless of the colonists' safety. But it should be remembered that few towns in the Empire were fortified at this time; static defences were not considered necessary and were not in keeping with the 'offensive' military thinking, then in vogue, which relied on attack being the best form of defence. Tacitus is most likely being wise after the event
3. Tacitus, *Annales* xiv, 31. *ad hoc templum divo Claudio constitutum quasi arx aeternae dominationis aspiciebatur, delectique sacerdotes specie religionis omnis fortunas effundebant*
4. *R.I.B.* 270–1, referring to the *vicus Mercurensium* and probably the *vicus Apollinensium*
5. The dogma that so-called charters were granted by the central government has recently been questioned by M. W. Frederiksen (*J.R.S.* lv, 183–98), who concludes that they were more often than not manufactured locally by free adaptation of various Roman laws
6. *Decuriones* are attested from Gloucester (*R.I.B.* 161), Lincoln (*R.I.B.* 250) and York (*R.I.B.* 674)
7. But a member who lost his fortune was not made to resign: *Digest* (Ulpian) L.4, 6; (Hermogenianus) L.2, 8. See also p. 172 for a decurion of York, who was only 29 when he died
8. *Lex Ursonensis* 91 (*I.L.S.* 6087)
9. Pliny, *Epis.* iv, 22
10. *Lex Ursonensis* 105 (*I.L.S.* 6087)
11. *ibid.* 94
12. *Seviri augustales* are attested at York and Lincoln: *J.R.S.* xi, 102, referring to M. Aurelius Lunaris, *sevir* of both coloniae; *R.I.B.* 678 referring to M. Verecundius Diogenes, *sevir* of York
13. *R.I.B.* 707. M. Ulpius Ianuarius, aedile of the *vicus Petuariensis* donated a stage to the local theatre. See also *Lex Ursonensis* 70–1 (*I.L.S.* 6087)
14. *Arch. J.* ciii, 61
15. Haverfield, *E.H.R.* xxxiii, 289; Stevens, unpublished lecture to the Society of Antiquaries. But see p. 117 below
16. A. Piganiol, *Les Documents Cadastraux de la Colonie Romaine d'Orange* (XVI Supplement

to *Gallia*, 1962)

17. Unless the *pagi* were formed initially from internal divisions within the Iron Age tribes, in which case a number can be suggested for the Brigantes

18. Mann has argued that a civitas capital could not be subdivided into intramural *vici* if it only ranked as a *vicus* itself. (ed. Jarrett and Dobson, *Britain and Rome* (1965), 111). Nevertheless constituent *vici* are known in one civitas capital (Metz, *I.L.S.* 4818) and possibly in another (Nantes, *I.L.S.* 7051), and there is little reason to suppose that either of these towns ranked higher than *vici* (Frere: *Antiquity* xxxv, 33). See also Bogaers: *J.R.S.* lvii, 232

19. See n. 13 above. Another inscription attesting an *aedilis* in a civitas capital comes from Sens (*Agedincum*): *I.L.S.* 7049

20. *R.I.B.* 311

21. *R.I.B.* 933. The tombstone is now lost

22. *Digest* (Ulpian) L.9. 4

23. W. Meyers, *L'Administration de la Province Romaine de Belgique* (1964), 115–24

24. *Lex Malacitana* 51 (*I.L.S.* 6089)

25. Frere (1967), 258

26. Atkinson (1942), 101

27. Frere (1967), 304

28. F. Haverfield, *The Romanisation of Roman Britain* (1915), 18; K. Jackson, *Language and History in Early Britain* (1953), 97; I. A. Richmond in *Civitas Capitals of Roman Britain* (1966), 19; S. S. Frere, *Britannia* (1967), 311. See also J. C. Mann in *Britannia* ii, 218

29. *J.R.S.* liv, 182: *ac quis te cinae(de) . . . ; equa ella; culo*

30. Richmond (1963), 105

31. *Antiqs. J.* xlii, 12 (fig. 5)

32. *Antiqs. J.* xviii, 68

33. J. P. Hanson, *Roman Theater-Temples* (1959)

34. J. M. C. Toynbee, *Art in Britain under the Romans* (1964), 359

35. R. E. M. Wheeler, *Roman Art and Architecture* (1964), pl. 190

36. Frere (1967), 261 quoting a capacity of about 2700 seats in the amphitheatre at Silchester

37. Toynbee (1962), 202 and pl. 227

38. *ibid.* 160 and pl. 88; also *Arch. J.* ciii, 54

39. Chedworth: *R.I.B.* 127; York: *R.C.H.M.* (1962), 135

40. Such as those overturned during the second-century fire in the forum at Wroxeter. Atkinson (1942), 127

41. There is an amusing account, in L. Apuleius, *Metamorphoses* of the intervention by a magistrate, after goods had been bought, by which the purchaser lost both goods and money

42. *Arch.* xc, 85

43. *Antiqs. J.* xlii, 8

44. Specialist commodity markets were not unknown in the Empire, and presumably were a development of the system whereby shopkeepers with a common trade often occupied the same street or quarter of a town. See H. J. Loane, *Industry and Commerce of the City of Rome* (John Hopkins University Studies in Historical and Political Science, LVI, no. 2)

45. *J.R.S.* xlix, 113

46. *Antiqs. J.* xlii, 6, 10, 12. In a number of towns regulations existed governing the demolition of buildings. It would seem that this could be done only if the owner guaranteed reconstruction; failing which a penalty equal to the value of the building had to be paid: *Lex Ursonensis* 75 (*I.L.S.* 6087); *Lex Tarentina* 4 (*I.L.S.* 6086); *Lex Malacitana* 62 (*I.L.S.* 6089). To what extent similar laws were made governing buildings in Britain is not known, but they might be suspected

47. *Antiquity* xxxviii, 105

48. *R.I.B.* 712. Since the evidence for shops is common to both towns and villages, it will be drawn from sources other than towns when necessary, to create a more intelligible picture

49. (ed.) J. S. Wacher, *Civitas Capitals of Roman Britain* (1966), 76

50. *ibid.*

51. *R.I.B.* 194, 213, 274

52. *Cod. Theod.* ix.21.6; extracting silver from coinage was punishable by death

53. *R.I.B.* 105, 151

54. *R.I.B.* 132, 149

55. Tacitus, *Annales* xiv, 38

56. Tacitus, *Agricola* xix, 4. Reduction of taxes may have been made possible by increased production, which must have been beginning to have an effect by Agricola's time

57. Rivet (1969), 197

58. Adam Smith, *The Wealth of Nations* (1775)

59. Collingwood & Myres (1937), 198

60. It should be stressed that the views put forward are only those obtaining at present. Great care must be exercised in consulting works on town fortifications as so many of the suggestions have been made only as working hypotheses, each in turn being replaced by another as it became outdated. Yet even in 1968, a book could still be published quoting Corder's theory of town-wall construction (*Arch. J.* cxii, 20); excellent though that paper was when first published in 1956, it has now

been left far behind by more up-to-date evidence. Probably the best current review of this complex subject is to be found in Frere (1967), 248–57, although even here some additions and corrections are required owing to more recent discoveries

61. This was certainly the case by the end of the second century (*Digest* I, 8, 9, 4; L, 10, 6) although we cannot be certain that the same rules applied in the first century

62. Ammianus Marcellinus, xxxvii, 8

63. Britain is not, however, the only province where such irregularity occurs. At Andernach on the Rhine there are no bastions on the river frontage, and at Salona in Dalmatia there is a strong concentration of bastions on the north walls, but few elsewhere

64. By the mid-fourth century it was quite normal for troops to be billeted in towns, as regulations laid down in *Cod. Theod.* vii, 8–11 show

65. S. S. Frere in (ed. J. S. Wacher) *Civitas Capitals of Roman Britain* (1966), 100

Chapter 3 (pages 79–103)

1. *R.I.B.* 12
2. *J.R.S.* lvi, 210; Merrifield (1969), 81
3. Tacitus, *Annales* xiv, 33
4. *Arch. J.* ciii, 63
5. Frere (1967), 324
6. Richmond (1963), 187
7. *R.I.B.* 5
8. *R.I.B.* 21
9. cf. the fourth-century Ptolemais inscription: R. G. Goodchild in *Quaderni di Archaeologia della Libia*, iv, 83. I am grateful to Miss Reynolds for this reference
10. Grimes (1968), 38. But see also Merrifield (1969), 110 for a revised date
11. B.M. *Guide to the Antiquities of Roman Britain* (1958), 48
12. *R.I.B.* 19
13. *J.R.S.* lvii, 63
14. *ibid.* 62
15. *R.I.B.* 17. There is also a tombstone from York showing a scroll-carrying centurion: R.C.H.M. (1962), 128, no. 95
16. For these dispositions see *J.R.S.* lvii, 61–4
17. *C.I.L.* xiii, 3162. The inscription refers to T. Sumnius Sollemnus who assisted the governor, Ti. Claudius Paulinus, on the staff of Legio VI Victrix. Strictly therefore this inscription does not help in the identification of the capital of Britannia Inferior, although in practise the governor was probably stationed at York. I am grateful to Professor

Frere for this comment. See also *Arch. Ael.*[4] xi, 130–3 for the boundaries of these new provinces

18. References to a *palatium* and *domus Palatina* occur in S.H.A. *Severus*, 22, 7
19. R.C.H.M. (1962), 55
20. *Not. Dig. occ.* xxiii, 10
21. *op. cit.* xi, 37
22. *op. cit.* xi, 20; xii, 15
23. *Antiquity* xxxv, 316
24. *Eborius episcopus de civitate Eboracensi provincia Britannia.*
    Restitutus episcopus de civitate Londiniensi provincia superscripta.
    Adelphius episcopus de civitate colonia Londiniensium
    Exinde Sacerdos presbyter, Arminius diaconus.
    The text is corrupt and *Lindensium* should probably be read for *Londiniensium* in lines 5–6
25. *R.I.B.* 103
26. *Epigraphische Studien* iv, 85
27. Admittedly though, at least one veteran of Legio VI, G. Julius Calenus, and another of Legio XIV, are known from Lincoln, although this is hardly sufficient to suggest a substantial connexion between those legions and the colonia
28. *Antiquity* xxxv, 320

LONDON

29. Cunliffe (1968), 234. The depot at Richborough may have been chiefly concerned with the collection and forwarding of the annona
30. Unless it is represented by the possible pre-Boudiccan street known below Lombard Street: Merrifield (1965), 118
31. *Arch. J.* cxv, 84
32. *Bull. Inst. Arch.* iv, 63
33. Merrifield (1965), 39. His alternative suggestion envisages this planned area as being part of the military installations
34. *Annales* xiv, 33
35. Most other buildings in London at this time were built with timber-frames and wattle and daub walls
36. *Current Archaeology* ii, 220
37. *Antiqs. J.* xxv, 48–52. Reproduced in Merrifield (1965), 90 with additions
38. See p. 427, n. 2
39. A number of provincial capitals were not promoted, and until positive evidence is forthcoming for London, it is unwise to pursue the matter further
40. Grimes (1968), 15–40
41. Frere (1967), 195

42. Grimes (1968), 50
43. *J.R.S.* lvii, 197; Merrifield (1969), 119; *T.L.M.A.S.* xxii, 5
44. Merrifield (1969), 119
45. The wall of London may not be as homogeneous as is often thought; its width varies from 7ft (2·1m) to about 9ft (2·7m)
46. Grimes (1968), 56; Merrifield (1969), 131; Marsden in *T.L.M.A.S.* xxi, 153
47. Grimes (1968), 63
48. J. S. Wacher, *Excavations at Brough-on-Humber, 1958–61* (1969), 54, 81. P. Salway et al. *The Fenland in Roman Times* (1970), *passim*; B. Cunliffe in (ed. A. C. Thomas) *Rural Settlement in Roman Britain* (1966), 72. H. Ramm in (ed. R. M. Butler) *Soldier and Civilian in Roman Yorkshire* (1971), 181
49. For Brough see J. S. Wacher, *op. cit.* 219; for London see Grimes (1968), 62 and Merrifield (1965), 269
50. *Descriptio Nobilissimae Civitatis Londiniae*
51. *Antiqs. J.* xlii, 38
52. Merrifield (1969), 24. Recent work on the Southwark side of the river sectioned a major street, 30ft wide, and many times resurfaced. If this is the main road leading to the bridge, however, it would imply a position for the latter which is upstream from the modern bridge, and contrary therefore to Merrifield's suggestion. *Britannia* i, 292
53. Grimes (1968), 71
54. Merrifield (1969), 127; Grimes (1968), 77
55. *J.R.S.* lix, 213
56. *Antiqs. J.* xlix, 128
57. Over a dozen fragments dating from the second and third centuries have been found in two seasons at Wanborough. Found in a medieval context there would probably be no hesitation in ascribing them to this later period
58. Down and Rule (1971), 77
59. But see p. 94 above for an alternative suggestion
60. Merrifield (1965), 146
61. Merrifield (1965), 239 (no. 170) gives N.E.–S.W., which he informs me is incorrect
62. *R.I.B.* 2
63. *L.M.C.* 51
64. Grimes (1968), chapt. IV
65. *J.R.S.* lix, 224
66. *Britannia* i, 292

Chapter 4 (pages 104–177)

1. *Arch. J.* ciii, 57–84
2. *V.C.H. Essex* iii (1963), 1–23
3. R.C.H.M. (1962), p. xxxv

COLCHESTER

4. *T.E.A.S.*[3] ii, 137; iii, 2
5. *Arch. J.* cxxiii, 29 and *T.E.A.S.*[3] iii, 2
6. Hull (1958), 160, 189. See also *T.E.A.S.* xxv, 301 for plans of buildings recently excavated in Insulae 29 and 30
7. *V.C.H. Essex* iii, 9
8. *Arch. J.* cxxiii, 39
9. Most conveniently seen in J. J. Wilkes, *Dalmatia*, 369
10. *T.E.A.S.* xxv, plan facing 302
11. *T.E.A.S.* xxv, 15
12. Hull (1958), 160 ff
13. Frere (1967), 323
14. *Britannia* iii, 164 ff
15. Tacitus, *Annales* xiv, 32
16. *I.L.S.* 2740
17. *Britannia* ii, 27
18. *T.E.A.S.*[3] iii, 43
19. Tacitus, *Annales* xiv, 31
20. Hull (1958), 62
21. *T.E.A.S.*[3] iii, 68
22. *T.E.A.S.* xv, 179; Hull (1958), 16
23. This explanation is virtually a return to the hypothesis originally put forward by Sir Mortimer Wheeler: R.C.H.M. *Essex*, iii, 21
24. *V.C.H. Essex*, iii, 93, 96
25. *Arch. J.* ciii, 63
26. *Arch. J.* cxiii, 40
27. Hull (1958), 31
28. *R.I.B.* 194
29. *Lex Ursonensis* 76 (*I.L.S.* 6087)
30. *V.C.H. Essex* iii, 11
31. *ibid.* 22
32. *Britannia* ii, 272
33. Hawkes and Hull (1947), 56
34. Information from Mrs Niblett
35. *V.C.H. Essex* iii, 113
36. Hull (1963), 91
37. Hull (1963), 43
38. *R.I.B.* 200–1
39. *R.I.B.* 203
40. *R.I.B.* 202
41. Toynbee (1962), 186, pl. 172
42. *Geog.* ii, 3, 22
43. *E.H.R.* lii, 197
44. *V.C.H. Essex* iii, 16
45. In (ed.) J. S. Wacher, *Civitas Capitals of Roman Britain* (1966), 74

LINCOLN

46. *C.I.L.* xiii, 6679
47. As Richmond does in *Arch. J.* ciii, 29
48. If the name had been *Flavia Lindensium* it would surely have survived, and equally if founded under Nerva, like Glevum it would

have kept its *Nervia*. At *Sala* (Asia), imperial coins were first minted under Domitian when the title *Domitianopolis* was adopted, but later dropped, presumably for the same reason. B. V. Head, *Historia Numorum* (1911), 656

49. *R.I.B.* 249 (Leg. XIV Gemina); 252 (Leg. VI Victrix)
50. e.g. Collingwood and Myres (1937), 188
51. *Arch. J.* cxvii, 54. However, only one possible town has so far been identified
52. Whitwell (1970), 20
53. Contemporary descriptions of the gates are conveniently collected in Richmond's article in *Arch. J.* ciii, 29–35. The plans should, however, be ignored as they do not include the most up to date discoveries and are therefore erroneous
54. *ibid.* 32
55. Whitwell (1970), 29
56. R. G. Collingwood and I. A. Richmond, *Archaeology of Roman Britain* (1969), 101. The grounds on which this suggestion is made are not discussed
57. This analysis of the gates depends on the explanations put forward by Whitwell (1970), 28–30
58. Based on observations by F. H. Thompson and J. B. Whitwell: *Arch.* civ, 201
59. *Arch. J.* ciii, 31. An internal diameter of only 9ft (2·7m) is small by the standards of other towns, and only at Chichester are they as small. There, however, the bastions were of a peculiar horseshoe shape. Whitwell (1970), 28 quotes 'nine feet in diameter', which would be impossibly small
60. *Arch. J.* cxii, 20–42
61. *Arch. J.* civ, 203
62. They are summarised in detail by Richmond: *Arch. J.* ciii, 38
63. *Arch. J.* cxi, 106 and repeated by Whitwell (1970), 32
64. The aqueduct at Fréjus branched before reaching the town, one half going to the port.
65. *Arch.* lv, 232
66. I am grateful to Mr A. G. Corbett, Dept. of Engineering, Leicester University for providing these figures
67. W. Haberey, *Die Römischen Wasserleitungen nach Köln* (1971), 29
68. Compare Nîmes 31 miles (50km); Fréjus 25 miles (40km); Lyons (from Mt. Pilate) 46½ miles (75km); Metz 13½ miles (22km); Cologne 48 miles (77km). The late Sir Ian Richmond, shortly before his death, in discussion with the writer, considered this the most likely solution to the problem
69. Miss Colyer, who directed the main part of the excavations on this sector, has asked me to point out that the description of the defences provided here is only tentative and may require modification after all the material has been examined in detail
70. The nearest analogies to gates of this plan in Britain are provided by the west gate of the Saxon Shore fort at Richborough and the north gate at Great Chesterford. In Germany, Andernach has two gates of similar plan
71. e.g. Antioch (Pisidia), Emporiae (Tarraconensis)
72. *R.I.B.* 270
73. *R.I.B.* 271
74. *Arch. J.* ciii, 42
75. Whitwell (1970), 113
76. *R.I.B.* 274
77. *J.R.S.* xi, 102. He was also *sevir* at York
78. Lewis (1965), 71
79. *ibid*
80. *J.R.S.* lii, 192, no. 8
81. See p. 84 above
82. *R.I.B.* 250; 252; 249; 266; 251; 262; 263
83. *Arch. J.* ciii, 52
84. *R.I.B.* 247
85. *R.I.B.* 2241. Milestones were sometimes, but not always, measured from the centre of the territory of the authority responsible for their erection
86. *R.I.B.* 2240
87. Whitwell (1970), 39
88. *R.I.B.* 2242
89. P. Salway *et al.* in (ed. C. W. Phillips) *The Fenland in Roman Times* (1970), 9–14, but see a contradiction by S. J. Hallam on p. 74 where a first-century date is attributed to it. See also Whitwell (1970), 94, quoting B. R. Hartley
90. See p. 134 above. A number of tiles stamped with the mark of Legio V have been found at Lincoln. This legion occupied the fortress at Xantern until AD 69. Tiles may, therefore, have reached Lincoln as ballast in ships, or perhaps as the export of a surplus. *Lincs. Hist. & Arch.* i, 29
91. Lincoln compared with York: Whitwell (1970), 101, quoting B. R. Hartley; the Fens: B. R. Hartley in *The Fenland in Roman Times*, 167
92. I. A. Richmond in *Civitas Capitals of Roman Britain* (1966), 83 and pl. IX
93. Myres (1969), 76
94. As may have happened in the Silchester (*Antiquity* xviii, 113) and Verulamium (Frere in *Civitas Capitals of Roman Britain*, 98) regions
95. Bede, *Hist. Eccles.* ii, 16

432

Notes

GLOUCESTER

96. *C.I.L.* vi, 3346 (*I.L.S.* 2365)
97. It is just possible that a different interpretation may be considered if *Ner* refers to a pseudo-tribe: G. Forni in *Studi Giuridici in memoria di Alfredo Passerini* (1955), 89; *Carnuntina* (1956), 40
98. If Frere (1967), 93 is correct in his assumption that Leg. XX moved to Wroxeter in 66 to take the place of Leg. XIV, it is probable that the new fortress at Gloucester was constructed by Leg. II. Nevertheless *R.I.B.* 122, found at Wotton, just outside Gloucester attests a soldier of Leg. XX
99. *Antiqs. J.* lii, 24
100. Tacitus, *Agricola* xvii, 17, 2. *subiit sustinuitque molem Iulius Frontinus, vir magnus quantum licebat, validamque et pugnacem Silurum gentem armis subegit, super virtutem hostium locorum quoque difficultates eluctatus*
101. It will be important to see if there is an overlap between Lincoln and Chester, where the date of building the fortress is known epigraphically: R. P. Wright and I. A. Richmond, *Catalogue of Roman Inscribed and Sculptured Stones in the Grosvenor Museum, Chester* (1955), 48, no. 199
102. *Britannia* ii, 246
103. It would seem that at least some buildings of this kind were built in the area later occupied by the forum: *Antiqs. J.* lii, 52
104. *Antiqs. J.* lii, 52
105. *Lex Ursonensis* 78 (*I.L.S.* 6087). E. G. Hardy (*Roman Laws and Charters* 35, n. 55) considered that a clause to this effect would be inserted in every colonial and municipal 'charter'
106. *J.R.S.* lvii, 195
107. *ibid.* xlix, 126
108. *T.B.G.A.S.* liii, 279
109. *T.B.G.A.S.* lxxxi, 28 and pl. I. For recent excavations on the defences see *Antiqs. J.* lii, 28
110. *T.B.G.A.S.* lv, 82
111. *Arch. J.* ciii, 70
112. *T.B.G.A.S.* xix, 154
113. *J.R.S.* l, 230
114. *T.B.G.A.S.* lv, 79
115. *J.R.S.* xlix, 126
116. *J.R.S.* lvii, 195
117. *J.R.S.* lviii, 212; lix, 242. For a detailed survey of Gloucestershire tile stamps see *J.R.S.* xlv, 68–72
118. Information from Mr R. P. Wright.
119. *Arch. J.* ciii, 72
120. *J.R.S.* xlv, 68–72; also for LLH and TCM, *J.R.S.* lix, 242; LLQ and VLA, *J.R.S.* lvii,

208
121. *R.I.B.* 161
122. *Arch.* ix, 228. Some doubt exists as to the provenance: see also *Arch. J.* vii, 357, where Colchester is suggested as the origin
123. *R.I.B.* 120
124. Hull (1958), 240; *R.I.B.* 191
125. *R.I.B.* 119
126. *J.R.S.* lvii, 195
127. *ibid.* lii, 180, pl. XXIV 3
128. *Antiqs. J.* lii, 63
129. Early Wharves: *J.R.S.* xxxii, 47; later quay: *T.B.G.A.S.* lv, 94; *J.R.S.* xxxii, 47
130. *Arch. J.* cxxii, 179
131. *T.B.G.A.S.* lv, 350
132. *J.R.S.* xlv, 69
133. *ibid.* 72
134. M. Suić, *Zbornik*, i, 27, fig. 12; G. Alföldy, *Bevölkerung und Gesellschaft der Römischen Provinz Dalmatien* (1965), 104. Centuriation which is not based on the municipal axes can be seen at Cremona: *J.R.S.* lxi, 32 and Orange: Piganiol (1962)
135. *J.R.S.* xxxii, 39
136. 776yds (709m) = 20 *actus*
137. *Antiqs. J.* lii, 58
138. *Arch. J.* ciii, 73

YORK

139. See Chapter 1, footnote 1 (p. 426)
140. *J.R.S.* xi, 101; M. L. Valensi, *Bordeaux, 2000 Ans d'Historie* (1971), 61. See also p. 166 for a discussion of this altar
141. *de Caes.* 20, 27
142. *J.R.S.* lvii, 63
143. A relic of the visit may possibly be seen in the statue base of Britannia erected by Nikomedes, an Imperial freedman of the Emperors (*R.I.B.* 643). The Emperors were most likely Severus and Caracalla, although Marcus Aurelius and Commodus cannot be ruled out. An Imperial freedman could, of course, settle anywhere in the Empire, but that one should have been at York is certainly a coincidence
144. *S.H.A. Severus*, 22, 7
145. R.C.H.M. (1962), p. xxxvi
146. *ibid.* 34, no. 34a–g. The same building numbers as those given by R.C.H.M. are used here
147. *R.I.B.* 644
148. *R.I.B.* 658
149. *R.I.B.* 662–3
150. For Brough see p. 393; also Wacher (1969), 26, no. 2. For *Praetorium Agrippina* see J. E. Bogaers, 'Praetorium Agrippina' (*Bull. Koninklijke Nederlandsche Oudheidkundige Bond*,[6] xvii, 210–39). Place-names with the

prefix *praetorium* also occur in other provinces, as recorded in the Antonine Itinerary

151. R.C.H.M. (1962), p. xxxvii
152. *ibid.* 51, no. 18, with additional information kindly supplied by Mr Ramm
153. *ibid.* 5
154. *ibid.* 49
155. *ibid.* 3, Road 10
156. *ibid.* 49, Street 17a
157. *ibid.* 51, Street 17c
158. *ibid.* 50, building 30
159. *ibid.* p. xxxvii. The width of the naves are: at Cirencester 38ft (11·5m); London 35ft? (10·6m); Silchester 27ft (8·2m)
160. *R.I.B.* 657
161. R.C.H.M. (1962), 52, buildings 21 and 26
162. *ibid.* 52
163. *ibid.* 52, building 19
164. *ibid.* 65, n. 1
165. As attested by two inscriptions mentioning *seviri Augustales* (p. 166 below)
166. R.C.H.M. (1962), 120, no. 59; 115, no. 30 and *R.I.B.* 650
167. *Arch. J.* ciii, 75. R.C.H.M. (1962), 120, no. 67
168. *R.I.B.* 641 and R.C.H.M. (1962), 120, no. 58
169. *R.I.B.* 649, 643, 646, 652–3, 659 respectively
170. For the building see R.C.H.M. (1962), 59; the dedications *R.I.B.* 648, 656
171. *R.I.B.* 698, quoting *I.L.S.* 9235 in support
172. Pliny, *N.H.* xxxv, 112; xxxvi, 184
173. Far better than appears in *J.R.S.* xi, pl. VIII.
174. *R.I.B.* 678, 687
175. *R.I.B.* 653; R.C.H.M. (1962), 116, no. 36 gives the reading as M. Minucius Mudenus
176. See also BROUGH-ON-HUMBER (p. 393) and Wacher (1969), 76
177. R.C.H.M. (1962), pl. 31; *Germ. Romana* v, taf. 11, 3
178. R.C.H.M. (1962), 63, no. 48, and for general discussion see p. 141
179. *Bonner Jahrb.* cxlii, pls. 30–1
180. In (ed.) J. S. Wacher, *Civitas Capitals of Roman Britain* (1966), 83
181. p. 142
182. *Arch. J.* xciii, 200
183. V.C.H. *Yorks.* ii, 479
184. R.C.H.M. (1962), 108
185. Butler (1971), 187; also additional information from Mr Ramm
186. Verulamium: *Antiqs. J.* xxxix, 4
187. R.C.H.M. (1962), 128, no. 96
188. *ibid.* 63, no. 47
189. *ibid.* 48
190. *ibid.* 65, no. 55 and unpublished excavations 1971
191. *Cod. Theod.* ix, 17

192. Ammianus Marcellinus, xvi, 8, 4
193. For a general account of the York cemeteries see R.C.H.M. (1962), 67–110, 121–34; for a detailed account of a particular cemetery: L. P. Wenham, *The Romano-British Cemetery at Trentholme Drive, York* (1968); for gypsum burials: H. G. Ramm in Butler (1971), 187–196
194. Ramm in Butler (1971), *loc. cit.*
195. Wenham (1968), 21
196. *R.I.B.* 684
197. *R.I.B.* 695
198. *R.I.B.* 685. For an alternative reading see R.C.H.M. (1962), 122, no. 77
199. *R.I.B.* 679
200. *R.I.B.* 683
201. *R.I.B.* 674
202. R.C.H.M. (1962), 130, no. 107. Julia Victorina is not mentioned as *coniux*. While not absolutely necessary, its absence might imply a date before AD 197
203. *ibid.* 132, no. 134. An interest in athletics is also implied by the marble statuette: *ibid.* 120, no. 60
204. *ibid.* 135, no. 149. The formula was commonly used by gladiators and charioteers
205. *ibid.* 114, no. 24
206. Wenham (1968), parts II, III
207. If we are right in our assumption that Trentholme Drive represents a poor-class cemetery and that tombstones and coffins represent a richer class, we have a basis here for an interesting social comparison. According to the inscribed tombstones from York, which give ages at death (sixteen in number), only two, with the possible implication of a third, give ages over forty. The average age at death is about 29, so there seems to have been little advantage in living in a higher social class. Disease struck all alike. But see the reservation by K. Hopkins in *Population Studies* xx, 245, on the use of tombstones to assess life expectations
208. However, Diogenes' cognomen might indicate an origin further east. Perhaps he was a freedman, who had been in the service of an Aquitanian master
209. Collingwood & Myres (1937), 171
210. *Descr. Graeciae*, viii, 43
211. *Arch. J.* ciii, 74; R.C.H.M. (1962), p. xxxvi. Also *Digest* L.15.1.3. (Ulpian)
212. Information kindly supplied by Mr Ramm
213. Wacher in Butler (1971), 166
214. Butler (1971), 179–99
215. Myres (1969), 75

Chapter 5 (pages 178–225)

CANTERBURY

1. A possible hinge from a legionary cuirass came from a Claudian level in Rose Lane: *Arch. Cant.* lxviii, 140
2. *Arch.* xliii, 151–64
3. Frank Jenkins, 'Men of Kent before the Romans.' *Canterbury Arch. Soc. occasional papers* No. 3 (1962), *passim*
4. See also D. P. S. Peacock in Hill and Jesson (1971), 182
5. Caesar, *de bello Gallico* v, 12–14
6. *Roman Canterbury*, No. 5, 13; *J.R.S.* xliv, 102
7. Frere (1962), 11; *J.R.S.* xlvi, 144
8. But not unknown: see *Caistor-by-Norwich*, p. 231
9. *Britannia* i, 85
10. which is dated to *c.* AD 100
11. Grenier, *Manuel d'Archéologie Gallo-Romaine*, 3, ii, 914
12. P. M. Duval, *Paris Antique* (1961), 180; Grenier, 3, ii, 900
13. If so, then the gravel area under the County Hotel and Stour Street might be interpreted as part of the *palaestra*
14. *Arch. Cant.* lxviii, 118
15. *J.R.S.* xxxix, 110
16. *Roman Canterbury*, No. 4. Part of the building is on show in the cellars of new buildings fronting Butchery Lane
17. *J.R.S.* xxxvii, 177; xxxix, 110
18. *J.R.S.* li, 191
19. *J.R.S.* xl, 113
20. *J.R.S.* xli, 139
21. *J.R.S.* xxxvii, 97
22. *J.R.S.* xli, 138
23. *Roman Canterbury*, No. 3
24. Lewis (1965), 78
25. Bede. *Hist. Eccl.* i, 26
26. *Med. Arch.* ix, 11
27. *J.B.A.A.*[3] xxviii, 1
28. *J.R.S.* xl, 114
29. *J.R.S.* xliii, 127; xlvi, 144; xxxix, 111; xlv, 145
30. *J.R.S.* xlvi, 144
31. *Antiqs. J.* xlviii, 15; xlix, 39; I, 17
32. *J.R.S.* xlvi, 144
33. *V.C.H. Kent*, iii, pl. XI; *J.R.S.* xlv, 143
34. E. Hasted, *The History of Canterbury* (1799), opp. p. 21; *V.C.H. Kent*, iii, pl. XI
35. *J.R.S.* xlvi, 144
36. *J.R.S.* lii, 190; *Arch. Cant.* lxxxiii, 273
37. *J.R.S.* xlvi, 144
38. *J.R.S.* xlv, 143; li, 191
39. *Roman Canterbury*, No. 2
40. *R.I.B.* 43
41. *Antiqs. J.* xxxvi, 40
42. *Arch. Cant.* lxxiv, 151
43. *Arch. Cant.* liii, 109
44. *Arch. Cant.* xlvii, 225
45. *Arch. Cant.* lxx, 247
46. *J.B.A.A.*[3] xxviii, 1
47. V.C.H. *Kent*, iii, 69; *J.R.S.* xxxviii, 97
48. *J.R.S.* xlviii, 149
49. *J.R.S.* xlvii, 225
50. *J.R.S.* xxxviii, 98
51. *Roman Canterbury*, No. 4. 16, 21
52. The building at Folkestone, associated with *Classis Britannica* tiles may not have been a villa, but a residence of some official of the fleet
53. Cunliffe (1968), 200
54. S. C. Hawkes and G. C. Dunning, *R.G.K.* 43–4, 155; *Med. Arch.* v, 1
55. Myres (1969), 77
56. S. S. Frere in *Civitas Capitals of Roman Britain* (1966), 92, fig. 20
57. *J.B.A.A.*[3] xxviii, 1

CHELMSFORD

58. *Itinerarium Curiosum* (1776), ii, 12
59. *E.H.R.* lii, 198. It might be noted that such names are virtually all of first-century date, which is itself an argument against Stevens' suggested transfer of the capital to Chelmsford at a later date
60. *Arch. J.* ciii, 61
61. An indication of the extent of the Trinovantian realm is provided by the distribution of south Italian amphorae which D. P. S. Peacock has studied: Hill and Jesson (1971), 173
62. It is interesting to compare the mention of the Catuvellauni in Dio's narrative of the invasion with the Trinovantes mentioned in the account of the Boudiccan rebellion by Tacitus. The latter tribe were not worthy of mention in the former context
63. C. Cichorius, *Die Reliefs der Traianssäule* (1896) lv, 199
64. *Geog.* ii, 3, 22
65. *It. Ant.* 474, 1
66. V.C.H. *Essex* iii, 64
67. *ibid.* 67
68. *Britannia* iii, 331 with extra information kindly provided by Mr P. J. Drury
69. Lewis (1965), 197
70. Information kindly supplied by Mr Drury Also *Britannia* ii, 271; *T.E.A.S.* iv, 3–29
71. *J.R.S.* lix, 223; *Britannia* i, 290; ii, 271; iii, 331
72. Most of the buildings so far excavated were of timber construction, and little use seems to have been made of masonry

VERULAMIUM

73. Wheeler (1936), 23
74. References to individual discoveries spread over several years are usefully collected in *Antiquity* xxxviii, 103–12. But see also *Antiqs. J.* xxxvii, 6; xxxviii, 13; *T. St Albans Archit. & Arch. Soc.* (1961), 31
75. *Antiqs. J.* xxxvii, 9
76. *Antiquity* xxxviii, 103
77. *Bull. Inst. Arch.* iv, 63
78. *Antiqs. J.* xxxvii, 4; xlii, 150
79. *Herts. Arch.* ii, 51
80. *R.I.B.* 1962. See also p. 408 below for further discussion
81. Wheeler (1936), 25
82. Collingwood and Myres (1937), 189
83. *Bull. Inst. Arch.* iv, 63; *Antiquity* xxxviii, 104
84. Frere (1971)
85. But it does not necessarily follow from this implication that the same ownership continued. Terrace houses can be erected by a single speculative builder who can then sell off each house as he chooses. The first houses in the *colonia* at Gloucester might serve to illustrate the point (p. 139): see *Britannia* iv, 348
86. For further discussion on this topic see p. 256 below
87. *Antiquity* xxxviii, 105
88. *T. St Albans Archit. & Arch. Soc.* (1895–1902), 199
89. Named the *principia* type of forum by D. Atkinson, *Excavations at Wroxeter, 1923–7* (1942), 349. But see also Ward-Perkins in *J.R.S.* lx, 7
90. J. le Gall, *Alésia: Archéologie et Histoire* (1963), 125
91. Frere (1971), 23
92. *Antiqs. J.* xvii, 28
93. *Antiquity* xxxviii, 108
94. e.g. Gosbecks, Woodeaton
95. Perhaps Matthew Paris, in describing documents reputedly discovered in the forum area by Abbot Eadmer's men (*Vitae Abbatum*, 994) was not so far wrong in describing the second most important deity of the town as Mercury. Indeed, wild though his description is, it is suggestive of a calendar of official religious celebrations of well-known type: cf. *Inscriptiones Italiae*, XIII, fasc. II
96. See V.C.H. *Herts.* iv, pl. IV for a block of masonry found by Page near the centre of the piazza; but this may have been only the bottom of a statue base
97. *Antiqs. J.* xxxvi, 7 and also *ibid.* xxxvii, 216 for further discussion on the inscription: for a revised text see Frere (1967), 202

98. V.C.H. *Herts.* iv, 131 and pl. IV
99. *Jahreshefte des Öesterreichischen Archaeologischen Instituts*, xi, 47, and more accessibly in J. J. Wilkes, *Dalmatia* (1969), 369–7
100. cf. Pompeii, where three separate buildings at the south end of the forum fulfilled identical functions as those at Verulamium. A. Mau and F. W. Kelsey, *Pompeii* (1899), 119. See also Ward-Perkins in *J.R.S.* lx, 10
101. Wheeler (1936), 93 and 86
102. *Antiqs. J.* xl, 18
103. Wheeler (1936), 113
104. For a conjectural reconstruction see Lewis (1965), 191
105. *Antiquity* xxxviii, 107
106. *Arch.* lxxxiv, 213ff
107. A similar possibility has been suggested at Canterbury: *Britannia* i, 90
108. Ward-Perkins (*J.R.S.* lx, 9) points out that the placing of temples against the rear wall of the enclosure is in contrast to the Gaulish practice of having a free-standing temple in the piazza
109. V.C.H. *Herts.* iv, 132
110. *T. St Albans Archit. & Arch. Soc.* (1953), 13
111. For conjectural reconstructions of these temples, see Lewis (1965), 182–3
112. *Arch.* xc, 86
113. Wheeler (1936), 94 and 102
114. *Antiqs. J.* xxxvii, 13 and pls. II, IIIa, IV, V; xxix, 17 and pl. I; xl, 16 and pl. I, III; *British Museum Quarterly* xxxv, 87; *Britannia* iii, 251
115. Frere (1971), 73
116. See p. 75
117. *Antiquity* xxxviii, 108
118. Wheeler (1936), pl. XXI
119. *ibid.* 63–75
120. *ibid.* 76
121. *Antiqs. J.* xlii, 153
122. *Antiqs. J.* xxxix, 2, 10
123. Suitably summarised in *Bull. Inst. Arch.* iv, 71–5
124. *Arch.* lxxxiv, 238
125. *ibid.* 232
126. *Antiqs. J.* xvii, 29
127. *Arch.* xc, 88
128. Frere (1971), 98. Cellars are not unknown features in and around Verulamium and have been found in Buildings I, 1; VIII, 2; XXVIII, 1 and outside the town over the river to the north-east. Note also cellars in the villas at Gorhambury and Park Street. For a collection of ironwork found in the Insula XIV cellar see Frere (1971), 105
129. In Insula XXVII: *Antiqs. J.* xl, 19
130. Wheeler (1936), 122
131. *Herts. Arch.* i, 49

132. But if they were later than the curtain wall it would not be difficult to achieve with flint and brick masonry
133. *Antiqs. J.* xl, 19; *Bull. Inst. Arch.* iv, 77
134. Wheeler (1936), 96
135. In *Civitas Capitals of Roman Britain* (1966), 97–8
136. *Antiqs. J.* xxxviii, 8
137. Wheeler (1936), 90
138. *ibid.* 109
139. *ibid.* 221; *Num. Chron.*[5] xii, 54
140. *Arch.* xv, 121; Toynbee (1962), pl. 190
141. Frere (1971), 57
142. *Antiqs. J.* xxvii, 14
143. *Antiqs. J.* xxi, 152; *V.C.H. Herts.* iv, 137; *Hearts. Arch.* i, 39
144. *J.R.S.* lvii, 188; lvii, 194; lix, 221
145. *J.R.S.* lvii, 194
146. *Antiqs. J.* xxxvii, 14
147. *J.R.S.* lix, 221
148. *T. St Albans Archit. & Arch. Soc.* (1961), 21
149. *Arch. J.* cii, 21; cxviii, 100

Chapter 6 (pages 226–288)

1. Tacitus, *Annales* xiv, 31: *quando in formam provinciae cesserant*
2. Tacitus, *Annales* xii, 31

CAISTOR-BY-NORWICH

3. *Britannia* i, 4, 5
4. Tacitus, *Annales* xii, 31
5. Tacitus, *Annales* xiv, 29–39; Dudley and Webster (1962); Frere (1967), 87
6. Suetonius, *Nero* 32
7. Tacitus, *Annales* xv, 45; xvi, 3
8. *Britannia* i, 16
9. *Arch. J.* iv, 72
10. *Britannia* ii, 9; for a report on the pottery see *Norfolk Arch.* xxvi, 197
11. *Britannia* ii, 1. For earlier accounts see *J.R.S.* xxii, 210; xxiv, 209
12. Also excavated by Atkinson; see *Britannia* ii, 20
13. *Norfolk Arch.* xxiv, 93
14. Information from Miss Barbara Green
15. In Norwich Castle Museum. Information from Miss Barbara Green
16. Toynbee (1962), 124
17. *Oxon.* xiv, 33
18. *J.R.S.* xxix, 214
19. *J.R.S.* li, 132 and pl. X, 1; *Civitas Capitals of Roman Britain*, pl. III; similar marks can also be seen at Silchester in pl. II
20. *Britannia* ii, 8
21. *Civitas Capitals of Roman Britain*, 60–9; Frere (1967), 249. See also p. 75

22. *J.R.S.* xxi, 232; xxv, 213
23. Hull (1958), 36
24. *Norfolk Arch.* xxiv, 93
25. *Civitas Capitals of Roman Britain*, 78
26. *J.R.S.* xxix, 214
27. *Antiquity* xl, 60
28. *Not. Dig. occ.* xi, 60
29. *Latomus* xxvi, 648
30. *It. Ant.* 474, 4; 6
31. Most conveniently summarised by A. L. F Rivet in *Civitas Capitals of Roman Britain*, 108
32. *J.R.S.* xxi, 232
33. J. N. L. Myres and Barbara Green, *The Anglo-Saxon Cemeteries of Caistor-by-Norwich and Markhall, Norfolk* (1973), 16
34. *J.R.S.* xvii, 217
35. *Britannia* i, 47, 52
36. By Sir Arthur Keith. The bones were apparently destroyed during the 1939–45 war, so that a re-examination is not possible
37. Information kindly provided by Professor Frere
38. Myres and Green (1973), 31

CHICHESTER

39. *Arch.* xc, 8; Cunliffe (1971), Vol. I, 10
40. *Antiquity* xlvi, 77
41. Cunliffe (1971), Vol. I, 17
42. Elsie M. Clifford (1961), 59; Cunliffe (1971), Vol. I, 73
43. Frere (1967), 68
44. *Agricola* xiv, 1; (ed.) Richmond and Ogilvie (1967), 189
45. I owe this suggestion to Professor Frere
46. Cunliffe (1971), Vol. I, 10, originated by E. C. Curwen, *Archaeology of Sussex* (1954)
47. *Agricola* xiv, 1
48. Cunliffe (1971), Vol. I, 10
49. Ptolemy. *Geog.* ii, 3, 28. There is some reason to think that the inclusion of Bath in the civitas Belgarum was an error of Ptolemy's. I owe this comment to Mr Rivet
50. See G. C. Boon in *Arch.* cii, 36
51. Cunliffe (1971), Vol. I, 75
52. *Arch. J.* cxxviii, 275
53. Chichester Civic Society E.C. *Report for 1971*, 13
54. *R.I.B.* 92
55. *R.I.B.* 91
56. *ibid.*
57. Dudley and Webster (1965), 58; *Antiquity* xlvi, 77
58. *Britannia* i, 77
59. *Sussex Notes and Queries* 13, 332
60. Down and Rule (1971), 16
61. *Sussex A.C.* c, 97
62. Down and Rule (1971), 27

63. *J.R.S.* liii, 151. See p. 155 for a plan showing what little was known of the street plan of the town in 1962
64. *J.R.S.* li, 189
65. Chichester Civic Society E.C. *Report for 1971*, 5
66. Down and Rule (1971), 15
67. *ibid.* 15; *J.R.S.* liii, 151; Chichester Civic Society E.C. *Report for 1972*
68. *Antiqs. J.* xvi, 149
69. *Sussex A.C.* c, 86
70. *ibid.* facing p. 80
71. A. E. Wilson, 'The Archaeology of Chichester City Walls' (*Chichester Papers* (1957) no. 2)
72. Down and Rule (1971), 143
73. *Sussex A.C.* c, 75
74. *ibid.* xc, 116; c, 84; The most recently discovered tower was found a short distance north of the probable site of the east gate. Its situation would imply that the gate itself lacked external towers. Chichester Civic Society E.C. *Report for 1972*
75. Down and Rule (1971), 13, 127
76. Chichester Civic Society E.C. *Reports for 1970 and 1971*
77. *Sussex A.C.* c, 99
78. *ibid.* xc, 99
79. *J.R.S.* lix, 87
80. *R.I.B.* 90
81. *R.I.B.* 94
82. *R.I.B.* 95
83. *R.I.B.* 93
84. Down and Rule (1971), 53
85. *Med. Arch.* v, 43
86. Conveniently summarised in *Antiqs. J.* l, 68

SILCHESTER

87. *Arch.* cii, 51
88. *ibid.* 39
89. If Hawkes is correct in suggesting the almost immediate surrender of the Dobunni (Clifford (1961), 62) after the Roman landing, then presumably one of the first tasks of the Roman army in the west would have been to secure their territory: hence the early construction of a road from Silchester to Dobunnic territory. Meanwhile the hostility of the southern tribes from Hampshire westwards was still being overcome and, as far as we can judge, most movements into the area were made along the coast from Chichester: hence a direct road from Silchester to Durotrigian territory was not given priority
90. *Antiquity* xxii, 172
91. *Arch.* cii, 40
92. *Arch.* lix, 366. Tiles were frequently reused and it is unsafe to rely on this alone. Yet its presence shows that there must have been masonry buildings at Silchester as early as Nero's principate, and a bath house might be thought to be a likely candidate
93. *Arch.* lix, 314. For a more up-to-date consideration see Boon (1957), 101
94. *Arch.* cii, 39
95. Suetonius, *Vespasian* 17: *in omne hominum genus liberalissimus explevit censium senatorium*
96. It was excavated in 1865-7: *Arch.* xlvi, 349, and re-examined in 1892: *Arch.* liii, 539. See also *Arch.* cii, 43 for a note on the date of the forum
97. *Arch.* cii, 43
98. *R.I.B.* 67. The equation with Segomo is not entirely satisfactory although suggested by Richmond (1963), 78, 190
99. *R.I.B.* 84, which places the find spot in the basilica, but see Boon (1957), 92
100. Frere (1967), 258
101. *Arch.* xcii, 135
102. It was primarily excavated before 1880, when little cognizance was taken of the streets, and partly re-excavated in 1893, when the excavator considered such a street a possibility: *Arch.* liv, 24
103. See CAERWENT, p. 386
104. *Arch.* lii, 754
105. *Arch.* lxi, 475
106. *Arch.* xcii, 129
107. North gate: *Arch.* lii, 753
    South gate: *Arch.* xlvi, 348; lii, 755
    East gate: *Arch.* xlvi, 346; lxi, 474
    West gate: *Arch.* lii, 756; lxi, 474
108. Mrs Cotton gave a date of AD 190-210 for the construction of the wall, but this may fall a little short of the actual date: *Arch.* xcii, 130. See B. R. Hartley in *Civitas Capitals of Roman Britain*, 59, n. 39 for revised date
109. *Arch.* xcii, 131
110. South-west gate: *Arch.* lv, 424
    North-east gate: *Arch.* liv, 357; xcii, 130
111. *Arch.* liv, 230
112. The excavators suggested that the walls had been built against older timber work
113. *Arch.* lviii, 419
114. *Arch.* lv, 422
115. *Arch.* lv, 232
116. *Arch.* lii, 744; lviii, 414. For further consideration of the Silchester temples see Lewis (1965), 20, 30
117. *Arch.* lxi, 206
118. *Arch.* liv, 447; lv, 413; lvi, 121
119. *Arch.* liii, 563; *J.R.S.* lii, 185
120. e.g. notably Caerwent (p. 386)
121. *Arch.* lvii, 113; I. A. Richmond in *Civitas Capitals of Roman Britain*, 79

122. *Arch.* lx, 156, 165
123. Boon (1957), 178
124. *R.I.B.* 87. Found in or before 1577 and now in the Museum of Archaeology and Anthropology, Cambridge
125. *R.I.B.* 69–71. Alternatively *peregrinorum* might refer to Roman citizens who dwelt at Silchester but whose domicile it was not
126. Boon (1957), 76
127. *Antiqs. J.* xxxviii, 114
128. *Med. Arch.* v, 26–7
129. *Med. Arch.* iii, 79
130. *Arch.* liv, 223. For later comments see *Med. Arch.* iii, 87, n. 36 and *Civitas Capitals of Roman Britain*, 96
131. *Antiquity* xviii, 113
132. See *Arch. J.* cxix, 114ff, for a report on Frere's excavations at Dorchester in 1962 which have thrown considerable light on the early Saxon occupation

WINCHESTER

133. Information kindly provided by Martin Biddle
134. Cunliffe (1964), 6; (1971), 11 (fig. 5)
135. Information from Martin Biddle
136. A fragment of a coin mould from near the Cathedral, even if Allen is inclined to date it to the post-conquest period, hints at the existence of a major settlement
137. *Antiqs. J.* xlv, 235; 1, 281
138. *Britannia* iii, 348, with additional information kindly provided by Martin Biddle
139. Ptolemy, *Geog.* ii, 3, 28; but see the caution on p. 436, n. 49 above
140. Summarised in *Antiqs. J.* xliv, 189, 214
141. *Arch. J.* cxix, 153; *Antiqs. J.* xliv, 203
142. Information kindly supplied by Mr Mackreth
143. *J.R.S.* xlviii, 150
144. *P. Hants. Field Club*, xxii, 57–71; *Antiqs. J.* l, 282
145. *P. Hants Field Club*, xxii, 52 ff.; *Antiqs. J.* l, 281–5
146. *J.R.S.* xviii, 207
147. *Arch. J.* vi, 398, 408
148. *Arch. J.* cxix, 155
149. *V.C.H. Hants.* i, 288
150. *Arch.* xxii, 52; C. Roach Smith, *Collectanea Antiqua*, ii, 54
151. *Britannia* iii, 349
152. See WROXETER (p. 371) for a raised hearth in a workshop opposite the forum
153. *Britannia* iii, 349, pl. XXIV, b
154. *Antiqs. J.* xlviii, 282
155. *occ.* xi, 60
156. Haverfield in *V.C.H. Hants.* i, 292; Collingwood in *Roman Britain and the English Settle-*

ments, 223; Wild in *Latomus* xxvi, 666
157. *R.I.B.* 88
158. *Antiqs. J.* xiv, 238
159. *Britannia* iii, 349
160. *Antiqs. J.* xlviii, 257; xlix, 302; l, 292
161. *Antiqs. J.* xlvii, 224
162. *V.C.H. Hants.* i, 286
163. *Arch. J.* cxix, 156
164. *Antiqs. J.* xliv, 206

Chapter 7 (pages 289–374)

CIRENCESTER

1. Clifford (1961), 43–67
2. Although this was not his full name, he will be called by the abbreviation hereafter
3. Dio Cassius, lx, 20
4. Deposition of both hoards must have taken place in the early 40s but it is impossible to be precise to within a year or so when dating individual issues
5. See p. 30 above for the reasons employed to reach such a conclusion. I am grateful to Mr John Robinson for discussing with me most of the points mentioned above and for allowing me to make free use of his suggestions, while he was preparing a doctoral thesis on the civitas Dobunnorum for the University of Leicester. I am also grateful to Dr Kent for his views on Dobunnic coins
6. Wacher (1971), 5
7. Clifford (1961), 21, with additional comments *Arch. J.* cxxii, 204
8. *Antiqs. J.* xliv, 11
9. *Antiqs. J.* xlii, 11; xliv, 11
10. *Antiqs. J.* xliv, 9
11. *R.I.B.* 114
12. *T.B.G.A.S.* xxi, 70; *P.S.A.* xxvii, 201; *Antiqs. J.* xlii, 5
13. The plan is rare in the Empire and can be most closely matched by the so-called Caesareum at Cyrene: *P.B.S.R.* (1958), 149
14. *Antiqs. J.* xlii, 8
15. H. J. Loane. *Industry and Commerce of the City of Rome*, 116, 122
16. *Antiqs. J.* xliv, 17
17. *Antiqs. J.* xlvii, 185
18. *Antiqs. J.* xliii, 23; xliv, 17
19. *Antiqs. J.* xlvii, 185
20. *Arch.* lxix, 179
21. *Arch.* lxix, 180; *R.I.B.* 105
22. *Antiqs. J.* xlii, 9. One plaster wall was lifted and restored, and is now on display in Corinium Museum
23. *Antiqs. J.* xliii, 19
24. *Antiqs. J.* xlvii, 188; *Britannia* i, 227
25. The full sequence of towers may not have

been completed. Excavations in the grounds of Watermoor Hospital revealed a massive beam set at the rear of, and parallel to, the rampart. This could be interpreted as part of the base for a wooden tower: *Antiqs. J.* xliv, 15

26. *Antiqs. J.* xli, 65
27. This measurement is in remarkably close agreement with the London and Chester Gates at Verulamium. All three gates are of the same general plan and probably contemporary in build
28. These pavements were first described in Buckman and Newmarch, *The Remains of Roman Art in Cirencester* (1850); but see also Toynbee (1962), 197
29. Toynbee (1962), 197. The pavement has been long since lost, but was drawn by Lysons
30. *R.I.B.* 103
31. *Antiqs. J.* xliv, 9
32. *Antiqs. J.* xlii, 7
33. In Stern (ed.), *La Mosaïque Gréco-Romaine* (Paris, 1965), also in Rivet (1969), 97 and most recently *Antiqs. J.* xlix, 235
34. Toynbee (1962), 7 and pls. 29, 37, 76
35. *R.I.B.* 105, 151
36. Toynbee (1962), 130
37. *T.B.G.A.S.* lxx, 51. It is worth noting that cultivated land existed inside the walls of Pompeii: *A.J.A.* lxxiv, 63
38. For elaboration see *Britannia* v, forthcoming
39. *Antiqs. J.* xlii, 9
40. *T.B.G.A.S.* lxxxv, 49
41. *Antiqs. J.* xlv, 101. The same, or a similar, surface was discovered in 1972 during excavations west of Purley Road
42. For a discussion see D. Atkinson: *T.B.G.A.S* lxxxvi, 21. Caution should, however, be exercised in view of the comments by M. Guarducci in *R.A.C.* xvii, 219 and xix, 144; J. Gwyn Griffiths in *Classical Rev.* lxxxv, 6; G. Ch. Picard in *Rev. Arch.* (1965), 101. Another objection can be made that the normal form of cross recognised by early Christians was the τ-cross, and so did not have four arms
43. Excavations in 1967, in the car park of the disused Western Region railway station, entirely failed to find any opening in the wall: *Antiqs. J.* xlix, 225. The situation here is complicated by the behaviour of the internal street leading to the postulated gate. It cannot be moved on the plan any great distance north or south from this point without striking known buildings
44. I am grateful to Mr McWhirr for making this information available to me in advance of his own publication

45. *R.I.B.* 110
46. *R.I.B.* 111
47. *R.I.B.* 112
48. *R.I.B.* 113
49. *Britannia* iii, 352
50. *Antiqs. J.* xii, 69
51. *Antiqs. J.* xliv, 14
52. In R. H. M. Dolley (ed.), *Anglo-Saxon Coins* (1961), 5
53. *Antiqs. J.* xliii, 21
54. In Leaholme Gardens (unpublished); and in Dyer Court, now the site of the Forum Car Park: *T.B.G.A.S.* lxxviii, 53, 84. The skeleton was there reported as associated with medieval pottery, but since no plan or section was published showing its position it is difficult to check. A report by the late Canon Grensted on the snail shells found in the skull, indicate that the body had come to rest in damp surroundings and in deep vegetation. The conditions in which this body were disposed are so similar to the description of the roadside ditch by Building XXIII, 1 that we might question the medieval pottery
55. Reviewed in Chapter 10
56. *Antiqs. J.* xliii, 26; xliv, 18
57. A. H. Smith, *Place Names of Gloucestershire* (1964), I, 64 gives 'town farm' for the derivation of Chesterton, presumably because it made no sense to him in any other way. We might now accept the more normal meaning of 'chester' as a fortified place
58. *T.B.G.A.S.* lxx, 52. Mr David Brown of the Ashmolean Museum has pointed out that this is but one burial from a cemetery of at least a dozen graves containing both male and female skeletons; it can be dated to the sixth century

DORCHESTER

59. *Vespasian* 4
60. Dudley and Webster (1965), 90
61. Wheeler (1943), 61
62. Richmond (1968), *passim*
63. *P.S.A.* iv, 188; *Arch. J.* xcvi, 114
64. *Antiqs. J.* l, 19; li, 4
65. V.C.H. *Somerset*, i, 295
66. Hill and Jesson (1971), *passim*
67. *Geog.* i, 103; Rivet has, however, suggested that *Dunium* should be equated with Hod Hill
68. Wheeler (1943), 12
69. R.C.H.M. (1970), 533
70. A legionary, or half-legionary, fortress at Dorchester was postulated by Frere (1967), 74. It should, however, be noted that recent

excavations and observations have entirely failed to demonstrate a military occupation below the town. I am grateful to Mr Bill Putnam for this information. The fort site should therefore probably be sought nearby

71. *R.I.B.* 1672, 1673
72. *P.S.A.N.H.S.* xcvi, 188
73. Richmond (1963), 79
74. Frere (1967), 205
75. As marked by Rivet: *A.N.L.* vi, 31; R.C.H.M. (1970), 535, n. 5. But see possible reservations in Chapter 9, p. 407
76. A detailed summary is contained in R.C.H.M. (1970), 531 ff. Where necessary, later references are to Inventory Numbers of Monuments
77. R.C.H.M. (1970), no. 196
78. R.C.H.M. (1970), nos. 177, 178 and 180
79. Summaries were published in *P.D.N.H.S.* xxix–xxxv. These have been collated and extended, by inclusion of hitherto unpublished material in the Dorset County Museum, by R.C.H.M. (1970), 589, no. 228
80. e.g. Vindonissa and Xanten
81. *op. cit.* 534
82. Information from Prof. B. Cunliffe
83. Summary R.C.H.M. (1970), 585, no. 227 See also *Antiqs. J.* xx, 435; *J.R.S.* lix, 229
84. R.C.H.M. (1970), 542. Later accounts appear in *Britannia* i, 298; ii, 279. I am indebted to Prof. Cunliffe for the comment on the early wall foundation, and to Mr Putnam for additional information
85. *Britannia* ii, 279
86. R.C.H.M. (1970), 553, nos. 182–7, based on interim reports in *P.D.N.H.S.* lix, 1; lx, 51 for the Colliton Park structures
87. Rivet (1969), 109
88. *Antiqs. J.* xlii, 7
89. R.C.H.M. (1970), 538
90. *R.I.B.* 188; although a more probable reading is given in R.C.H.M. (1970), 574
91. Wheeler (1943), 72. He considered the actual site of the temple to have been of ancient religious importance
92. Interim notes and plans in *P.D.N.H.S.* lxxxviii onwards; *Britannia* ii, 280. I am also grateful to Mr C. J. Green for some additional comments
93. R.C.H.M. (1970), 538

EXETER

94. The Iron Age of Devon and Cornwall is most conveniently summarised in Aileen Fox, *South-West England* (1964), Chapt. VII and in Charles Thomas, *Rural Settlement in Roman Britain* (1966), 74–98

95. A summary of the military situation in Dumnonia is contained in *P.D.A.E.S.* xxiv, 22 and Aileen Fox, *Roman Exeter* (1973), 6
96. Aileen Fox, *Roman Exeter* (1952), 7; also in *Civitas Capitals of Roman Britain* (1966), 46
97. *P.D.A.S.* xxvi, 4
98. Information kindly provided by Mr Michael Griffiths and Mr John Collis. The present excavations are part of a series being conducted by the Exeter City Archaeological Field Unit
99. Fox (1952), 37, 101
100. *P.D.A.E.S.* ii, 55
101. Fox (1952), 18, 101
102. *P.D.A.E.S.* v, 30
103. Fox (1952), 51
104. *P.D.A.E.S.* xxvi, 12
105. Caution should, however, be exercised in view of von Petrikovit's qualified rejection of typological dating for fortifications: *J.R.S.* lxi, 203. Yet, for Britain at least, a careful and detailed analysis definitely shows chronological differences between types
106. The somewhat compact gates at Housesteads have a space of 23ft 6in (7·2m) between towers
107. Fox (1952), 19; *J.R.S.* lii, 184; *P.D.A.S.* xxvi, 11
108. Fox (1952), Part iv
109. Information from Mr John Collis
110. *J.R.S.* lii, 184; *P.D.A.S.* xxvi, 9
111. *ibid.* 92
112. see n. 94 above
113. Fox (1964), 147; Charles Thomas, *Rural Settlement in Roman Britain* (1966), 92
114. Fox (1964), 16
115. *J.R.I.C.* NS l, 60
116. *Med. Arch.* iii, 89 ff
117. Cf. Frere in *Civitas Capitals of Roman Britain* (1966), 95
118. Frere (1967), 377

LEICESTER

119. D. F. Allen, *The Coins of the Coritani* (1963)
120. Kenyon (1948), *passim*
121. *J.R.S.* lviii, 186
122. Unpublished excavations by the writer
123. Or fortress. A fine, enamelled legionary belt-plate has been found: *Arch. J.* cxv, 84
124. Kenyon (1948), 10. Caution should perhaps be exercised here. An extensive cobbled layer on top of the undisturbed ground surface has been found covering much of the central area of the town. Admittedly in favour of Miss Kenyon's interpretation, she does not show it in all her sections. But the cobble layer could be a natural formation

125. *ibid.* 11
126. *J.R.S.* liii, 134
127. Unpublished excavation by the writer
128. *J.R.S.* xlix, 113
129. S.H.A. *vit. Hadriani.* 19.2: *in omnibus paene urbibus et aliquid aedificavit.* Fishwick has drawn attention to Hadrian's activities as a builder on his journeys through Gaul to, and from, Britain: *J.R.S.* lii, 50
130. Excavations on the forum and basilica, extending over a number of years have been published collectively by Miss J. E. Mellor and Mr M. A. Hebditch in *Britannia* iv, 1–83
131. Kenyon (1948)
132. Information kindly supplied by Mr B. R. Hartley, who has informed me that there is virtually no difference between the *termini post quos* of the two phases
133. Kenyon (1948), pls. xi, xxvi
134. *Britannia* ii, 201
135. Unpublished excavation by Leicester Museums
136. Kenyon (1948), 40
137. *J.R.S.* lvii, 183
138. *J.R.S.* xlix, 113
139. *J.R.S.* xlix, 113
140. The scheme of decoration is not unlike a representation of a theatrical proscaenium painted on the wall of a house at Herculaneum: R. E. M. Wheeler, *Roman Art and Architecture* (1964), pl. 190, and reproduced in Plate 4. The artist in Leicester, although possibly using a copy-book which was over 70 years old, added his own touches, such as the cupid with the shock of red hair. See also *Britannia* iii, 262
141. *J.R.S.* lii, 196; liv, 182
142. Information kindly supplied by Mr Leslie Cram, who has prepared a full report for publication
143. Despite frequent excavations in the past two decades, most of the mosaics known are earlier discoveries. They were summarised, together with other remains, by Haverfield: *Arch. J.* lxxv, 32
144. *J.R.S.* lix, 215
145. *R.I.B.* 2244; also *T.L.A.S.* xxix, 13
146. *J.R.S.* lvii, 183
147. *T.L.A.S.* xxviii, 19; xxix, 1; xxxii, 89; *J.R.S.* xlix, 113; lvii, 183; lix, 215
148. *Arch. J.* lxxv, 10
149. *J.R.S.* lviii, 186
150. e.g. Kenyon (1948), 38
151. *T.L.A.S.* xlii, 1
152. E. Blank, *Ratae Coritanorum* (1971), 11
153. *Cod. Theod.* ix, 21, 6
154. *Arch. J.* lxxv, 36

155. *Britannia* i, 286
156. *R.I.B.* 245
157. *A.E.* (1944) no. 57; *C.I.L.* xvi, 160
158. Rivet (1964), 65; Joyce Reynolds in *Civitas Capitals of Roman Britain*, 73
159. Frere (1967), 205; Bogaers in *J.R.S.* lvii, 233
160. *C.I.L.* vii, 1335, 4
161. *Arch. J.* lxxv, 25
162. *E.E.* iii, 147, no. 136
163. *E.E.* vii, 1143
164. *Britannia* iv, 36
165. Unpublished excavation by the writer
166. Myres (1969), 76

WROXETER

167. 'The Cornovii'. (ed.) Foster and Alcock, *Culture and Environment* (1963), 255
168. *R.I.B.* 291
169. *T.B.A.S.* lxix, 54
170. *J.R.S.* liv, 165
171. *J.R.S.* xlv, 88. The early military situation is discussed further by Webster and Stanley: *T.Shrop.A.S.* lvii, 112
172. Frere (1967), 117, n. 2
173. Atkinson (1942), 6
174. Bushe-Fox (1913), 21; (1916), 1
175. *J.R.S.* li, 158, for a plan
176. Frere (1967), 243, n. 1
177. Foster and Alcock (1963), 260
178. It is worth noting, not only in this connexion, but also in other similar cases, that there were normally no rights of expropriation resembling the modern compulsory purchase order: Suetonius, *Julius* 26.2; *Augustus* 56.2. Presumably the exception would have been where a local by-law existed requiring derelict or demolished buildings to be rebuilt within a certain time, or payment of a forfeit: *Lex Ursonensis* 75 (*I.L.S.* 6087); *Lex Malacitana* 62 (*I.L.S.* 6089); *Lex Tarentini* 4 (*I.L.S.* 6086). However Miss Reynolds has pointed out that Gaius, *Institutes* II, 51 makes provision for the acquisition of land if it has been negligently vacated, if the owner dies without an heir or if he is a long time absent from it
179. Atkinson (1942)
180. Atkinson (1942), 177; *R.I.B.* 288
181. Bushe-Fox (1913), *passim*
182. Information from Katherine Hartley. Her dating for the activities of Sennius requires Atkinson's date of AD 155–65 for the fire to be revised
183. Atkinson (1942), 129
184. *Arch.* lxxxviii, 184
185. *Antiqs. J.* xlvi, 229
186. *Uriconium* (1872), 108

187. *Arch.* liv, 147
188. *Arch.* lxxxviii, 180
189. *Arch.* lxxxviii, pl. LXIV b
190. Insula numbers after Webster & Stanley: *T.Shrop.A.S.* lvii, 114
191. *T.Shrop.A.S.* lvii, 121
192. *J.R.S.* liv, 165; p. 163 for plan showing correct position of bridge, which is incorrectly placed in *T.Shrop.A.S.* lvii, 114
193. *T.Shrop.A.S.* lvi, 133
194. *T.Shrop.A.S.* lvii, pl. XXI
195. cf. Corbridge: *R.I.B.* 1144, 1164–5; Chester: *R.I.B.* 460; also Chedworth: *T.B.G.A.S.* lxxviii, 21
196. Atkinson (1942), 121
197. Bushe-Fox (1916), 13
198. Vitruvius, VIII, 6, 2; for a full consideration see T. Ashby (ed. I. A. Richmond) *The Aqueducts of Ancient Rome* (1935), Part I
199. A number of excavators have investigated the defences with differing results. The most recent study is by Webster in *T.B.A.S.* lxxviii, 27, but even this is, by now, not entirely in accord with modern views on town defences. See also *T.Shrop.A.S.* lviii, 197, where the presence of bastions is suggested
200. Bushe-Fox (1914), 11; (1915), 13; (1916), 65
201. *Uriconium* (1872), 159
202. Atkinson (1942), 216
203. *T.Shrop.A.S.* lvii, 101
204. Atkinson (1942), 195
205. Bushe-Fox (1914), 2
206. For a suggested restoration see Lewis (1965), 69, 184. This use of the water channel suggests that, by the time it had passed the temple, it was only carrying surplus away
207. Lewis (1965), 71
208. Foster and Alcock (1963), 259
209. *Civitas Capitals of Roman Britain*, 17; Foster and Alcock (1963), 261; Frere (1967), 258
210. A somewhat similar pattern of ditched enclosures has been investigated at North Thoresby, Lincs., where a vineyard or orchard might have existed: *Lincs. Hist & Arch.* i, 55
211. Atkinson (1942), 195
212. Bushe-Fox (1916), 20
213. *T.Shrop.A.S.* lvii, 118
214. *R.I.B.* 295
215. V.C.H. *Salop* i, 249
216. *Uriconium* (1872), 165
217. Foster and Alcock (1963), 260
218. Seneca, *Epistulae Morales* 56
219. *Current Archaeology* xxv, 45
220. *J.R.S.* lviii, 206

Chapter 8 (pages 375–404)

CAERWENT

1. Tacitus, *Annales* xii, 31
2. *ibid.* 32: *non atrocitate, non clementia mutabatur*
3. Tacitus, *Agricola* xvii, 3
4. Foster and Daniel (1963), 159
5. *Carnuntina* (1956), 108
6. *Civitas Capitals of Roman Britain*, 56, referring to *Arch.* lxxx, pl. LXXXIV
7. *Arch.* lxxx, 231; summarised in *B.B.C.S.* xv, 164
8. *R.I.B.* 395; *Mon. Antiq.* ii, 125; iii, 13
9. Excavated in 1907–9: *Arch.* lx, 128; lxi, 569 Reconsidered by Nash-Williams in *B.B.C.S.* xv, 159
10. By Nash-Williams in 1923–5: *Arch.* lxxx, 231
11. *Arch.* lix, 297
12. *Arch.* lxxx, 268, fig. 11
13. *R.I.B.* 311
14. *Arch.* lix, 115
15. *Antiquity* xxxv, 33
16. *J.R.S.* lvii, 233
17. *Civitas Capitals of Roman Britain*, 109
18. As shown by Craster's excavations at the east gate: *Arch. Camb.* ciii, 58, and Grimes' on the north sector: *Arch. Camb.* lxxxvi, 210; for revised views on the dating of the respective fortifications see Frere (1967), 249 and Hartley in *Civitas Capitals of Roman Britain*, 56
19. Nash-Williams: *Arch.* lxxx, 251; earlier excavations: *Arch.* lviii, 119; lix, 87; lx, 111; Ward's summary: *Arch. Camb.* xvi, 1
20. West gate: *B.B.C.S.* xv, 231, east gate: *Arch. Camb.* ciii, 54
21. *Arch.* lxxx, 257
22. *Carnuntina* (1956), 114
23. *Arch.* lxii, 1; *B.B.C.S.* xv, 93
24. *R.I.B.* 309
25. *R.I.B.* 310
26. *R.I.B.* 949
27. *Arch.* lxiv, 447. Trouble with land-owners is not a recent phenomenon on excavations, as readers of this report will see
28. Lewis (1965), 197
29. *B.B.C.S.* xix, 338; for a summary of early Christianity at Caerwent, see Aileen Fox in *Arch. Camb.* (1946)
30. *Arch.* lix, 104
31. *Arch.* lvii, 301
32. *Arch.* lviii, 121
33. *Arch.* lviii, 138
34. *Arch.* lxxx, 263
35. *E.E.* lx, 1015. The reading might be thought a little fanciful, although Mr Boon has suggested to me that the published drawing

is partly upside down

36. *Arch.* lxi, 575
37. *Arch.* lxxx, 235
38. *Arch.* lxxx, 230

CARMARTHEN

39. *It. Ant.* 483, 8
40. *Geog.* ii, 3, 23
41. *J.R.S.* xxxviii, 58
42. R.C.A.H.M. *Carmarthen*
43. *J.R.S.* li, 127
44. V. E. Nash-Williams (revised M. G. Jarrett, 1969), 23–6
45. *Carm. Ant.* v, 4
46. e.g. Catterick and Brough-on-Humber: Butler (1971), 165–77. See also p. 393
47. *Carm. Ant.* vi, 7. Unfortunately, it has not proved possible to obtain a plan of Roman Carmarthen, and the reader is referred to the plan in this report
48. e.g. Silchester and Wroxeter. But the size differential should be taken into account
49. *Carm. Ant.* v, 3; vii, 58
50. For defences see *Carm. Ant.* v, 2; vi, 4
51. cf. the large shop on the east corner of Insula XXVIII at Verulamium (p. 216)
52. *Carm. Ant.* vi, 13

BROUGH–ON–HUMBER

53. *Geog.* ii, 3, 17
54. *Arch.* xciii, 12
55. *It. Ant.* 464.1. There are, however, difficulties in accepting the accuracy of this list, cf. Rivet in *Britannia* i, 41; and see p. 397 for reasons why the two sites may not be the same
56. *R.I.B.* 707
57. For the pre-1939–45-war excavations see: Corder (1934), (1935); Corder and Romans (1936), (1937), (1938) and *J.B.A.A.*[3] vii, 5. For the post-war excavations see Wacher (1969)
58. Butler (1971), 166
59. *Antiqs. J.* xviii, 262; *Hull Museums Publications*, 212 and 237
60. Wacher (1969), 5
61. Periods IIa–V; *ibid.* 5–29, with revisions in Butler (1971), 166
62. Stone from the Fishbourne palace was possibly plundered to help build the Saxon Shore fort at Portchester: Cunliffe (1971), I, 191
63. This thesis has been more fully developed in Butler (1971), 165
64. In Stern (1965), 96; Rivet (1969), 102
65. Wacher (1969), 4
66. *ibid.* 198, no. 704

ALDBOROUGH

67. Tacitus, *Annales* xii, 36
68. Tacitus, *Annales* xii, 40; *Histories* iii, 45
69. Wheeler (1954), *passim*
70. *Northern Hist.* i, 16
71. *Y.A.J.* xl, 1; *J.R.S.* lii, 166
72. Ecroyd Smith (1852), 7
73. *J.R.S.* lii, 166; a military bath-house may be a possibility
74. Ecroyd Smith (1852), *passim*
75. The most recent consideration of the defences, by Dorothy Charlesworth, is in Butler (1971), 155
76. *R.I.B.* 2276–8
77. *Y.A.J.* xl, 55
78. *J.R.S.* lv, 204
79. *Y.A.J.* xl, 55
80. *E.E.* vii, 937. Miss D. Charlesworth has kindly drawn my attention to views expressed by Mr R. P. Wright. He considers the mosaic to represent the Muses on Mount Helicon, the Greek letters being part of the name
81. The pavements referred to are illustrated in Ecroyd Smith (1852), with the Wolf and Twins pavement included in a supplement. See also Toynbee (1962), no. 184
82. I. A. Richmond, *The Roman Pavements from Rudston, East Riding* (1963)
83. *J.R.S.* lvii, 179
84. *R.I.B.* 708
85. *R.I.B.* 709–10
86. *J.R.S.* lv, 204

Chapter 9 (pages 405–410)

1. *E.H.R.* lii, 200; *C.W.* xlvii, 15; liii, 52. See also *R.I.B.* 933 and *J.R.S.* lv, 224
2. Salway (1965), 180
3. e.g. The *Abinnaeus Archive*; Egypt is, however, a rather special case
4. *R.I.B.* 583. Another centurion with similar duties is given in *R.I.B.* 587. See also Richmond in *J.R.S.* xxxv, 15
5. VIII, 43, 3
6. *Vita Sancti Cuthberti*, iv
7. *J.R.S.* xlvii, 202
8. *Gesta Pontificum Anglorum*, iii
9. Finds made down to 1924 are collected in *C.W.*[2] xxiv, 94
10. *R.I.B.* 951, 943
11. *R.I.B.* 949, 946
12. *R.I.B.* 955–64
13. *R.I.B.* 2059
14. *R.I.B.* 933; *J.R.S.* lv, 224
15. *I.L.S.* 5969
16. *R.I.B.* 1672–3
17. *P.S.A.N.H.S.* xcvi, 188

18. *J.R.S.* lvii, 233
19. *R.I.B.* 1843–4. Bogaers has also overlooked the civitas Carvetiorum of the tombstone and milestone mentioned above under Carlisle. By no stretch of the imagination can it be identified with its capital of Luguvalium. Indeed, the Angles' name for the town was *civitas Luel*, according to Bede
20. *J.R.S.* xxxix, 108; xl, 110; *Britannia* i, 296; ii, 278, with additional information kindly supplied by Mr John Casey
21. *R.I.B.* 2235
22. *J.R.S.* lvi, 223
23. R. G. Collingwood and I. Richmond, *The Archaeology of Roman Britain* (1969), pl. X, a; *Civitas Capitals of Roman Britain*, pl. IV
24. *J.R.S.* xlviii, 3
25. E. T. Artis, *Durobrivae* (1828); *V.C.H. Hunts* i, 225, 230; B. R. Hartley, *Notes on the Pottery Industry of the Nene Valley*. One maker of mortaria stamped his wares: *Cunoarus Vico Duro(brivae)*, Frere (1967), 209, n. 3
26. *Antiquity* xxxv, 29–36; *J.R.S.* lvii, 232

Chapter 10 (pages 411–422)

1. Recent accounts of the period: C. F. C. Hawkes, 'The Jutes in Kent' in (ed.) D. B. Harden, *Dark Age Britain* (1956), 91; *Antiquity* xxx, 163; *Athenaeum* xxxv, 316; Stevens in *E.H.R.* lvi, 353; J. N. L. Myres, 'Adventus Saxonum' in (ed.) W. F. Grimes, *Aspects of Archaeology in Britain and Beyond* (1951), 221; *J.R.S.* l, 21; *Latomus* xxvi, 436; John Morris, 'Dark Age Dates' in (ed.) M. G. Jarrett and B. Dobson, *Britain and Rome* (1966), 145; V. I. Evison, *The Fifth Century Invasions South of the Thames* (1966); *Med. Arch.* v, 1. S. S. Frere in *Civitas Capitals of Roman Britain* (1966), 87; Frere (1967), chapt. 17. J. N. L. Myres, *Anglo-Saxon Pottery and the Settlement of England* (1969); John Morris, *The Age of Arthur* (1973)
2. *J.R.S.* l, 31 ff.; *Britannia* iii, 277
3. *Latomus* xxvi, 436
4. *Britannia* ii, 218
5. *De vita Christiana*, attributed by Morris to the period *c.* AD 411. Doubts have been cast by Liebeschuetz, *Latomus* xxvi, 436, on whether the passage refers to Britain at all. Even if it does not, the general picture described may not be so far removed from the truth when applied to Britain

6. *J.R.S.* l, 21. The two protagonists appear to have been Vortigern and Ambrosius Aurelianus. See also *Britannia* iii, 277
7. *Roman Britain and the English Settlements* (1937), 317
8. E. A. Thompson, *The Early Germans* (1965), 131; *Past and Present* xiv, 2
9. e.g. in the Rhineland: Amm. Marcellinus, xviii, 2
10. The epidemics have been reviewed by J. F. Gilliam: *American Journ. of Philology*, lxxxii, 225–51
11. Procopius II, xxii–xxiii
12. Hydatius 126; *Chron. Min.* ii, 24
13. *Chron. Min.* ii, 81–2; 26
14. *de excidio Britanniae* xxi (Wade-Evans, 2nd edition, 1959)
15. Dobson and Jarrett (1966), 151
16. Stevens: *E.H.R.* lvi, 363; Myres: Grimes (1951), 228
17. Evagrius, ii, 6. I am grateful to Mr C. E. Stevens for this reference
18. H. Zinsser, *Rats, Lice and History* (1935), 143. Zinsser mistakenly places this epidemic in the Danubian provinces, and also confuses the authors, attributing the source to Eusebius
19. (ed.) R. C. Latham and W. Matthews, *The Diary of Samuel Pepys*, vi (1665–6), 1972. Nearly 69,000 supposedly died in London alone and over a quarter of a million in Naples. Hecker estimated that a quarter of the inhabitants of Europe died during the Black Death, but in many parts the gross mortality exceeded this figure. (J. F. C. Hecker, *The Epidemics of the Middle Ages* (1844), 30)
20. Armand, *Histoire Médico-Chirugical de la Guerre de la Crimée*
21. Hill and Jesson (1971), 203–13
22. Amm. Marcellinus, xvi, 2, 12
23. *Roman Britain and the English Settlements* (1937), 434. Although towns are mentioned collectively in the Chronicles, remarkably few are mentioned by name and none apparently was the site of a battle. It is essential also that we should try to distinguish between foederati and the later immigrants, who came and settled of their own free-will.
24. *Chron. Min.* i, 660
25. (ed.) Barley and Hanson, *Christianity in Britain, 300–700* (1968), 97

Index

Note: numerals in **bold type** indicate main sections, those in *italics* footnotes